Praise for *The Bat*

A *New York Times* bestseller

"The classic political campaign of our time has its classic retelling now in Haynes Johnson's and Dan Balz's *Battle for America*. In addition to the compelling narrative of the events we remember, they have, through their post-election reporting, solved almost all the mysteries about what was happening behind the scenes in the Obama, Clinton, and McCain camps." —David S. Broder, *The Washington Post*

"Magisterial . . . Captures the thrill of the campaign and its meaning. Balz and Johnson are the true heirs to Teddy White."
—George Stephanopoulos, ABC's *This Week with George Stephanopoulos*

"Balz and Johnson's material is rich and built upon extensive firsthand interviews. . . . [Filled] with details that range from poignant to chilling."
—Art Winslow, *Los Angeles Times*

"Even readers who followed the election closely will find revelations and new perspectives in this gripping account of a fascinating election season." —*Booklist*

"A superior piece of political reportage and interpretation . . . Essential for watchers of politics and a model for similar electoral analyses in the future." —*Kirkus Reviews*

PENGUIN BOOKS

THE BATTLE FOR AMERICA

Dan Balz is the lead political reporter for the *Washington Post*. He has also served as the paper's national editor, political editor, and the White House correspondent. He lives in Bethesda, Maryland.

Haynes Johnson is a Pulitzer Prize winner and the author of fifteen books, six of them national bestsellers. He holds the Knight Chair in Journalism at the University of Maryland and lives in Washington, D.C.

The BATTLE for AMERICA

The Story of an Extraordinary Election

Dan Balz and Haynes Johnson

PENGUIN BOOKS

PENGUIN BOOKS

Published by the Penguin Group
Penguin Group (USA) Inc., 375 Hudson Street, New York, New York 10014, U.S.A.
Penguin Group (Canada), 90 Eglinton Avenue East, Suite 700, Toronto,
Ontario, Canada M4P 2Y3 (a division of Pearson Penguin Canada Inc.)
Penguin Books Ltd, 80 Strand, London WC2R 0RL, England
Penguin Ireland, 25 St Stephen's Green, Dublin 2, Ireland (a division of Penguin Books Ltd)
Penguin Group (Australia), 250 Camberwell Road, Camberwell,
Victoria 3124, Australia (a division of Pearson Australia Group Pty Ltd)
Penguin Books India Pvt Ltd, 11 Community Centre, Panchsheel Park, New Delhi – 110 017, India
Penguin Group (NZ), 67 Apollo Drive, Rosedale, North Shore 0632,
New Zealand (a division of Pearson New Zealand Ltd)
Penguin Books (South Africa) (Pty) Ltd, 24 Sturdee Avenue,
Rosebank, Johannesburg 2196, South Africa

Penguin Books Ltd, Registered Offices:
80 Strand, London WC2R 0RL, England

First published in the United States of America by Viking Penguin,
a member of Penguin Group (USA) Inc. 2009
This edition with a new afterword published in Penguin Books 2010

1   3   5   7   9   10   8   6   4   2

Copyright © Dan Balz and Haynes Johnson, 2009, 2010
All rights reserved

THE LIBRARY OF CONGRESS HAS CATALOGED THE HARDCOVER EDITION AS FOLLOWS:
Balz, Daniel J.
The battle for America 2008 : the story of an extraordinary election / Dan Balz and Haynes Johnson.
p.   cm.
"A James H. Silberman Book."
Includes bibliographical references and index.
ISBN 978-0-670-02111-6 (hc.)
ISBN 978-0-14-311770-4 (pbk.)
1. Presidents—United States—Election—2008.   2. Political campaigns—United States—
History—21st century.   3. United States—Politics and government—2001–
I. Johnson, Haynes Bonner,—   II. Title.
E906.B35   2009
973.932—dc22   2009017129

Printed in the United States of America
Designed by Nancy Resnick

For Tim Russert,
friend and colleague,
who defined the race
only to miss the last chapter

and to our wives,
Nancy Balz and Kathryn Oberly

Heroes and philosophers, brave men and vile,
have since Rome and Athens tried to make . . .
transfer of power work effectively. No people
have succeeded at it better . . . than the Americans.

—Theodore H. White, *The Making of the President 1960*

Contents

BOOK FOUR: THE REPUBLICANS

BOOK FIVE: THE ELECTION

EPILOGUE: THE INAUGURATION

AFTERWORD TO THE PAPERBACK EDITION

To the Reader

We began research for this book in 2006 out of a conviction that the presidential election of 2008 promised to be one of the most significant in American history. More than two years later, it has turned out to be that and more—the election of a lifetime, one that will be studied for years for its shattering of historical barriers and its long-term consequences for the United States.

In the decades we have spent chronicling American politics, nothing has equaled this election for the richness of its characters, for the light it sheds on questions of race, gender, religion, class, and generational changes, and for the stakes it raises for the future. It was an election that took place against a background of two wars, the collapse of the world's capital markets, a gathering global recession, soaring national debt, and pervasive doubts about the direction of the country from traditionally optimistic Americans. These problems created deep anxiety and presented challenges for the presidential candidates faced with some of the most daunting issues the United States has confronted, not least the gravest economic crisis since the Great Depression. How well those issues were addressed during the election will define the nation's course, for better or worse, in years to come. In the end, public hunger for change produced an outpouring of voters hopeful that a new president and a new approach would lead to a better America.

A word about our methods and sources: We were present at many of the scenes recounted in this narrative, and we conducted recorded interviews, covering hundreds of hours of conversations, with the principal political players, their strategists and advisers, and the voters who rendered final judgment on those who won and lost. Many were on the record, but many others were agreed to on the condition that we grant anonymity to encourage candor as the campaign unfolded.

Our narrative focuses on three candidates who battled to win the White House: Barack Obama, Hillary Clinton, and John McCain, who represent strikingly different strands of the American story. At the same time, the history of this election cannot be told, or understood, without taking into account the record of the failed presidency that preceded it. Though George W. Bush no longer was on the ballot, his shadow hovered over all that followed.

The BATTLE
for AMERICA

TAKEOFF

Waiting

"We didn't have bank accounts, we didn't have credit card accounts, we didn't have any staff, we didn't have a list of people who were going to do our first serious fund-raisers."

—David Plouffe, Obama's campaign manager

Sunday, March 4, 2007, Selma, Alabama

B arack Obama is sitting aboard his modest six-seater chartered aircraft on the tarmac at Selma—waiting. He's just finished his part in the commemorative ceremonies marking the anniversary of the Bloody Sunday voting rights march across the Edmund Pettus Bridge, where forty-two years earlier civil rights demonstrators had been trampled, tear-gassed, and viciously beaten with whips and billy clubs.

As he waits to begin the flight to Boston for political fund-raisers the next morning, he's accompanied by just two aides: his press spokesman, Dan Pfeiffer, and his six-foot-five-inch "body man," Reggie Love, who can barely stuff his frame into his small seat. But that doesn't matter. Obama's in a good mood. His speech has been well received, and he believes he more than held his own against the imposing figures of Hillary and Bill Clinton, among other notables present for the ceremonies.

For Obama, Selma marks the first time he and Hillary Clinton have crossed paths since announcing their campaigns for the White House weeks before. Inevitably, given the intense media focus on their rivalry, their appearance has been hyped in the press as a critical Obama versus Clinton moment and attracts a huge press gathering. That alone makes Selma a formidable political challenge, but there are others.

With its symbolism as the scene of the last great battle of the civil rights era, leading directly to passage of the Voting Rights Act of which he and every elected black officeholder is a direct beneficiary, Selma gives Obama a chance to demonstrate that his candidacy stems from the history of the civil rights movement. It also provides an opportunity to put to rest doubts expressed among black Americans that he's "not black enough" to carry the banner of the movement forward.

It's an argument Obama knows well, frustrating though it is, especially since he is only the third black person to be elected to the United States Senate since Reconstruction. With surpassing irony, no American politician has expressed more revealingly the agonizing conflicts of race—or, in his case, the biracial conflicts—than his account of his African father, "black as pitch," and Kansas mother, "white as milk." His remarkable memoir, *Dreams from My Father: A Story of Race and Inheritance*, first attracted attention to him as a promising political figure twelve years before. Its pages are filled with brooding, self-revelatory passages about his struggle to come to grips with his mixed racial identity, including his painful description of how as a teenager he stopped acknowledging his mother's race because he feared he would be seen as ingratiating himself to whites, writing, "Privately, they guess at my troubled heart, I suppose—the mixed blood, the divided soul, the ghostly image of the tragic mulatto trapped between two worlds."

Out of this soul-searching of a thirty-four-year-old emerges the cool, disciplined politician of steely determination in pursuit of his unlikely dream of becoming president of the United States. Obama knows all too well that Clinton stands as the odds-on, even inevitable, winner of the nomination—and for good reason: She is the best known, has the most formidable political organization, the most money, the greatest expertise. She's backed by a network that has helped win the White House twice, something no Democrat had accomplished since FDR, and can recruit almost anyone she wants. And everyone knows her name.

Beyond all that, she and Bill Clinton have a special claim on the allegiance of black voters. So popular is Bill among blacks that he's been called, admiringly, "the first black president." She also begins her campaign enjoying the endorsements of leading blacks from the civil rights era, including Congressman John Lewis of Georgia. Lewis, who was nearly clubbed to death on that Bloody Sunday in Selma, is among those this day who linked arms with her and Obama while crossing the Pettus Bridge in reenactment of that historic march to freedom.

Against the politically intimidating Clinton advantages, Obama begins his "improbable quest" literally with almost nothing. "We didn't have bank accounts, we didn't have credit card accounts, we didn't have any staff, we didn't have a list of people who were going to do our first serious fund-raisers," remembers David Plouffe, who has been tapped as the campaign manager. At first, they don't even have a Web site.

Now, as Obama waits at the Selma airport, before him on the tarmac sit two large, sleek Gulfstream jets. As he watches, two motorcades of black SUVs roll onto the tarmac and up to the jets. Out of one SUV comes Bill Clinton, followed by his Secret Service detail and his aides. The second, even larger motorcade brings Hillary Clinton and her entourage. Within minutes, the former president's plane is taxiing down the runway. Obama's small plane is scheduled to depart next. The pilot tries to start their engine, but he can't. The battery is dead. Don't worry, the pilot tells Obama, airport crews are searching for a long extension cord. They'll plug it into a generator in the lobby and run it from the terminal back to the plane to jump-start the engine. Still, the plane won't start. While Obama and his aides are cramped inside the plane, sweltering in a cabin without air-conditioning, they watch as Hillary's Gulfstream takes off. Bemused, Obama tells his young aides, "I guess this really is a grassroots campaign."

The Warrior

"A lot of people are writing you off."

—A reporter to John McCain

**Four months later, Friday, July 13, 2007,
Concord, New Hampshire**

It wasn't the kind of campaign trip to New Hampshire John McCain
originally planned. The Granite State was *his* state, the state he counted
on to rescue him from political disaster. By this Friday in July 2007, the
McCain campaign has imploded. Not only has it run out of money with
what appears to be reckless mismanagement, but McCain has just had to
fire key members of his staff; others voluntarily leave his side. Days later,
he is traveling back to New Hampshire on his first trip after his campaign's
apparent collapse.

Now here he is, in Concord, speaking to a luncheon audience, hoping
to rescue his presidential dreams by rekindling support from citizens of
New Hampshire loyal to the old John McCain.

After his address, he holds a news conference. The scene is chaotic.
McCain stands surrounded by the media pack, who pound him with question after question about what happened to his campaign. Amid this torrent
he tries to strike a cheerful air, but as he faces his questioners, he can see
that even old friends in the press corps now doubt him.

Fast and furious, the questions come:

Q: You criticized [Congress] spending like a drunken sailor.
MCCAIN: Yeah.
Q: Yet it seems like some of your campaign staff got their hands on
    the liquor. How can you justify the spending that went on?

MCCAIN: Well, I've fought wasteful spending for a very long period of time, and I'm fighting this, and when I see mistakes, I correct them.

Q: You talked a little bit earlier about the mistakes in the campaign, and you're taking blame for any mistakes that were made.

MCCAIN: I'm not taking, quote, blame, I'm taking responsibility. . . . That's the way I was brought up in the military. You take responsibility when you're in charge.

Q: Senator McCain, are there any circumstances under which you could imagine yourself not still being a presidential candidate when the New Hampshire primary's held?

Smiling, he gives a quick reply, intended as a humorous quip to draw an appreciative response from his once admiring and supportive press pack: "Contracting a fatal disease," John McCain answers.

Dead silence. No laughter. Nothing.

"Anything short of that?" the reporter asks.

McCain replies, "Not that I know of." Then, three times, he gives the same response: "You never know . . . You never know . . . You never know."

Still the questions come, until finally, "Senator, when it comes to hope, which is more hopeful—the chance of progress in Iraq or the chance of you getting the Republican nomination?"

Here, John McCain laughs. "You mean, in the words of Chairman Mao, it's always darkest before it's totally black." A pause, then, "I don't know the answer to that. I'm sorry, old friend, it's hard for me to answer a question like that."

All he can do, he says, is take his case back to the good people in his favorite state of New Hampshire. He says, "They know me, and I'm very pleased to have the opportunity of really spending a lot of time with them."

A brave front, but it doesn't inspire much hope for his chances. On McCain's next campaign trip to New Hampshire shortly after his ordeal in Concord he's flying commercial, carrying his own bag, traveling with a single aide, and ignored by the press. For John McCain, it's either a final humiliation or a test of the power of the old prisoner of war to endure, even to prevail.

The Uniter

"A heck of an interesting tale."

—George W. Bush

Flashback, January 11, 2001

The winter sky is darkening as the chartered airplane speeds toward Waco, Texas. Inside the cabin, President-elect George Walker Bush sits in the aisle seat in the first row on the right.

After two days of meetings and briefings in Washington, Bush is returning home for the last time before his inauguration in nine days. Four weeks earlier, thanks to an intensely controversial ruling of the United States Supreme Court, he becomes the first candidate in 124 years to lose the popular vote and still become president.

Often guarded or defensive in interviews, Bush is more relaxed and candid than we remember from many previous interviews.* He's also unusually reflective as he describes the extraordinary events that began with election day and continued for thirty-seven days, holding him, his opponent, Al Gore, and the nation in a state of suspense unmatched in any previous presidential election: shouting protesters, angry charges, spin and counterspin, court challenges and counterchallenges. All expose an American political system imploding before the eyes of the world.

In the end, by a five-to-four vote the U.S. Supreme Court for the first time intercedes and determines the outcome of a presidential election. The court overturns Florida's state court ruling, halts the recounts, orders them ended. The election results are to stand as tabulated. Out of nearly

---

* Co-author Dan Balz, who covered Bush's gubernatorial and presidential campaigns for the *Washington Post*, conducted this interview on the plane as part of a *Post* political team series on the aftermath of the 2000 election, later published as *Deadlock: The Inside Story of America's Closest Election*.

six million votes cast in Florida, Bush leads by 537. Gore wins the popular count by 543,816. Because of the Supreme Court's ruling, however, Bush has 271 electoral votes—one more than needed.

Bush's inaugural will take place against a backdrop of the divisive controversies of the Clinton years, which resulted in only the second impeachment of a president in history. Clinton still ignites Bush's conservative base with anger, but he will be leaving office with an unusually high public approval rating of 65 percent.* He also bequeaths favorable conditions to his successor: a nation at peace, facing no visible foreign threats, with projected surpluses for years to come. The rosy forecast for Bush's inauguration day is nearly $6 trillion in surpluses that would accumulate between 2001 and 2011. If a national political consensus can be achieved, America has the ability to do almost anything it wants.

As Bush's plane speeds toward Texas, he envisions the opportunities these challenges present for his presidency. When he addressed the nation for the first time as president-elect from the House chamber of the Texas State Capitol the day after the Supreme Court ruling, Bush told Americans, "I believe things happen for a reason." What did he mean by that? we ask as the plane begins its descent to Waco.

Bush, who campaigned as a "compassionate conservative," whose intent was to be, as he had told the American people, a "uniter, not a divider," amplifies that theme. Leaning across his aisle seat, he cites Lincoln's warning about the dangers of an American house divided. His presidency, George W. Bush says, provides those like him, who have been entrusted with power, a chance "to rise above the expectations of what a divided house means, and at the same time to diminish cynicism. I believe it is an opportunity for people who go to Washington—both Republicans and Democrats—to come together."

His last words before touchdown still echo: "It's a heck of an interesting tale, isn't it?"

---

* By contrast, Truman, Nixon, Carter, and G. H. W. Bush all had sunk to approval rates in the 20s before leaving office, while Johnson's rating at the end of his presidency was at 49 percent, Ford's at 53 percent, and Eisenhower and Reagan recorded 59 percent and 64 percent, respectively.

At the Gate

Seldom in American history had a president experienced such a roller-coaster ride. After 9/11 Bush received the highest approval rating ever recorded. By January 2007 his popularity was plummeting toward depths not recorded since Nixon at the time of his forced resignation.

Washington, January 2007

In modern American history, no presidential election seemed as wide open—or as consequential. The 2008 campaign attracted one of the largest and most impressive fields of candidates ever, and one marked by a historical precedent: For the first time in more than half a century, a presidential race begins without either a president seeking reelection or his vice president attempting to succeed him.

The Democratic field is especially strong. Even the less likely candidates—John Edwards, Bill Richardson, Chris Dodd, and Joe Biden—are substantial politicians and credible nominees. Edwards is the glamorous southerner and former senator from North Carolina who ran a strong race for the Democratic nomination in 2004 and then ended up as John F. Kerry's vice presidential running mate. Kerry later told a friend he regretted picking Edwards as his running mate. Edwards and his wife, Elizabeth, blamed the Kerry team for strategic blunders. So as Kerry held open the possibility that he might run again, Edwards plunged into the 2008 campaign less than a month after Bush's second inaugural, soon to harbor a dark secret about an affair with a campaign aide.

Biden of Delaware is one of his party's most respected voices on foreign policy and has been a senator for nearly three decades; Richardson is the most prominent Hispanic politician in the country, now the governor of

New Mexico after having served as United Nations ambassador and secretary of energy during the Clinton years; Dodd is one of the Senate's
leading legislators, having earned that reputation after almost three decades of Capitol Hill experience.*

Among Republicans, the field is less strong, if only because no one
seems to fit the mold of past nominees, especially the commanding figure
of Ronald Reagan. McCain aside, Rudy Giuliani, the former mayor of New
York, is the most intriguing—best known for his leadership of a shaken city
after the September 11, 2001, terrorist attacks leveled the World Trade
Center. Mitt Romney looks most like a president, with his square jaw and
boyishly handsome face, seen posing beside the perfect political family. He
has a dynastic name too. His father, George, was a popular Republican
governor of Michigan and a leading GOP presidential candidate in 1968.
Romney's religion poses an obstacle. In a party dominated by conservative
southern evangelicals, can a Mormon ever win? Conservative credentials
are not the problem for Mike Huckabee, the former governor from Arkansas. Like Bill Clinton, he can boast of having come from a town called
Hope. He has a warm and winning personality, and conservative views. But
nobody takes him seriously. Lurking in the background, but already the
subject of political speculation, is the dark horse candidacy of Fred Thompson, former senator as well as screen and TV actor.

Besides an impressive field of candidates, yet another factor elevates
the 2008 election to historic status. By 2007, the United States faces severe economic challenges. At the same time, America is involved in two
wars, still confronts the threat of Islamist terrorist attacks, and stands in
danger of seeing its power decline. All of this induces a deep sense of
anxiety among voters.

Two-thirds of them tell pollsters they believe the country is headed seriously in the wrong direction. Month by month that negative feeling inten-
sifies. The housing market is collapsing, setting off a wave of foreclosures
with shock waves that ripple through America's banking and financial sec-
tors. The middle class is imperiled as unemployment rises, triggering layoffs and buyouts. The Gallup Poll finds a majority of voters more
pessimistic about their financial future than at any point in decades. The
stock market has plummeted from a 2007 high of 14,164 on the Dow Jones
Industrial Average to just over 8,500 a year later and continues to fall. All

---

* Two others sought the Democratic nomination: Ohio Representative Dennis Kucinich and former
Alaska senator Mike Gravel. As the most liberal candidates in the race, neither had a significant impact
on the outcome.

of this grim news is a prelude to much worse. In the weeks before the election, the failure of leading Wall Street firms and banks spawns a crisis of confidence that raises the specter of a financial collapse rivaling the darkest days of the Great Depression three-quarters of a century earlier.

The gloomy news inspires the oldest theme in American politics—time for change—and sets the stage for what political commentators inadequately call "a change election," an election that could mark the end of the conservative era dating from Ronald Reagan's presidency nearly thirty years earlier. Those years marked the rise and fall of the Democratic Party. In 1964, a year after the assassination of John F. Kennedy, Lyndon Johnson won the greatest landslide in American history with 61.1 percent of the vote over Barry Goldwater, eclipsing even Franklin D. Roosevelt's margin over Alf Landon in 1936. Yet two years later Republicans emerged from the 1966 elections in control of half of the statehouses, including seven of the ten most populous states. Democrats fell into such public disfavor that they lost seven of the next ten presidential elections. Only once did they carry barely more than half of the votes cast—with Jimmy Carter's 50.1 percent in 1976.

That same brief time span, from 1964 to 1966, marked the beginning of the Republican Party's rise from seeming political irrelevance to that of America's leading political power. By the summer of 1965, after the great moment in Selma, the common cause of blacks and whites marching together was shattered. Racial riots swept the Watts section of Los Angeles. Over the next two years they spread to cities across the country. At the same time America was experiencing growing waves of protests, many violent, about the bitterly divisive Vietnam War. LBJ's Great Society, which had passed the liberal reforms of Medicare, Medicaid, and advances in women's and minority rights, was over.

By 2007, as the candidates gather, nothing better illuminates the changes and challenges facing them and their two political parties than the standing of George W. Bush. He has become an increasingly distant, almost irrelevant figure, so much so that it's hard to recognize the hopeful president-elect who flew back to Texas before assuming the presidency.

His words on that memorable flight six years earlier are in poignant, near tragic contrast to a presidency gone awry, of hopes dashed both by events and by his own decisions in the White House. His political capital is eroded, his Republican Party in turmoil, his country trapped in an unpopular war and sinking deeper into debt, and his fellow citizens more polarized than when he first took his oath of office—all the opposite of what he hoped for when he talked about wanting to elevate the politics of the era and bring the country together. In between came 9/11, the invasion of Iraq, the fruitless search for weapons of mass destruction, "Mission Accomplished," Abu Ghraib, Hurricane Katrina, the Republican loss of Congress.

Seldom in American history had a president experienced such a roller-coaster ride. After 9/11 Bush received the highest presidential approval rating ever recorded (90 percent) in all the years since the Gallup Poll began its first opinion surveys during Franklin Roosevelt's presidency. By January 2007 his public standing hovers at sixty points below its peak and plummets toward depths not recorded since Nixon at the time of his forced resignation. The final chapter on Bush's presidency has not yet been written; he still has two years left in office. But at the least, his has been a damaging presidency that will leave his successor a legacy of some of the most daunting policy problems at home and abroad ever faced by a new president.

Of the candidates who begin the battle, only three—Obama, McCain, and Clinton—emerge to dominate the race for the nomination. Their challenge is to convince voters they can produce significant change after years of public disaffection from all things political. Obama and Clinton carry a special burden: to prove they can break through the barriers erected by the virulent record of American racism and sexism.

Obama, born in 1961, is the biracial figure initially viewed suspiciously by many blacks as not representative of the black experience and by many whites as an elitist black whose values are different from those of the America they know. His entry into politics came long after the destructive political climate of the sixties that divided the generations, pitted region against region, group against group, and launched the divisive "culture wars" that have influenced political battles since. If elected, he will be the first African-American president, and one of the youngest.

McCain was shaped by the legacy of a family of World War II military leaders. His defining experience was as a prisoner of war in Vietnam, and his campaign carried a Shakespearean element: the former prisoner of war who again has become a "POW." His steadfast support of the war policies of George W. Bush, who crushed his presidential hopes seven years before, now becomes his greatest political liability.

Clinton is a classic representative of the post–World War II baby boom generation, the Goldwater girl who turned against the Vietnam War and became a progressive Democrat. Her generation came to political power in the wake of immense change—the civil rights movement, the antiwar movement, the feminist movement—that created a revolution in American life, affecting everyone and everything, from the nature of the society to the structure of its institutions. Those explosive times left a legacy of both great achievement and despair, as riots, assassinations, scandals, and impeachments deepened public cynicism about politics and politicians. With the possible exception of Eleanor Roosevelt, Clinton has been more influential than any previous First Lady. But she also carries the baggage of the scandals of the Clinton years and the fierce opposition of critics who despise all things Clinton. If elected, she will be the first female president.

It is with those three candidates, talented but so different, so representative of their times, that we begin.

BOOK ONE

THEY'RE OFF

CHAPTER ONE

Obama

"So you will not run for president or vice president in 2008?" Tim Russert asked. "I will not," Obama replied.

—January 22, 2006

Ten months after that exchange, when he again faced Tim Russert in the well-chilled studios of NBC News in Washington, along the angular wooden table where news has so often been made on *Meet the Press*, Obama knew Russert would ask him once more about his plans to run. Obama was prepared for it. This time, he was ready to make some news of his own.

Tim Russert was a political celebrity in his own right whose stature eclipsed most of those who appeared with him as guests. *Time* magazine had named him among the one hundred most influential people in the world, and it was on his television program that all politicians and public figures craved to be seen. When Obama had last appeared on *Meet the Press*, Russert had recalled Obama's pledge to serve out his full six-year Senate term and not seek higher office after having been elected in November 2004. Russert had pressed Obama for another declaration of his intentions. "My thinking has not changed," Obama said. Russert, leaning forward, his eyes fixed steadily on Obama, tried again. "So you will not run for president or vice president in 2008?" Obama replied, "I will not." Ten months later, he was on *Meet the Press* again.

The night before, while driving back from Philadelphia after completing the first week of a book tour during which clamorous crowds were urging him to run for president, Obama discussed with his top strategist, David Axelrod, and his communications director, Robert Gibbs, the questions Russert would likely ask the next morning. They all knew that Russert, famous for throwing quotations back in the faces of politicians, was certain to air segments from Obama's last appearance and demand a response. "We have to say we're thinking about this," Obama told Axelrod and Gibbs. They agreed.

Russert waited until the very end of *Meet the Press* to play the earlier tape. Turning to Obama, he repeated Obama's final "I will not run" words and waited for a response. Obama hesitated a fraction of a second. "Well, the—that was how I was thinking at that time," he said. "And, and, you know, I don't want to be coy about this, given the responses that I've been getting over the last several months, I have thought about the possibility. But I have not thought about it—about it with the seriousness and depth that I think is required. My main focus right now is the '06 election, and making sure that we retake the Congress. After, oh—after November 7, I'll sit down and, and consider, and if at some point I change my mind, I will make a public announcement, and everybody will be able to go at me."

Russert pressed the point. "But it's fair to say you're thinking about running for president in 2008?" he asked. "It's fair, yes," Obama replied. "And so when you said to me in January, 'I will not,' that statement is no longer operative." Again, Obama paused briefly. "The—I would say that I am still at the point where I have made no decision to, to pursue higher office, but it is true that I have thought about it over the last several months."

"So it sounds as if the door has opened a bit," Russert concluded.

Obama acknowledged, "A bit."*

Those words shattered all assumptions about the 2008 presidential campaign. Whatever had gone before—all the trips to Iowa by lesser-known candidates, all the talk about Hillary Clinton's invincibility—was suddenly the subject of major reevaluation. A media, already fascinated, treated Obama's appearance with Russert as major news. Even though the real top political story of the moment was the possible takeover of Congress by Democrats just two weeks away, both the *Washington Post* and the *New York Times* carried the Obama story on their front pages the next day: "Crowd-Pleaser from Illinois Considers White House Run," read the *Times* headline.

---

* Long after he won the nomination, Obama recalled that moment: "I was never comfortable about being coy about my intentions," he told us. "When I had been on his show after getting elected [to the Senate], I was absolutely convinced that I would not be running. I was telling the truth then. By the time I was on that show in the fall of '06, I was thinking about it. And for me to say no—particularly given that two months later I might have already announced—I didn't think it made too much sense."

Long after he secured the nomination, after the most grueling contest in the history of the Democratic Party, during an interview aboard his campaign plane Obama reflected on what pushed him into the race after only two years in the Senate. "Objectively you've got to say there's a certain megalomania there that's unhealthy. Right?" he said with a chuckle. "Axelrod said this to me and he always reminds me of this. One of the things he said to me is he wasn't sure I would be a good candidate because I might be too normal. Which is why it's amusing, during the course of this campaign, the evolving narrative about me being aloof and elitist.

"Axelrod's right," he continued. "I'm not somebody who actually takes myself that seriously. I'm pretty well adjusted. You know, you can psychoanalyze my father leaving and this and that, but a lot of those things I resolved a long time ago. I'm pretty happy with my life. So there's an element, I think, of being driven that might have operated a little differently with me than maybe some other candidates. The way I thought about it was more of a sense of duty, in this sense. I thought to myself, there aren't that many people put in the position I'm put in. Some of it's just dumb luck. Some of it maybe has to do with me embodying some characteristics that are interesting for the time that we're in. But when I made the decision to do this, it wasn't with the certainty that I was the right person for the job. It was more the sense of, given what's been given to me, I should probably just give it a shot and see whether in fact there's something real there.

"But I went into it with some modesty, thinking to myself, it may be that this really is all hype, and once people get a sense of my ideas and what's going on there that they think I'm some callow youth or full of hot air, and if that turned out to be the case, that was okay. I think for me it was more of a sense of being willing to do this, understanding that the odds were probably—I gave myself twenty-five percent odds, you know, maybe thirty—which are pretty remarkable odds to be president of the United States, if you're a gambling man."

By late 2006, Barack Obama was already the most exciting presidential candidate of either party. Clinton had the money, the experience, and the political machinery. McCain had run before, plus he had the compelling war hero profile. Both Clinton and McCain had long been preparing for their campaigns, while Obama was arriving at the starting gate seemingly out of nowhere in a rush of expectation and hype. Who, really, was he, and why had he struck such a strong chord among public and press?

To say Barack Obama was ambitious, confident, even cocky is an understatement; but then the same can be said of nearly all who dream of becoming president of the United States. What distinguished Obama was his determination not to wait until he had forged a longer political record of achievement, and the historic conjunction of events that made possible so unlikely a candidacy.

Part of Obama's appeal was understandable. To an American public always open to the new, always susceptible to the political prospect of change, especially in difficult times, everything about him promised a sharp break from the past. His personal story was intriguing, and somewhat familiar, thanks to his best-selling memoir, *Dreams from My Father*, written years earlier after his appointment as the first African-American editor in chief of the *Harvard Law Review*. The mere factual recitation of his biography suggested elements of a fable, a classic tale of rising from humble roots to triumph over adversity, the kind Americans have always relished: the black father from Kenya, the son of a goat herder, who came to the United States to study in Hawaii, there to meet and marry a fellow student, a white woman born in Wichita, Kansas, whose father served with Patton's army and whose mother became a World War II Rosie the Riveter war plant worker; the family ultimately following the old American pattern of heading west after the war and settling in Hawaii; the collapse of the biracial marriage after the father abandoned his wife and two-year-old son, Barack, in 1963 to return to Africa, where he became an alcoholic*and died in a 1982 car crash; the mother's remarriage to an Indonesian businessman who moved his new wife and young son to Jakarta, where Barack attended local schools until the age of ten; then, yet another move, with Barack returning to Hawaii to be raised by his white grandparents and attend a private school while his mother remained in Jakarta.

The rest of his story filled out the legend: attendance as a scholarship student at Occidental College in California, then Columbia University, then Harvard Law; community organizing on Chicago's South Side; legal work in a firm specializing in civil rights law; teaching constitutional law at the University of Chicago; the budding political career.

However helpful his personal story, two speeches actually made his

---

* In a curious coincidence, both Obama's father and John McCain's, an admiral, were alcoholics.

campaign for president possible. The first was in October 2002 before an anti–Iraq war rally in Chicago.

That speech came at a decisive moment in Obama's life, a time of self-doubt and frustration. At forty-one years old, he was in his sixth year in the Illinois Senate, relatively little known outside Illinois political circles. His career at that point could hardly be called soaring; just two years before, he had lost his attempt to take the congressional seat held by Democratic Representative Bobby Rush. He was tired of life in Springfield, the state capital, and envious of younger politicians on the rise. He was planning to run for the U.S. Senate in the 2004 Democratic primary, but had not yet formally announced. As he wrote in *The Audacity of Hope*, "I began feeling the way I imagine an actor or athlete must feel when, after years of commitment to a particular dream, after years of waiting tables between auditions or scratching out hits in the minor leagues, he realizes that he's gone just about as far as talent or fortune will take him. The dream will not happen, and he now faces the choice of accepting this fact like a grown-up and moving on to more sensible pursuits, or refusing the truth and ending up bitter, quarrelsome, and slightly pathetic."

As the debate over Iraq intensified in Washington, Clinton, McCain, John Edwards, John Kerry, and many others were preparing to support a congressional resolution giving Bush a blank check to go to war in Iraq. Obama decided to speak out against the war, though he was warned by friends to choose his words carefully. Whatever he said could affect his political future. For that reason, for one of the few times in his young career he used a prepared text.

Here, in part, is what he said that day: "I don't oppose all wars. After September 11, after witnessing the carnage and destruction, the dust and the tears, I supported this administration's pledge to hunt down and root out those who would slaughter innocents in the name of intolerance, and I would willingly take up arms myself to prevent such a tragedy from happening again. I don't oppose all wars. All I know is that in this crowd today, there is no shortage of patriots, or of patriotism. What I am opposed to is a dumb war. What I am opposed to is a rash war. What I am opposed to is the cynical attempt by Richard Perle and Paul Wolfowitz and other armchair weekend warriors in this administration to shove their own ideological agendas down our throats, irrespective of the costs in lives lost and in hardships borne. What I am opposed to is the attempt by political hacks like Karl Rove to distract us from a rise in the uninsured, a rise in the poverty rate, a drop in the median income—to distract us from corporate scandals and a stock market that has just gone through the worst month since the Great Depression. That's what I'm opposed to. A dumb war. A rash war. A war based not on reason but on passion, not on principle but on politics."

He condemned Saddam Hussein, calling him "a brutal man, a ruthless man, a man who butchers his own people to secure his own power," with a record of having "repeatedly defied UN resolutions, thwarted UN inspection teams, developed chemical and biological weapons and coveted nuclear capacity." The world would be better off without him, Obama said, then added, "But I also know that Saddam poses no imminent and direct threat to the United States or to his neighbors, that the Iraqi economy is in shambles, that the Iraqi military is a fraction of its former strength, and that in concert with the international community he can be contained until, in the way of all petty dictators, he falls away into the dustbin of history."

In words that would be seen as prescient, he summed up the case against American intervention: "I know that even a successful war against Iraq will require a U.S. occupation of undetermined length, at undetermined cost, with undetermined consequences. I know that an invasion of Iraq without a clear rationale and without strong international support will only fan the flames of the Middle East, and encourage the worst, rather than the best, impulses of the Arab world, and strengthen the recruitment arm of al-Qaeda."

His speech didn't attract national attention, didn't affect the outcome of the debate over Iraq, and didn't then elevate Obama's political stature. But it did attract the growing antiwar groups and passionately liberal activists who exercised great influence in the Democratic Party. Of all the candidates, Obama had staked out the earliest, clearest, and most eloquently expressed opposition to the war.

Obama was not expected to win even the 2004 Democratic Senate primary. He faced two better known, and better funded, candidates: Dan Hynes, the state comptroller, was the son of one of Chicago's most prominent and powerful Democrats; Blair Hull had made hundreds of millions of dollars as a stock trader and investor. Obama began the race far behind. Then, as the primary neared, Hull's collapse—a scandalous divorce that included charges of abuse and an admission of cocaine use—aided Obama's rise. Obama won the primary with 53 percent of the vote to become the Democratic nominee for the open seat.

Instant good fortune came that April when he spoke at a John Kerry presidential campaign stop in Chicago. Kerry was so impressed by what he heard that he became an Obama patron who set in motion a crucial event.

Kerry was searching for the right keynote speaker for the Democratic convention in Boston that July. Obama's advisers quietly began lobbying the Kerry team. Obama was out campaigning for the Senate seat when the call came from Mary Beth Cahill, Kerry's campaign manager. After it ended, Obama told the others with him in his car that he wanted to use his life story to speak about an America liberated from the red/blue divisions that then defined the political landscape. Later he made it sound as if his selection was merely a lucky matter over which he and his aides had little influence. "I have never exactly figured that out," he told Larry King during an October 2006 TV interview, responding to King's question about how he was chosen. "Somehow they thought that I could be useful at the convention. And so we started hearing that they might want me to speak there, which we didn't think too much of. And then at some point we got a call that they actually wanted me to be the keynote speaker."

Between sessions in the Illinois Senate, working late at night, or even taking refuge in the Capitol men's room, Obama kept scribbling away on scraps of paper to set down his thoughts and finally turned them into a speech draft. After finishing the legislative session in Springfield on Saturday, July 24, he arrived in Boston at close to midnight. On the flight he recalled his only other trip to a Democratic convention, four years earlier in Los Angeles. The car rental company had rejected his credit card, he couldn't even get a floor pass, and eventually he left, early and disconsolate.

Before he began final practices for his prime-time speech, now just two days away, he was booked to appear on the Sunday morning talk shows. Communications director Robert Gibbs roamed the convention floor, keeping a wary eye on his young star.

"Is your candidate an orator?" we asked Gibbs that morning.

"Not really," he said matter-of-factly.

What he didn't tell us that morning was that the practice sessions were not going well. Obama's delivery was flat and unimpressive. As he went through his lines, his advisers listened silently. Obama was frustrated by their lack of response. His team then brought in Michael Sheehan, the best speech coach in the Democratic Party, who tutored Obama from beneath the podium of the convention's Fleet Center. Obama had thought that to reach twenty thousand in the arena and a television audience in the millions he had to bellow. You don't need to shout, Sheehan told him. You don't need to scream. Just tell your story. Talk as if you're talking to someone. "With each rendition," Axelrod said, "it just became more and more organic to him, more and more flowing."

On the afternoon before his speech, David Mendell, who was covering the Illinois Senate campaign for the *Chicago Tribune*, followed Obama through the security fences protecting the Fleet Center. Obama looked even more confident than usual, Mendell thought; then he asked Obama how he was feeling about his speech. "I'm LeBron, baby," Obama replied, referring to LeBron James, the teenage phenomenon who was dazzling the National Basketball Association. "I can play on this level. I got some game."

His friend Marty Nesbitt marveled at the buildup surrounding Obama the day before the speech. "Wait until tomorrow," Nesbitt recalled Obama telling him, according to a later account in the *New Yorker*.

That night, moments before the speech, a nervous Axelrod and Gibbs were preparing to head out into the arena to watch their candidate. Obama patted Axelrod on the shoulder. "Don't worry," he said. "I'll make my marks."

As Obama began tracing the story of his own life, and of his biracial family, he was hitting his marks perfectly. "My parents shared not only an improbable love," he said. "They shared an abiding faith in the possibilities of this nation. They would give me an African name, Barack, or 'blessed,' believing that in a tolerant America your name is no barrier to success. They imagined—they imagined me going to the best schools in the land, even though they weren't rich, because in a generous America you don't have to be rich to achieve your potential."

The delegates were riveted on the young black man wearing a dark suit, white shirt, and pale blue necktie. Now they were on their feet filling the hall with thunderous applause as Obama delivered what became his signature message:

"Now, even as we speak, there are those who are preparing to divide us—the spin masters, the negative ad peddlers who embrace the politics of 'anything goes.' Well, I say to them tonight, there is not a liberal America and a conservative America—there is the United States of America. There is not a black America and a white America and a Latino America and an Asian America—there's the United States of America. The pundits, the pundits like to slice and dice our country into red states and blue states; red states for Republicans, blue states for Democrats. But I've got news for them, too. We worship an awesome God in the blue states, and we don't like federal agents poking around in our libraries in the red states. We coach Little League in the blue states and yes, we've got some gay friends in the red states. There are patriots who opposed the war in Iraq and there are patriots who supported the war in Iraq. We are one people, all of us pledging allegiance to the Stars and Stripes, all of us defending the United States of America. In the end—in the end—in the end, that's what this election is about. Do we participate in a politics of cynicism or do we participate in a politics of hope?"

In just twenty minutes, Barack Obama's political career had changed forever. The reaction to his speech was overwhelming. From commentators high in their booths broadcasting across the country to delegates in the hall, there was a sense of discovery and possibility. It was John Kerry's convention, but Barack Obama was the star. In the days and weeks and months after Boston, that star would continue to rise. "I knew from the moment he finished that things had changed in a way they were never going to go back," Axelrod said.

He was now a national celebrity, but still a Senate candidate with a race to finish. There again, fortune smiled on Barack Obama: His path to the Senate was already assured by the surprise withdrawal a month before the convention of his Republican opponent, Jack Ryan, after an embarrassing sex scandal. Illinois Republicans scrambled to find a replacement. In August, they settled on a most improbable candidate: perennial presidential hopeful Alan Keyes, an African-American from Maryland, not Illinois, a bombastic conservative who had no realistic chance to win. On November 4, 2004, Obama defeated Keyes by a landslide, carrying 70 percent of the vote to 27 percent for Keyes. It was the widest victory margin for a state-wide race in Illinois history. On that same election day, Obama's patron John Kerry became the latest in the long line of Democratic presidential candidates—seven out of the last ten—to lose to a Republican and set up George W. Bush's second term in the White House.

Once the candle was lighted in Boston, it never went out. Obama arrived in the Senate to great fanfare. His office was inundated with requests—

sometimes three hundred a week—for press interviews, speaking engage-
ments, appearances at political dinners. He had passed no legislation, given
no major speeches, and carved out no areas of expertise, yet he was treated
as a rock star. On the day of Bush's second inaugural, only two weeks after
being sworn in, Obama was stopped repeatedly as he made his way around
the Capitol. Republicans wearing Bush-Cheney buttons wanted to have
their pictures taken with the new senator with the million-dollar smile
and the compelling personal story. It was left to his seven-year-old daughter, Malia, to offer a humbling note. On the day he was sworn into office,
Obama and his family were walking around the Capitol grounds. "Are you
going to try to be president?" Malia asked playfully. "Shouldn't you be vice
president first?"

In his second year in the Senate, Obama stepped up his outside political
activity, appearing at Democratic Party events in Kansas and Minnesota
and Ohio. Ben Nelson, the conservative Democrat from Nebraska, asked
him to speak at a dinner in Omaha. Obama, he said, was about the only
national Democrat he would invite into his state. Everywhere Obama went
the crowds were far larger than those for other national candidates. And
everywhere people were urging him to run for president.

All this was part of a plan by his staff to raise Obama's national profile
and not foreclose the possibility of running for president in 2008. Though
a 2008 campaign seemed highly doubtful at the time, Obama was taking
deliberate steps to strengthen his position if the opportunity presented
itself. Pete Rouse, his chief of staff, prepared a memo, dated January 16,
2006, outlining the strategy. "It makes sense for you to consider now
whether you want to use 2006 to position yourself to run in 2008 if a 'perfect storm' of personal and political factors emerges in 2007," he wrote.

Rouse believed then that the odds Obama would run in 2008 were
exceedingly low. He was doing what a good adviser does, which was to
consider all contingencies. "If making a run in 2008 is at all a possibility,
no matter how remote, it makes sense to begin talking and making decisions about what you should be doing 'below the radar' in 2006 to maximize
your ability to get in front of this wave should it emerge and should you and
your family decide it is worth riding," Rouse wrote.

The summer of his second year in Washington, Obama followed the
path of previous presidential hopefuls by making a well-publicized foreign
trip—this one, chosen with symbolic and personal meaning, to Africa.

His seventeen-day itinerary included South Africa, where he criticized the government for its indifference to the AIDS crisis on the continent, and a refugee camp in Chad where refugees from the Darfur catastrophe were living. The centerpiece of his journey was a return to his father's native Kenya. There the outpouring was extraordinary: crowds surging close whenever he reached out to shake a hand; streets jammed; markets empty; a song written in his honor playing on loudspeakers. He and his wife, Michelle, took voluntary AIDS tests to encourage others to do the same. They visited Obama's grandmother Sarah Hussein Obama in the small village of Kogelo.

The African trip had a profound effect on Obama. For the first time, he later told advisers, he began to think about how his election as president might change America's image around the world, and how people would view the United States if an African-American was its leader.

In late summer, he accepted an invitation from Tom Harkin to speak at the Iowa senator's annual steak fry in September. For Obama and his team, the Iowa trip was a deliberate attempt to create some buzz, though those around him were still uncertain he would run in 2008. To further stoke presidential speculation, however, Rouse, formerly the top aide to Majority Leader Tom Daschle, asked another Daschle person, Steve Hildebrand, to join Obama. Since Hildebrand had been well-known as Gore's Iowa caucus guru, this was seen as another signal of Obama's presidential ambitions. Other Democratic candidates, including Clinton, had been recruiting Hildebrand, but he had never met Obama. That weekend Hildebrand became a convert. Soon, he was the most enthusiastic advocate for a 2008 race.

In October, Obama began a national publication tour for his second book, *The Audacity of Hope*, a title he borrowed from a sermon by his longtime Chicago pastor, the Reverend Jeremiah Wright Jr. The book was published not long before Obama's second appearance with Tim Russert on *Meet the Press*. His goal was to propel *Audacity* to the top of the bestseller lists, Obama told his aides. Don't you know, they said, you will be competing with John Grisham's first venture into nonfiction? That didn't bother Obama. When *Audacity* first hit the best-seller list, it was ranked number two behind Grisham. "It's great," he told Gibbs. "I want to be number one."

It was in that period that Obama and his key group privately began giving serious consideration to a presidential run. "During the book tour and then in rallies for '06 candidates, we were just getting enormous crowds and a lot of interest," Obama later explained to us. "At that point, I think my team and myself—my team and me—started thinking about what does this mean and is there something to the message I'm delivering that is right for these times, and is there something I could do at this moment that is different from what another Democratic candidate might be able to do."

On November 8, 2006, the day after the midterm elections, Obama and his advisers gathered around the conference table in Axelrod's Chicago offices for a major discussion about running for president. The group included Obama; Michelle; Axelrod; Gibbs; Rouse; Hildebrand; David Plouffe, slated to be his presidential campaign manager, if there was to be a campaign; Alyssa Mastromonaco, his scheduler; and close friends Valerie Jarrett and Marty Nesbitt. They agreed to set deadlines for a campaign that would have to go, as Obama put it, "from zero to sixty."

During one of their early meetings, Plouffe, relatively new to Obama's inner circle, had starkly posed Obama's choices. Your next two years could be remarkable times for you and your young family, Plouffe said. You could have pretty much every weekend off, take vacations, enjoy your lives. The alternative is a schedule that will keep you on the road constantly, with intense scrutiny, and that's going to be very hard. He cautioned Obama to keep two things in mind: While everyone's throwing rose petals in front of you now, you're not the front-runner in this race and you're going to have a lot of people who don't support you. On the other hand, if you win, you'll be the leader of the most powerful nation on earth.

"They didn't tell me anything I didn't know," Obama later told us, smiling as he recalled the meetings. "I was in a very good place. I was doing well in the Senate. We had gotten some legislative accomplishments I was very proud of. We'd just gotten the majority and I'd helped achieve that majority, so I was well positioned to get committee assignments I wanted, to maybe get some things done I'd been looking at for a long time. My books had sold, so I had some financial freedom I hadn't had before. My daughters were at just the most magnificent age there is. So I think I understood this was going to be a big sacrifice."

Asked about the best advice he received during that period, Obama replied, "Well, I have to say, it was advice I gave to myself. Which was, don't do this unless you actually believe that you'd be the best president. . . . There might be some people who would run for president to sort of boost their profile. I was already about as well-known as any politician in the country, with the exception of maybe Hillary and a handful of others. So I didn't need to run just as a gesture."

During that period, Obama privately consulted key political figures to get their assessment on whether or not he should run. Among them were Dick Durbin, the senior senator from Illinois, Tom Daschle, the well-respected former Democratic leader of the Senate, and Edward M. Kennedy, keeper of the Kennedy legacy. All urged him to run.

In the meantime, Axelrod had prepared a private presidential strategy memo for Obama dated November 28, 2006. An outgoing president nearly always defines the next election, Axelrod wrote, and people almost never seek a replica—certainly not after the presidency of George W. Bush. The basic qualities people saw in Bush—especially those voters likely to participate in Democratic primaries, but Independents and disaffected Republicans as well—were stubbornness, hyperpartisanship, a tendency to place ideology over reason, and a predilection to side with special interests. In 2008 people were going to be looking for a replacement, someone who represented different qualities. Where Bush was stubborn and unwilling to admit error, they were going to be seeking someone open and willing to bring together people with different points of view. Where Bush was hyperpartisan, they were going to be looking for someone to transcend the morass in Washington.

In Axelrod's opinion, Obama's profile fit this historical moment far better than Hillary Clinton's. If he was right, Obama could spark a political movement and prevail against sizable odds. "You are uniquely suited for these times," Axelrod wrote. "No one among the potential candidates within our party is as well positioned to rekindle our lost idealism as Americans and pick up the mantle of change. No one better represents a new generation of leadership, more focused on practical solutions to today's challenges than old dogmas of the left and right. That is why your convention speech resonated so beautifully. And it remains the touchstone for our campaign moving forward."

The second half of the Axelrod memo was more personal and pointed. "We should not get into a White Paper war with the Clintons, or get twisted into knots by the elites." He argued that the issue of experience was overrated but said strength was not, and he conceded that Clinton, because of all she had weathered, was seen by voters as a candidate of strength. "But the campaign itself also is a proving ground for strength."

His assessment of the field concluded that there were only two real rivals. Clinton, he wrote, "will try to command the race early with an array of White Papers. Her goal will be two: to suggest that she has the beef, while we offer only sizzle; and that she is not about the past but the future. But for all her advantages, she is not a healing figure. As much as she tacks to the right, she will have a hard time escaping the well-formulated perceptions of her among swing voters as a left-wing ideologue."

Edwards, he wrote, "is not to be discounted." The Edwards message of anticorporate populism and the widening gap between rich and poor had real resonance. "He connects viscerally with working class and rural voters, which is reflected in his impressive early lead in Iowa. He is a dynamic, relentless campaigner and debater." But Edwards, he added, had a potential problem raising the necessary funds to win the nomination, and there were also questions about whether he had the heft to become president.

"Finally," Axelrod wrote, "a word on the politics: Many have counseled you to wait and acquire more experience and seasoning before you jump into a race for the presidency. But history is replete with potential candidates for the presidency who waited too long rather than examples of people who ran too soon. . . . You will never be hotter than you are right now. And with the longevity favored by the Washington establishment comes all the baggage. You could wind up calcified in the Senate, with a voting record that hangs from your neck like the anchor from the Lusitania. . . . In short, there are many reasons to believe that if you are ever to run for the presidency, this is the time."

Axelrod's memo was most notable for its unsparing critique of his client. "The disarming admissions of weakness in your book [*Dreams from My Father*] will become fodder for unflattering, irritating inquiries." In parentheses, he alluded to questions Obama might face as a candidate: "How *many* times did you use cocaine and marijuana? When did you stop? Who did you buy it from? Did you *sell* drugs? Have you broken any other laws?"

He continued, "This is more than an unpleasant inconvenience. It goes to your willingness and ability to put up with something you have never experienced on a sustained basis: criticism. At the risk of triggering the very reaction that concerns me, I don't know if you are Muhammad Ali or Floyd Patterson when it comes to taking a punch. You care far too much what is written and said about you. You don't relish combat when it becomes personal and nasty. When the largely irrelevant Alan Keyes attacked you, you flinched.

"All of this may be worth enduring for the chance to change the world. And many, many people who believe in you are ready to march because we think the world so badly needs the change and leadership you have to offer. (Perhaps by running and winning, you can help change our politics too.)

"If you pull the trigger," the memo ended, "I am confident that we can put together a great campaign and campaign message of which we can all be proud."

Obama took two trips in December as he and his advisers refined their campaign strategy. The first was to California and the Saddleback Church of Rick Warren, the evangelical pastor and author of *The Purpose Driven Life*. Obama appeared as part of a summit on AIDS and the church, and he won a standing ovation. But it was the second trip, his first ever to New Hampshire, that moved him irretrievably into the 2008 campaign.

The pretext for traveling to New Hampshire was a book signing for *Audacity* in Portsmouth, where he spoke at an events center on the out-skirts of town. Long before his arrival, the parking lot was jammed and the conference center packed to overflowing—all 750 tickets were gone within hours. Outside, hawkers were selling Obama-for-President shirts, cam-paign buttons, and paraphernalia while inside, veteran political operatives were talking of how Obama had tapped into a public yearning for a leader who can change attitudes and bring the country together.

Later in Manchester, fifteen hundred people paid twenty-five dollars each to see Obama. He was introduced by New Hampshire Governor John Lynch, who joked that the party had originally invited the Rolling Stones until learning they could sell more tickets by having Obama there. When Lynch said, "Senator Obama, should you choose to run—" he was imme-diately interrupted by cheers and applause. Obama spoke for half an hour, ending with what sounded like a candidate's rallying cry: "America is ready to turn the page. America is ready for a new set of challenges. This is our time. A new generation is prepared to lead. You are part of that and I am grateful to be a partner with you on that."

Chuck Campion, who ran Walter Mondale's 1984 New Hampshire campaign and had come up from Boston with his wife to see firsthand what the Obama phenomenon was about, marveled at the scene. "In all my history," he said, "nobody's ever had a crowd this big, this early."

Throughout the day Obama was trailed by a press corps that rivaled that of most candidates on the eve of a New Hampshire presidential primary. They sat at row after row of tables in the back of the banquet hall hammering out leads that described Obama's visit in the most extraordinarily flattering terms—a swooning press reaction later called, accurately, "Obamamania." The TV talk show host Chris Matthews typified this kind of reaction when he remarked much later that he got "a thrill up my leg" after listening to Obama.

Before Obama spoke in Manchester, he held a press conference. He hadn't made a final decision about running, he said, and didn't believe ambition alone justified a candidacy. "I guess what I'm saying is, I don't want to be driven into this decision simply because the opportunity is there," he said, "but rather because I think I will serve the country well by running." Did he think what he was offering was different from other Democrats? "I think there's a certain tone that I've taken in my career that seems to be resonating right now. I will say this, that I am suspicious of hype. The fact that I've become—that my fifteen minutes of fame has extended a little longer than fifteen minutes is, I think, somewhat surprising to me and completely baffling to my wife. And I think what's going on is that people are very hungry for something new. I think they are interested in being called to be part of something larger than the kind of small, petty, slash-and-burn politics that we've been seeing over the last several years, and to some degree I think I'm a stand-in for that desire on the part of the country. . . . I think right now people are feeling they want commonsense, nonideological solutions to practical problems that they face, and so they're wondering could I be somebody who would help be partners in that."

When he finished, he looked toward one of his aides and asked, "Who's got my tea?"

Before announcing his candidacy, Obama vacationed in Hawaii. But he found no refuge there. A photograph of the bare-chested Obama on the beach in his swimsuit showed up in *People* magazine. He called Plouffe in Chicago. This is a drag, he told his would-be campaign manager. Plouffe wondered what he meant. I've been on the streets my whole life, Obama told him. I can't really move around. As he listened, Plouffe thought to himself, Maybe he's not going to do this. But Obama returned ready to run. On January 16, 2007, twenty-four months after being sworn in to the Senate, he filed the required notice of his presidential exploratory committee and announced his intentions with a video on his new Web site.

Obama set February 10 for his formal announcement in Springfield, Illinois, where he had served for eight years in the state senate. He chose the grounds of the Old State Capitol, where in 1858 Abraham Lincoln delivered his famous "House Divided" speech during his losing campaign for the United States Senate against Stephen A. Douglas. Obama's advisers liked the symbolism of having the first serious African-American presidential candidate standing where the Great Emancipator had spoken. They also hoped the scene might remind people of another Obama connection to Lincoln: Obama, like Lincoln, would come to the presidency with only limited national experience.

Obama, who liked to write late into the night, delivered a draft of his speech to his advisers about 4 a.m. on the Thursday before the Saturday announcement. Two speechwriters reworked it, but there was little time for Obama to practice. He arrived in Springfield on Friday night, where he was scheduled to tape an interview with CBS's *60 Minutes*. He had gone through the speech a few times the previous day, but had time for what one aide remembered as "one indifferent read-through" before returning to his hotel. Back in his suite, several friends prepared to leave to give Obama time to sleep. He insisted they stay and talk. "I remember looking at him," recalled Valerie Jarrett, one of his closest friends and a Chicago confidant, "and saying, 'Are you okay?' and he said, 'Yes, I'm fine. Are you okay?'" She replied, "No, I'm not. I'm a nervous wreck."

Saturday dawned with brilliant sunshine and bone-chilling temperatures, hovering in single digits as the announcement time neared. When she saw the weather forecasts, Michelle Obama urged his political team to move the event indoors. Obama's advisers resisted. They wanted not only the Greek-revival Capitol topped with a white-and-red cupola in the background but also the television shots that would show a sea of supporters huddled together as the candidate spoke. On the grounds of the Old State Capitol, and in the streets adjacent, people began to assemble—and then more people and more people until there were more than fifteen thousand of them, bundled against the frozen central Illinois morning. Even the advisers had not anticipated a crowd this large. Obama, his wife, and their daughters made their way onto the stage to a gigantic roar. He spoke of destiny and "the improbable quest" he was beginning that day:

"I recognize there is a certain presumptuousness—a certain audacity—to this announcement. I know I haven't spent a lot of time learning the ways of Washington. But I've been there long enough to know that the ways of Washington must change. The genius of our founders is that they designed a system of government that can be changed. And we should take heart, because we've changed this country before. In the face of tyranny, a band of patriots brought an empire to its knees. In the face of secession, we unified a nation and set the captives free. In the face of Depression, we put people back to work and lifted millions out of poverty. We welcomed immigrants to our shores, we opened railroads to the West, we landed a man on the moon, and we heard a King's call to let justice roll down like water, and righteousness like a mighty stream. Each and every time, a new generation has risen up and done what's needed to be done. Today we are called once more—and it is time for our generation to answer that call. For that is our unyielding faith—that in the face of impossible odds, people who love their country can change it."

From across the grounds came the roar of the crowd and the muffled applause from thousands of hands in heavy gloves. Families hoisted up their children for a better view and raised their digital cameras to capture history. They had come, many from hundreds of miles away, because they believed they *were* witnessing history. A new political movement was arising.

As in Boston, Obama had met the moment. Now he had a campaign to run. If somehow he managed to defeat Clinton in the primaries, further ahead presumably lay John McCain. How would the Republicans run against him if he became the Democratic nominee? In December 2006, when Obama was asked that by *Chicago Tribune* editors and reporters, he quickly answered, "War hero against snot-nosed rookie."

CHAPTER TWO

Johnnie Boy

The war in Iraq was "necessary, achievable, and noble. . . . Don't let anyone tell you otherwise."

—John McCain, defending Bush's Iraq war decision
to the 2004 Republican convention

John Sidney McCain III, "Johnnie boy" to his mother, was the presumed front-runner for his party's nomination in 2008. Years earlier, in 2000, he was an insurgent, a maverick, an irritant to the establishment. He was never a party man. In fact, he was distrusted within his party, seen as a too-willing collaborator with the Democrats and an unreliable conservative. The religious right disliked him, though his voting record on abortion was solidly pro-life. Economic conservatives saw him as a turncoat; they could not forgive his opposition to Bush's big tax cut in 2001, though he was the Senate's most hawkish opponent of pork-barrel spending. Only on defense and national security did McCain have the respect of those within his party, and then grudgingly so. Worst of all, he was seen as too eager to butt heads with the president.

McCain always believed he would be in a strong position to win a general election after Bush's 2004 reelection opened the way for a successor. McCain's problem was getting to that election. To win the nomination, he knew he needed to move from outsider to insider.

John McCain is a complex man whose character was formed as a military aristocrat and in a lifetime of public service. His father and grandfather were four-star Navy admirals, and like them McCain attended the Naval Academy in Annapolis. Unlike them, he graduated near the bottom of his class in 1958 (894th out of 899). He was a rebellious cadet and became a Navy pilot eventually assigned to combat duty in Vietnam. His service there became the stuff of a legend that shaped the rest of his life.

By 1967, McCain had made lieutenant commander and was on bombing runs over North Vietnam from the aircraft carrier USS *Forrestal*. That July, he narrowly escaped death after a fire swept the *Forrestal*, enveloping his plane on the carrier deck. McCain was badly burned, sustaining injuries from metal fragments to leg and chest after a bomb exploded. The fire killed 134 men, but he escaped and helped another pilot to safety.

The events at the center of the McCain story began three months later, on October 26, 1967. On his twenty-third bombing mission over North Vietnam a missile, fired from a Hanoi battery, struck McCain's A-4E Skyhawk. He bailed out and parachuted to Truc Bach Lake below, where North Vietnamese found him, unconscious, nearly drowned, suffering broken bones in both arms and a leg. They bayoneted him, crushed his shoulder with a rifle butt. They took him to Hoa Lo Prison, the infamous "Hanoi Hilton," where American prisoners of war were routinely and brutally tortured.

His five and a half years of captivity spanned the closing years of Lyndon Johnson's presidency, with the nation divided, and four years of Richard Nixon's White House tenure, which later ended with Nixon's resignation in disgrace in the wake of the Watergate scandal. While America was experiencing those national disasters, McCain was undergoing his own personal traumas. He was beaten, often repeatedly, and bound with ropes, all part of an interrogation process to compel "confessions" from prisoners. During the early months of his captivity, McCain was even denied medical treatment, and for two years he was held in solitary confinement. It was not until much later, after his captors learned that his father had been named commander of all U.S. forces in Vietnam, that they offered him, as a propaganda show of mercy, an opportunity to be released. McCain refused unless the other prisoners came out with him. Finally, on March 14, 1973, he was released. He had lost fifty pounds, his hair had turned white, and he was unable to raise his arms above his head.

John McCain, promoted to captain, returned to Washington to serve as Navy liaison to the Senate. It was there that he learned politics firsthand. He was offered promotion to admiral, but turned it down to enter politics himself in 1982 as Republican candidate for the House from Arizona, where he had moved. He won, served two terms, then in 1986 won the Senate seat held by retiring Barry Goldwater, the pre-Reagan political father of modern conservatism.

From the beginning, John McCain was a politician with restless energy and a short attention span. He could be merciless in his joking putdowns of young staffers. He had a quick temper and did not hesitate to use it on his colleagues. He survived an ethics investigation over a political influence scandal stemming from the collapse of savings and loan institutions in the 1980s and was dubbed by the media as one of five senators making up the "Keating Five." But whatever his strengths and weaknesses, friend and foe alike agreed on one fact about John McCain: He was a genuine American hero.

McCain's 2008 candidacy was born out of the despair and bitterness of a failed run for the White House against George W. Bush.

After McCain decisively defeated Bush in the 2000 New Hampshire presidential primary, their next encounter was in South Carolina, the state where the Civil War began and home to flag-waving, military-supporting citizens. South Carolina broke John McCain's spirit. The primary was vicious, as the Bush forces, their candidate on the ropes, savaged McCain. The worst could never be traced directly to Bush's team, but McCain and his advisers were certain they were responsible.

In one account, Mark McKinnon, Bush's media adviser, is described as listening to plans being laid by Bush's South Carolina operatives to attack McCain and thinking, "They let the dogs off the chain." There were telephone calls claiming McCain had fathered an illegitimate black daughter.* There were deceptive "push polls" designed to inflict damage on candidates by employing propaganda and false rumors to deceive poll respondents into thinking they were being asked questions based on facts. There were negative ads and snarling exchanges between the two candidates and ugly rumors about Cindy McCain being a drug addict and John McCain a homosexual who was mentally unstable as a result of his long imprisonment and torture. The attacks shook McCain badly. "Frankly, it's the first time in the campaign that I've been a little rattled," he said after hearing an account of a phone call to one household in which he was described as a liar and a cheat. He took down his own negative ads and sought to return to the style of campaigning that had helped him win New Hampshire, but to no avail. Bush won the primary easily, 53 to 42 percent.

---

* McCain's wife, Cindy, had brought back to the United States a three-month-old abandoned girl from a Bangladeshi orphanage run by Mother Teresa. They adopted her and named her Bridget.

A few days later, McCain won Michigan, but his campaign was already in a death spiral. Bitter and dispirited, he retaliated with a speech in which he attacked the right-wing evangelical preachers Jerry Falwell and Pat Robertson as "agents of intolerance." By early March he was out.

Two months later, McCain stood next to Bush in a Pittsburgh hotel in what he agreed was a "take your medicine now" event to announce his support for the victor. He had to be coaxed by a reporter before finally uttering the right words. Through gritted teeth, he said softly, "I endorse Governor Bush." Then, in what seemed like a sarcastic coda, he added, "I endorse Governor Bush. I endorse Governor Bush. I endorse Governor Bush. I endorse Governor Bush. I endorse Governor Bush."

McCain returned to the Senate the leader of a rump movement of moderates, independents, reformers, and citizens fed up with the ways of Washington. His relations with the new White House were distant and chilly. John Weaver, his top political adviser, was so angry over what had happened in the campaign that he signed up as a consultant with the Democrats. Senate Democratic leader Tom Daschle quietly approached McCain and encouraged him to switch parties. McCain mulled over the idea but would not do it.

Then he began to flex his muscles. With Democrat Russell Feingold of Wisconsin, he put together a coalition to pass the most significant campaign finance reform act since Watergate. In Bush's second term, McCain fought the president over torture policy and forced him to give ground. He led a bipartisan group known as the "Gang of 14" that defused a tense standoff over Bush's judicial nominees. Conservatives, looking ahead to probable Supreme Court vacancies, were infuriated. Dr. James Dobson, the conservative leader of Focus on the Family, called the McCain-led deal "a betrayal." What his detractors overlooked was that McCain's compromise assured confirmation of some of Bush's most conservative and controversial court nominees.

McCain had never given up his dream of becoming president. What he needed most was a rapprochement with Bush to ease his way back into good standing with the Republican establishment. Bush's reelection campaign paved the way. The first step came that spring of 2004 with a telephone call from Weaver to Mark McKinnon, media guru to Bush. Weaver wanted the White House to know that McCain was eager to campaign for the president and believed he could be vitally important in attracting swing voters. McKinnon set up a meeting between Weaver and Karl Rove, who had been enemies for many years. The two agreed to bury their differences, opening the way for McCain to become Bush's most important surrogate.

Nothing captured that shift in political loyalties more powerfully than what took place during a joint appearance at a campaign rally in Pensacola, Florida, on August 10, 2004. Television cameras recorded the scene and the crowds cheered as George W. Bush and John S. McCain, standing together on the stage, embraced in a bear hug. Then, with McCain's head resting awkwardly on Bush's shoulder, the president gave his former rival a peck on the cheek.

Later, McCain spent a night at the Bush ranch. There the president and several aides deliberately left Rove and McCain alone at the house. Some of Bush's aides were worried about that private meeting, and were anxious to get back before any damage might be done. Bush took the opposite view. "The president said, 'No, let's wait, let's let them marinate a little,'" recalled Mark McKinnon. McCain and Rove talked about the electoral map, about how McCain could help through the fall. Knowing of McCain's admiration for President Theodore Roosevelt, Rove later gave McCain a pair of Teddy Roosevelt cuff links as a souvenir for his help in Bush's reelection.

One of McCain's most important contributions, the moment he showed his loyalty to the president as never before, came on the opening night of the Republican National Convention in New York at the end of August. There he offered a strong defense of Bush's decision to go to war in Iraq, articulating the case far better than the president or other administration officials had. The war, McCain said, was "necessary, achievable, and noble." The choice, he added, "wasn't between a benign status quo and the bloodshed of war. It was between war and a graver threat. Don't let anyone tell you otherwise."

McCain was far ahead of Clinton or Obama in preparing for 2008. As she was worrying about reelection in New York and Obama was barely thinking seriously about running for president, McCain took his initial trips to early states. His first stop was Concord, New Hampshire, on April 7, 2006—a fund-raiser for Republicans in the state legislature. About two hundred people turned out to hear him that night. He told some old jokes that he had used for years before addressing three topics at the heart of his message. First, spending in Washington was out of control and Republicans had to curb their own appetites and return to fiscal discipline. Second, il-

legal immigration was out of control but the only answer was a comprehensive solution that included a path to citizenship for undocumented workers
already in the country. Third, winning in Iraq remained vital to America's
security. He said, "The consequences of failure are immense. . . . If we
leave Iraq, if you read Zarqawi, bin Laden, all of these other terrorists,
they're not going to just be satisfied with Iraq. They're coming after us."

On those three bullet points he was in agreement with the Republican
base on spending, at odds with them on immigration, and out of step with
the country on the war. His candidacy was off to a shaky start.

After the fund-raiser, McCain was driven to the Hancock Inn for the
night. It was rainy and the roads were enveloped in clouds and fog, so it
wasn't until 8:30 p.m. that he came down to the dining room to join John
Weaver, Mike Dennehy, his New Hampshire political adviser, and Dennehy's wife, Sarra, as well as several reporters.

He was relaxed and engaging—the McCain voters had seen in the 2000
campaign. He talked at length about the immigration bill then under consideration in the Congress, and was passionate about the need for action.
He was critical of some Republicans who opposed his bill and lavished
praise on Edward M. Kennedy, his Senate partner in pushing for comprehensive legislation. "He is a lion in winter," McCain said. He was also
deeply worried about the political cost to his party if Republicans killed
immigration reform. "We all know the parties that have attracted immigrants into this country have been the ruling parties," he said. "It's just a
historical fact."

A man approached the table. "Senator, pardon me for intruding. I'm
from Massachusetts and you probably don't hear this enough from us, but
I'm a Republican, I'm an admirer, and I wanted you to know there are a
few of us." McCain smiled. "I think you're covered under the Endangered
Species Act," he said to laughter around the table.

The talk turned to Iraq. What could Bush do about the situation there?
McCain had long advocated sending additional forces but was now pessimistic about that course of action. "I think it's getting more and more up
to the Iraqis, because we're not going to increase troop presence there," he
said. "We all know that. We're not."

He was careful not to criticize Bush but expressed great frustration
with Donald Rumsfeld and the Pentagon. He recalled one of his early trips
to Iraq after the invasion when he met a British officer who told him
bluntly the United States needed more troops. When he returned to Washington, he went to the Pentagon for breakfast with Rumsfeld and several

senior military officers. "I say, 'Mr. Secretary, you don't have enough troops. We've got to have more troops over there.' [Rumsfeld says,] 'Commanders on the ground have not asked for additional troops.' I said, 'With all due respect, Mr. Secretary, I don't expect the commanders on the ground to ask for help. It's the nature of the beast.' I said, 'But you've got to look at the overall situation and it's clear from historical lessons you've got to have more boots on the ground.'"

McCain had traveled to Iraq with Hillary Clinton in 2005. Now a reporter asked about her views on the war and how they might affect her presidential aspirations. McCain said, "I think she's in a difficult spot given the fact that her party is moving further and further to the left on the issue."

Would she be a strong presidential candidate? Yes, he said, without hesitation. "She's smart. She's tough. She's disciplined. . . . I think to underestimate her would be the height of foolishness for any Republican. I could probably imagine a couple of remote scenarios where she doesn't get the nomination, but in most scenarios, she's got the nomination. That's not a stroke of genius."

Would you offer her the vice presidency? someone asked in jest. "In a New York minute," he said with a laugh.

Back then to serious questioning. Was she too polarizing to win a general election? one of the reporters asked. "First of all, it depends who she runs against, and I'm dead serious when I say that—my own ambitions or lack of ambitions aside," McCain said. "So how is she able to position herself depending on who she's running against?" He then looked over at Weaver. "Correct me if you think I'm wrong, John, but I think 2000 and 2004 were radical departures from traditional presidential politics, because Rove was able to energize the base enough so that you just expanded the base out and won the election. Every other time, as we all know, it's the fight for the center." He continued, "So if she's able to solidify her base early, which apparently she's able to do, then she can swerve over to the center. . . . I think she may have an easier time moving to the center than perhaps we might like."

In describing the course for Clinton, he was sketching out his own hoped for path: Consolidate—or in his case at least mollify—the base early and then move to the center for the general election.

The dinner closed with McCain offering a lengthy explanation of his relationship with Jerry Falwell, at that point the most visible symbol of his effort to win over the GOP base. There were reports that McCain and

Falwell had patched up their differences. Falwell even invited him to deliver the commencement address at Liberty University. The previous weekend, NBC's Tim Russert had grilled McCain so relentlessly about Falwell, among other issues, that as the program was ending, McCain deadpanned, "I haven't had so much fun since my last interrogation" as a prisoner of war.

"[Falwell] sought the meeting, came in and sat down and said I want to put our differences behind us. I said absolutely," McCain told those around the table at the Hancock Inn. "Then the conversation continued. I discussed with him my position on the gay marriage amendment, because I knew that was a hot-button issue with them and they're not in agreement with me on the federalism aspect of it. [McCain opposed a constitutional amendment but supported state bans on gay marriage.] And he said, 'I'd like you to speak at the commencement of my university.' . . . Ronald Reagan's spoken there. Bush One spoke there. Bush Two, I think, has spoken there. . . . The one thing that some people don't get is that I put that stuff behind me." He rapped his knuckles on the table to emphasize each word. "It's not a huge deal, but I didn't ask to see him. I didn't seek to communicate with him. We received a call one day that said Reverend Falwell would like to see you. Fine. . . . You've got to do that. And I find then that people don't hold grudges against me."

The next morning, McCain appeared at a town hall meeting at Keene State College. Harking back to 2000, he said, "It seems like only yesterday," except the reception was not as friendly. A student asked a pointed question about Falwell. Not satisfied with McCain's first explanation, the student said, "This is a radical religious movement that Jerry Falwell is part of and don't you think that a respected person such as yourself, and rightfully so, don't you think that legitimizes that movement?" McCain then defended the Christian right. Religious conservatives had become the backbone of the party structure, he said. "Should we eject people from our party because we may have disagreements?" he asked. "I think the great strength of the Republican Party is for us to all get involved, debate, and come to a consensus."

Minutes later, a man stood up to challenge McCain on immigration. He called illegal immigrants "parasites" and declared, "A criminal is a criminal." Ten minutes later, another man raised the immigration issue. Why is the bill under consideration in Congress likely to be any more effective than the

one passed twenty years earlier? "It's very different from the 1986 law," Mc-
Cain explained, but it was clear his questioner did not agree.

Then a woman stood up. Her list of grievances was long and she concluded by saying, "This country no longer belongs to me. I'm not getting
anything I really need and my grandchildren are being saddled with a nine-
trillion-dollar debt. Why should I vote Republican?" McCain, prickly now,
told her Democrats were even more profligate than Republicans. "So
maybe you should vote for vegetarians," he scolded.

"The Republicans are in charge of three houses," she responded. "You
have no excuse."

As the audience applauded, McCain answered, more politely. "Yes,
ma'am," he said. And then, "I knew we should have cut this thing off." The
quip brought laughter from the crowd, but it was now clear the climate he
would face as a candidate in 2008 was far different from eight years earlier,
and the closer he tied himself to Bush, the more precarious his path.

McCain's makeover extended beyond courtship of establishment Republicans and leading social conservatives. It included a dramatic shift in
his position on Bush's tax cuts. In 2001, McCain was one of just two Republican senators to oppose the new president's massive $1.35 trillion tax
cut plan. Two years later, he was one of three Republican senators to oppose another round of tax cuts, arguing they were irresponsible. In 2004
he said he would not support extending the cuts. That soon changed. With
Republicans pushing to make the tax cuts permanent in 2006, and McCain
now courting the tax-cutting wing of the party, he suddenly shifted positions and voted with his party to extend tax cuts for dividends and capital
gains, saying, "American businesses and investors need a stable and pre-
dictable tax policy."

What was emerging was a far different McCain from the one who ran
in 2000. He was no longer maverick enough to satisfy the Independents
who once embraced him, but neither was he yet reliably conservative
enough to generate passion within the base.

The final step in his political makeover was to sign off on a campaign
apparatus patterned after Bush's 2004 reelection committee, a huge operation that was in sharp contrast to the lean campaign he ran in 2000.
McCain approved an initial blueprint that called for spending $154 million
to win the Republican nomination. The plan was laid out in great detail in
a spreadsheet, later provided to us. There were itemized projections for
travel (chartered airplanes would cost the campaign a quarter million a
month); for Cindy McCain's staff and traveling expenses; for super-offices

in New York and California; for political offices in two dozen states; for communications and policy and research; for an e-campaign; and for advertising (production of the first ads was slated for July 2007, with the spots budgeted to begin airing in November).

All it required was money. McCain's team envisioned raising $48 million in the first quarter of 2007, a figure that no campaign had ever achieved. They anticipated $36 million from major donors, more than $5 million from direct mail, almost $2 million on the Internet. The numbers were unbelievable. But McCain's advisers were committed. "We have to look as much like Bush on fund-raising as we can," Rick Davis, CEO of the burgeoning enterprise, told us. That McCain was now adopting the Bush model was a supreme irony.

When the Republicans lost the House and Senate in November 2006, McCain didn't worry about formally announcing his campaign for president. He had already been running for two years. Days after the midterm election, he filed papers with the Federal Election Commission declaring himself a candidate.

CHAPTER THREE

Hillary

We are more Thatcher than anyone else. . . . Being human is overrated.

—Mark Penn's advice to Hillary

In January 2007, no one loomed larger in presidential politics than the newly reelected junior senator from New York, Hillary Rodham Clinton. Her path to the starting gate was unique. No former First Lady had ever sought the presidency; no female politician had ever begun a presidential campaign as the favorite; no First Lady had ever suffered the public humiliation Hillary did over her husband's affair with White House intern Monica Lewinsky.

Clinton's decision to run for the Senate from New York in 2000 seemed folly to many, including some of her own advisers. When she began, she was a cautious and sometimes wooden candidate who came to appreciate even more her husband's natural gifts as a candidate, she ruefully told her advisers. New Yorkers had anticipated a titanic battle between a sitting First Lady and then New York mayor, Rudy Giuliani. But after he was diagnosed with prostate cancer, Giuliani quit the race. In his place, Republicans offered a callow Long Island congressman named Rick Lazio. She won easily.

On the night of her election, Trent Lott, the Republican leader of the Senate, gave her fair warning of the reception she could expect. "I'll tell you one thing," he said. "When this Hillary gets to the Senate—if she does, maybe lightning will strike and she won't—she will be one of one hundred, and we won't let her forget it."

Instead, what they got was a consummate politician. Clinton was diligent, prepared, and respectful of the upper chamber's traditions and of her elders. She sought out the senior Democratic senator and guardian of its traditions, Robert C. Byrd of West Virginia, who tutored her in the arcane ways of the Senate. "I think of her as a pupil of mine," Byrd later said. She made friendships across the aisle. She joined a prayer group that included a number of evangelical Republicans. She co-sponsored legislation with conservatives like Rick Santorum of Pennsylvania, though it pained him to explain their relationship. She teamed up with House Majority Leader Tom DeLay, who had led Republicans in pressing for Bill Clinton's impeachment and remained an outspoken opponent of her husband. She worked with Republican Senator Lindsey Graham of South Carolina to improve conditions for reservists and members of the National Guard. She joined McCain and Graham on a congressional trip to the Baltic region. What happened there soon became legend on Capitol Hill—a vodka-drinking contest in which the New York senator matched the men drink for drink. When we asked Graham about the incident in March 2005, his eyes brightened and he began to chuckle. "What goes on a trip stays on a trip," he said. "Let's just say that Hillary Clinton's one of the guys."

Clinton waited patiently until a seat on the Armed Services Committee opened up, then seized it. On the committee, she rarely missed a hearing and, as the panel's junior member, waited for her turn to question the generals and admirals and civilian leaders of the Pentagon. "She had an extraordinary grasp of our military culture, our soldiers, our families and what it was like for them," General John Keane said in the summer of 2006.

Nor did she neglect her home state of New York. Traveling with her in early September 2005, we watched as she moved through a procession of meetings to highlight her success in bringing money to complete a section of interstate highway near Elmira, to fund a high-tech facility in Canandaigua, to create markets for fruit and vegetable growers, upstate wineries, and New York City restaurant owners. In Penn Yan, she drew a laugh when she said the reason she spent so much time working on agricultural issues was "I like to eat and drink."

She was happy in the Senate, pledging to serve the full six years of her term when elected in 2000 and holding firm to that pledge when, in 2003 and early 2004, supporters urged her to enter the Democratic nomination battle. In November 2003, she traveled to Iowa to emcee the annual Jefferson Jackson Dinner featuring all the presidential candidates, sparking more talk about how she towered over others in the party.

After the 2004 election, there was no escaping the speculation about a Clinton race, nor did she make any serious effort to discourage it. Before turning full attention to 2008, she had one overriding goal: winning reelection as impressively as possible in 2006. She hoped a good performance among upstate Republicans would persuade skeptical Democrats that she could win in other Republican areas around the country. Unlike her potential rivals, she did not even visit Iowa or New Hampshire that year, so intent was she on rolling up a huge victory at home.

Her Senate reelection campaign offered the powerful opportunity to build a fund-raising base that would follow her into a presidential campaign. If she raised money successfully, and spent wisely, she would be able to begin her presidential race with more money in the bank—perhaps $20 or $25 million—than many of her rivals could expect to raise in the first two or three quarters of 2007. But the Senate campaign became a financial disaster. Though she eventually raised $51.5 million, she burned through $41 million of it against an opponent who spent just $6 million. She ended 2006 with only $11 million in the bank for her presidential campaign. A year later, she would pay dearly for this mismanagement. She wanted a huge reelection victory and got it, carrying 67 percent of the vote. But it came at a price. Some of her advisers believed there had been too much focus on the reelection effort and not enough on getting ready for 2008. "My own gut is they put way too much premium on that," one of the Clintons' closest friends said later. "We should have used '06 to get ready to run for president."

For all of Clinton's effectiveness as a senator, questions lingered as she prepared to run: What did she really believe? Was she, as her husband had been, a New Democrat, a centrist who would challenge the party's liberal constituencies? Was she a radical feminist, as the right-wing talk show hosts liked to depict her? Was she the Clinton of Hillarycare, the ambitious and ultimately disastrous effort to reform the nation's health care system? Was she the Clinton who had been the target of the most relentless assaults on her character and whose own strong counterattacks dismissing her enemies as part of a "vast right-wing conspiracy" only triggered greater controversies?

Her attempts to answer these questions did little to clarify her political identity. She answered a call from the centrist Democratic Leadership Council to head a project for a fresh agenda for the 2006 midterms. But the speech she delivered at the DLC's 2005 summer meeting in Columbus, Ohio, was gauzy Democratic boilerplate, not a new vision of the party. In the spring of 2006, she began a series of policy speeches with the intention of giving people a fuller sense of what she believed. But even her aides had difficulty describing what was distinctive about her philosophy or ideology.

At the same time, she seemed unwilling to reduce herself to political sloganeering. "I don't think like that," she told us in May 2006. "I approach each issue and problem from a perspective of combining my beliefs and ideals with a search for practical solutions. It doesn't perhaps fit in a pre-existing box, but many of the problems we face as a nation don't either."

Everyone had a different label for her. One of her outside advisers called her "a modern centrist," another "a progressive without illusions," a politician who has been "consistent but complicated." Mark Penn, her chief strategist, saw her as a "responsible progressive." The late Molly Ivins, the tart-penned Texas liberal, saw her as a combination of "triangulation, calculation and equivocation," and the Reverend Jerry Falwell, before he died, told us she was a liberal "ideologue."

The public at large had pervasive doubts: Did Americans really want to return to the bitter controversies and tawdry scandals of the Clinton years? Even more troubling was an undercurrent we heard. "Dynasty," said one such voter, female and Democrat and admiring of Clinton personally. She meant, she explained, the dominance of two families over the nation's destiny that had characterized presidential control for the last twenty years. Starting in 1988, George H. W. Bush's presidency was followed by two Bill Clinton terms. They were followed by George W. Bush's two terms from 2000 to 2008. Now Hillary's candidacy raised the prospect of possibly another two-term Clinton reign.

Clinton resisted any public talk of a candidacy, but in late summer 2006 her advisers began putting together the machinery for a White House bid, starting with the team that had carried her into the Senate. The presumed manager-to-be was Patti Solis Doyle, a Chicagoan who had worked for Hillary Clinton since 1992. The chief strategist would be Mark Penn, who was as close to Hillary and Bill Clinton as anyone in their political world. Mandy Grunwald, who had joined Bill Clinton's 1992 campaign and remained part of the political family, would be in charge of media. Howard Wolfson, a former executive director of the Democratic Congressional

Campaign Committee, would be the communications director. Neera Tanden, Clinton's chief issues adviser, would be policy director. One other person who would play a critical role was Harold Ickes, who had served as deputy White House chief of staff under President Clinton and as a long-time confidant to Hillary. These people were experienced, winners, tough-minded and feared—but as a team they were dysfunctional. They often were at war with each other. They did not adequately supervise control of their financing. They debated endlessly over the campaign message and strategy. They failed, in short, to run a taut, disciplined political operation. They also misjudged their opposition. Ickes recalled a long strategy meeting that summer where Obama's name came up. He was not regarded as a serious threat. Ickes bet Obama would not even run. Solis Doyle predicted he would.

While her immediate advisers were united in wanting her to run, Clinton loyalists beyond the inner circle had misgivings. Mike McCurry, a self-described "Hillary partisan" who had been Bill Clinton's White House press secretary, was one of them. "I thought running was a bad idea for her, because of the viciousness and the polarization she would start with as baggage," he told us in the fall of 2007, months after the decision to run had been made. "To be successful, she'd have to shed a lot of that. You know, front-runners don't fare very well."

McCurry said he made these points to people he had worked with in the White House who were very close to her, but he was speaking as some-one not directly plugged into her select inner team. "I'd say, 'Look, when you're talking her through this [decision whether to run], someone has to make the case that this is going to be awfully hard. It will get very personal. Whatever's out there about President Clinton lurks in the shadows all the time; you never know what bombshell may drop the next day. . . . And why go through that when you are, right now, one of the most popular United States senators? People really admire how hard you work, and they like you; you're appreciated on both sides of the aisle; within the confines of the Senate you're not an incendiary, polarizing figure. You're a real leader, and you've got credibility leader qualities written on you.' . . . That was my message literally."

Clinton herself had no doubt the campaign would be tough and at times painful, but worth the prize. "She loved the United States Senate," recalled campaign chairman Terry McAuliffe. "She knew how brutal the campaign would be. I think what in her mind she had to get over was [whether] it was worth what she was going to have to go through, considering she was in a place she loved." At one point she told McAuliffe, "I have no illusions about how tough this is going to be. I am ready for what they throw at me."

Shortly before Christmas, Penn sent Hillary an eleven-page, single-spaced memo entitled "Launch Strategy Thoughts." Part of his memo, first unearthed by Josh Green of the *Atlantic*, was pure flattery. At one point he wrote, "We have incredible image strengths—we have the highest levels of early enthusiasm for any Democratic candidate in modern history—people don't just like Hillary Clinton, they love her; they are enthusiastic about her, and that enthusiasm is growing, not shrinking."

The memo was critical of the party's two previous nominees, Al Gore and John Kerry, whom he regarded as weak. People knew where President Bush stood, both in 2000 and 2004, Penn wrote, adding, "What on earth were Gore and Kerry going to do if they got elected? Few could figure that out. They were too busy trying to explain the past rather than give the voters a clear vision of the future. Gore became obsessed with Monica Lewinsky and Kerry with Vietnam. Kerry became a relentless voice of criticism, not or [sic] leadership or creativity."

In boldfaced type he wrote, "Hillary occupies a completely different ground than past nominees. People see in Hillary Clinton someone who works hard to get results, someone who is tough enough to make decisions, someone who is smart enough and experienced enough to understand the complexities of the modern world and yet passionate enough to fight for causes she believes in. She also heads a movement of women looking to achieve the true promise of America—that a qualified woman could be president of this country."

He went on, "And we have to be careful not to fall into the trap of reliving the past—this election can't be about the old Clinton years, but about the future. Bush did not run on the record of his father, though he benfitted [sic] from the name and association. New Times, New Ideas, a New Clinton."

Penn argued that former British prime minister Margaret Thatcher should be Hillary's role model: "She represents the most successful elected woman leader in this century—and the adjectives that were used about her (Iron Lady) were not of good humor or warmth, they were of smart, tough leadership. . . . We are more Thatcher than anyone else. . . . She was brought to power by a disastrous 'socialist' government while we are coming in after a disastrous conservative government."

Penn saw Obama as a potential obstacle who "represents something big—an inspirational movement. But the more you analyze what he says, the more you wonder what is behind the hype." He recommended they "research his flaws, hold our powder, see if he fades or does not run. Attacking him directly would backfire. His weakness is that if voters think about him five minutes they get that he was just a state senator and that he would be trounced by the big Republicans."

Another obstacle was the Democratic base, which Penn described as "the most liberal, activist, difficult group of voters in America." He called for neutralizing them. "The brie and cheese set drives fundraising and elite press but does not drive the vote. . . . Kerry beat [Howard] Dean. Gore easily defeated [Senator Bill] Bradley." To deal with this constituency, Penn called for outreach to the blogs and more criticism of Bush's policies in Iraq. He ticked off other potential problems, from concern among Democrats that she could not win a general election to the potential threat in Iowa posed by John Edwards.

He also spoke to the charge that Clinton was insincere. "In the polling, this was the most damaging attack—the smart attack for Republicans or primary opponents," he wrote. To counter this, Penn recommended avoiding "anything that even smells like a position change. We are perilously close on Iraq and we should stick to criticism of current policy as much as possible."

Penn described Clinton as she was: the "establishment, experienced leader candidate. While humility is always a great trait, leadership of a party that is looking for leadership is what we have to offer—we are the candidate with the money, the ideas, the operation, and the determination to win. Our goal in this first quarter is to show we have the muscle to win—to live up to the financial expectations. We want to show Obama how it is really done. First trips must be big, fundraising must be big."

He warned her not to take voters in the early states for granted. "We have to focus on the local races, treating each state like it is Upstate New York. . . . I believe that if you win Iowa it is over," he wrote.

Toward the end, Penn turned to the touchiest issue of all: how to make

Clinton seem more appealing. "Bill Gates once asked me, 'could you make me more human?' I said 'being human is overrated.' Now don't get me wrong. Connecting with people and understanding their problems with passion is a critical part of leadership. But the idea that if only you were warmer and nicer so many more people would like you and [you] would be in the White House is wrong. True, more people would like you. Fewer would vote for you."

His memo concluded by addressing the issue that most threatened her hopes of winning the nomination: Her support for the resolution authorizing Bush to go to war in Iraq had created a breach with the left in the Democratic Party—and an opening for Obama.

Clinton's Senate advisers Philippe Reines and Andrew Shapiro had been urging her to make one more trip to Iraq before launching her candidacy. Many of her political advisers told her she could wait no longer to start the campaign. But Penn thought she should make the trip before announcing. "I believe we have to visit Iraq before we can visit other places in the world," he wrote. "The Iraq war is the major animating issue. Time and again, it is not about how you voted in the past, but what would you do about it. This gives us a chance to make it clear that Iraq and fixing it is central to what you are about—the reason that you would leave the Senate for the White House—what you see happening there, what is happening to the middle class here, what is happening to America's respect in the world. They are the reasons you are jumping in. . . . The alternative is to skip Iraq, throw your hat in the ring earlier and do it all as a straight political month. It is what the others will be doing which is why I like plan A."

On Thursday, January 11, 2007, Clinton, Evan Bayh, and John McHugh, a Republican congressman from upstate New York, left Andrews Air Force Base for the Middle East. The itinerary included Kuwait, Iraq, Afghanistan, and Pakistan. Six days later, back in Washington, she told reporters at a press conference, "The president's team is pursuing a failed strategy in Iraq as it edges closer to collapse, and Afghanistan needs more of our concerted effort and attention." She outlined a series of proposals designed to lead to the start of a phased withdrawal of U.S. forces. If the Iraqis then failed to meet certain benchmarks, the administration would be required to seek a new authorization from the Congress for the war effort.

She was now ready to run. Three days later, she launched her candidacy with a video on her campaign Web site. Sitting in a chair in a sunlit room overlooking the garden at her home in Northwest Washington, a radiant Clinton told the world, "Let's talk. Let's chat." In a statement, she declared, "I'm in and I'm in it to win."

BOOK TWO

THE PEOPLE

CHAPTER FOUR

"Very Scary Times"

"How many think the next generation will be better off than yours?" the pollster asked the all-Republican group of voters. Not a single hand was raised.

—From a Peter Hart focus group

Optimism has been the hallmark of the American people. Through good times and bad, through wars and economic downturns, they have clung to the belief that, however difficult their own time, their children's lives would be better than theirs. No longer was that true as the 2008 election year began. That sense of an America confronting dire conditions and unique challenges defined the mood of voters. We found that was true both in our interviews across the nation and in our attendance over a long period of time at "focus groups" chosen to reveal attitudes about the candidates and the issues.

To a startling degree, Democrats, Republicans, and Independents, liberals, moderates, and conservatives agreed about the troubled state of the nation, no matter their disagreements over policies and political personalities, their regions and individual backgrounds. These voters were eager, almost desperate, to "turn the page," as Barack Obama's call for fundamental change put it—and they needed to rally behind a candidate who offered the best hope of delivering on that promise. In the beginning, they were unsure whether Obama, or anyone else, met that test even as the problems facing the nation worsened.

In the spring of 2007, nearly nine months before the first primary and a year and a half before the election, the pollster Peter Hart conducted the first of ten focus groups. These sessions, each lasting up to three hours and sponsored by the Annenberg Public Policy Center of the University of Pennsylvania, were designed to track the attitudes of voters as the campaign unfolded. The voters represented the range of the American electorate, demographically, politically, and ideologically and by race, age, and gender. The three focus groups that met before 2008 began set the stage for all that followed and proved to be remarkably revealing about the political currents that would mark the entire year.

Once that first group of Republicans, Democrats, and Independents was seated around a long conference room table, Hart asked them to quickly give him a word or phrase to describe how they felt things were going in America. Their bleak responses poured forth:

"Alarming."

"Depressing."

"Disturbing."

"Insecure."

"Turbulent."

"Lack of leadership."

"Political disunity."

At that point, the Iraq war was *the* dominant issue, one that darkened nearly everyone's opinion about America, regardless of political leaning. Republicans who had supported George W. Bush and Democrats who had opposed him agreed that U.S. policy toward Iraq was not working and needed to be changed.

The group's feelings about the candidates were sketchy, inconclusive, or ill-formed—with one exception. That was Hillary Clinton. She was, by far, the most polarizing of candidates. Nearly every voter had a strong, often passionate opinion about her, ranging from adoration to loathing. Again, the quick responses told the story. She was either a "strong leader" or "deceitful"; "dishonest" or "phenomenal"; "fake" or "determined." Hart, struck by the intense emotional attitudes about Clinton, commented afterward, "Of all the candidates I have ever observed, or surveyed for or about, only Senator Edward M. Kennedy in 1980 resembled this kind of profile. Like Clinton, the view of Kennedy was complex and multilayered. It was not a single challenge he had to overcome but a complex mix of elements. What was clear for Kennedy in that campaign, and now seems clear for Clinton in this one, is that her campaign needs a moment when voters 'open their windows' and are willing to listen and reevaluate Hillary Clinton and see her in a fresh light."

The focus group saw Barack Obama as the most intriguing candidate, describing him as "smart," "charismatic," "articulate," and "independent." Obama emerged from that first session as a potential leader among Democrats, Republicans, and Independents. However, most of those voters wanted to learn more about him; they still felt they knew too little to get behind him.

"He seems young," said Fay Citerone, fifty-three, a liberal Democrat and an IT professional for a manufacturer. Though she had reservations about Clinton, she was leaning toward her and wanted to see a woman in the White House. Yet Obama intrigued her. "We've known about him for three or four years in public life," she explained. "I just haven't seen enough about him. He's a question mark." We followed Citerone's future political path throughout the year as she wrestled over which Democrat to support, occasionally shifting from one candidate to another in the face of new campaign evidence about them. In the end, she became a perfect mirror of how Americans voted—and why.

Six months later, in early November, Hart conducted his second focus group, an all-Republican, more ideologically conservative panel. All had voted for Bush for president in both 2000 and 2004, but their responses about the state of America were as pessimistic, if not more so, than the earlier session in which half of the voters were either Democrats or Independents:

"Troubled."

"Very conflicted."

"So much sharp division."

"Very uneasy times."

"Shaky."

"A lot of turmoil."

By then, concerns over Iraq had begun to fade, though the war remained a negative for most voters. Fears of a declining economy—rising gas prices, the deteriorating housing market, increasing loss of jobs—were becoming the number one issue.

Then Hart asked them what they thought the lives of the next generation of Americans would be like compared to theirs. Raise your hand, he told them, if you believe their lives will be better. Not a single Republican raised a hand, and they immediately began talking about their worries about the future.

"It's very scary times," said a grandmother of five. "I don't want my grandchildren to inherit what we are setting up for them."

"We're saddling our kids down with debt," said another voter. "If we continue to break down, it's going to be chaotic and difficult for them to emerge successfully in the future."

The housing market is going to get worse, said another: "Right now, kids out of college in that first job can't afford a starter home. What's it going to be like ten to twenty years from now? I mean, where are they going to live? Are they going to live with Mom and Dad until they're thirty? I mean, what's going to happen?"

The grandmother spoke again about her fears for the generation after her. "It's scary for me to think about what they'll have to go through," she said. "Right now they are all very, very spoiled. They all have everything they want. I don't know how they'll handle things when they go out on their own. It also worries me that a lot of what's going to happen to this country is going to be dependent on our debt. We're becoming so indebted. . . . Who's buying our loans? Who is going to own us? Who owns us right now, and who's going to own us later on? That is my greatest fear: that we are going to be bought. We are going to give ourselves to another country because of debt."

All these conservative Republican voters shared these negative views, and their concerns were not only about America's current problems, however severe. They were worried about something more troubling, less characteristic of the way Americans usually feel about their future.

In the decades we have covered the nation's elections, Americans have experienced fears and problems aplenty. We have listened to hundreds upon hundreds of citizens in their homes and offices as they discussed their concerns about the state of the nation—about the Cold War, the Bomb and the threat of nuclear holocaust; about the fear that the society was coming apart amid riots spawned by assassinations and antiwar protests; about recessions and market crashes; about political scandal and fears about a system that was broken. But the attitudes that tumbled out in 2008 were different. They were not about any one problem, but something more pervasive: a sense that America had reached a historic turning point. At worst, they feared the country was in danger of sliding into a deep decline signaling either that its greatest days were past or that Americans faced a less secure and diminished future.

A month later, Hart's third focus group—this one entirely Democrats and Independents—reinforced all these feelings and set the stage for what was to come during the election year itself. Once more, the quick responses about the state of the nation were uniformly negative:

"Rocky."

"Shaky."

"Disgraceful."

"Chaotic."

"Wrong direction."

As with other groups, these voters were fixated on the sinking economy. Iraq was receding into the background, though the policies that had led the United States into that war continued to be widely unpopular. As one voter said, "People are dying for what?" Now there was more talk of bankruptcies; of "never-ending strain" on finances; of frustration over not being able to understand what was happening and why, especially in a Washington out of touch and a preserve of privilege; of an untrustworthy news media. "If you turn on the news, you can't get four people and have a conversation," said one man. "You have four talking heads that scream at each other in sound bites and platitudes. Outside of Tim Russert's program, I don't know if there's a program worth listening to." A pause, then a follow-up: "With the exception of Jon Stewart, the comedian, that is." That led someone else to talk about the power of the Internet and the way people depended upon it, and the blogs, for their news. "The Internet has grown and provided us more information," he said, "but it's so segmented people only read or listen to what appeals to them. So no one's getting an overall view."

Yet for all the negative comments, neither in these focus group sessions nor in our conversations elsewhere did voters fall into the cynicism or despair that had marked so many earlier elections. They were not turned off, or tuned out. They were following the election intensely and repeatedly said they believed it to be one of the most, if not *the* most, critical elections of their lives. "The stakes are very high," said one of those Democratic voters. "What comes to my mind is that maybe we should say it's morning in America again, like Reagan said. I don't want Reagan back, but we're going to have to have somebody to change the whole way we've been acting and doing things."

This remark triggered instant reactions:

"I'm looking for someone who's going to surround themselves with the best possible people," said one person, "and also someone who's open to finding new ways to approach issues."

"Also someone who can show the rest of the world that we are still the greatest democracy in the world," came another voice.

"I want to trust the government," said another person, "and then feel like I not only believe them, but I agree with them, and feel like they're working in our best interests."

"I'd like to see an America again where we could be proud to be an American," yet another said, "so that when we go overseas, which I have done, I don't have to be embarrassed anymore."

The most revealing moments came when the conversation turned to race and gender. Three of the Democratic women in this group were African-Americans; earlier, they all said they were Clinton supporters, even though they found Obama appealing for his "fresh new face . . . his idealism." Then one of the women said of him, "He has to be better than anybody. Just like women have to be twice as good as anybody else, Barack has to be that much better."

And what about Hillary? Hart asked. Does she need to prove something in order to win the presidency? "She does," the woman replied. "You know, she can be in the boys' club, and the minute things get hard, she has to prove she's not weak. She's not going to be a girl and cry about it. A large part of the population has the perception that women are weaker than men. Certainly she has shown strength. She's not going to cry. Everybody knows that. I think the same thing of Barack. He's got to be twice as good."

Hart then asked a question that drew an emotional outpouring from the African-American women who were Hillary supporters. What if Barack becomes the nominee? he asked them.

"I'd be so shocked," one said. "It's his time, but it's not going to happen in my lifetime. He's a mold in the making, but he's not there yet."

"I would fear for his safety," the second black woman said. "You know, the way some people think and act toward different races. I just—I don't know, I think it's going to be tough."

Which was the greatest bias, Hart asked, toward race or gender?

"Race, race!" one of the black women shouted. "No matter whether this gentleman is intelligent enough to be president or not, it's just the bottom line that he's black. He could be a rocket scientist and they don't want anybody black in office."

"It's not his time," said another black woman, a Hillary supporter. Then, impulsively, she blurted out, "I don't know whether I should say this, because I know he's not going to win, and [that's why] Hillary really is my next choice."

Do you think the country's ready for an African-American? Hart asked.

"No, I don't."

Because?

"Because the bottom line is the country is racist, and no matter what this man does, and how intelligent he is, nobody wants to see a black man be president and to be controlled by somebody who is African-American."

Suddenly the conversation was charged with emotion—and with disagreement. "I think there's a lot of people who don't care about race," one of the white male voters said. "And I don't think they would purposely not vote for him because he's black."

"Oh, yes," came the response, strongly disagreeing with the white male's remark.

"Oh, yes, I do too," another of the black voters said.

Another trend that proved critical to the election was becoming clearer: the transforming power of young voters.

"I think this new generation is going to turn a lot of things on its heels," commented a white woman when the discussion turned toward changes taking place in America. "I think they think differently. They act differently. Their attitude toward war, toward work, their lifestyles are so very different from my generation. I came of age in the sixties and seventies and it's time for them. They want the stage, and I think they're going to make their presence known, and they should."

Another woman agreed. "I look at it from a slightly different view," she said. "There's a certain segment of society—older, more set in their ways—and it's a horrible thing to say but once they're gone I think it will be very different."

It already *was* different. Everywhere we traveled, from beginning to end of the long campaign, the way Obama appealed to young voters remains an indelible memory.

One example. The place: outside an Obama campaign headquarters in the Philadelphia suburb of Wynnewood, Pennsylvania, a group of young white women, all students, about to join other all-white young Obama volunteers inside. Why Obama? we ask Eliza Reynolds. She'd been listening to her committed friends, she explained. "When someone's real, I think our generation gets so much more involved because we're used to bullshit in our faces. We're a TV generation, we're an Internet generation, and pop-up ads and so forth is so fake to us. Hillary looks so fake. You see her smiling and it makes you want to crunch up. 'Oh, look at that. I don't want that. That doesn't speak to me.' Then you see Obama speaking and he's not trying to push too big words at you, anything that's complex. He's saying stuff that's simple, that's real, that really gets to you, you know. He's a really impressive speaker, you know. Inspiration should not be undervalued, you know."

Young voters in 2008 signaled a major shift in political behavior. They were becoming more liberal than they had been a generation ago, and identifying more with Democrats than Republicans, trends documented by extensive survey research.

Since 1966, the year that saw the shift from liberalism to conservatism, from Democratic dominance to Republican ascendancy, an annual survey of entering freshmen at two- and four-year public and private colleges and universities has been conducted each fall by UCLA, in association with the American Council on Education. More than nine million students, at some fifteen hundred institutions of higher learning, have participated. Over the decades the annual surveys had tracked a steady turning away from public life, public service, political and social activism in reaction to the idealism of students in the sixties. Year after year, young Americans placed increasing emphasis on making money and on materialism. That trend continued—or accelerated—through the Bush election of 2000. "Looking Inward, Freshmen Care Less About Politics and More About Money," read the survey headline about that freshman class of '04. "If this fall's perplexing presidential race provided a lesson in politics," the survey reported, "college freshman may have slept through the class." Their attention had "reached an all-time low."

But that was before the Iraq disaster, before the downturn in the economy, before Katrina and other problems severely discredited Bush's presidency. By the fall of 2006, in its forty-first annual survey of more than 270,000 students, a striking change had occurred. That year's headline reported, "Interest in Politics Increases as Students Move Politically from Center." And they were discussing politics more than at any point in the past four decades. This heightened interest produced the largest turnout in twenty years by voters under the age of thirty, and played a large role in the midterm elections of 2006 that brought Democrats to control of Congress. At that point, students identifying as "liberal" were at the highest point since 1975, 30.7 percent, while those identifying themselves as "conservative" were 23 percent. The survey concluded, "This indicates that freshmen are moving away from a moderate position in their political viewpoints."

Data showed growing support for greater governmental involvement in key issues. Nearly three-fourths of those surveyed believed the government should do more to control the sale of handguns and should give greater support for gay rights (61.2 percent agreed that "same sex couples should have the right to marital status"), while only a fourth thought "it is important to have laws prohibiting homosexual relationships." On abortion, 78.4 percent of liberals agreed it should be legal; only 31.8 percent of conservatives concurred. Again, reflecting overall trends, moderates were closer to liberals in their views. By more than two to one, liberals favored abolishing the death penalty and legalizing marijuana. On whether the government was doing enough to control environmental pollution, 88.5 percent of liberals thought the government should do more. So did 79.3 percent of middle-roaders—and 62.5 percent of conservatives. When students were asked whether a national health plan was needed to cover everybody's medical costs, 83.9 percent among liberals agreed, as did 74.2 percent of middle-roaders and 57 percent of conservatives.

In a strong reversal from earlier surveys, the 2006 one reported "a significant increase in commitment to service among American freshmen." A year later, it reported, "It appears this was not a one-time phenomenon. . . . Student desire to 'influence social values' also continues an upward trend and is at its highest point since 1993."

By the 2008 election, the United States was experiencing its latest—and greatest—wave of immigration, a human tide making America increasingly diverse. When the Census Bureau tabulated its mid-decade figures, not only had the United States hit a historic population milestone of 300 million,* but one in every three U.S. residents represented a minority. Hispanics, with 42.7 million, were the largest and fastest-growing group. They were followed by blacks, with 39.7 million, and Asians, with 14.4 million.

The country was populated by rising numbers of foreign-born and second-generation Americans. More than half were from Latin America, a fourth from Asia, 14 percent from Europe, and the rest from other regions

---

* One census statistic underscores the extraordinary nature of American mobility: In that 300 million population, 237 million cars were registered, with 198.1 million people licensed to drive them over the networks of highways and interstate freeways binding together the nation.

of the world such as Africa or Oceania (Australia, New Zealand, and island nations of the Pacific).

Those new demographics were changing voting patterns across America, both for election of the new president and for the future. Sunbelt and western states like Arizona, New Mexico, Colorado, and Nevada were in play for the Democrats as the election year began. In the last half century, Democrats had carried Arizona only once, Colorado twice, Nevada just three times. New Mexico had been the most reliably Democratic of the group, but had gone for Bush in 2004. Through the 1970s and 1980s, Republicans had counted on California, the Rocky Mountain West, the South, and the Great Plains to produce a virtual electoral lock in presidential races. This was the springboard for the election of every Republican president from Richard Nixon to Ronald Reagan. Despite the shift of California to the Democrats, this geographic coalition delivered the presidency to the father-and-son Bush team.

Americans were still moving to the Sunbelt, continuing to make it the fastest-growing region in the nation. The South contained 36 percent of America's total population, the West 23 percent, the Midwest 22 percent, and the Northeast 18 percent. But the rising Latino population threatened to break the long Republican hold on those southwestern states. Already, Hispanic voter turnout in presidential elections had risen—from under 2.5 million in 1980 to over 7.5 million in the 2004 election—bringing with it increasing numbers of Hispanic officeholders at all levels of local, state, and national government. By 2008, the number of Hispanics in Congress had increased from nine to twenty-two, including three in the U.S. Senate. The potential shift of several southwestern states posed serious problems for the largely all-white Republican Party.

The new America that emerged was different in almost every respect—socially, culturally, demographically, economically, attitudinally, and politically. Into a new millennium came an America in which memories of past triumphs and tragedies were no longer dominant. The traumas of those times—from assassinations to Watergate to Vietnam to riots—had faded. Even the Clinton years of promise and problems seemed part of a distant historical era.

Candidates beginning their campaigns had to find ways to connect with the new versus the old America, the past versus the present. How would they propose resolving the nation's economic woes? How would they advocate charting a new direction in America's foreign policy at a time when U.S. prestige had never been lower? How would they restore faith in the operations of government to ensure that needed progress was made? As potential presidents, they all faced the challenge of addressing these subjects—and more. A country that yearned for change was already in the midst of confounding ones. America in the aftermath of September 11, 2001, an economic downturn, and a deeply unpopular president was a country in transition and in trouble at home and abroad. As ever, people hoped for a new beginning, with new leadership, if it could be trusted, to chart a better course. Now it was up to the politicians to deliver such a message, and the people to decide.

BOOK THREE

THE DEMOCRATS

CHAPTER FIVE

Hillary for President

"We face a lot of evil men."

—Hillary Clinton in Iowa, January 28, 2007

For much of 2007, it looked as if Hillary Clinton would win it all. She had an inner circle that had been tested through two Senate campaigns and a network that had helped win the White House twice. She could recruit almost anyone she wanted. Her political offices on K Street in Washington were close to overflowing as she neared the announcement of her candidacy, and soon she would move to more spacious, and less expensive, quarters across the Potomac River in suburban Virginia.

Obama began with almost nothing. His minuscule campaign apparatus was divided between Chicago and Washington. On January 17, 2007, when he filed his papers forming an exploratory committee, his tiny Washington office was staffed by just four people. They bought a wireless router the day before the launch to provide everyone with Internet access. The next day they bought a printer. Their only TV was in a back room shared with other people from another company. "Every day we had to haggle with people who were watching *Wheel of Fortune* so we could control the TV and watch the news," his spokesman, Bill Burton, recalled. The same almost pitiful shortage of staff and resources was true when the Obama team set up their ground operation in Des Moines, Iowa. Upon his arrival there, Steve Hildebrand, the veteran organizer establishing their Iowa beachhead, stopped at a Verizon Wireless store to pick up a cell phone with a local 515 area code. He then called the number in to Obama's Chicago headquarters, where it was listed on a press release. "Iowa for Obama" had a phone but no office.

In the opening weeks of the campaign, Obama found the campaign trail more physically taxing and mentally challenging than he had imagined.

Despite Plouffe's December warning, he was at times overwhelmed by the pace and demands of a full-scale presidential campaign. Wherever he went, there were enormous crowds—almost seven thousand in Ames on his first trip to Iowa; ten thousand in Oakland; more than twenty thousand in Austin—but sometimes people who came to hear Obama went away feeling let down. His message did not then seem to match the hype surrounding his candidacy. By contrast, Clinton found ways to inject the unexpected into her appearances. During a question-and-answer session in Davenport, Iowa, she was asked how well equipped she was to deal with a dangerous world full of evil men. "Well, the question really is, we face a lot of dangers in the world, and in the gentleman's words, we face a lot of evil men," she said. "People like Osama bin Laden come to mind. And what in my background equips me to deal with evil and bad men?" She rolled her eyes and smiled. The audience, assuming she was referring to her husband and his affair with Monica Lewinsky, erupted with a roar of laughter and hoots and whistles that built and rolled through the room for a full thirty seconds.

She was game for everything. At a Democratic National Committee meeting that month, Obama delivered his speech and soon left the building. Clinton stayed for hours to meet and talk personally with the members. At the International Association of Fire Fighters, Clinton opened with a girlish "Thanks so much—and thanks for last night too" that drew a loud "Ooohhh" from the predominantly male audience. She talked about 9/11 and the heroic role that firefighters had played. Obama talked about veterans' care and fell flat.

"I'm actually always sort of a slow starter," Obama told us later. "The same thing happened during my U.S. Senate race. My stump speeches tend to come to me organically. I try a bunch of things out. And sometimes they work and sometimes they don't. So in those first couple of months, I wasn't operating on this tight script." He recalled the opening months of his U.S. Senate race. "I'd be talking to an audience of thirty people in a living room somewhere or in a diner or a VFW hall. So you're off Broadway and nobody's paying attention . . . ," he said. "But the problem for us was, we were *already* on Broadway. The media was following us nonstop. In April of 2007, we had twenty-three thousand people show up in Austin, Texas. So suddenly you've got these enormous crowds, huge spotlight, and I'm still sort of working out my riff."

The gap between Clinton and Obama became clear in late March when the Service Employees International Union hosted a candidate forum on health care in Las Vegas. Obama's appearance was a near disaster. No union in the country, with the possible exception of the California Nurses Association, had put more emphasis on health care than SEIU. But Obama was utterly unprepared while his rivals arrived fully primed.

First to speak was John Edwards. Two days earlier he and his wife, Elizabeth, had announced that tests showed a recurrence of her breast cancer, only now it had spread to her bones. Her condition was described as untreatable. Amid a wellspring of public sympathy for their ordeal, and expressions of admiration for Elizabeth's courage and the portrait of the loving, supportive couple they drew before the public, they vowed his campaign would continue.

On that morning in Las Vegas, John and Elizabeth were together for their first public appearance since their press conference announcing the return of her inoperable cancer. As he addressed the union audience he was crisp, forceful, and totally engaged. "What we have is a dysfunctional health system in America," he said. "What we need is big, bold, dramatic change." Edwards deftly fielded questions about his wife's health and their commitment for him to stay in the race. He was also straightforward about the cost of his health care plan and how he would pay for it.

Obama came next. He made no mention of Elizabeth Edwards and her courageous battle and had no plan to present, saying, "Everybody on this stage will have a plan." The moderator, *Time* magazine's Karen Tumulty, had pressed his campaign ahead of time for information about his health care agenda but got nothing in return. She handed off the questioning to a member of the audience, Morgan Miller, who would later become known as the "Obaminator" to her friends because of her pointed questioning of the candidate. She expressed dismay at how little information was available on his campaign Web site. "What really are your top issues?" she asked. Obama was hesitant and defensive. "Keep in mind, our campaign right now is a little over eight weeks old," he said. When asked about how he would pay for expanded access to health care, he fudged. "I have not foreclosed the possibility that we might need additional revenue in order to achieve my goal," he said. "But we shouldn't underestimate the amount of money that can be saved in the existing system." He received only polite applause.

Clinton took the stage next, and Obama could see the contrast between them. After praising Elizabeth and John Edwards, she said, "We're supposed to limit this to three minutes. As some of you know, I can talk three hours or three days on health care." Though Clinton did not have a plan at that point either, it was quickly apparent how expert she was. Health care was her passion, and it showed. It is a disgrace, she thundered, to have millions of Americans left out of the health care system. "We need a movement. We need to make this the number one voting issue in the '08 election," she said as her words were drowned out by rising applause. "We're going to get it done this time." She was even more impressive during the questions. When she finished, someone in the audience yelled out, "You go, girl!"

Obama knew he had lost the day. Now he understood better what Plouffe had told him in December about the pressures of a presidential campaign. "Her presentation was sharp and she knew how to arouse the crowd. . . . He was impressed by it," Axelrod said. "Basically he had leaped into the deep end of a very cold pool and I think it was a shock to the system. It took him a while to figure out how to swim. . . . As bright and as gifted as he is, this was all new to him. He went through a period that was very difficult. He was tired. But he felt challenged as well. Little by little he began to learn the rhythm and the pace and the requirements."

When we talked to him about that Las Vegas forum more than a year later, Obama vividly recalled it. "We had made a strategic decision that we weren't going to put our health care plan out yet," he said. "I thought to myself, this is conversational. I'm going to have a conversation with Karen [Tumulty] about how I see health care. And Hillary came in and made a full-blown stump speech presentation. She was standing up, she was playing to the crowd."

A few days after the SEIU forum, Obama spoke before a convention of the Building and Construction Trades in Washington. He opened with a dismissal of the group's significance. "I've got to vote at noon so I'm going to have to cut this short," he said. He was as good as his word, speaking briefly and then departing. On his way back to the Capitol, Obama confided to a colleague that he had not done well before the union audience. He was, he admitted, exhausted after only two and a half months as a candidate. He asked Gibbs to follow him over to the Capitol for the vote. Gibbs was struck by Obama's demeanor. He looked miserable. "You could tell he was wiped out from the whole thing," Gibbs said.

One issue posed a grave threat to Clinton's candidacy. She was badly out of step on Iraq in a party whose antiwar wing had grown increasingly stronger and more vociferous.

Not since Vietnam had Americans been so traumatized by a war. Though unpopular and powerful as a political issue, Iraq did not have the same corrosive effect on American society as Vietnam. That earlier war had personally affected every young American of military age subject to a draft; Iraq was a war fought by an all-volunteer force. Although the public attitude toward the professional military had improved since the Vietnam era, there was a growing distance between those who wore the uniform and those who did not. You could be passionately against the war but totally unaffected by it directly. At the same time, the heated exchanges on the campaign trail made it difficult to reach measured positions on how to extricate the United States from the disaster. And the campaign debates rarely addressed a greater issue: how to maintain American forces abroad and repair the damage done to a military that, as in Vietnam, was stretched to the breaking point.

For these reasons we traveled to West Point to get a military perspective about the impact of Iraq, now and in the future. There, on a bitterly cold and blustery day, with snow swirling over the bluffs of the Hudson and against the background cadences of chanting cadets jogging along the streets, we talked with a remarkable young officer, Ray Kimball. After graduating from West Point in 1995 and twelve years of active service holding command and staff positions, Major Kimball teaches history to what he describes as "the next generation of leaders" at West Point. After his combat duty in Iraq, he earned master's degrees in history and Russian, East European, and Eurasian area studies from Stanford University "It's a time of enormous change and stress on our military—without question, the greatest stress since Vietnam," Major Kimball told us. "We're seeing the flight of talented people. We're seeing the loss of our human capital—our captains and majors and sergeants—who are the building blocks of the Army of 2010, 2015, 2020, and 2025. One of our biggest concerns involves our enlisted soldiers. We have significantly lowered our standards. There's been a rise in requiring people to get moral waivers for heavy crimes before they can enter the service. It concerns me that part of the way we're bringing in folks is by putting a dump-truck load of money in front of them. I worry what that does to our professional military standards."

Major Kimball was closely following the presidential election. "I would like this election to be a referendum on what we want from our armed forces—and, in a larger sense, our government," he said, "because if we're going to be asked to do jobs like Afghanistan and Iraq, the status quo can't continue. . . . These are tough, complicated things we're asking the military to do. So if you want to sign up the nation to do these things, then you better be ready to pay the costs in manning and training and equipping people. You need to be willing to pay later in benefits, in health care, in education. If you're not willing to bear those costs, something has to give way."

At this point, the historian in Major Kimball emerged. "There's a larger question, a greater issue, in all this," he said. "We are disconnecting the military from the society it serves. You know, we've had the term 'citizen soldier' for 225 years and it's a concept I believe in. I heard this month that the Army's magazine for the reserves and National Guard was describing them as 'warrior citizens.' The fact that we're putting citizens second is wrong. George Washington said it: 'We took up the role of soldiers, we did not lay down the role of citizens.' Citizen comes first. Period. End of story. And it worries me that Americans in the main are not as familiar with the military role and experience as they have been in the past."

As the campaign began, Obama had the purest position on Iraq, having opposed the war before the invasion. He could draw a sharp distinction with Clinton over Iraq. Politically, the war provided his candidacy energy and ready-made support among the Democratic activists who were key to the nomination.*

Clinton was isolated on the issue and increasingly uncomfortable. On her first trip to Iowa, she was hit with a hostile question about the war, prompting a long and defensive answer. She was being told bluntly by allies in the early states that her position was unsustainable. That she was so slow to recognize her problem was surprising for an otherwise astute politician. "The first stage was acceptance of the problem," said one Clinton adviser. "And then the second stage was coming up with a solution."

Clinton had been shifting her position for months, but the political winds were shifting even faster. Clinton's goal was to strike an uneasy balance—critical enough of Bush's policies to persuade her critics on the left, while preserving her hard-earned reputation as a Democrat with a muscular foreign policy to carry into the general election.

Her starting point was always the vote in 2002. Her vote was not an

---

* John Edwards voted for the war in 2002 but soon after the 2004 campaign recanted in a *Washington Post* op-ed. "I was wrong," he said of his vote.

endorsement of the president's policy of preemption, she said, but she supported the war resolution without reservation. "This is a very difficult vote," she said. "This is probably the hardest decision I have ever had to make—any vote that may lead to war should be hard—but I cast it with conviction."

Once the invasion was over and Saddam toppled, Clinton supported the overall mission, but increased her criticism of the administration's handling of the postwar conflict. She spent Thanksgiving 2003 in Iraq and in February 2005 returned there, traveling with John McCain. From Baghdad, the two appeared on NBC's *Meet the Press*. She said vigorous debate about administration policy was needed, but added, "It is not in America's interests for the Iraqi government, the experiment in freedom and democracy, to fail."

From Washington, moderator Tim Russert asked whether that meant she disagreed with those calling for a timetable for withdrawal. She said it would be wrong to send a signal to the insurgents that the United States would be out at a date certain. "We want to send a message of solidarity," she added.

By the autumn of 2005, the president's approval rating had dropped dramatically. Bush was in a frantic bid to shore up support for his presidency and his war policy; Clinton was looking to put more distance between herself and the unpopular president and the unpopular war. On the eve of a presidential address on Iraq, she took the unusual step of sending an e-mail to her constituents, outlining her views on the war. Those sixteen hundred words were by far her most detailed—and critical—statement on the war.

If her careful wording hinted at a repudiation of her vote, her aides vigorously denied that interpretation. Still, by neither admitting her own mistake nor embracing a timetable for withdrawal, she remained out of step with a growing segment of her own party.

There matters stood through much of 2006, as one after another Democratic lawmaker advocated timetables for getting out of Iraq. Pressure continued to increase for Clinton to do the same. In an interview in May 2006, once again she held back. A few weeks later she was booed before an audience of progressive Democrats when she said, "I [do not] think it is a smart strategy to set a date certain. I do not agree that that is in the best interest of our troops or our country."

On NBC's *Today* show just before Christmas 2006, she took another step away from the vote. "Obviously, if we knew then what we know now, there wouldn't have been a vote," she said. She had been saying that for more than a year. But this time, she added, "*And I certainly wouldn't have voted that way* [italics added]." That comment passed almost unnoticed.

In January, she announced her opposition to Bush's new plan for a "surge" to send additional troops into battle in Iraq, but continued to resist signing on to a timetable. "I'm not going to support a specific deadline," she said.

Even though she had dramatically escalated her rhetoric, Clinton could not satisfy her antiwar critics. The press turned the issue into a dominant theme of her candidacy, ignoring her pre-Christmas *Today* show statement. Grassroots activists continued to express their unhappiness with her. By now, she had stood behind her vote for too long to "cut and run." But she kept looking for ways to express her dissatisfaction with the president. In early February, at the Democratic National Committee's winter meeting, she found one. She said then, "If I had been president in October of 2002, I would not have started this war. . . . If we in Congress don't end this war before January 2009, as president, I will."

Still, it was not enough.

Her advisers now concluded there should be as little daylight as possible between her and Obama, or between her and the majority of Senate Democrats. Wherever the Democratic caucus moved, she would try to move with them. Next, she should forcefully point out that, as a senator, Obama's votes on the war were virtually identical to hers, thus challenging Obama's antiwar convictions. Finally, she must lay out her opposition to the war and her policy for ending it as clearly as she could—and in the place where she needed it most, Iowa.

The bad blood between the Clinton and Obama camps broke into the open during a Harvard University Institute of Politics conference on March 19, 2007. Through most of the day, their conversation was civil—and tepid. But that night the antagonisms, bile, and bitterness between the rival campaigns burst into public view. It began when a Kennedy School of Government student asked about Clinton's Iraq war resolution vote. "The question I have for you," the student said, "is how do you convince those of us who might otherwise be inclined to support her that she has the judgment not to get us involved in another quagmire?" That question triggered a slashing exchange between David Axelrod and Mark Penn. The two chief strategists viewed politics through different lenses. Penn relied on data, cold and impersonal as it was, to frame his attitudes about candidates and voters. He divided the electorate into subgroups and looked for policies that would appeal to them. Axelrod believed candidates and voters responded less to issues and specific policies than to broader narratives and personal character. He found Penn's approach soulless. Penn had wanted the Clinton campaign to challenge Obama on the war. Bill Clinton agreed and was doing so in private gatherings with Democrats. Now Penn decided to take the fight public by launching an attack on Obama: that Obama had waffled when asked how he might have voted on the resolution had he actually been in the Senate; that during his first year in the Senate, he had been virtually silent on the war. "Senator Obama voted for the $301 billion of funding," Penn said. "So did Senator Clinton. Senator Obama voted against a definite withdrawal date. So did Senator Clinton."

Axelrod, a few feet away from Penn on the stage, was seething. He tried to interrupt. Penn kept talking. When Axelrod finally got the microphone, he accused Penn of distorting the record. The country wouldn't be in the mess it was, he said, had Bush followed Obama's recommendations on Iraq.

This was more than a difference over policy. It was personal. Axelrod disliked Penn, felt him to be arrogant. Penn resented the advantage Obama was getting for his stand against the war. He continued his attack. He asked, is this election going to be about what happened in 2002 or about the future? "Who is going to do the best job in Iraq?"

Axelrod answered sharply. "Are we going to spend ten months savaging each other or are we going to try and lift this country up?" he said. "And we choose to lift this country up."

As the audience broke out in applause, Penn tried to cut them off. "Are we going to look at everybody's records," he said, "everybody's votes—tell everyone out there the truth about who supported what, who voted for what, when, or are we going to selectively tell people?"

In May, Clinton took her most dramatic actions to silence her critics. Earlier, Senator Russell Feingold of Wisconsin had proposed a measure calling for a troop withdrawal to begin within 120 days of passage and to be completed by March 31, 2008. Both Clinton and Obama indicated they would support a motion to cut off debate on the measure to which it was attached. Although the Senate refused to shut off debate, Clinton had sent the signal she wanted. She was fed up with the president and was prepared, as one adviser put it then, to "throw the kitchen sink at him."

But the cloture vote was mere symbolism. Two weeks later, the Senate voted on a $120 billion spending bill that included $100 billion for Iraq and Afghanistan. For Clinton, the bill presented her with an excruciating choice. Should she bow to reality, support a bill certain to pass, and risk losing enough support among the Democratic base to threaten her nomination? Or should she stand firm against the president, yield to the howls of protest from the antiwar activists, and face Republican charges in the general election of turning her back on the troops?

Two of her Senate rivals quickly announced how they would vote. Chris Dodd said he would oppose the spending bill. Joe Biden, chairman of the Foreign Relations Committee, declared he would vote for it. Obama, like Clinton, refused to tip his hand.

Clinton's campaign advisers were unanimous—surprisingly so. All recommended a no vote. Her Senate office also urged her to go against. Only a few outside advisers cautioned against a no vote. Clinton was torn, convinced that Obama would support the funding measure. What if he votes no? one adviser asked her later in the day. "He's not going to," she replied.

Her advisers were not convinced. A "yea" by Clinton and a "nay" by Obama would violate her "no daylight" policy—and would hand Obama another major weapon. But a no vote would seem to violate her nearly five-year effort to preserve her credentials as a future commander in chief.

She and Obama were among the last two senators to cast their votes that night. In a statement, she said, "Tonight I voted against the Emergency Supplemental Appropriations Bill because it fails to compel the president to give our troops a new strategy in Iraq. I believe that the president should begin a phased redeployment of our troops out of Iraq and abandon this escalation." Obama said, "I opposed this war in 2002 precisely because I feared it would lead us to the open-ended occupation in which we find ourselves today. . . . We should not give the president a blank check to continue down this same, disastrous path."

Just fourteen senators opposed the measure. Although she would never apologize for her war resolution vote in 2002, she had now moved dramatically to a point where she was in a minority within her own Democratic caucus. Other than his original opposition to the war, while he was a state senator in Illinois, Obama would have nothing further to use against her, her advisers believed. In Des Moines a few weeks later, she outlined her commitment to ending the war. By midsummer, she and her aides were convinced they had largely neutralized Iraq.

Debates gave Clinton yet another opportunity to separate herself from the field. Like all front-runners, she was wary of debates, particularly early debates, because she knew expectations would be highest for her and she would be the target of all the others. But the cable networks were in fierce competition for ratings and audience share, and the campaign was a major attraction for viewers. Debates could fill the entire prime-time hours— with the added benefit of all-day live coverage from the debate site. So the pressure was extraordinary. Despite efforts by Clinton and Obama to resist, the first debate was scheduled barely three months into the campaign—the first of what would become more than two dozen Democratic debates (Republicans had more than twenty) over a full year.

Though they were billed as "debates," in reality they were staged appearances where candidates traded carefully crafted, poll-driven sound bites and moderators often sought to trap the candidates with "gotcha" questions. But the candidates had no alternative to participating in them. Despite the criticisms of debates, they *did* draw viewing audiences, *did* spark interest in the election.

The first debate was held on April 26, 2007, on the campus of South Carolina State University, a black land-grant institution in Orangeburg and the site of a deadly protest during the civil rights movement. On the day of the debate, there was a festive air at the college. MSNBC was broadcasting live from the campus throughout the day. Representative James Clyburn, the newly installed African-American House Democratic whip, had graduated from South Carolina State and had fought to bring the debate to his alma mater. Clyburn had not taken sides in the Democratic battle, but he would later play a critical role when he clashed with Bill Clinton over racial issues.

The debate confirmed that the Democratic field was deep and experienced. Edwards, Biden, Dodd, and Richardson more than held their own, but all eyes were on Clinton and Obama, and there was one striking moment between them. Toward the end of the night, moderator Brian Williams, the NBC anchor, turned to Obama and asked, "Senator Obama, if, God forbid a thousand times, while we were gathered here tonight, we learned that two American cities had been hit simultaneously by terrorists, and we further learned beyond the shadow of a doubt it had been the work of al-Qaeda, how would you change the U.S. military stance overseas as a result?"

Obama began running through a checklist: Make sure there was an effective emergency response. Check with the intelligence agencies to see if there are other threats. Check to see who might have carried out the attack "so that we can take potentially some action to dismantle that network." What we can't do, he added, is "alienate the world community based on faulty intelligence, based on bluster and bombast. Instead, the next thing we would have to do, in addition to talking to the American people, is making sure that we are talking to the international community. Because, as has already been stated, we're not going to defeat terrorists on our own."

It was a legalistic response, and at first blush there was little to quibble with—until his rivals were asked the same question. Edwards said, "The first thing I would do is be certain I knew who was responsible, and I would act swiftly and strongly to hold them responsible for that." Richardson didn't even get the question, but volunteered, "I would respond militarily, aggressively," he said. "I'll build international support for our goals. I'd improve our intelligence, but that would be a direct threat on the United States, and I would make it clear that that would be an important, decisive military response, surgical strike, whatever it takes."

Clinton was equally militant. "I think a president must move as swiftly as is prudent to retaliate," she said. "If we are attacked and we can determine who was behind that attack, and if there were nations that supported or gave material aid to those who attacked us, I believe we should quickly respond. Now, that doesn't mean we go looking for other fights. You know, I supported President Bush when he went after al-Qaeda and the Taliban in Afghanistan. And then when he decided to divert attention to Iraq, it was not a decision that I would have made had I been president, because we still haven't found bin Laden. So let's focus on those who have attacked us and do everything we can to destroy them."

The debate moved to other topics, but Obama clearly understood what had happened. When his next question came, he returned to the issue of a new terrorist attack. "One thing that I do have to go back on, on this issue of terrorism," he said. "We have genuine enemies out there that have to be hunted down. Networks have to be dismantled. There is no contradiction between us intelligently using our military, and in some cases lethal force, to take out terrorists, and at the same time building the sort of alliances and trust around the world that has been so lacking over the last six years. And that I think is going to be one of the most important issues that the next president is going to have to do, is to repair the kinds of challenges that we face."

Obama knew he had flubbed the question. Long after, with the nomination in hand, he could laugh it off. "I still remember the first debate," he told us, "where Brian Williams asks what are you going to do if we get attacked, and I'm thinking, well, first thing I have to do is make sure everybody is okay and make sure we've got emergency services in place. Then I'm going to talk to my intelligence folks and figure out do we know how this was done and then I'm going to consult with my allies to let them know. So I'm going through this stuff [and] by the time I get to the third step, the time was up, and I think Hillary was next and she said, 'I'm going to bomb those folks.'" At this point he started laughing hard. "And you could see . . . it was a disaster."

This was exactly the contrast Clinton's advisers had hoped to draw—one candidate prepared and ready to serve as commander in chief, the other tentative, hesitant, lawyerly but not strong and forceful in his leadership—more interested in multilateralism than in protecting the United States of America. The next day, Clinton's team jumped on Obama, issuing a statement that drove home their talking point without directly mentioning him. "Hillary was the candidate," her campaign said, "who demonstrated that she would know how to respond if the country was attacked."

The debates continued to establish Clinton's dominance. In New Hampshire in early June, she calmly deflected criticism from Edwards. The next month in South Carolina she again drew a sharp contrast with Obama when he unexpectedly pledged that, as president, he would willingly meet with the leaders of such rogue nations as Iran and North Korea without preconditions during his first year in office. "Well, I will not promise to meet with the leaders of these countries during my first year," Clinton interjected. "I will promise a very vigorous diplomatic effort because I think it is not that you promise a meeting at that high a level before you know what the intentions are. I don't want to be used for propaganda purposes. I don't want to make a situation even worse."

This looked like another Obama gaffe. Flying back to Washington that night, Penn urged Clinton to keep pressing Obama. The following day, her campaign recruited former secretary of state Madeleine Albright to lead the attack against Obama. But Clinton also took matters into her own hands—to the surprise of many of her advisers. During a telephone interview with reporter Ed Tibbetts of the *Quad City Times* in Iowa, she launched a personal attack on Obama, telling Tibbetts, "I thought he was irresponsible and frankly naïve."

By midsummer, Clinton's team, which had worried about the debates, had come to a dramatically different conclusion. "They have clearly been our friends in a big way—that no one expected," Wolfson said. Another Clinton adviser explained, "I'd argue she's doing herself more good through these debates than any other single thing in the campaign." But he knew that the string might not continue indefinitely. "One of these days she's going to screw up, and you guys are dying for her to screw up just for the story line," he told us one morning shortly before Labor Day. "She can't keep winning these things over and over again."

As Labor Day approached, the Clinton machine continued to hum. Iowa would be challenging; that was clear to all. But at her national headquarters, the main focus was on national trends and numbers. She maintained a healthy lead in the national polls. Her campaign was being described as a juggernaut, her prospects for the nomination almost inevitable. She was miles ahead of Obama and everyone else on the issue of who had the experience to be president. Obama's only opportunity, her advisers concluded, was if he were able to transform the change issue into a weapon that could stop her momentum. Her campaign intended to deny him that opportunity and targeted the Labor Day weekend as the time to launch a new strike—by turning the change issue against him.

It was warm and sunny when she and Bill arrived in Concord the day before Labor Day, only the second time the Clintons had campaigned together. In a rare change of pattern, the campaign chartered a press plane (though she and her husband would be on their own jet). Press aides alerted reporters that she planned to unveil a new stump speech. When the traveling press arrived on the grounds of the state capitol, they quickly saw what her message would be. Campaign workers had erected a stage with banners that read, "The Change We Need." Others read, "Change + Experience." She drew a roar of approval from the enthusiastic crowd when she shouted, "Are you ready for change in the United States of America?"

Hillary Clinton had never gone directly at Barack Obama's core strength the way she did now. Her advisers always paid lip service to the fact that voters wanted change, but they were more concerned about voter resistance to electing the first woman president. She needed to show strength to demonstrate she could be commander in chief. Creating a sense of inevitability about her candidacy combined with an image of strength topped any message of change: Strength and experience always trumped change—or so they thought.

Her Labor Day weekend stump speech was the result of weeks of discussions, with considerable input from Clinton herself. It would be, in the words of one aide, a moment of "shock and awe" that would pin Obama back on his heels. Her advisers saw it as a pivot from successfully establishing herself as the candidate most ready to be president to challenging the ground he occupied. Co-opting part of his change message would enable her to checkmate Obama before he got moving.

"Change is just a word without the strength and experience to make it happen," she told the Concord audience. "And I know some people think you have to choose between change and experience. Well, with me, you don't have to choose. I have spent my entire life fighting for change. . . . I will bring my experience to the White House and begin to change our country starting on day one."

Then, in a line that aimed squarely at Obama, she added, "We need to dream big, but then we have to figure out how to make those dreams a reality in the lives of Americans."

From Concord, the Clintons drove to the Hopkinton state fair. Then it was on to Nashua for a nighttime rally, then to Iowa the next morning for a labor rally, and finally to Des Moines for another big rally at the state fairgrounds. During those two days, she repeated her new stump speech over and over. As she delivered it a final time before heading back east, Bill Clinton stood behind her on the stage, mouth agape, staring aimlessly into the crowd. "He's totally exhausted," said an aide.

Later in September came the unveiling of her signature domestic issue, health care. Back in December, she told an adviser, "If I can't do universal coverage, what's the point of running?" That was far from a casual remark. Her failure to enact universal health care during her husband's first two years in the White House had helped Republicans seize control of Congress in the 1994 elections, a devastating defeat for the Democrats and personally a bitter one for her. Now she made it known that if elected she intended to push aggressively for universal coverage. What she lacked through most of the early campaign was a plan to get there. On Monday, September 16, at a hospital in Des Moines, she finally unveiled one.

Her new plan was carefully crafted and politically astute, offering detail where necessary and avoiding it where possible. Clearly, she had learned her lesson from the health care debacle. Since most people who have insurance want to keep what they have, she built her plan on the existing system of employer-based insurance, with alternatives for those who did not have insurance through their work. Her plan, unlike Obama's, imposed a mandate, requiring that everyone purchase some kind of insurance.

By 2008, 41 percent of working-age Americans—or seventy-two million people—were having difficulty paying medical bills. Seven million older adults aged sixty-five and beyond faced the same problems. And those problems worsened throughout the election year as the economic crisis brought rising numbers of layoffs and cutbacks—or termination—of health insurance benefits. For someone like Dr. Janis Orlowski these kinds of figures form a background for her daily experience as chief medical officer at the Washington Hospital Center, the largest nonprofit hospital in the Washington, D.C., metropolitan area and ranked among the nation's top hospitals. Conditions there are a perfect example of the promise and problems of the American health care system, and illustrate why health care remains a potent political issue.

"In this hospital," she told us, "I have Supreme Court justices. And I have undocumented, unhealthy individuals who fall off a roof and suddenly no one knows who they are. I provide them top-quality, state-of-the-art health care. They return to whatever level of recovery they can, then they can't find a place to go. They have no family, no means to care for themselves. At this time I have ten individuals in our hospital who have been here for thirty days. Why? I cannot place them appropriately in an outpatient setting. And you know where they're sitting right now? In my hospital, with us taking care of them. In the end, my patients are paying for their care. Why? Because of the issue of the uninsured patient or the undocumented one. You asked me how our health care issues fit in with this presidential election. This is a critical election, the most critical I can remember. I have three newspapers delivered to my doorstep every day. So I should be an educated citizen. I have the [*Washington*] *Post*, I have the *New York Times*, and I have the *Wall Street Journal*. I read all day long on health care, so if anything I should be educated on the candidates' thoughts on health care. But I have to tell you I have only a very vague idea of what they plan to do with health care. I hear sound bites about health care: 'We're going to bring health care to everyone. We're going to make smart decisions. We're going to have a program to insure the uninsured.' Great. That's what we need. But how?"

Reflecting on the way the political system deals with health care, Dr. Orlowski said, "We know what the issues are, but they're not addressing them. If we know that we have these health care problems, why are we not educating the public about them?"

Clinton followed the health care speech with the most extensive media blitz of her campaign, which included a string of interviews with columnists. That weekend, she granted interviews to all five major Sunday talk shows.

The next day, after Hillary Clinton's "most dominating week of the campaign to date," co-author Dan Balz wrote the following snapshot for the *Washington Post*'s Web site:

"The Hillary Clinton who appeared on five Sunday morning shows was a formidable political candidate: poised, polished, knowledgeable. The package she presented was designed to send a message to her Democratic rivals: catch me if you can. She now sits atop the Democratic field, in a tier by herself. . . . The rush to anoint Clinton as an inevitable nominee overlooks the history of nomination battles, which is that few candidates win these contests without a struggle or without at least one serious setback or stumble—either self-inflicted or inflicted by the voters." What could trip up Clinton? "The most likely is a defeat and that certainly appears most possible in Iowa. . . . Clinton holds a sizeable lead in national polls, and she has, on average, double digit leads in the other early states. But in Iowa, the polls show a three-way contest that also includes Barack Obama and John Edwards—and what happens in Iowa and New Hampshire will affect all the other states."

A late September *Washington Post*/ABC News poll put her lead over Obama at 53 to 20 percent. A University of New Hampshire poll showed her lead growing from nine to twenty-three points between July and September. Even in Iowa, the one state where she was struggling, a *Des Moines Register* poll the first week of October showed her leading Obama and Edwards, after trailing earlier.

A September 29 strategy memo prepared by Penn showed the bullishness inside her campaign: "We are on strategy. The other campaigns are not. . . . If you are sitting over there at the Edwards or Obama camps you are realizing you are not going to win on policy, so you will try to win on personality and character. They never quite get how a blend of substance and issues can define character. . . . Having won the national battle, we should be focused on the key states where ending it decisively is increasingly within reach."

We sat down with Penn two weeks later. "We're at an unexpected moment in the campaign," he said. "The numbers that are coming back are better than anybody expected." He sounded upbeat as he talked about what he believed the campaign had done right to put Clinton in such a strong position. She had been firmly established as the candidate of strength and experience, while Obama, he argued, was in a rut with his theme of change. "I don't think Obama is catching on in Iowa," he went on. "He's not an Iowa person. . . . We're in a better position than anyone imagines at the moment."

Privately, Penn was warning Clinton to steel herself for the attacks that might be coming. On September 30, he advised her that it was time to prepare a series of ads as possible counterattacks. He believed that some columnists, supporting Obama, were furious she was doing so well and that opponents would be assaulting her not on policy but on character. They would call her dishonest, untrustworthy. All she could do was get ready. She agreed.

Howard Wolfson had earlier proposed preparing ads highlighting her motivation for public service and her personal beliefs as a way to inoculate her against coming attacks on her character. Penn shot down the idea, according to a member of the inner circle. Voters don't care about private character, he argued, only public character and what a politician can deliver.

The Unraveling

"Hillary is not the first person in Washington to declare 'Mission Accomplished' a little too soon."

—Obama to Jay Leno, October 16, 2007

On the morning of August 8, Axelrod arrived at his Chicago office shortly before ten o'clock. "We're on this bucking bronco but we've got to ride it," he said ruefully. "We'll find out later whether it was the right horse to get on or not, but we're on it now so we've just got to sit tight in the saddle and ride the thing."

It was the day after the fifth debate, hosted by the AFL-CIO and held outdoors at Soldier Field before a raucous crowd of union members. Obama had come under fire for his foreign policy statements over the last three weeks, beginning with the CNN-YouTube debate in South Carolina. In a speech, he had made an implied threat to mount cross-border raids into Pakistan by U.S. soldiers if actionable intelligence showed there was a chance to capture or kill "high-value terrorist targets"—a point Axelrod pushed to include to make the speech more newsworthy. He stumbled over considering nuclear weapons to fight terrorism there. In Chicago, his opponents were instantly on the attack. Chris Dodd called Obama "highly irresponsible." Clinton said it was "a very big mistake to telegraph that and destabilize" the Pakistani government.

Obama fired back, but clearly he and his campaign had been put on the defensive. The exchanges bolstered the continuing story line: He wasn't seasoned enough to be president. And even though he was raising significant amounts of money and drawing big crowds, he wasn't making up ground against Clinton in the national polls.

The winter months had tested Obama's capacity to meet the demands of a 24/7 presidential campaign—the punishing physical ordeal, the microscopic dissection of his every word, the longing for time with family, the feeling he was always on. Now the summer and early fall were a test of his patience and resilience. Even Obama and his advisers recognized that Clinton had won the early rounds.

"I think that they've run a good campaign," Axelrod said that day in August. "She herself has performed at a very high level. . . . She's very, very disciplined and she's very tenacious. She obviously wants this in a big way. Strength is an important quality in a presidential candidate, and given all the things that she's endured, people think she's strong."

Despite his own difficulties, Obama was privately sympathetic when Clinton made a rare stumble during a debate at the YearlyKos Convention of liberal bloggers. Inexplicably, during that debate she had offered a broad defense of Washington lobbyists after her opponents questioned her acceptance of contributions from them. Edwards and Obama immediately criticized her sharply. What could she have been thinking? Axelrod asked Obama. He was struck by Obama's response. "She made a mistake," Obama said. "You know what? Nobody can appreciate it but a candidate. This is hard. Running for president is not easy. You get tired, you make mistakes. She made a mistake." He added, "It's hard for me and I'm fifteen years younger than she is. And she's working hard, she's tired, she made a mistake.'"

That private remark highlighted Obama's own frustrations. His senior advisers had worried at times that his sour mood was affecting morale throughout the campaign. After a summer fund-raiser, several top advisers joined Obama for a late dinner. Obama could sense where the conversation was heading. "Okay," he said, "is this where we have an intervention?" He knew he had to be more positive, he said, adding, "You guys told me what it would be like, but it's hard."

At another point, Gibbs flew from Chicago to Washington to join Obama on a campaign trip to Iowa. His purpose was to have a candid talk about the candidate's morale and to allow Obama to vent his frustrations. "Are you having any fun?" Gibbs asked. Obama launched into a lengthy response. He was deeply frustrated. He was unhappy with his debate performances. He was annoyed with the long-distance critiques from his advisers. He was exasperated by the way the message was being managed. He was irritated with press coverage suggesting he was leaving audiences underwhelmed. He was troubled by talk that his campaign lacked substance. "He felt like he was stuck in this washing machine of this circular narrative that he couldn't get out of," Gibbs said. Gibbs tried to sound sympathetic while urging Obama to find something positive to focus on, saying that as difficult as things seemed, going forward was no more difficult than turning back. Still, Obama could find nothing positive to say about the experience.

Reggie Love, Obama's young personal assistant, was working his Black-Berry. He piped up, "Boss, if it's any consolation, I'm having a blast."

"Reggie," Obama replied with a withering look, "it's not."

What sustained Obama most through those difficult months was his campaign's amazing fund-raising machine. Early in 2007, during a conversation with Edwards, we asked how his first-quarter fund-raising might compare with Clinton's and Obama's. Nobody, Edwards said, would come close to Clinton; his goal was to stay within reach of Obama. Edwards was wrong on both counts. When the first-quarter reports came out, Obama's numbers stunned the Clinton campaign. Because she had transferred $10 million from her Senate campaign, and raised more general election money in that quarter, she had an overall lead for the period. But Obama became the story. He brought in $25 million that quarter and actually raised more money that could be used in the primaries than did Clinton. Three months later, Obama produced another eye-popping quarter of fund-raising. He raised $32.5 million—$31 million of it for the primaries—topping Clinton's total of $27 million. "Obama's Money Puts Clinton's Inevitability in Doubt," said a headline on CNN's Web site.

Obama was pleased with his fund-raising operation but little else. On July 15, he met with his senior staff at Valerie Jarrett's home. One adviser recalled it as the moment Obama began to take a more direct role in the operations of his campaign. He was blunt in his critique and the exchanges among some of his advisers became testy. Beyond fund-raising and the operation overseeing the Internet and new media, the campaign was not performing well, Obama said. The message still wasn't where it should be. The political operation wasn't up to speed. The campaign lacked crispness and good execution. He believed his campaign was becoming too insular and wanted new people added to the inner circle. He told his team they were all doing B work. If they continued on that course, they would come in a respectable second. "Second is not good enough," he said.

The July–August fight over foreign policy marked a turning point for Obama's confidence. Though he was frustrated by the criticism of his statements, he was exhilarated by the debate they touched off. "That was one of the best moments of the campaign," he later told us. Obama's political advisers may have been nervous. Obama was not. The night of the South Carolina YouTube debate, Axelrod was in the spin room, pummeled by reporters about whether his candidate had committed a major mistake. He sought to explain away Obama's comment about meeting leaders without preconditions. The next morning Obama ordered him to stand firm.

"We were driving back from South Carolina to the airport and this was already starting to swirl on the blogs as a gaffe," Obama later told us. "I said, 'Don't back down. If we go down, we're going down swinging.' It was a moment where I felt confident enough to trust my instincts and also confident about the fact that I wasn't going to be intimidated by the pundits. One of the things I learned was to stop reading clips and stop reading blogs, because you have these voices swirling in your head. This was a moment where I said, 'You know what, I'm just going to make sure that whatever I do accords with what I believe.'"

As he told his aides, he was convinced he was right about what he had said about meeting with leaders of rogue nations and going after terrorists inside Pakistan. That, he insisted, was consistent with the message of his campaign: He would change business as usual in Washington, a position he believed the American people supported. At first, his top advisers were not so sure. They were nervous enough to commission polling in New Hampshire to see whether the public backed Obama on his foreign policy statements. They came away convinced Obama was right. (At the same time, Clinton's advisers reached the opposite conclusion. Their research persuaded them that Obama had reinforced doubts about his readiness to be president.)

On a steamy Monday afternoon in mid-August we caught up with Obama after a rally at a recreation center in Keene, New Hampshire. He was relaxed and confident and, to a surprising degree, eager to take on Clinton, even though so far he had appeared tentative. Though he had faced tough questions during the previous month, he said he had found the exchanges invigorating and, he believed, helpful to his candidacy. "If you look at the specifics of each issue, I feel very confident and comfortable with my position," he said. "But it runs contrary to some of the conventional wisdom in Washington."

He expressed no doubt about his position on the terrorists in Pakistan.

"Critics could argue that we shouldn't talk about it," he said, "and I absolutely reject that notion because I think that the American people have to understand what's at stake in our foreign policy, and if we're fighting on the wrong battlefield and we're losing ground on the battlefield where we have to win—in Afghanistan along the Pakistan-Afghan border—that's something that has to be discussed in this campaign."

He believed his exchange with Clinton had crystallized her political strategy. "They want to project Senator Clinton as the seasoned, experienced hand. I don't fault them for that," he said. But "what the Oval Office needs right now is good judgment. Experience can be a proxy for good judgment, but it isn't always. And it is striking that all the people who were on that stage in Chicago [at the AFL-CIO debate] talking about their experience and criticizing me for the lack of it were the same people who went along and displayed incredibly poor judgment in going along with a war that I think has been a disaster. So I'm happy to have that debate about what is the relevant experience you need to lead this country."

Even though polls showed Clinton holding commanding leads over him, he could say, "I don't spend a lot of time focused on the polls nationally. . . . The fact is I'm not as well-known as Senator Clinton is. If her name recognition is 99.9 percent, mine is probably—in terms of people actually knowing who I am—closer to 60 percent."

He was less positive about his performance in the debates. "There's no doubt that the sixty-second format debates, or even ninety seconds, are tough for me," he admitted. "I tend to be a storyteller. I like to connect with people by talking about where we've been and talking about where we're going and the aspirational aspects of my message are rooted in people's stories and stories about this country. It's very hard to do that in ninety seconds. I think that having a different format would benefit me. There's no doubt that if we had more of a conversation, or we had a roundtable and it was a little more open-ended and maybe we structured it so that it focused on one topic would play to my strengths. And there's no doubt that the sort of sound-bite debate style—some candidates have mastered that art more than I have."

He was even more revealing when he spoke about what it was like to move so swiftly from freshman senator to top-tier presidential candidate. It was hard being away from home, he said, and he missed his wife and daughters. Being around them fortified him. He said he also was fighting against trimming his sails or becoming overly cautious. "I think one of my strengths is that when people hear me talk, I think that part of what they like is it sounds like I believe what I'm saying and that I'm not calibrating everything to meet what's considered politically acceptable," he said. "So I don't want to lose that, and that I think has been a challenge. Overall, though, look, if you had asked me on February 11th, the day after I announced, would you be happy with being a strong second place in the polls, having raised as much money as the Clintons, being basically tied or close in all the early states, having three times the number of donors and volunteers as any other campaign on either the Republican or Democratic side, I'd probably take it."

Despite those upbeat words, Obama's campaign was at a low point—"not firing on all cylinders," as one senior staffer put it. However much Obama pointed to evidence of progress and success, neither he nor his advisers and the wider circle of donors and loyalists were happy with how things were going. "There was obviously significant turbulence late summer, early fall," Gibbs said. There was no escaping the bad news: "There was a time in the late summer and early fall that people thought the fad's worn off and the guy's going to die in the early fall."

So now Obama was under pressure to take Clinton on. "The greatest push we got was you've got to kneecap her, that you've got to go really negative," Gibbs said. "We just never thought that was the way you win the nomination. But some of that donor pull is hard to resist because you realize that if those guys get crabby it could be tough. We understood that all of what had attracted people to Barack would erode if we did something that people got turned off by. That doesn't mean we didn't have discussions, but despite unsolicited advice to just, as Barack said, to kneecap her, we realized that wasn't a smart thing to do."

Through this period, Obama was struggling to sharpen his message. During a short vacation in August he talked to Jarrett about his frustrations. He needed to redo his stump speech, he told her; he didn't feel he was connecting the way he wanted to. Jarrett often traveled with Obama and that fall heard him talk frequently about his frustrations. "He would say, [it's] like a lock and I have to unlock [it] and he said I am getting there," she recalled. "I can figure this out." Jarrett mimicked the candidate holding an imaginary lock in his hand trying to find the combination that would open it. Obama was looking for a way to transcend the one-on-one conversations with voters he was having and find a message that would captivate masses of them.

In October, Jarrett traveled to Iowa with Obama for a meeting with members of his national finance committee, who were peppering Obama's advisers with doubts and complaints. Obama was well aware of the concerns, and what he said that day stayed with Jarrett for months afterwards. "He said, 'I know you guys are nervous, I know it's much bumpier than you thought it would be, but I'll hold your hand and we'll get through this,'" Jarrett said. "He said, 'I'll hold your hand if you're nervous, I'll be right there with you, but we're going to get through this, we're going to do this together.'"

Obama told us that trip was an important moment of confidence-building. "I just told people, I said, 'If you guys thought this was going to be easy, you must have not been listening to us. We always knew this was hard and that I'm the underdog, but we can win this thing if you don't waver.'"

Did he really say he would hold their hands? "Yes," he replied, "and that's right when things started to turn around."

By mid-October, Clinton's campaign exuded supreme confidence. In an appearance on Jay Leno on October 17th, Obama tried to puncture those hopes. "Hillary is not the first person in Washington to declare 'Mission Accomplished' a little too soon," he quipped that night. Two weeks later her unraveling began.

All the focus was on Obama as he headed into their next debate in Philadelphia on October 30. Not only was he under increasing pressure from his aides to take Clinton on more aggressively, but also they wanted him to display the fighting temperament his critics said was missing. When Adam Nagourney and Jeff Zeleny of the *New York Times* interviewed him shortly before the debate, they reported that Obama had glared and said "no" when asked whether he lacked the stomach for a real confrontation with Clinton. "It is absolutely true that we have to make these distinctions clearer," he said. "And I will not shy away from doing that." The *Times* headline set the stage for the next encounter: "Obama Promises a Forceful Stand Against Clinton."

By debate day, the boxing metaphors were running wild, with *Hardball*'s Chris Matthews leading the charge. "It's fight night!" he exclaimed as he opened his MSNBC show a few hours before the debate. "Expectations are running high for challenger Barack Obama. Will he come out swinging against Hillary? Will John Edwards get into the mix? Could this battle turn into a brawl, with Hillary walking away unscathed and maybe even stronger?" He turned to NBC correspondent Andrea Mitchell. "Is this his last chance?"

If the debate had ended after ninety minutes, the story might well have been that Clinton had survived the toughest series of attacks in any debate so far. Obama challenged her to speed up the release of documents in the National Archives that would shed light on the advice she had given her husband during his two terms in the White House. He accused her of failing to offer the country a clear contrast with Bush and the Republicans. But Obama was hardly as aggressive as the pre-debate chatter had predicted. That role fell, as before, to John Edwards, who ripped into Clinton as a creature of a corrupt power structure. "I think what voters have to ask themselves is: Do you believe that the candidate who's raised the most money from Washington lobbyists, Democrat or Republican, the candidate who's raised the most money from the health industry, drug companies, health insurance companies, the candidate who's raised the most money from the defense industry, Republican or Democrat—and the answer to all of those questions is: That's Senator Clinton. . . . And I think that if people want the status quo, Senator Clinton's your candidate. That's what I believe."

The role Edwards played for Obama that night—as in other debates—proved extremely helpful. From late summer, he began leading the attack on Clinton, both on the stump and in debates. A Clinton adviser complained, "Edwards decided to turn himself into a kamikaze." Edwards was particularly aggressive at the YearlyKos Chicago convention, where he and Obama attacked Clinton for taking money from lobbyists.* Through the fall, he escalated his attacks. "I felt like I needed to do it," he later told us, "because I didn't see it being done in any other way. I thought if we floated through the debates, she would win the nomination." Obama was able to piggyback on those attacks without seeming overly negative himself, and without paying any price in the press for going negative.

Edwards also offered Obama advice during the debates. "You've got to focus, you've got to stay focused," he said he told Obama during a commercial break in Philadelphia. Later, he told us that Obama would come prepared to confront her but then back off. "He'd do it and then he'd shift back to the intellectual, detached kind of way of talking about things while I was pounding away on her and [stayed] very focused on her."

---

* The YearlyKos audience, reflecting the views of the progressive blogosphere, was hostile to Clinton. As the candidates took their debate places, Edwards said a man in the front row opened a placard reading, "Stop Lying, Hillary." Edwards recalled, "He held that thing up the entire debate, never put it down."

Through most of the Philadelphia debate, Clinton was calm. Then the topic turned to an issue close to home, a plan by then governor of New York Eliot Spitzer to make illegal immigrants eligible for driver's licenses. "Well, what Governor Spitzer is trying to do is fill the vacuum left by the failure of this administration to bring about comprehensive immigration reform," she said. "We know in New York we have several million at any one time who are in New York illegally. They are undocumented workers. They are driving on our roads. The possibility of them having an accident that harms themselves or others is just a matter of the odds. It's probability. So what Governor Spitzer is trying to do is to fill the vacuum. I believe we need to get back to comprehensive immigration reform because no state, no matter how well intentioned, can fill this gap. There needs to be federal action on immigration reform."

NBC's Tim Russert, one of the moderators, asked the others onstage whether anyone opposed the idea. Chris Dodd quickly spoke up. "Look, I'm as forthright and progressive on immigration policy as anyone here. But we're dealing with a serious problem here. We need to have people come forward. The idea that we're going to extend this privilege here of a driver's license I think is troublesome and I think the American people are reacting to it. . . . Talk about health care, I have a different opinion. That affects the public health of all of us. But a license is a privilege, and that ought not to be extended, in my view."

Clinton attempted to reenter the conversation. "Well, I just want to add, I did not say that it *should* be done," she said, "but I certainly recognize why Governor Spitzer is trying to do . . ."

As she tried to keep talking, Dodd would not hold back. "Wait a minute," he said. "No, no, no. You said—you said yes . . . you thought it made sense to do it."

"No, I didn't, Chris," Hillary replied, her indignation rising.

In fact, she was right; she had not said exactly that. But it didn't matter. The debate had taken a sudden, fateful turn. When NBC anchor Brian Williams tried to move the conversation to another topic, Edwards would not let it go, charging Clinton with talking out of both sides of her mouth. "I think this is a real issue for the country," he said. "America is looking for a president who will say the same thing, who will be consistent, who will be straight with them. Because what we've had for seven years is doubletalk from Bush and from Cheney, and I think America deserves us to be straight."

Obama jumped in. "Well, I was confused on Senator Clinton's answer.

I can't tell whether she was for it or against it. And I do think that is important. One of the things that we have to do in this country is to be honest about the challenges that we face."

At Clinton headquarters in Virginia, senior staffers were watching the debate with half an eye. But they suddenly snapped alert as they saw their candidate melt down in front of a national television audience in a two-minute exchange. For the next several days, Hillary's response to the immigration question dominated the commentary. Nearly all was critical. "This is classic Clinton," an anti-Clinton blogger said. "Say anything, DO anything to get elected. Friends, Reject the Clinton Dynasty . . . why should we continue to be ruled by 2 families. . . . Reject the Clintons and their baggage. America deserves better."

Clinton advisers tried to spin their way out of the problem, playing the gender card as hard as they ever had. The debate, they argued, showed a bunch of men attacking "one strong woman." At Wellesley, her alma mater, she told students, "In so many ways, this all-women's college pre-pared me to compete in the all-boys club of presidential politics." But as hard as they tried, there seemed to be no way to undo the damage. Obama's team recognized the balance had changed. "You said, 'Okay, now there's something to work with here,'" recalled Jim Margolis, the Obama campaign's media adviser. "It was a key moment at a time when we needed a few."

For months the Clinton campaign had successfully kept the focus on her experience, her strength, her readiness to be president. At every debate she had reinforced those attributes with mostly unflappable performances. Now, nine months of good work were in danger of coming apart in what was being called one colossal stumble. It was an example of the unpredict-ability of political campaigns and the consequence of not dealing with weaknesses. In a matter of seconds another side of her political character emerged. Here was a Clinton who appeared evasive, a Clinton who shifted positions, a Clinton you couldn't trust—in short, the side of Clinton that led many voters to doubt whether they wanted her in the Oval Office. After the campaign was over, spokesman Phil Singer said, "It was a real-time example of one of . . . the negatives on her." Suddenly Hillary no longer seemed invulnerable, transcendent, the inevitable winner.

Nearly a year later, in an *Atlantic* article on the debates, James Fallows concluded, "Hillary Clinton seriously blew only one answer of the count-less hundreds she delivered. That was her fumbling response on whether she thought illegal immigrants should get driver's licenses. . . . In other circumstances, she would have batted away this issue as she routinely did much tougher questions. . . . But . . . the blog and cable-news controversy over her 'stumble' and 'equivocation' significantly cut her then-large national lead over Obama and gave him an opening."

Hillary Clinton's stumble over immigration proved to be highly damaging to her campaign. Coming just two months before the Iowa caucuses, the timing could not have been worse.

CHAPTER SEVEN

Iowa: Round One

"They understood something intuitive in Iowa. . . . They understood that this process is ego-driven, even at the lowest level."

—Former governor Tom Vilsack, a Hillary supporter,
on Obama's operation

In the long war for the Democratic nomination, Iowa was the epic battle. There would be other critical turning points, but nothing matched Iowa. No one had ever witnessed a campaign quite like it, a Democratic struggle for the heart and soul of a small, rural, almost all-white state. The battle raged for a full year, collectively cost more than $70 million, consumed almost more of the candidates' time than all the other states combined, and drew by far the most media attention—all for the support of just 240,000 voters out of an American population of more than 300 million.

Clinton was the dominant national front-runner through most of 2007, but never in Iowa. Her first Iowa poll, taken as she was getting ready to launch her candidacy, showed Edwards, who had never abandoned the state after 2004, at 38 percent and Clinton tied with Obama at just 16 percent. For Clinton—who liked to remind people that though she represented New York, she was born and raised in neighboring Illinois—Iowa was always a struggle, a frustrating state where the Clintons had no network and no particular history. It was a place where she never felt comfortable, with an electorate that never fully warmed to her and a caucus process that she and her husband came to loathe. All had devastating consequences for her candidacy.

The contrast between her Iowa campaign and Obama's was significant, if not always visible. Obama, the novice, surrounded himself with an Iowa-savvy team of advisers and made a critical strategic bet: to put almost all his emphasis on the state. Then he gamely stuck with this plan through his low months in the late summer and early fall of 2007 when doubts about his candidacy reached a crescendo. "I pushed Plouffe on this and I give Plouffe a lot of credit," Obama would tell us later. "I was steady but I did ask him, I said, 'David, we're not running a national strategy, we're getting the you-know-what kicked out of us, and do we know that these national polls are not going to infect what's happening in Iowa?' And he held fast. He said, 'Look, I have confidence in what we're doing there.'"

Clinton, far more experienced, surrounded herself with a cadre of senior advisers who did not know Iowa or its caucus process. They were slow to organize and waited too long to make a full commitment. Even then, they spent months debating how much to put into their operation and how to position her. Her vote for the Iraq war provided Obama an opening in a state with a history of antiwar sentiment. As James Carville later noted, her polls suggesting she had put Iraq behind her could never fully measure how her vote ultimately provided Obama's campaign with energy, resources, and antiwar support. Her vote, he believed, was crippling.

In the aftermath of Iowa, a consensus emerged that Obama had simply out-organized Clinton on the ground—that he won it because of his superior get-out-the-vote operation. The reality is far more complicated. Obama put together a phenomenal organization in Iowa, but Clinton's became extraordinarily capable as well. She lost because she wasted months by picking the wrong staff and because of continuous internal arguments over a winning strategy. Perhaps most critical of all, she was never able to match the energy and enthusiasm that Obama inspired among new young voters. With his change message, Obama struck a unique chord. Winning Iowa did not secure his presidential nomination, as it did John Kerry's four years earlier, but Obama's triumph made it far more difficult for Clinton to win the nomination.

The presence of John Edwards also made Iowa different. In 2004, he finished a strong second to Kerry and never stopped campaigning there. Just before New Year's Day 2007 in New Orleans, Edwards announced his candidacy. Later that day, he flew to Des Moines. More than a thousand people were waiting for him when he arrived at the Iowa Historical Museum. The sheer size of the crowd was a reminder that Edwards would be a formidable candidate, making Iowa unique in being the battleground for a true three-person fight. The overflow crowd that night also signaled that Iowans were ready for a presidential campaign of historic proportions.

Hillary Clinton was the first of the big two to arrive. Her chartered plane touched down in Des Moines on the afternoon of Friday, January 26,

2007, the first time in more than three years that she had even visited the state. Bill Clinton had never had to run in the Iowa caucuses; when he sought the presidency, everyone stayed out of the caucuses in deference to favorite son Tom Harkin. The Clintons were unfamiliar with the state's peculiar political culture. She was running behind Edwards in the polls and bunched in a pack that included Obama and Tom Vilsack, the former Iowa governor. But for the next two days, she looked as if she owned the state. Her first stop was the Drake Diner, where she ordered a milkshake and fries and sat for an interview with David Yepsen, the political columnist for the *Des Moines Register*. Confirming her star quality, their interview was repeatedly interrupted by a parade of well-wishers.

Saturday began her real political activities, starting with the Iowa Democratic Party's state central committee. There she demonstrated that she would follow Mark Penn's advice about projecting the strength of Margaret Thatcher. "When you're attacked, you have to deck your opponents," Clinton told the party officials. That afternoon, she held her first big campaign rally in a Des Moines high school gymnasium before a thousand people. Banners adorning the wall read, "Let the Conversation Begin," a theme from the announcement of her candidacy the previous Saturday. "Well, I'm Hillary Clinton and I'm so glad to be in Iowa," she told the crowd. "I'm running for president and I'm in it to win it. I'm going to do it the old-fashioned way. I intend to come and talk to you and listen to you in your living rooms and your church basements and your union halls—wherever you are gathered."

After speaking for about fifteen minutes, she invited questions. The first came from a woman who said she was thrilled to see a woman running for president. "It's about time—if not past time—that we had a woman as president of the United States," this Iowan said, but then pointed out that all forty-three presidents had been men, and asked, "How is your campaign prepared to tackle that issue?"

Clinton answered, "I don't think I'm the only woman here who feels sometimes you have to work a little harder. Right. . . . All I have said is there will probably be more stories about my clothes and hair than some of the people running against me. . . . The fact that I'm a woman, the fact that I'm a mom, is part of who I am. But I'm going to ask people to vote for the person they believe would be the best president of the United States."

A voice from the audience called out, "You go, girl!"

"Go with me," Clinton shouted back.

The next day in Davenport she was supposed to greet people at a local diner, but because of the tremendous curiosity about her candidacy, her event was shifted to the county fairgrounds. This time she got tougher questions, including one about the health care debacle over which she had presided. It took her ten minutes to answer. When asked about her vote for the Iraq war resolution, she excoriated Bush over his handling of the war. But the most memorable moment came when she gave that teasing answer to a question about how she would deal with a dangerous world of evil men, evoking memories of the Monica Lewinsky affair with her husband. "What in my background equips me to deal with evil and bad men?" she said. Later, at her first press conference, reporters pressed her to explain what she really meant by her reply to that question. "I thought I was funny," she said with a shrug after several tries. "You know, you guys keep telling me to lighten up. I get a little funny, and now I'm being psychoanalyzed."

This first Iowa trip proved to be unexpectedly moving for Clinton and her team. They were overwhelmed both by the size of the crowds and the warmth of the reception, and by the sense that they were all beginning a historic journey many of them believed would elect the first woman president. "We all underestimated how emotional it was for her and for all of us," said Lorraine Voles, one of the few members of Clinton's team who had Iowa roots. "We were all just like, oh my God."

Two weeks later, Obama arrived for his first visit. During the short flight from Springfield to Cedar Rapids, he and Michelle, in good humor, roamed the aisle of his chartered airplane, chatting with reporters in the back cabin and reporting that their daughters seemed less than overwhelmed by the historic nature of his candidacy. Obama's first event was at a town hall meeting at John F. Kennedy High School, where he told the crowd, "This is just a naked political pitch. I want your support. I want your vote. I want your time. I want your energy." By the time he got to Waterloo for an evening town hall rally, his state director, Paul Tewes, had told him, gently, that in Iowa, presidential candidates ask people to "caucus" for them, not vote for them, part of the quick learning curve he was on as he began his campaign.

In Waterloo, where he spoke for less than thirty minutes, his reception was electric. He knew his opposition to the Iraq war would play well with Iowa's strong antiwar activists, and it did. At his mention of Iraq as "a

senseless war," he was interrupted by cheers and applause that lasted half
a minute. As he closed, he told the audience, "The biggest challenge we
face is not just the war in Iraq. The biggest challenge isn't just health care.
It's not just energy. It's actually cynicism. It's the belief that we can't change
anything. The thing that I'm hoping most of all during the course of this
campaign is that all of you decide that this campaign can be a vehicle for
your hopes and dreams. I can't change Washington all by myself."

"Right behind you," someone yelled out from the crowd.

At every stop, the crowds exceeded expectations. In Cedar Rapids and
Waterloo, the town halls were filled to overflowing. In Iowa Falls, a breakfast planned for thirty people attracted two hundred. In Ames, more than
seven thousand filled the Hilton Coliseum. Given the emotional response
of Iowans to him, Obama's advisers knew the key to success was to capture
all that energy and convert it into support in the caucuses.

Obama's campaign saw the national nomination battle through the prism
of Iowa; Clinton's team saw Iowa through the prism of a national campaign. The distinction was critical. The initial trips to Iowa showed that
both Clinton and Obama had star appeal, though he was still the underdog. What would prove decisive was which campaign best understood how
to build a winning campaign in a caucus state.

Unlike a primary, where polls are open from early morning to early
evening and ballots are cast in secret, caucuses usually are held at a specified time and can require a commitment of several hours. They attract
mainly a small group of party activists. Some people cannot participate
because they work during the caucus hours. Others find the process intimidating. Thus caucus voters represent only a small fraction of the total
voters. The Iowa caucus voters are required to stand before friends and
neighbors and publicly declare support for their candidate. If a candidate
does not reach a prescribed threshold of votes, typically 15 percent of the
voters in the room, voters are lobbied by representatives of other candidates and then can switch their votes to a new candidate. It is a confusing
and often chaotic process, one that in years past has been criticized, but it
has also made Iowa activists among the most attentive and discerning voters in the country. For the candidates, it presents a test of how to fashion
a strategy to win.

Obama had two powerful advantages. All of his top advisers—both in
Chicago and in Iowa—were veterans of Iowa campaigns. Most came out

of the organizational side of politics—vitally important in understanding the requirements of a caucus state—rather than from a campaign's media, message, or communications side. Campaign manager Plouffe came from the staff of former House majority leader Richard A. Gephardt, who had twice run in the caucuses. Top strategist Axelrod had worked for Paul Simon's presidential campaign in 1988, for Edwards in 2004, and for Vilsack's gubernatorial races. Steve Hildebrand, the deputy campaign manager, ran Iowa for Al Gore in 2000. Paul Tewes, Obama's new Iowa state director, had been Gore's field director in Iowa and was also a business partner of Hildebrand. Marygrace Galston, Tewes's deputy, was a field organizer for John Kerry in Iowa in 2004. Emily Parcell, the political director for Iowa, had worked for Gephardt. Mitch Stewart, the Iowa caucus director, had been one of Edwards's regional field directors. Larry Grisolano, who oversaw the media and polling, was an Iowa native and veteran of many campaigns there. Pete Giangreco, who handled direct mail and was Grisolano's business partner, also had worked campaigns in Iowa for years.

No one in Clinton's tight inner circle had real Iowa experience, nor was there any top adviser steeped in the intricacies of caucus organizing: Only Lorraine Voles, part of the communications team, and JoDee Winterhof, the Iowa director, had lived and worked in Iowa before. Clinton's first Iowa trip in January was also the first time a number of her advisers had ever set foot there. That experience gap gave Obama's team a huge head start—and the confidence to make early decisions that later paid enormous dividends. Obama's advisers concluded that his candidacy would rise or fall with the early states and that of those, Iowa was first among equals. As Giangreco put it, "Everything was subservient to Iowa."

Early in the campaign, David Plouffe showed his mettle. It was two weeks after Obama's first visit, when the Iowa and Chicago headquarters teams met in Des Moines for a daylong retreat. That weekend, Plouffe signed off on a hugely ambitious blueprint for organizing Iowa. Traditionally, the approach to organizing in the state began with the list of voters who had attended the previous caucuses. In 2004, 124,000 people had participated in the Democratic caucuses. The Iowa Democratic Party's voter lists, which every campaign bought for up to $100,000, contained the names of 99,000 of them. But Obama's research showed that his likely support among these Democrats would not be enough to overcome Clinton's or Edwards's appeal.

"They understood something intuitive in Iowa and probably something intuitive about this race nationally," said Tom Vilsack. "To win in Iowa, they were not going to be able to rely on the same hundred and ten, hundred and twenty thousand Democrats who generally show up at a caucus. They had to blow the roof off of the numbers of people attending caucus. . . . In other words, you go to people who aren't normally courted and you make them feel like they are the most special people on earth."

Obama's Iowa team was envisioning a bold plan to build a new electorate. Instead of operating out of a headquarters office in Des Moines, and a relatively few field offices elsewhere, Obama should create as many regional offices as his money would allow. Tewes, the state director, projected a need for two dozen or more, which eventually increased to thirty-seven.

"We wanted to open up all these offices real quick and have our people out [there]," Tewes explained. This was at odds with the traditional approach. "We said no, we wanted, for at least eight or ten months, to have the same people working the same area," Tewes said. "But that required having a lot more people up front and a lot more offices up front, which required obviously spending more money up front."

Plouffe grasped the importance of what Tewes and others were proposing, gave general approval to their concept, and when it became clear that Obama would have far more money than anyone originally thought, the campaign accelerated its timetable. "It made a huge difference," Tewes said, "because a lot of our organizers were fixtures in the community. They had been there for ten months. The office was on Main Street. It was like a scene from *The Andy Griffith Show*. It was just a place to go and talk about politics. No amount of TV can buy those kinds of relationships."

Nate Hund, one of those grassroots Obama organizers, was a perfect example. When the caucuses were over and he was getting ready to leave the little town of Algona, where he had spent months, local leaders encouraged him to stay and run for mayor. Despite his affection for Algona, he moved on.

Plouffe made another critical decision: Obama would avoid, as much as possible, local and county Democratic Party fund-raisers and gatherings. The Iowa staff balked, but it was Plouffe's hunch that among hardcore activists who showed up at those meetings, Obama would be the third choice behind Clinton and Edwards. He wanted Obama to appear before Democrats who weren't the party activists and, when possible, Independents and even Republicans. Like much about Obama's focus on organization, the success of this plan only became evident later as the Obama operations gathered momentum in attracting new groups of supporters. "We were a bit skeptical ourselves of this plan to bring in all these new caucusgoers," said Mitch Stewart, "just based on the lore of Iowa—you know, that there's a certain set of groups that generally show up and it's our responsibility to persuade those folks as opposed to bringing in a whole new slew of people. And Plouffe and Paul [Tewes] saw right away the ability to bring in a new group of people."

Tewes also envisioned massive outreach to Independents, Republicans, and Iowans who were not registered to vote. He wanted parallel operations aimed at every possible constituency in the state: African-Americans, veterans, farmers, labor, Latinos, teachers, women, gays and lesbians, environmentalists, sportsmen, Native Americans, the disabled, peace groups—and, most important, young voters.

The decision to invest so heavily in the Iowa plan was made in the rush of the opening weeks of the campaign, but it proved to be one of their smartest strategic gambles. "It took a lot of guts on Plouffe's part to say this is the deal, this is what we're going to focus on," Giangreco said. "I think there was a moment over the summer of '07 where Hillary Clinton could have locked Iowa down. But the fact was that no one on that campaign had ever done Iowa, no one understood Iowa at all."

Tom Vilsack was one of the first to sound the alarm. The former governor had declared his candidacy for president in late 2006, the first major Democrat to do so. He had the kind of credentials that, in past campaigns, might have made him a serious contender: a leader among the nation's governors during his two terms in office, a midwesterner, a Roman Catholic, a politician with a deep interest in policy. None of that counted for much in a year when Democrats could choose from two rock stars like Clinton and Obama—and in a nomination battle that included a third candidate, Edwards, who had a strong base in Vilsack's home state. By the end of February 2007, he was out.

Not long after ending his own candidacy, he and his wife, Christie, signed on with Hillary Clinton. Vilsack was devoted to her candidacy and, by mid-spring, terribly disturbed at what he was seeing. Edwards was already moving swiftly to sign up members of the now-available Vilsack network. Obama was putting down roots across the state. But Clinton was stalled in neutral. During a spring trip to Washington, Vilsack encountered Terry McAuliffe at a restaurant. He told the former head of the Democratic

National Committee, who was national chairman of the Clinton campaign, "Terry, you've got to really organize a caucus. It's not like a primary. It's about time and it's about resources and it's about personal relationships and it's about schmoozing people repeatedly. It's highly personalized and the organization you're setting up doesn't reflect that and we need to change." McAuliffe replied, "You need to tell that to the candidate."

Patti Solis Doyle, Clinton's campaign manager, asked one of Vilsack's top advisers, Teresa Vilmain, to go to Iowa and report back on the state of the campaign. Vilmain was known as one of the most effective organizers in the Democratic Party, an Iowa native who had maintained close family and political ties to the state. When she arrived in May at Clinton headquarters in Des Moines, she found a train wreck in the making. The headquarters office had no receptionist, no interior walls for offices, no copying machine, and no budget approved by Clinton's national office. Nor had the national office approved a plan for organizing the state. JoDee Winterhof had complaints of her own. She was struggling to get more of Clinton's time in the state, fighting to have the senator make more phone calls to prospective supporters, and battling headquarters over the budget. Vilmain checked in with Tom and Christie Vilsack. They told her, "This isn't working."

While Solis Doyle was trying to persuade Vilmain to take over the Iowa campaign, the Clinton team suffered another huge embarrassment. A memo by deputy campaign manager Mike Henry, advising Clinton to consider skipping Iowa, was leaked to the *New York Times*. Henry, who oversaw the Clinton political and field operations, was growing worried about the cost of the nearly two dozen primaries scheduled for Super Tuesday, February 5, 2008. He wrote, "Worst case scenario: this effort [Iowa] may bankrupt the campaign and provide little if any political advantage."

Parts of the Henry memo would prove prophetic. Given the cost of keeping her large enterprise afloat over the coming months, an all-out campaign in Iowa would leave Clinton with just $5 to $10 million to compete on Super Tuesday. By skipping Iowa, Henry argued, Clinton would "change the focus of the campaign from a traditional process (Iowa first) to a more strategic campaign that favors us and enable us to amass more convention delegates by campaigning aggressively in the larger states holding greater numbers of delegates. If she walks [away] from Iowa she will devalue Iowa (our consistently weakest state)."

Within minutes after contents of Henry's memo appeared on the *New York Times* Web site, Clinton campaign officials dismissed it as the meaningless work of one person in the campaign. Clinton immediately made a round of calls into Iowa to assure Democrats that she would compete energetically for support in the caucuses. A few days later, she delivered that message in person. "It's not the opinion of the campaign," she said of that memo in an interview with Kay Henderson of Radio Iowa. "It's not my opinion."

Vilmain heard about the memo as she was getting ready to leave Washington for a scouting trip to Nevada. She headed back to Iowa to contain the damage. And she exchanged tough words with Henry, whose office she had been sharing. Henry never gave her a warning that he was preparing to recommend pulling out of the state, she complained angrily. "How can I have confidence in you?"

Two weeks later, the campaign announced that Vilmain would take over Iowa. When she arrived for good the weekend of June 16, her assessment was extraordinarily gloomy: The campaign had no momentum. Clinton was not spending enough time in the state. Washington was in "a delusional state of mind" about what it took to organize Iowa. No one in Washington knew what they didn't know about caucuses.

Vilmain thought Edwards had the most impressive operation. Obama was flooding the state with organizers, although it wasn't clear how effective they were. Clinton had limped through the spring with just eleven people on her Iowa staff. More troubling, Iowans still did not know Hillary Clinton. They knew *of* her, but few knew, for example, that she had been born and raised in the Chicago suburbs. There also seemed to be little empathy for her. Edwards might have a 28,000-square-foot house and have spent four hundred dollars for a haircut, but Iowa Democrats trusted his sincerity when he talked about ending an America of haves and have-nots. The bottom line was that Clinton was three months behind Obama in organizing and both of them were behind the pace Edwards was setting. The situation, Vilmain told people, was painful.

Tom Vilsack was equally pessimistic. He said, "There was no written document, so to speak, that laid out precisely what needed to be done, who needed to do it, and what the timelines were. Or if it had been approved, nobody had read it or nobody was following it. Meanwhile, Senator Obama was getting his young people out in neighborhoods all over the state, knocking on doors. . . . So all of a sudden, all these unknowns [voters] who weren't on anybody's radar screen—they're getting phone calls, they're getting visits, every couple weeks they're getting e-mails. Now they're feeling part of something special, a movement, a cause. And they don't brag about it, they don't talk about it. They don't even tell anybody they're doing it. And we're struggling to get the plan in place."

•

CHAPTER EIGHT

Iowa: Round Two

"We're going to get our ass kicked."

—Terry McAuliffe to Hillary and Bill Clinton
on the night of the Iowa caucuses

The Iowa State Fair is one of the most celebrated stops on the road to the White House. It begins in the heat of August, when the sweet corn is at its sweetest. The presidential candidates flock to the fair to mingle with thousands of prospective voters, gaze at the famous butter cow (a life-size animal sculpted from butter), flip pork chops on a hot grill, hold forth at the *Des Moines Register*'s Soap Box, see a giant pig in the livestock barns, and consume some of the unhealthiest food on the planet, from corn dogs to deep-fried Twinkies. The better-known candidates draw clusters of autograph seekers and requests for photographs. The rest hope their ritual stop will earn them a line or two in the paper or, better yet, a small photo on the inside pages.

On the night of July 2, 2007, the Clinton campaign had turned a corner of the fairgrounds into their own piece of political Americana. The fair was still weeks away, and the Clintonites had the grounds to themselves for a special outing, the moment Clinton's Iowa team had argued and lobbied for. Because Bill Clinton was the most popular Democrat in the state, they wanted him to campaign alongside his wife to jump-start the sputtering organization. Endless conference calls were held to get the planning just right.

"There were no less than twenty calls," one Clinton staffer recalled, a reminder that with the Clintons, nothing comes easy, without bureaucracy, or without excessive control. In the end, it was turning out fine, the setting a soft summer night just as they had hoped. On the big flatbed of an eighteen-wheeler, the advance team had created a stage and ringed it with bales of hay adorned with little American flags. On the back of the bleachers, larger American flags were hung, with the largest flag of all displayed on the columns of the exhibition building to form the backdrop for photographers while the Clintons were onstage. Placards bearing the campaign's newest slogan were everywhere: "READY for Change! Ready to LEAD!"

The Clintons were more than an hour late—Bill in a bright yellow shirt, Hillary in a bold pink jacket and blouse. Bill's introduction of her was for him brief—just ten minutes. He spotted a man in the crowd holding a sign that read, "Husbands for Hillary," and played the good spouse. "I'd be here tonight if she asked me, if we weren't married . . . because . . . in 2008 I will celebrate my fortieth year as a voter and in those forty years— tumultuous, fascinating years for America—she is by a long stretch the best-qualified nonincumbent I have ever had a chance to vote for president in my entire life."

For the next two days, the Clintons owned Iowa. They dominated the news, held forty public or private events and were seen by nearly seventy thousand people, including tens of thousands at a Fourth of July parade in Clear Lake. There, more than four hundred volunteers, along with the former president, hurled twenty thousand pieces of candy into the sweltering crowd. Hillary had never done a parade like that, she said after it was over. In New York, politicians hook arms, and crowds along the route scream and yell, but not always nicely. "Everyone waved at me here," she went on, "and I'm just happy because they waved at me and all five fingers were showing." At every stop, while her entourage ate pie and ice cream and sweated in the summer heat, the Clintons made up for months of lost time with voters, while signing up county coordinators and other volunteers in a desperate scramble to build an organization to match those of Obama and Edwards.

For two and a half days the Clintons seemed to get Iowa—a light bulb went off, said one Iowan. Now they could get down to the business of winning. They already had made a decision to play hard in Iowa. Michael Whouley, a hard-nosed Boston pol—he had helped bring John Kerry back to life in Iowa in 2004 and was one of the most feared organizers in the Democratic Party—helped persuade them at a meeting at their home in Chappaqua.

Even then the national campaign hesitated, haggling with the Iowa staff over budgets, timing of visits, and spending. Hillary also seemed reluctant to do what other candidates took for granted, wondering why she had to go to some of the smaller counties to meet with twenty-five or fifty activists at a time. She preferred to stay at only a few hotels in the state, which forced her schedulers to plan her trips accordingly. In October the Clinton team prepared three maps showing where she, Obama, and Edwards had traveled since January 1. She had done a total of sixty-nine stops in thirty-seven of the state's ninety-nine counties; Obama had held one hundred events in fifty-two counties; Edwards, one hundred forty-one events in eighty-seven counties. The maps highlighted what everyone knew: Clinton's opponents were significantly outworking her.

She resisted the constant demands to make phone calls to party activists and influential Iowans. "She's terrible about phone calls—hates them," one supporter recalled. But "when she's on the phone, she's amazing. She's engaging, she asks about the kids, she asks about—you know, it's a real conversation. But she can't get off the phone, and so she just hates doing it." Bill Clinton was no better. "The president doesn't make a political call in the state before Labor Day," another Iowa supporter complained. "Then you couldn't get him *not* to make one in December, when it was too late."

In addition to accelerating organizational efforts, the July 4th tour had another purpose: to reintroduce her to Iowans. She was still regarded by many as chilly and distant, an impression at odds with her warmth and generosity to those who knew her well. While the Clinton team was attempting to refurbish her image, Obama's was making him better known by launching television ads and sending a DVD to voters across the state. Clinton's first ads featured policy issues and treatises on middle-class economics. Inside her campaign, a long-running debate raged over her ads. The campaign team ordered up a biographical ad, shot in black and white, with Clinton telling the poignant story of her mother, who at age ten took the train to California with her even younger sister to move in with an aunt. "It was beautiful," Solis Doyle said later. "Brings a tear to your eye." But it was never shown.

Even after her July 4th trip, Clinton's problems continued. The Iowa leadership wanted more and more of her time, and later that summer an Iowa staffer wrote a memo saying the race was currently unwinnable given the money, time, and travel available to them. "People scoffed at it," recalled another staffer. Clinton's time was precious. She had fund-raising demands and other states in which she had to campaign. Most discouraging to the Iowans that was so much of Clinton's time was being eaten up by her responsibilities in the Senate. Consequently, she squeezed in her campaign time around her Senate voting schedule. At one point in the summer, Vilsack said to her, "You're going to have to decide whether you want to be a senator or president." He recalled her response. "'Well, I understand that. The August recess is coming, and that's when we're going to start doing what has to be done.' So she said . . . 'we're going to get serious about this in August.' And she did."

By October, she appeared to have made up considerable political ground. The campaign believed Iraq had eased as a major problem. Her health care plan attracted considerable attention in the local press. Her organization was coming together rapidly. Most important as a sign of her resurgence, an early October *Des Moines Register* Iowa Poll showed her leading Obama and Edwards, leaping from third to first in four months. Yet the same weekend, a conversation we conducted with ten activists from Linn County (Cedar Rapids) exposed a troubling undercurrent. Eight months earlier, on her first trip to Iowa, we had assembled the same group with the help of the Democratic county chairman for a story in the *Washington Post*. We discovered both the potential for her candidacy and the obstacles she faced. Surprisingly, given the *Register* poll, eight months later those activists still had major questions about her. She was too polarizing to win an election, one of the activists said. Another said she could never bring the country together. Asked what advice they would give her, one person said, "She just has to become more real."

There was one other event in October that, had it played out then as it did later, might have changed the Democratic race. The *National Enquirer* published an article headlined "Presidential Cheating Scandal! Alleged Affair Could Wreck John Edwards' Campaign Bid." The story claimed that Edwards had had an extramarital affair with a woman who had traveled with him on the campaign trail. An Edwards spokesman denounced the report as "false, absolute nonsense." The mainstream media ignored the story. Elizabeth Edwards briefly disappeared from the campaign trail, but her absence was assumed, incorrectly, to be related to her battle with cancer.*

On October 15, 2007, the Clinton high command held a summit meeting at the law offices of O'Keefe, Lyons & Hynes in Chicago. The Chicago location assured secrecy—the sight of Clinton's national headquarters leader-

---

* During the summer of 2008, after the *Enquirer* published additional details and long after he had quit the race, Edwards confessed to the affair but denied that he was the father of the infant born to the woman.

ship descending on Des Moines would have set off alarm bells across the state—as well as providing neutral territory for them to conduct a pointed discussion of her Iowa prospects. From Washington, the group included Penn, Solis Doyle, Ickes, Grunwald, and Henry. The Iowa contingent included state director Vilmain, Dave Barnhart, a Whouley protégé who had arrived the month before to serve as caucus director, Winterhof, the one-time director and now a senior adviser, and Karen Hicks, a skilled party organizer based in New Hampshire.

Clinton's Iowa campaign saw Edwards as a greater threat, but beating Obama was their top priority. One fact most worried her Iowa organizers: Many more of Edwards's supporters had participated in caucuses before and were more likely to show up again. In the early fall, when Clinton's people crunched the numbers from hundreds of thousands of telephone calls and personal contacts with Iowans, they discovered that an alarming percentage of her supporters—nearly seven in ten—said they had never caucused. Many were older, particularly older women. The Iowa team believed that the Washington staff saw Clinton in better shape than she was (though headquarters always regarded Iowa as her most difficult state) and the Iowans came to Chicago with an agenda, to dispel any sense of false optimism about the state of play in their state and to ask for a substantial budget increase to fund an unprecedented door-to-door operation to educate their supporters about the caucus process.

Penn opened the meeting with a polling presentation that, from the viewpoint of the some of the Iowans, was outrageously optimistic. Tensions between Penn and the Iowa team already existed. They did not believe he understood the caucuses. Penn, in turn, believed the Iowa team was too hidebound, too wedded to past caucus history. The Iowa staff listened to Penn's presentation and feared that national headquarters wanted to spend not a penny more than necessary to win their state. National was not going to pay for any landslides in Iowa. As Iowa's caucus director, Dave Barnhart was particularly upset. When Penn was finished he offered a contrary view based on a different set of numbers. Barnhart recalled later his goal was to explain to them "basically just say, 'Look, with the current resources, this is what we think we can deliver. If everyone's okay with that, great, but we need to quit talking about winning the state.'"

A few days earlier, the Clinton campaign had completed five focus groups, two in Sioux City with Clinton supporters who had never before attended a caucus. As they watched live on their laptops in Des Moines, senior staff couldn't believe what they were hearing. "Our people didn't know caucuses," Vilmain recalled. "They were totally befuddled." One elderly woman arrived thinking she was at a caucus. "When she said that, you just wanted to throw up," Barnhart said. Other focus group participants thought they would have to pay to attend the caucuses, or that the caucuses were open only to elected officials or the party elite. Another Clinton staffer called the results an "Oh, shit!" moment for the campaign. They needed a totally new approach to prepare their supporters for caucus night. At the Chicago meeting, they asked for money to hire another hundred people whose only job would be to go door-to-door, sit down in homes with voters identified as Clinton supporters, show them a DVD about how caucuses operate, and give them a pep talk about how important it was for them to show up for Hillary Clinton on January 3.

Ickes was not impressed with the proposals. He believed the Iowa team had come forward with an insufficient request. At best, he said, it might assure Clinton of second place, and if so they might as well just forget about Iowa and save the money for Super Tuesday. "Why don't you come back with a budget we can win on?" he demanded. The Iowa team revised their budget, asking for even more money. Headquarters quickly approved, and from that day forward the Iowa campaign never lacked for resources. Whatever Iowa wanted, Iowa got. One member of the Iowa team said later, "And then we had everything we needed and more. . . . It was enough, it was just too late."

As Clinton's team was meeting to resolve their differences over Iowa, Obama was meeting with his senior leadership to review the progress—or lack of it. For weeks, he had been pummeled by donors, friends, journalists, and pundits questioning his strategy. They told him that it was time to start moving his national poll numbers up to stop Clinton from gaining an insurmountable advantage; that his strategy of focusing on Iowa was a loser; that it was time to realize he was running a national campaign; that it was time to go negative. His fund-raisers were so skittish that one even talked of trying to force out some of his top advisers, though nothing ever came of it.

Obama pollster Joel Benenson vividly remembered the directness with which Obama opened the meeting. He remained confident that the campaign could be won, but said, "But right now we're losing, and we've got ninety days to turn this around." Then he pressed Plouffe about the Iowa strategy, asking why his campaign manager was certain that Clinton's big lead in national polls would not infect Iowa's electorate. "He questioned us sharply," Axelrod said. "There's no doubt that he wanted assurance that we knew what we were doing. . . . We said by the measures we apply, things are on the right track. The metrics in Iowa were good."

But Obama came to love Iowa and particularly his team of young organizers. "What gave me confidence was the quality of the people on the ground," he told us later. "We had *the* best statewide organization, I think, in the annals of American politics. Those kids, they were just great. So you'd land in Iowa, it was like an island unto itself and you would just feel this sense of, something's going on here."

Out of that autumn research came three pillars of an Obama message: First, bring the country together to usher in a new politics (however ill-defined that "new politics" might be). Second, strongly emphasize the need to fight the special interests. Obama's advisers told him nobody believes Clinton can do that. You can. Third, level with the people, tell them even unpleasant truths to enhance Obama's reputation for authenticity, which his campaign believed Clinton lacked. An October 12 memo highlighted the conclusions, and took particular note that Clinton was vulnerable to attacks on her character. Obama's advisers believed it was time to start drawing contrasts with Clinton, to heighten voters' doubts about her and to cement her image as the insider in a year of change. Larry Grisolano, who oversaw polling, research, and paid media, had this expression: If Clinton wants to run as the candidate with Washington experience, we've got to make her pay a price for that Washington experience.

Next to the caucuses themselves, the Iowa Democratic Party's Jefferson Jackson Dinner on November 10, 2007, was the most significant political event of the yearlong campaign in Iowa. Nearly ten thousand activists, and all the candidates, were expected to attend. From past history, the Iowa campaign staffs knew the evening could be a turning point. Four years earlier John Kerry had resurrected his slumping candidacy with a fiery speech at the dinner, which turned out to be the beginning of the end of Howard Dean's campaign.

The morning of the dinner, Vilmain gathered her troops in a cavernous room in the Hy-Vee Center to review the instructions for the evening and practice the chants their supporters would use when Clinton spoke: *Turn up the heat*, they would respond after she delivered their promptlines. Later in the afternoon Obama and Michelle led a huge, boisterous band of supporters into the Veterans Memorial Auditorium to practice the campaign's rally-ending mantra—*Fired up! Ready to go!*—with the Isiserettes Drill and Drum Corps providing the beat.

An hour or so before the dinner began, the campaigns packed the balconies with their supporters. Obama's looked like a youth brigade, Clinton's a sea of elderly Iowans. Mark Penn and Mandy Grunwald walked into the press room early in the evening and disparaged Obama's forces. "Ours look like caucusgoers," Grunwald said. Obama's, Penn added, did not look old enough to vote. But in the balconies, the potential nightmare of caucus night was playing out before the Clinton staffers' eyes. "It was like a third-world country," Barnhart said. Only one concession stand was open, and the lines for it were so long that some people had to wait an hour and a half to be served. They ran out of water. By 8 p.m., some of Clinton's elderly supporters began to leave, saying they would watch on television at home. Aides began posting people at exits to urge them to stay and return to their seats. "We were calling them the hemorrhage group because we were hemorrhaging people," Barnhart said. "And so we had lost about a third of our people before Hillary even took the stage."

It had taken a monumental effort to get Clinton's national leadership even to focus on the dinner. Less than a week before, they were still haggling over her speech. "It took them forever," said a Clinton adviser in Iowa. "They were trying to figure out the JJ [Jefferson Jackson] message five days out. And you couldn't get anybody's attention."

Obama had been preparing for the dinner since his team's strategy meeting in mid-October. His Iowa advisers included veterans of Kerry's campaign who knew its importance.

On November 3, a week before the dinner and one year before the 2008 election, Obama had delivered what the campaign dubbed the "year-out speech" in South Carolina. It was, in fact, a dry run for Jefferson Jackson. A few hours after delivering the speech, Obama told us during a telephone interview from the road, "Now is the time for us to start fleshing out the argument that I've been talking about why I should be the Democratic nominee instead of the other candidates who are running in the primary." When we suggested that Obama was portraying Clinton as embodying the worst of the political system, he disagreed. "I would reject that she represents the worst of the system . . . but as I said, she's run a textbook campaign and the textbook that is issued by Washington conventional wisdom says that you should be vague and avoid definitive answers in campaigns in part to make yourself a smaller target to Republican attacks, but the argument I'm making is that unless we can be candid with the American people it's going to be hard for us to govern."

Then why was he having trouble gaining traction with voters and still behind in the polls? we wondered. "It's important to recognize that we're running against the dominant brand name of the Democratic Party," Obama replied. "That's why we focused on the early states where we can be much more directly engaged with voters and spend time with them. This is always going to be a harder argument to make than just to check off the traditional list of Democratic proposals or speak to the enumerated concerns of the various Democratic interest groups. This has more to do with pushing beyond traditional campaign politics."

After speaking in South Carolina, Obama flew to New York to appear on *Saturday Night Live*. Axelrod called speechwriter Jon Favreau from the greenroom. He said Obama liked the speech but it would need to be cut in half to use at the Jefferson Jackson Dinner. He said Obama needed the draft by morning. Since the dinner rules prohibited the use of notes or a teleprompter, every candidate had to memorize the speech. With the new draft in hand, Obama arrived in Iowa Tuesday night for a rally in Cedar Rapids and then headed for Davenport to begin a two-day trip along the Mississippi River and then back across southeast Iowa to Des Moines. "I can remember walking by his hotel room one day that week and the TV was up really, really loud," Robert Gibbs recalled. What was going on? he wondered. Only days later, he realized Obama had been practicing his speech then, but with the TV sound loud so he couldn't be heard outside his room.

The dinner started about 6 p.m. and dragged on for hours. It was approaching 11 p.m. when Clinton, the next to last speaker, was introduced. She delivered a strong speech, although her call to *Turn up the heat* left many of her own staffers cold. Then it was Obama's turn. As in Boston and in Springfield, he hit his marks, drawing a sharp contrast between himself and Clinton, though he never mentioned her by name. "Telling the American people what we think they want to hear instead of telling the American people what they need to hear just won't do," he said. "Triangulating and poll-driven positions because we're worried about what Mitt or Rudy might say about us just won't do. If we are really serious about winning this election, Democrats, we can't live in fear of losing it. . . . This party—the party of Jefferson and Jackson; of Roosevelt and Kennedy—has always made the biggest difference in the lives of the American people when we led, not by polls, but by principle; not by calculation, but by conviction; when we summoned the entire nation to a common purpose—a higher purpose. And I run for the presidency of the United States of America because that's the party America needs us to be right now."

The next morning, David Yepsen, the most influential political columnist in the state, wrote, "Should [Obama] come from behind to win the Iowa caucuses, Saturday's dinner will be remembered as one of the turning points in his campaign here."

Obama's speech created an immediate surge of energy for his campaign, and a growing sense that caucus night in Iowa could become a climactic showdown. At that point, Obama seemingly could do no wrong.

Four days after the Jefferson Jackson Dinner, the candidates met in Las Vegas for another debate. "Look out," Edwards warned Obama, she's coming after you. Clinton was aggressive that night but it was the moderators who tried to trip up Obama, and on the very question that had caused Clinton so much trouble in Philadelphia. Asked his position on whether illegal immigrants should be allowed to have driver's licenses, Obama waffled. "I am not proposing that's what we do," he said. After much pressing, he said he did support them. Unlike Clinton, Obama paid no price for his equivocation. That drove Clinton's team mad.

"We are back to April, when Obama had the endless lift of the national media hyping his candidacy," Penn wrote in a November 23 memo. "Particularly dangerous now is David Yepsen, who is touting his candidacy and who is realistically the most powerful journalist in America at the moment. . . . A chorus of Hillary-bashing press coached Obama relentlessly that he had to attack and that he cross their line with their help. . . . But Edwards managed to attack so harshly that Obama somehow got the best of both worlds: the benefits of attacking her but not being seen as too negative in his campaigning." Penn noted that the attacks by Obama and Edwards had raised Clinton's negatives by ten points and had hurt her on honesty and answering tough questions. "In general it put a fog over our candidacy." Penn knew that Obama had tapped into two real sentiments: people's desire to be unified and their hunger for authenticity. He knew Clinton was seen as polarizing, but recent events, he believed, had given Clinton the opportunity to change the debate from a referendum on her to a choice for the voters. They had to break through "his façade into the real Obama."

On December 2, with a new poll showing Obama now leading in Iowa, Clinton struck back. "I have said for months that I would much rather be attacking Republicans, and attacking the problems of our country, because ultimately that's what I want to do as president," she said. "But I have been, for months, on the receiving end of rather consistent attacks. Well, now the fun part starts. We're into the last month, and we're going to start drawing the contrasts."

Earlier that day, Clinton had lashed her own campaign team during a morning conference call. "She was just fed up," said one staffer who was on the call. "She just got on the conference call and just lit into everyone." Her anger was prompted, in part, by being told by aides that things still weren't clicking in Iowa, particularly on the message front. The previous night, during a cocktail reception for the *Des Moines Register*, she was told by the local reporters that they rarely heard from her campaign about Obama. That news, too, set her off. "We're getting outhustled here," she said, according to a staffer who listened in. "And it's not a field problem, it's not a political problem, it's a messaging and communications problem. Their message is beating us here, their press team is beating us here, their overall communications is just better than us here, and we have to do something."

Solis Doyle was at home that morning, listening in as well. Clinton's ire included the entire senior staff at headquarters. A member of that staff remembered Clinton's frustration and anger. "This is crazy," Clinton said. "This is all about Iowa, we need to win there, decision makers need to go do Iowa. . . . Everybody's got to go." By the next day Solis Doyle was in Des Moines, followed by others. They stayed until the caucuses were over.

There *was* cause for alarm. Clinton's internal polling showed serious slippage. Five days before the Jefferson Jackson Dinner, a three-way track had her at 32 percent, Edwards at 31 percent, and Obama at 25 percent. Five days later, Obama had surged into the lead. Later in November, Clinton's polling showed her ahead once more, with 35 percent as against 27 percent each for Obama and Edwards. But the December 4 track brought worrisome news. Now the race was essentially a dead heat—Clinton and Obama at 29 percent each, Edwards at 31.

In the meantime, inside Clinton's campaign, the battle over whether she could afford to attack Obama continued to rage. Penn remained hawkish, as did Bill Clinton. One of the campaign's top advisers said later of Bill Clinton, "He really started poring over Mark's research and said we *have* to go negative, we *have* to attack this guy. If the press isn't going to take a fair shot at him and a fair look at him, then we're going to be the ones that have to do it."

At a meeting at the Clintons' Washington home on December 1—the day before Hillary's angry conference call—Bill Clinton vented his frustrations about the campaign. "He basically said," one person recalled, "We've got to make the negative ads, got to get 'em ready, we've got to put them up and we've got to go negative on this guy. Nobody else is doing it. We've got to do it'. . . . It was pretty much an order." That night, Penn told Hillary, "I see no way we can win if we do not take him on."

Clearly the Obama attacks on Clinton were hurting her, in part because her campaign had never taken steps to inoculate her. "The campaign against us, which the Obama campaign has never gotten enough notice for having run—is that she's dishonest, can't be trusted, disingenuous," a senior Clinton adviser said later, "and we never did a goddamn thing to anesthetize ourselves against it."

But Clinton faced a dilemma the campaign was never able to solve in Iowa. Her advisers were right to anticipate the attacks, but they misjudged how the attacks would be delivered. They prepared negative ads and responses to what they thought would be the likeliest attack ads from Obama and Edwards. But neither of them used television ads to deliver their attacks. Instead, they went after her in debates and speeches and campaign appearances. Her ads had to remain on the shelf.

Much of the Iowa team objected strenuously to Clinton's negative turn in early December, arguing that voters there would react badly if Clinton went on the attack. "The emphasis on being nice was overwhelming," Phil Singer said. If anybody but she attacked Obama verbally, the press ignored them. And if she did it, she might alienate undecided voters she was trying to convert. The Iowa team wanted a totally different approach. "We brought her mom out, we brought Chelsea out. We brought people from her past to introduce her," Solis Doyle said. "We cut these great ads with Dorothy [Rodham], Chelsea. They went over so well we put them on in New Hampshire, where we were losing ground because we were losing ground in Iowa. And it was working. I just think it was too little too late."

Caucus day arrived with a sense of anticipation and expectation in Obama's campaign, nervousness and concern inside Clinton's. That morning, Tom Vilsack was prowling the corridors of the Polk County Convention Center, where the television networks were conducting round-the-clock interviews. Like all of Clinton's supporters, he was trying not to show his nervousness. If turnout was not extraordinarily high, he remained optimistic that Clinton could win.

What is remarkable is how close the two campaigns were in their projections of likely supporters. Obama's campaign estimated turnout would be about 167,000, possibly 180,000. Only Gordon Fischer, the former Iowa Democratic chairman and now a loyal Obama supporter, predicted that as many as 200,000 might turn out. No one on Obama's team believed him. Based on the 167,000 projection, the Obama campaign was certain they could produce 54,000 people, which would give Obama about 33 percent of the total allocation of delegates.

Clinton's team estimated turnout at around 150,000, though some thought it could rise to 160,000. The campaign estimated that 50,000 to 53,000 Clinton supporters would show up. So meticulous was the Clinton team that they had taken the unusual step of striking identified supporters off their lists if it was clear those voters were either too infirm or not enthusiastic enough to show up to caucus. Almost 16,000 people were eliminated this way.

On the afternoon of the caucuses, Clinton had lunch at the Latin King restaurant in Des Moines and met with several of her Iowa team in a back room. We feel good up to 165,000, they told her. Anything above that made them nervous. On caucus morning, the Iowa team reviewed Penn's final tracking. The *Des Moines Register*'s final poll had shocked everyone, giving Obama a clear lead and projecting a big turnout. Penn's three-way numbers showed Clinton at 32 percent, Obama at 31, and Edwards at 28. But Penn also had done another random-digit dialing survey. That showed Obama at 41 percent, Clinton at 30, Edwards at 24. What if turnout hits 180,000? someone asked. Then it's too late to do anything about it, someone remembered Penn responding. Besides, Penn said, if you believe in your assumptions, there's no reason to abandon them because of the *Register* poll.

Obama had two organizational advantages at that point. First was the campaign's emphasis on younger voters. During the Christmas holidays they had devised elaborate means of tracking college-age supporters, handing them off from an organizer at their campus town to an organizer in their hometown. They also had developed a spreadsheet of every high school in the state, with organizers identified for each. Obama's second advantage was his campaign's outreach to Independents and Republicans. But the true focus of the Obama team was any voter under age forty. Students might not be reliable, but the others likely were.

Earlier, Clinton had gone after Independent women, but Obama's team launched a last-minute push to go back to virtually every Independent voter in the state as well as selected Republicans. Their message was simple: If you want information about the caucuses, call this 800 number. "We had twelve lines dedicated to incoming 800-number calls," Tewes said. "Four days before [the caucuses], we had to add another eight. And we still couldn't keep up. People wanted to know where their caucus location was, wanted to know the hours, what a caucus is." Eventually, twenty lines were dedicated to the Independents. "You just felt like something was going on," he said.

Hillary Clinton is superstitious. She generally does not like to watch election returns. Early on the evening of January 3, as thousands of Iowans were heading to the caucuses, she was in her suite at the Fort Des Moines hotel.

Barack Obama was confident. "You could just feel we were firing on all cylinders," he later told us. "The field stuff was working. . . . The intensity was there. My message was working. The crowds were excited. The last night before caucus night, we flew into Dubuque. It was zero degrees. There was like half a foot of snow on the ground. We got in at eleven at night into Dubuque and there were like two thousand people packed into this auditorium going crazy. You could just feel that we were going to be in pretty good shape."

Obama had never been to a caucus, and after all the miles he had traveled through Iowa, he wanted to see what one looked like. With Plouffe and press aide Tommy Vietor in tow, he set out for a caucus site in Ankeny, just north of Des Moines. They arrived at Ankeny High School about 6:15 to a parking lot overflowing with cars and long lines through the door. "This is democracy in action, and I've lost my voice," a raspy Obama told one supporter.

It was a scene that left the normally undemonstrative Plouffe still giddy six weeks later. "It was a manifestation of all that work for a year of what we'd hoped to put together," he said. There was an elderly man with a long white beard and a red T-shirt who looked like Gandalf from *The Lord of the Rings*. There were young African-Americans and single moms and families, a portrait, Plouffe said, of what they had hoped to build with their campaign. "It was a wonderful, wonderful night for democracy."

One hundred forty miles away, Tom and Christie Vilsack were arriving at the Ward One precinct caucus in Van Allen Elementary School in Mt. Pleasant. "Who are these people?" Vilsack thought. "I've never seen these people before." The population of Mt. Pleasant is about nine thousand. Vilsack's wife is a native and Vilsack has lived there most of his adult life. For him to walk into a caucus and not recognize scores of people was unnerving. Even then his first reaction was not one of panic. He thought the turnout was good for Clinton, very good for Obama. He still believed she could hold her own. It wasn't until the caucus process moved to its second phase, when the supporters of the candidates who did not reach 15 percent began to move to other candidates, that he started to worry. Clinton was getting very few of the second-choice supporters.

By the time he and Christie were flying back to Des Moines to meet with the Clintons and their advisers, he realized she was going to lose. Vilsack was in anguish. He gripped his wife's hand, but through the entire flight the two never talked, sitting silently in the small plane as it made its way over frozen fields and small towns. "I felt that I had failed somebody that I cared deeply about," he said. "I couldn't even articulate what it was that I should have done differently or how I should have approached this differently, but I felt there was a great deal of trust placed in me and I didn't deliver."

At Obama headquarters, as early reports of long lines gave way to more precise estimates of how many people were coming out, it was clear that turnout would far exceed projections, and with it came the confidence that Obama was about to spring a stunning upset on Clinton. In Clinton's boiler room, the realization of what was happening brought looks of panic and feelings of nausea. By the end of the evening, turnout reached 239,872. Obama's percentage of the delegates was 37.58, Edwards's was 29.75, and Clinton's was 29.47.

Clinton's team was totally unprepared. "We thought we would either win Iowa or Edwards would win Iowa," Wolfson said. "Either of those outcomes was fine." One Clinton supporter remembers it as one of the worst experiences of her life. "I was in the boiler room the night of the caucuses," she said, "and I was watching people's faces turn green. Patti. Teresa. Karen. Howard. Silence. Green. Sickening looks on their faces." Teresa Vilmain recalled approaching Terry McAuliffe, the campaign chairman, fund-raiser, cheerleader and confidant of the Clintons. "Prepare them," she said. Though the final numbers were not in, she doubted that Clinton would even finish second.

McAuliffe already had gotten a call from Bill Clinton to come up to their suite. McAuliffe told him they were going to lose—badly. You've got to be kidding me, the former president said. He got Hillary and McAuliffe repeated the news. "We're going to get our ass kicked," he said. A call went out for others in the senior staff to come to the suite. Hillary went downstairs at one point to deliver her concession speech. Later she gathered the entire Iowa staff to thank them. But mostly that night, she, Bill, and her stricken top advisers fumed and argued over what they should do in the wake of her third-place finish.

One adviser in the room said of Hillary's emotions, "disappointed is not strong enough and outrage is too strong." Another said, "She wasn't screaming and yelling and lashing out. She was disappointed to have lost. Upset. Surprised. Not to have lost, but to have finished where we finished." Jerry Crawford, one of the savviest veterans of Iowa politics and a longtime Clinton ally, described her that night as the "ultimate prizefighter who has taken the ultimate punch and pulls herself together and doesn't get knocked off stride and goes downstairs and performs." But she was more than disappointed; she was intensely frustrated. Vilsack recalls her words. She said, "I'm doing what you all asked me to. Every time you ask me to do something, I've done it. Would you just give me a clear understanding of precisely what my mission is here?"

Bill Clinton was in a fighting mood. He thought there had been shenanigans at the caucuses and wanted to get to the bottom of it. Even more, he was annoyed that they had not taken on Obama earlier. He had wanted attacks on Obama's ties to the corrupt Chicago developer Tony Rezko. He had wanted a vigorous effort to undermine Obama on Iraq. "He wanted to go negative," recalled one person in the room. His attitude was, "We should have done it in Iowa, we should have kept doing it. We need to do it in New Hampshire." "He's the Comeback Kid," said another person in the room. "He was anxious to start the comeback." Penn was in full agreement about attacking Obama, as he had been for months. Vilsack, who had strongly opposed going negative in Iowa, now said he agreed. Grunwald said some of the negative ads had already been prepared, and the Clinton team huddled around her laptop to watch them. Solis Doyle was described by others as shell-shocked and mostly silent, though she was opposed to going negative. Wolfson strongly resisted going negative. It's hard to run against a movement, he warned. Grunwald, who knew the New Hampshire electorate better than anyone there, cautioned against a quick shift toward negative campaigning in New Hampshire.

The meeting in Clinton's suite ended inconclusively. She had a flight to catch for New Hampshire. Vilsack remembers Clinton packing her bags, getting ready to leave. "See you in October," he said, his way of telling her she would still be the Democratic presidential nominee in the general election to come. Clinton flashed a smile. On his way out, Vilsack caught a glimpse of Clinton's mother, Dorothy Rodham. "I'll never forget this as long as I live," he said. "Mrs. Rodham was in the bedroom, this adjoining bedroom by herself. And she was hurting for her daughter. You could tell. Her head was down. She just didn't know what to do." The Clintons flew off in their own plane; most of the staff piled into the press plane for the ride to New Hampshire. Solis Doyle and Mike Henry planned to return to Washington temporarily. As the others were leaving, they saw the embattled pair, Solis Doyle and Henry, campaign manager and deputy campaign manager to an enterprise now in turmoil and disarray, sitting in the darkened coffee shop in the Fort Des Moines. Whatever pain they felt that night would only increase in the days and weeks ahead.

Obama delivered a memorable speech. A great victory had now been turned into a movement.

"You know, they said this day would never come," Obama told his delirious supporters. "They said our sights were set too high. They said this country was too divided, too disillusioned to ever come together around a common purpose. But on this January night, at this defining moment in history, you have done what the cynics said we couldn't do. . . . Years from now, when we've made the changes we believe in, when more families can afford to see a doctor, when our children—when Malia and Sasha and your children—inherit a planet that's a little cleaner and safer, when the world sees America differently, and America sees itself as a nation less divided and more united—you'll be able to look back with pride and say that this was the moment when it all began. . . . This was the moment when we finally beat back the policies of fear and doubts and cynicism, the politics where we tear each other down instead of lifting this country up. This was the moment."

Then he was off to New Hampshire.

CHAPTER NINE

Five Days in New Hampshire

"Why should we believe you can win a national election?" a New Hampshire voter asked Clinton. She replied, "I have been through the fires."

Hillary Clinton's chartered airplane landed in Manchester sometime around 4 a.m. on Friday, January 3. It was brutally cold, the temperature hovering just above zero and piles of snow everywhere. Her morning started badly with a senior staff conference call.

She tried to sound strong and determined and, if not upbeat, at least positive. Iowa was behind them, she said. Let's go forward. But the call quickly revealed a campaign team in a deep funk and ill-equipped to help her. She was met with virtual silence when she said hello. Solis Doyle was not on the call. Penn and Wolfson, who normally dominated the morning calls, had nothing to offer, and when asked later neither of them could remember much about it. Grunwald, Clinton's media adviser, echoed her boss and tried, gently, to encourage Penn or Wolfson to weigh in. Again there was silence, according to several accounts.

Clinton said they had made mistakes in Iowa and she wanted to move immediately to correct them in New Hampshire—the most important being a campaign to go after younger voters. She wanted to reach out to college campuses. "She made it pretty clear that she was not happy that she was not given, or getting, better information about what she was to do in New Hampshire," said one person listening. Another later said he believed what she wanted that morning was a conversation about what to do next. But her most trusted advisers were either AWOL or too shaken by the loss in Iowa, too tongue-tied, too depressed to respond. The call was filled with awkward pauses and empty spaces. According to another person listening—who later described as gross negligence the lack of support

Clinton got at that moment—"She said in a very calm voice, 'Well, I guess I'll do it myself . . .' That was her attitude. 'I'll do it myself.' It wasn't mean, it wasn't vicious. I actually felt horribly sorry for the woman. I felt like this woman had been misserved."

Finally, Clinton had had enough; she curtly ended the call with another expression of her displeasure. "Thank you all," she said as she signed off. "I've enjoyed talking to myself the last twenty minutes."

The conference call marked a temporary transfer of power. Hillary and Bill Clinton would take it back from her inner circle at headquarters. *They* would now run the campaign. *They* would plot the strategy. *They* would give the orders. *They* would largely ignore the team that had guided the campaign for the previous year. *They* would turn instead to a combination of old friends, aides, local advisers, and loyalists who were offering advice directly to them. Now Hillary especially would turn to her New Hampshire team, who knew the state's electorate intimately and knew well of the Clintons' long-standing connection to voters there.

For months, the New Hampshire team had been working to build a firewall in the event of a cataclysmic Clinton loss to Obama in Iowa, a third-place defeat few truly expected. Now they only had five days to turn back Obama's momentum.

In Nashua at about 8 a.m. she met backstage in a cavernous, chilly airplane hangar with Nick Clemons, the New Hampshire state director, and Guy Cecil, the national political director, who had been working the state for weeks. She told them she was prepared to do whatever they recommended. She wanted more events where she could meet voters informally, events that would show voters how much this primary meant to her. "I'm going to work harder than anyone else in this state to win New Hampshire," she told them. At one point that morning, someone suggested that she not take questions at her first scheduled event. Clinton responded testily that her campaign had become too imperious, her events too much like White House events. She wanted to get in closer touch with the voters. She especially wanted contact. "I want to take questions at every single event," she said.

There was a sense of urgency in her voice when she opened her first post-Iowa rally in the hangar that morning—and a look of concern on her husband's face. What the Clintons feared was a rush to judgment, an Iowa-driven gale-force wind at Obama's back. She told the audience, "New Hampshire voters are going to be weighing and assessing everything in the next five days. It's a short period of time, but it's enough time. Time for people to say, wait a minute." When she turned to questions, someone asked, "Why should we believe you can win a national election?" She replied, "I have been through the fires."

Obama also arrived in the middle of the night, exhilarated but exhausted. If Clinton was redoubling her efforts, if she was about to shed some of the baggage she had carried in Iowa and begin the kind of campaigning that New Hampshire voters expected, Obama was in danger of riding the wave coming out of Iowa and letting himself get too comfortable. If he won in New Hampshire, Obama could become the Democratic nominee more easily than anyone had thought.

A big midday rally in Concord would kick off Obama's final days of campaigning, to be followed by an important speech that night at a New Hampshire Democratic Party dinner.

The Obama team's conference call that morning was lighthearted. There was good-natured joshing with his New Hampshire team about the onus being on them to finish what Iowa had started. They talked about the polling. Even before Iowa, Obama had been gaining in New Hampshire. As of that morning the race remained tight. They discussed what bounce Obama might expect from his Iowa victory, and how long it would last. And they wanted to make sure the crowd for their Concord rally would be good, and give Obama time in the afternoon to rest and get ready for his evening speech. That night, Obama won the rhetorical sweepstakes at the party fund-raising dinner while Clinton seemed to be struggling to find her message. Day one in New Hampshire seemed a continuation of Iowa.

On Saturday morning a monumental traffic jam was building around Nashua North High School. Cars overflowed the school parking lot and were illegally left along snowbanks or on the edges of intersections. A procession of cars inched down the narrow road trying to get anywhere close to the school, where Obama was scheduled to appear at 10 a.m. The line of people snaked from the front door around the parking lot and up the walkway by the road. Nearly three thousand people showed up that morning, too many to fit into the gymnasium; some ended up in an overflow room next door. That alone seemed to be the story—the massive outpouring being generated by Obama's candidacy. He was used to attracting big crowds, but there was something about this one that turned heads and caused seasoned campaign advisers and skeptical reporters to let down their guard. Coming off the high of the Iowa victory, Obama appeared to be on an unstoppable roll.

A member of his New Hampshire team later said, "I think that's when in some respects we lost sight that there was a race going on in New Hampshire. New Hampshire voters are known for being extremely independent minded. They weren't going to want Iowa to tell them what to do." And David Axelrod said, "[Clinton] looked like she was fighting for it and that she was very much on ground level. We looked like we were sailing above and taking victory laps and I think we were all vaguely uncomfortable with it. We had just gone through this whole struggle in Iowa where we were contending for every vote and now [we're] all coming in hoisted on people's shoulders and all that and it didn't seem right."

Had Obama sent his staff into the crowd at the Nashua high school that morning, his advisers might have understood why it didn't seem right. Like many others, we were more impressed with the lines than with what people at the rally were saying. Only later, when we reviewed our notes, did the voices add up to something other than an Obama march to victory. Some were like David Batchelder, who said he was impressed with Obama's hopeful message and had decided to support him over John Edwards. But a number of others were still undecided and still shopping. "He's got a new message," said Bob Gosselin, an Independent voter. "Whether he's got enough experience to pull it off is the question." Ken Cody, also undecided, had set out early that morning from the New Hampshire seacoast to see Obama, but he was also interested in Clinton. Cody said he was impressed with Clinton's policy expertise and experience but credited Obama with having leadership skills that she did not show. "That's the balancing act," he said. "He creates a lot of excitement but I don't think people have had a chance to look under the covers. That's a little scary to me." In short, there was evidence, for anyone willing to pay attention to it, that even in the middle of an enthusiastic Obama rally, some voters were still undecided—perhaps more than anyone realized.

Clemons's team made the decision to scrap the plan to focus simply on Clinton's identified supporters. Instead, they would put as much or more emphasis and energy into reaching out to undecided voters and persuading them to vote for the underdog Hillary Clinton. "We knew that they would be seeing poll after poll after poll after poll after poll showing Obama with a growing lead," said Guy Cecil, the lone adviser from the national headquarters intimately involved in New Hampshire. "And we didn't want to leave them to chance."

The next day, Clinton's schedule called for her to go door-to-door in Manchester. Normally with just a few days to the election, she would stop only at houses of supporters, urging them to be sure to vote in the primary. She returned to her campaign bus puzzled. "Why are we going to the doors of 'threes'?" she asked Clemons. (Campaigns rate voters on a scale of one to five—ones being solid supporters, twos leaners, threes undecided, fours and fives leaning toward or solidly for someone else.) "Because we have to," Clemons replied. "We don't have enough 'ones' to win." Later, Clemons explained that he had also reassured his candidate, telling her, "We've got it covered on the ground, despite what you're hearing from the members of Congress and senators who were here. We know what we're doing. We haven't lost our minds."

For most of Friday and into Saturday, even as she made her way around the state, she and Bill listened, absorbed, talked, and ultimately redesigned the look, feel, and sound of her campaign. On Saturday, she told someone that, since Iowa, she had already heard directly from more than thirty people who offered ideas on message and strategy.

E-mails poured into her BlackBerry. These were her friends, former aides, loyalists, and others who, out of deference to the campaign leadership, had for months sought to send their advice through the proper channels but had felt shut out by the headquarters team. For many in this group, Penn was a marked man. They felt his strategy of stressing inevitability and experience had led to her defeat in Iowa, and that he had failed to recognize the power of the change message. Many wanted Penn fired, even though he had a powerful hold on the Clintons. The critics also were after Solis Doyle, despite her close ties to Hillary. Until then they had deferred to her as campaign manager. After Iowa, she seemed to them in over her head, unable to help chart a clear course or manage the inner circle of difficult personalities, rivalries, jealousies, and hatreds. The old Clinton network teemed with gossip, complaints, conspiracies, and ideas. They overshadowed the senior advisers, who were powerless to object. One Clinton loyalist said of the inner circle, "They were so down on their knees you didn't have to kick them."

What made New Hampshire so intriguing was that its political culture and demographic profile seemed to be far more promising for Obama than Iowa had been. Already, it was obvious that the Democratic race was dividing the electorate into two demographic camps: older, less affluent, less

educated voters for Clinton; younger, wealthier, more liberal voters for
Obama. In many of the demographic groups where Obama had found
his greatest strength in Iowa, New Hampshire's Democratic primary electorate had at least as many or more of those voters. There were fewer older
voters, twice as many Independents, more wealthy voters, more better-
educated voters. However, no outside politicians had deeper ties or a
stronger bond to the state than the Clintons after Bill Clinton's miraculous
recovery in 1992 that brought him back from near death to a second-place
finish and the self-proclaimed title of "Comeback Kid."

Hillary's allies believed a single demographic group held the key to repeating Bill's comeback: women. In New Hampshire, women made up 57
percent of the Democratic electorate. Iowa had never elected a woman to
statewide office or to the House. New Hampshire's world had many successful women, including former governor Jeanne Shaheen. After the 2006
elections gave the Democrats control of the state legislature, both the
speaker of the New Hampshire House and the president of the Senate
were women; both supported Clinton.

Events over the final four days before the vote built up Clinton's appeal
to female voters. On Saturday night, ABC News, New Hampshire's
WMUR-TV, and the *Manchester Union Leader* staged a debate marathon
at Saint Anselm College consisting of back-to-back ninety-minute debates
featuring the remaining candidates from both parties. The Iowa returns
had forced Joe Biden and Chris Dodd out of the race. Just four major
Democratic candidates were left: Clinton, Obama, John Edwards, and Bill
Richardson, although Richardson was hardly a factor. During the debate,
Clinton, as she had promised, was aggressive, her voice rising in irritation.
But what worked most to her advantage was a two-against-one attack in
which Obama and Edwards pounded and at times seemed to belittle the
woman in the race.

Edwards later explained, "I thought I had to win Iowa, and when I
didn't win Iowa, I had to get to a two-person race quickly, and I thought
Obama was going to win New Hampshire." So when Clinton attacked
and Obama defended, Edwards counterattacked on behalf of Obama.
Later, Obama called Edwards's performance "a weird thing." For his
part, Edwards conceded he had miscalculated. "I think it helped her," he
said. "And *I* thought it went exactly the way I wanted it to go. Shows you
how smart I was."

In the early stages of the debate, Clinton attacked both Obama and
Edwards for their thin legislative records. "Words are not actions," she

said. "And as beautifully presented and passionately felt as they are, they are not action. You know, what we've got to do is translate talk into action and feeling into reality." Then she hit out at Obama for changing positions on a series of issues. When Edwards finally got a chance to speak, he said, "Every time he speaks out for change, every time I fight for change, the forces of status quo are going to attack. Every single time. . . . I didn't hear these kinds of attacks from Senator Clinton when she was ahead. Now that she's not, we hear them."

In the second half of the debate, WMUR's Scott Spradling pointed out to Clinton that although New Hampshire voters saw her as the most experienced and electable, they seemed to like Obama more than her. "Well, that hurts my feelings," Clinton said with a kind of little-girl expression on her face, provoking laughter. "I'm sorry, Senator," Spradling responded. Clinton kept going: "But I'll try to go on. He's very likable. I agree with that. I don't think I'm that bad." Obama then broke in. "You're likable enough, Hillary," he said. "Thank you," she said. Later Obama realized that what he meant to sound supportive came off as plain rude.

Obama left the debate unaware that his remark might be a problem. His advisers were relieved the debate was over; it was past time to get him back in touch with real voters. Clinton's advisers were concerned that she had not done all she could have early in the debate; many voters, they feared, missed her best moments.

Penn had produced a memo the night of the debate, entitled "Where is the bounce?" In the first days after Iowa, he argued, the race had changed little. By Sunday, however, public and private polls were all showing a substantial boost for Obama, putting him ahead by twelve points on Saturday and by ten points on Sunday. Clinton's New Hampshire team knew she was in deep trouble, but this was not Iowa, where she had always struggled. In New Hampshire, she had been ahead by twenty-three points in September. It was far harder to win over a voter who had never backed her than to regain the support of someone who had once been a Clinton supporter but now had slipped to undecided or even leaning to Obama. That was particularly the case for women, her advisers believed. They were hopeful that she could win back some of them. On Saturday they saw the first glimmers of a comeback. By Sunday they could see even more.

The anecdotal evidence flew in the face of the polls. Her coordinator of volunteers reported a huge influx of supporters into the state to help reach out to voters. The uncommitted voters were continuing to come her way. Obama was drawing big crowds, but so too was Clinton. On Sunday she campaigned at the same Nashua high school where Obama had been the day before—and nearly matched the size of his crowd. Her change message was now woven into her words on the economy. In an effort to promote her own less elegant style, she chipped away at Obama's alluring profile. "You campaign in poetry, you govern in prose," she told the Nashua crowd. The next day, Bill Clinton went after Obama on Iraq, calling the claim that he really had been a consistent opponent of the war a "fairy tale." His remark drew little attention in New Hampshire, but gathered strength in the days after the primary.

The day after the Iowa defeat the Clinton team had decided she could not afford to launch a truly negative campaign against Obama. "It was a small minority that wanted to do the negatives," said one Clinton adviser. "A vocal minority." Bill Clinton and Penn were still in favor, but the entire New Hampshire team was opposed. They had spent months campaigning on a positive message. To shift the tone, they argued, would look transparently desperate. But below the radar, they sent out a mailer challenging Obama's pro-choice credentials. Obama's team discovered the abortion mailer on Sunday and decided to have a surrogate answer—a decision they later regretted. But on that Sunday, everything looked solid for Obama, still bleak for Clinton.

Around midnight on Sunday, Nick Clemons's cell phone started to ring. "Private number" flashed up on the phone. It's Bill Clinton, he thought. The former president had been calling everyone he knew in New Hampshire all weekend, trying to make sense of what was happening. He knew the state intimately and the rhythms of its campaigns. How can we be so far behind in the polls here so quickly? he wondered. Is there an opportunity for us to make up the ground? Clemons believed that Clinton was really thinking, Can we still do well enough to claim a victory even in losing, and what do we still need to accomplish that? He was still torn about the campaign's decision not to attack Obama hard. Should we have hit him earlier, should we have shone more of a spotlight on Obama before he became this "movement"? What was the New Hampshire team doing to win the primary? Clemons gave a frank appraisal. Things were better than they had been, but not good enough. He wanted to keep expectations within bounds. At that point, the goal was to prevent an Obama blowout on Tuesday. "We were thinking if we could just keep [Obama's margin] under six or seven [points], people hopefully would see that as a win," Guy Cecil recalled. "That's where our mind-set was."

On Monday, Hillary Clinton was at Café Espresso in Portsmouth. Her New Hampshire press secretary, Kathleen Strand, was in the back, distracted, when a reporter tapped her on the shoulder. I think your candidate just made national news, the reporter said. Strand saw cameras flashing and a commotion. Hillary had just started to cry, someone else told her. Strand's first thought was that after tangling with her opponents in Saturday's debate, Clinton was now in tears. "Dear God!" Strand thought, then immediately got in touch with Clemons and the New Hampshire headquarters. "I think we have a problem," she reported.

Strand's instincts were wrong; not having seen the moment, she could not understand its impact. What they really had was an opportunity, a break in Clinton's steely exterior that let a glimmer of her humanity peek through for all of New Hampshire, and the world, to see. She was seated at a table with a group of sixteen voters, mostly women, taking questions, when suddenly she lost her composure. A freelance photographer wondered how she managed to handle all the pressures of a fierce campaign and keep going in the face of defeat, then asked, "How do you do it?"

Clinton tried to sound lighthearted about challenges but was quickly overcome with emotion. "It's not easy, and I couldn't do it if I didn't just passionately believe it was the right thing to do," she said. She paused and leaned her chin on her left hand. "You know, I have so many opportunities from this country. I just don't want to see us fall backwards." At that point her voice began to waver and her eyes grew moist. The audience applauded. She seemed to recover, switched her microphone to her other hand, and started in again. "You know, this is very personal for me. It's not just political. It's not just public. I see what's happening." Then her voice began to crack again. "And we have to reverse it. And some people think elections are a game. They think it's about who's up or who's down." By now she was regaining her composure and the determined politician side of her took over: "Some of us put ourselves out there and do this against some pretty difficult odds. And we do it, each one of us, because we care about our country. But some of us are right and some of us are wrong. Some of us are ready and some of us are not. Some of us know what we will do on day one and some of us haven't really thought that through enough. . . . This is one of the most important elections America's ever faced. So as tired as I am—and I am—and as difficult as it is to kind of keep up what I try to do on the road, like occasionally exercise and try to eat right. It's tough when the easiest food is pizza. I just believe so strongly in who we are as a nation. So I'm going to do everything I can to make my case, and then the voters get to decide."

The entire incident lasted just two minutes, but it dominated the news of the last full day of the primary campaign. It was all anyone was talking about on cable TV; the clip of her "breakdown," or "crying," was played over and over. A hot debate ensued. Was this episode genuine or concocted, a true flash of emotion by a vulnerable candidate with her back to the wall or a calculated Clinton moment designed to curry sympathy with voters who saw her as cold and aloof? Throughout New Hampshire—throughout the country!—the word spread instantly that something big had happened in Portsmouth.

Obama was on his bus when someone got an e-mail alerting his campaign. By then a clip was already online. There was some chortling on the bus by staffers who made fun of Clinton. Then Obama spoke up. "He said, 'You know, guys, this isn't easy,'" Axelrod recalled. "'She's out there busting her ass and I know what it's like, so ease up a little.'"

When asked that afternoon, Edwards claimed he hadn't seen it, but he seemed to belittle Clinton. "Presidential campaigns are a tough business, but being president of the United States is also a very tough business," he said. When Obama's team heard about Edwards's comment, they winced. After what had happened at the debate, they feared it would look like more piling on—and they believed that when Clinton was portrayed as a victim, she would benefit.

Back at Clinton's headquarters, Chuck Campion was parked in Clemons's office. Campion had run New Hampshire for Walter Mondale in 1984 and knew how quickly fortunes can change there. He had come in to lend a hand to Clemons for the final days. When Strand's call came in, he spent most of the rest of the day monitoring the coverage, watching the TV clip and the reaction to it. Hours later, Clemons came back into his office and saw Campion finally turning off the television. "I think this is going to be good for us," Campion said.

Obama closed out his New Hampshire campaign the way he began it, with a display of energy, jubilation, and powerful rhetoric. The scene that awaited him at Concord High School had become almost commonplace during the primary's final days: long lines of people waiting expectantly for the doors to the gymnasium to open, traffic lining side streets, cars parked illegally. When the doors opened around 10 p.m., his supporters did not just stream into the gymnasium, they hopped and danced and chanted, exchanging high-fives and hugs and kisses, swept along by the pounding music on the public address system and a dizzying sense of anticipation.

Obama did not arrive until after 11 p.m., just in time to make the late newscasts, his voice by now hoarse. Still, he spoke for forty minutes, interrupted constantly by applause and cheers and the beating of drums and chants of *O-Bam-A! O-Bam-A!* Near midnight, he introduced new language into his stump speech. "People are confused about why we are generating this energy," he said, "And it has exactly to do with this, the notion that somehow we have been locked in these constraints. People telling us what we cannot do. . . . There is a moment in the life of every generation, if it's to make its mark on history, when that spirit has to shine through, spirit that says we are casting aside our fears and our doubts and our cynicism . . . when we embrace the difficult, daunting task of remaking a nation."

By then, within Obama's campaign there was no doubt about Tuesday's outcome, nor within Clinton's or among the hundreds of reporters trailing the two candidates. Everyone was preparing the stories for the next night and the day after, shrewd analyses of how Clinton had lost, where it had gone wrong, how Obama had demolished the Clinton machine, and whether she was truly finished. When Obama's rally ended, with the Brooks & Dunn anthem "Only in America" playing in the background, reporters crowded around Axelrod, seeking a snippet to add to the string they were gathering for their final Clinton campaign obituaries. "If you win big tomorrow, do you think that will secure you the nomination?" one reporter asked. Cautiously, Axelrod responded, "I expect that we're going to be contesting this for some weeks to come and we're prepared to do that. . . . We're ready to deal with whatever comes." What's a measure of success tomorrow? another reporter asked. "Winning is a success." Did he see any likelihood that an Obama win would force Clinton out of the race? "No," he replied. "I think she's a strong and formidable candidate. As I said, they're the greatest political franchise of our generation. We're settled in for a long contest."

Backstage, Obama had asked his pollster, Joel Benenson, how it looked. Benenson had stopped polling on Sunday night, but had no doubt about the trend lines. "I said, look, I think it's tightened up," he recalled. "I said I think if everything goes right you could win by ten or eleven but I said I still think we win by eight." On the next morning's conference call, others recall Benenson's virtually guaranteeing victory.

Obama had a light schedule on election day: a late start, a big rally at Dartmouth, quiet time until the returns came in, finally the victory speech that was already in good shape. It was a beautiful day, sunny and unseasonably warm, a welcome break after a harshly cold and snowy December in both Iowa and New Hampshire. Valerie Jarrett remembered the almost idyllic drive with Obama's entourage back from Hanover after the rally. "I will never forget," she said. "David Axelrod said we should enjoy this moment, because in every campaign there are ups and there are downs and there are downs in our future so let's enjoy this victory in New Hampshire. . . . I had no idea it would be so soon."

We once asked Ann Lewis, Hillary Clinton's friend and adviser, to describe Clinton's political philosophy. She pointed to the words of John Wesley: "Do all the good you can, By all the means you can, In all the ways you can, In all the places you can, At all the times you can, To all the people you can, As long as ever you can." By that, Lewis sought to explain Clinton's devotion to issues like health care, children's well-being, and education. In New Hampshire that John Wesley credo defined her entire candidacy. She would wrest every opportunity out of every minute of every day until the polls had closed and she could no longer affect the outcome.

Clinton was up before dawn on primary morning, carrying coffee to the polling places, chatting with poll workers, voters, volunteers, and supporters. She hit five precincts that morning. Her image on New Hampshire television screens throughout the day was of an embattled Hillary Clinton fighting hard for every vote. Bill Clinton called in from the precinct where he had been sent that morning. Cecil recalled his saying, "I'm telling you guys, something is happening. There are lots of people that come to this thing saying they were undecided."

Late in the afternoon, Hillary was resting at her hotel in Concord when her New Hampshire team got wind of preliminary exit polls showing Obama ahead by nine points. Lynda Tocci, who was directing Clinton's get-out-the-vote operations, barely blinked. We can cut that in half, she boasted. Let's get back out there. Let's put everybody we've got on the streets. That not only meant volunteers and paid staff, it also meant the candidate—if they could cajole her into one more appearance. They put in a call to Huma Abedin, Clinton's personal aide, and begged her to urge Clinton to come to Manchester and stage an event aimed at getting coverage on WMUR's early evening newscasts, which would blanket much of the state. How are you able to guarantee coverage? Abedin asked. The event would be held outside WMUR's studios, she was told. Soon, Clinton and about fifty supporters were in front of the cameras with the message that the race was close, every vote counted, and that she still needed help to prevent Obama from winning.

Exit polls showed a race far different from the one everyone had expected. Yellow lights flashed in every newsroom in America, putting on hold the long-planned stories of what a double loss would mean for Clinton's candidacy—and for Obama's. In the Clinton and Obama boiler rooms, the first returns painted a similarly surprising picture. Clinton won three wards in Portsmouth—far better news than they had anticipated. They knew they were looking at a close race now, although still likely a narrow loss.

In Obama's boiler room, state director Matt Rodriguez seemed to know with the first batch of real votes that the worst was coming. Precincts he had expected to win were going for Clinton. He told Leslie Miller, the New Hampshire communications director, "We're going to lose." Meanwhile, Clemons was sending Bill Clinton the raw data flowing into the boiler room and the former president was crunching the numbers himself at his hotel. He was upbeat. At one point when he called in, someone shoved a piece of paper in front of Clemons: "Lower his expectations," it read. By 10 p.m., Bill Clinton was urging the New Hampshire team to declare victory. Still they hesitated. Finally, the Associated Press declared her the winner, and only then did her advisers accept the reality of what she had accomplished.

At Obama's hotel, long before the race had been called, Plouffe and Axelrod and Gibbs walked upstairs to Obama's room. He came out into the hallway. They told him it looked as if he would fall a couple points short. According to one person there, Obama said, "You know, it was that crying thing, wasn't it?" He added, "We were a little too cocky, weren't we?" He leaned up against the wall and then, with a smile of resignation, "This is going to go on for a while, isn't it?"

Michelle Obama's view, according to those present that night, was that this was a test not only for Barack and the campaign but also for his supporters. How solid are they, she asked rhetorically, because it's not going to be easy.

In the holding room before he went out to concede the election, Obama came up to Jarrett and put his hands on her shoulders. "Are you okay?" he asked. "If you're okay, I'm okay," she replied. "I take my cue from you." "He said, 'Would I have liked to have won? Yes,'" she recalled. "'You know how competitive I am. But I'm fine.'"

For all the calm he seemed to exude that night, Obama understood the blow he had just taken. His campaign had once hoped he could finish second in Iowa and ride that win to a victory in New Hampshire. The opposite had happened. He knew how much more precarious the road ahead now appeared, knew that having let Clinton come back, he faced an even more daunting test of character, resolve, and organization. "New Hampshire was a gut check," he told us later. "In New Hampshire, all our momentum from Iowa had been broken and we're looking at a bunch of contests, including February 5th, where suddenly Hillary's national name recognition was very valuable. You know, we could have lost after New Hampshire."

He explained what happened. "What our pollsters told me was, every undecided woman swung to Hillary that last three days," he said. "All of them. Which just doesn't usually happen. I think the combination of her choking up, an inartful comment by me during the debate that wasn't intended in any way the way it came out, but I understood it came out as sort of dismissive, John Edwards doing a weird thing and kind of ganging up on her, despite the fact that I had won [Iowa]. . . . And I just think the sense that, gosh, you know, we shouldn't just hand it to this guy, and she's really fighting for this thing and has paid her dues, I think all those things just converged for people to say to themselves, let's keep this going a little bit."

The New Hampshire loss revealed characteristics in Obama that served him well through the long campaign—his facility to stay calm under pressure, his capacity for self-reflection, his willingness to take corrective action, his determination to keep his team focused. He described the campaign's reaction to the New Hampshire loss as one of his proudest moments of the campaign. "I think I came out of that thing not pleased, but telling my staff and my supporters it probably shouldn't be this easy for me to win, that we probably do need to earn this thing, because we're going to have a tough time, should we get the nomination, against Republicans and we need to have one of these under our belts. First of all, to not want it to happen again, but to also understand that we're going to have to earn this thing."

The day before the primary, when they were all anticipating victory, Obama had told speechwriter Favreau that one thing he wanted to get across in his victory speech was that he didn't want it to seem that winning the nomination was going to be too easy. He did not want his campaign, or his followers, to get too cocky. After the primary results, that was no longer any problem. Now they needed to bolster their spirits.

Favreau and Ben Rhodes, another Obama speechwriter, had little time to turn the victory speech into a concession, and in fact there were very few changes made in the original, save for the congratulations to Clinton.

The speech became a rallying cry to dispirited followers and a show of determination in the face of a shattering defeat. "We know the battle ahead will be long, but always remember that no matter what obstacles stand in our way, nothing can withstand the power of millions of voices calling for change," Obama said. "We have been told we cannot do this by a chorus of cynics who will only grow louder and more dissonant in the weeks to come. We've been asked to pause for a reality check. We've been warned against offering the people of this nation false hope. But in the unlikely story that is America, there has never been anything false about hope. For when we have faced down impossible odds, when we've been told that we're not ready, or that we shouldn't try, or that we can't, generations of Americans have responded with a simple creed that sums up the spirit of a people."

He finished with an uplifting note:

"Yes, we can. . . . And so tomorrow, as we take this campaign south and west; as we learn that the struggles of the textile worker in Spartanburg are not so different than the plight of the dishwasher in Las Vegas; that the hopes of the little girl who goes to a crumbling school in Dillon are the same as the dreams of the boy who learns on the streets of L.A.; we will remember that there is something happening in America; that we are not as divided as our politics suggests; that we are one people, we are one nation, and together we will begin the next great chapter in America's story with three words that will ring from coast to coast, from sea to shining sea—Yes. We. Can."

The next day, at a private fund-raiser in Boston, Obama told donors his campaign had been "like Icarus flying too close to the sun." One person in the room recalled him saying, "We're trying to effect real change and real change doesn't come this easily. We know that they're going to fight back and they're going to fight back hard and it's going to be a long, hard struggle." In a strange way, he said, it feels right that he didn't win. He had put it more starkly the night before as he was talking with his advisers in the hotel. Matt Rodriguez said he would never forget the candidate's words at that moment. "This reminds me of a Frederick Douglass line," Obama said. "Power concedes nothing without a struggle."*

On primary night, there was a sense of crushing disappointment around Obama. Favreau sat in the holding room, his head down, as Obama called Clinton to congratulate her. Deval Patrick, the governor of Massachusetts and a close friend of Obama's, came over to Favreau. Patrick did not know the young speechwriter. "Keep your head up," he told him. "We're going to win this thing." By the end of the night, spirits began to revive. After his concession speech, Obama went back to his hotel for a birthday celebration for his sister. Everyone sang "Happy Birthday" and talked about the road ahead. Plouffe organized a conference call for the entire staff, which became a defiant call to arms and a challenge to all of those who had spent a year in the trenches only to slam into a wall in New Hampshire. He closed the call with a memorable exhortation: "Now let's go out and win this fucking thing!"

Obama's defeat was a lesson from Politics 101: Campaigns matter. In New Hampshire, his effort was as much an extended victory party after Iowa as it was a campaign. He was asking New Hampshire voters to ratify what had happened in Iowa. That was not enough to trump what Clinton rightly understood about New Hampshire's stubbornly independent-minded electorate.

The Obama team had missed the signs, so focused were they on continuing the powerful narrative of Obama's post-Iowa momentum. In Iowa, Clinton's closing argument had been: Pick me because I'm experienced. In New Hampshire, it was: Pick me because I care so deeply about what has happened to this country and to you. Her tearful moment in Portsmouth and her debate performance at Saint Anselm brought women back to her side. She won New Hampshire by seventy-six hundred votes, with 39.4 percent of the vote compared to Obama's 36.8. Final preelection

---

* Douglass's actual words were: "If there is no struggle there is no progress.... Power concedes nothing without a demand. It never did and it never will."

polls had suggested Obama would carry the women's vote, as he had in Iowa. Exit polls showed Clinton winning women by twelve points. The New Hampshire firewall held.

In her victory speech, Clinton said, "I listened to you, and in the process I found my own voice. I felt like we all spoke from our hearts, and I am so gratified that you responded. . . . for all the ups and downs of this campaign, you helped remind everyone that politics isn't a game. This campaign is about people, about making a difference in your lives, about making sure that everyone in this country has the opportunity to live up to his or her God-given potential. That has been the work of my life. . . . So we're going to take what we've learned here in New Hampshire, and we're going to rally on and make our case. We are in it for the long run."

She had taken her campaign onto her own shoulders and survived. But as she prepared to break camp after her stunning victory, she presided over a divided house. Her dispirited and squabbling senior staff had contributed almost nothing to her success in New Hampshire. Now they were on the verge of a calamitous breakdown.

CHAPTER TEN

Disintegration

We need to change the leadership.

—Message to Patti Solis Doyle, January 8, 2008

Patti Solis Doyle was in her Concord hotel room the morning of the New Hampshire primary when a new message popped up on her BlackBerry. She stared at the tiny screen in disbelief. Devastated, she put in a telephone call to Harold Ickes, a veteran of Democratic presidential politics and of Clinton's world. He was eating breakfast in the same hotel. Ickes often ignored his phone. But the vibrations on the table caught his attention and he decided to answer. To his dismay, he heard a distraught Solis Doyle on the other end of the line.

Solis Doyle began by saying, A number of friends who have our best interests at heart have concluded that we need to change the leadership of the campaign. Ickes asked, "Are you reading to me?" Yes, she replied, from her BlackBerry. She continued: Maggie Williams will be coming in with full authority on all hiring and budget matters. I want you to remain as a valued member of the senior management team. You can retain the title but Maggie will have effective control of the campaign. Ickes asked, "Who's this from?" When she told him, "Hillary," Ickes replied, "Well, you're lying to me." She said, "No, I'm not." Ickes wolfed down the rest of his Belgian waffle and walked quickly to Solis Doyle's room, where he found her in tears.

What began that morning—what had really begun in the hours after Iowa—would, at the very least, mar Hillary's victory in New Hampshire that night. While Clinton's New Hampshire–based team of advisers was still focused on pulling off a political miracle, almost all of her national team had given up hope. They were huddled—bunkered, really—in the Centennial Hotel in Concord. Most spent the day in the staff room in a running debate over how to revive Clinton's candidacy—if that was even possible after what they assumed would be two consecutive losses to Obama. Solis Doyle spent much of the day cloistered in her room, visited occasionally by a few staunch allies in Clinton's dysfunctional inner circle. They had heard about the e-mail and became deeply involved in the drama about a staff shakeup.

For that day, and many to come, the Clinton team was in a state of turmoil that had begun five days earlier in the boiler room in Des Moines as they watched the Iowa caucus returns. How could Hillary and Bill Clinton remake the team that had begun the race a year before with such soaring hopes and with every expectation that many of them would end up in the White House? Now, with a New Hampshire loss seeming a certainty, they suddenly faced the prospect of being held responsible for one of the most stunning collapses in presidential annals.

All day, cable television had been filled with rumors of big changes in the works. That morning's *New York Times* identified as possible victims the four top people in the campaign: Solis Doyle, chief strategist Penn, media adviser Grunwald, and communications director Wolfson. Solis Doyle and Penn seemed most vulnerable, but no one really knew how much the Clintons would break up the operation if she lost. Even as Hillary pressed ahead in New Hampshire, largely on the strength of her own character, the paralysis of her senior staff deepened. Solis Doyle's Black-Berry message signaled that things were about to get worse.

Ahead lay a decisive month, with contests in Nevada and South Carolina leading to Super Tuesday, with more than twenty contests. That was when Hillary would wrap up the nomination, or so the conventional wisdom had held. Instead, those became the weeks when the Clinton team experienced a collective breakdown that lasted until Obama had a lead among pledged delegates big enough to make him virtually unbeatable. Far from being the overpowering political machine of legend, the Clinton campaign turned out to be a world filled with destructive internal conflicts, a place of tensions and enmities. The campaign team fought over strategy and message. Senior staffers either warred with each other or jealously protected their positions; factions fought factions; individuals maneuvered for advantage. During this critical month, there seemed to be no way to stop the infighting or the damage it was causing to the effort to win the nomination.

Stories of the inner wars quickly became legend. Reporters feasted for months on the internal strife that had become endemic through the course of the campaign. Much later, the *Atlantic Monthly's* Joshua Green published campaign memos that illuminated the strife through much of 2007 and early 2008. On March 6, the *Washington Post's* Anne E. Kornblut and Peter Baker (later with the *New York Times*) published a remarkably revealing article rich with on-the-record quotes from campaign officials firing at one another and airing dirty laundry in public. The *Post* article prompted an anguished e-mail from Bob Barnett, noted Washington lawyer and Clinton campaign intimate, to top campaign officials. His subject line said it all: "STOP IT!!!!"

Hillary Clinton bears prime responsibility for the breakdown of her campaign at a time when she could least afford it. She was the architect. She established a team without a clear leader. She allowed the lines of authority to blur by failing to put anyone in charge. In the end, there was no one to take full responsibility for the operation and its decision-making. Her mistake, *Politico* columnist Roger Simon later concluded, was in valuing loyalty over experience. "The Clinton campaign was not nearly as good as it looked from the outside," Simon said. "Make no mistake. It was not Penn, it was not Ickes, it was not Patti Solis Doyle, much as they were reviled within the campaign. Hillary Clinton was warned about what was going on, and more than once. In the end she ran the kind of campaign she wanted to run."

She created an operation in which it was always easier to stop something than do something. The tight inner circle numbered just five people, talented and with strong personalities: Penn, Solis Doyle, Wolfson, Grunwald, and Neera Tanden. Solis Doyle was a sunny personality. She was the campaign manager in title but not the dominant leader and could not crack heads to enforce decisions. Penn was brilliant, even his opponents gave him that. But he could be difficult in his personal relationships. He was a centrist who in 1996 helped design President Clinton's small-bore reelection initiatives like school uniforms. Penn had written a book called *Microtrends* that sliced the electorate into segments. In Iowa, he put labels like "Seasoned Salties" (older women) and "Latte Drinkers" (mostly upscale men) on different demographic groups. Of Clinton's advisers, he was the most aggressive, regularly advocating that the campaign begin attacking Obama. In a March 2007 memo, he had urged the campaign to take note of Obama's "lack of American roots" and said he could not imagine the country electing someone in a time of war "who is not at his center fundamentally American." He said the campaign could not attack directly on this but argued, "Let's own 'American'" in its message. He was overruled. Others resented what they saw as his ability generally to run roughshod over the rest of the campaign. He chafed at what he felt was lack of real power to implement his ideas—less power than he believed he had in 1996.

Grunwald earned her stripes in Bill Clinton's 1992 campaign as a smart and very tough operative. She oversaw the advertising team but often battled with Penn over what those ads said and looked like after New Hampshire. Wolfson led a communications operation designed to fend off the New York tabloids and a national press corps that the Clinton team saw— often correctly—as hostile to their candidate. The communications team was fast on rapid response and geared to win every news cycle, but rarely known for its light touch. Tanden did policy, but not much politics. She had served as Clinton's policy guru for years and had her ear on such major initiatives as health care.

Others in the headquarters group exercised powers of their own. Ickes oversaw delegates and helped Solis Doyle with the budgets, but did not feel fully empowered to deal with political operations. He was one of the few insiders with long experience in presidential politics, shrewd and sometimes prickly, who had helped create the system of nomination rules that ultimately proved Clinton's undoing. He was also a sworn enemy of Penn; their contentious relationship dated back a decade. Mike Henry, the deputy campaign manager and political director, had developed a solid reputation in Virginia politics, but ran a political operation that others in the campaign came to regard as weak and overwhelmed. To remedy that, Solis Doyle and Ickes recruited Guy Cecil from the Democratic Senatorial Campaign Committee, who was asked to oversee New Hampshire and the February 5th Super Tuesday states. He quickly became Henry's rival and nemesis. Phil Singer was Wolfson's deputy, skilled in the thrust and parry of campaigns, but volatile. On the fund-raising side, Jonathan Mantz was a clearly talented finance director, but he was appalled when he realized how rapidly and foolishly the money was being spent. Terry McAuliffe, the campaign chairman, was a fund-raising powerhouse, a pal of the former president, and the campaign's self-designated chief cheerleader.

Hillary Clinton created a campaign in which authority always seemed to rest with someone else. Her team spent endless hours in conference calls hashing out everything, yet struggled in after-action reports to pin down responsibility for mistakes. For much of 2007, this team seemed highly effective, though even the smoothest of campaigns might have foundered against a newcomer who was tapping so effectively into the public mood. When Hillary stumbled badly in Iowa, the knives came out—as they often do in losing or struggling campaigns. As a group, the inner circle was seldom upbeat, often pessimistic, worried, embattled—all the more so when things were difficult. James Carville, the Clinton loyalist who was rarely directly involved, was struck by two things. First, how much everyone loved Hillary. Her advisers were devoted to her. But, Carville said, "it always struck me how joyless that campaign was."

Hillary's e-mail caught Solis Doyle by surprise, although she later realized she should have known, not only because of the swirl of rumors but also because of a tense private discussion she had with Clinton the day before. Because of that meeting, the e-mail was devastating. She and Clinton had talked about how gloomy the projections seemed. The senior staff believed, as everybody did, that they were going to lose New Hampshire, possibly by double digits. They thought the Culinary Workers were going to go for Obama in Nevada right after New Hampshire, and they knew South Carolina looked increasingly solid for Obama. Solis Doyle also knew that if they lost four in a row, their money, already tight, would dry up.

Solis Doyle's meeting with Clinton took place a few hours before Clinton choked up in the Portsmouth diner. All that day, according to an informed source, Solis Doyle wondered whether the bleak electoral outlook that she had described to Clinton contributed to the emotions Hillary displayed for the world to see. They talked alone for most of their meeting—Bill Clinton came in at a later point—but mostly it was a frank discussion between the candidate and her campaign manager about the state of the campaign. Solis Doyle outlined possible options based on her belief that New Hampshire was lost. Among them was a proposal for Clinton to quit the race, withdraw gracefully, return to the Senate, and begin salvaging her career in the job she loved. The informed source said Solis Doyle did not recommend that course to Clinton but pointed out to her that it was certainly an option. Clinton reportedly was furious after their conversation, incensed by what she regarded as her campaign manager's defeatist attitude.

Solis Doyle also told Clinton that she needed fresh blood in her campaign. She knew that a second straight loss would result in a chorus of demands for heads to roll, including hers; and she was prepared to accept that fate. But she also urged Clinton not to stop there. She recommended that Penn, the most divisive figure inside the campaign, go too. Among new people, she recommended that Clinton bring into the campaign Doug Sosnik, who had served as political director in the Clinton White House, and Steve Richetti, another Clinton White House veteran. She had long pushed for another pollster to supplement Penn, and urged Clinton to hire Geoff Garin, one of the party's most respected pollsters, a suggestion she had made before. She also recommended that Carter Eskew be recruited to help improve the campaign's advertising. Why would any of them come into the campaign under such difficult circumstances? Clinton wondered. They have nothing to lose at this point, Solis Doyle replied. She suggested they reach out to Maggie Williams, who was Hillary's chief of staff in the White House. Clinton was dubious that Williams would come aboard. She'll do it for you, Solis Doyle said.

Solis Doyle later told others she believed it was a mistake to have such a gloomy discussion the day before the primary and agreed only because Clinton wanted an unvarnished assessment. That made Clinton's e-mail all the more upsetting. She did not mind being fired. She was a big girl. It was the way Clinton did it. Solis Doyle sent an e-mail back saying she would leave the campaign.

Once that e-mail from Hillary was sent, her departure was certain, though it took another month. "Did I think that the job and the place is bigger than I am? So many times," she said as she reflected on the experience. But she also believed that she had presided over Hillary's feuding team effectively. Not everyone agreed.

Solis Doyle was the daughter of Mexican immigrants. Her older brother Danny Solis worked as a community organizer with Obama and later became a Chicago alderman. She grew up on Chicago's heavily Latino southwest side, graduated from Northwestern University, and, with the help of her brother, started her political career working in city hall and later in the reelection campaign of Mayor Richard J. Daley. She was recruited for Bill Clinton's 1992 campaign by Daley's campaign manager, David Wilhelm, who managed the Clinton campaign. Solis Doyle became Hillary Clinton's first hire. Over the course of sixteen years, she rose steadily to become one of Clinton's most trusted advisers. They were so close that Hillary had read at Solis Doyle's wedding.

When the time came to organize for the 2008 election, Clinton named Solis Doyle as her campaign manager. Among those who argued against her was Terry McAuliffe, the close friend of both Bill and Hillary. David Axelrod, a longtime friend, had warned Solis Doyle not to take the job. He knew the Clinton culture, that when things went sour, everyone would take cover. He told her she was better off being the candidate's best friend than the candidate's campaign manager.

Solis Doyle had many detractors both in the campaign and in Hillaryland. They grew in numbers through January and into February, as Clinton's campaign suffered through its lowest weeks and the weaknesses in strategy, operations, organization, and management became clearer. The most serious charge against her after Iowa and New Hampshire was that she had badly mismanaged the budget.

So depleted were their finances that when the campaign looked beyond New Hampshire, Nevada, South Carolina, and the nearly two dozen Super Tuesday contests on February 5th, they discovered that they would be virtually broke. Even worse, according to her critics, she had failed to keep Clinton informed. When Clinton learned in January how little money was left, according to a report, she was dismayed that her only recourse was to loan her campaign $5 million.

In September, Ickes had written a memo warning of a sizable deficit by January—$12 to $15 million—at the rate the campaign was spending money. He advised Solis Doyle to keep Clinton fully informed and in his few budget meetings with Clinton laid out those projections.

The campaign spent enormous sums in Iowa: in the neighborhood of $25 million. Hillary Clinton complained repeatedly about the budgetary sinkhole that Iowa became. Even in the middle of the Iowa campaign, she could not understand why they were spending so much for so few voters. Twenty-five million for a hundred and fifty thousand voters? "She thought it was a huge waste of money," Solis Doyle said. But Clinton was told there was no other way to play Iowa, and besides, Obama was doing the same. The Clinton campaign spent lavishly elsewhere, based on the assumption that there would be a knockout blow by February 5th. "The culture of our campaign was a high-priced culture," one senior official said. "Much more was spent on scheduling and advance than we should have spent. They were used to a lifestyle and a culture that I think resulted in money being spent that we could have saved. . . . Those decisions were not made blindly. They were made with a lot of debate."

Carville recalled being with Bill Clinton and McAuliffe in mid-December when Hillary won the endorsement of the *Des Moines Register*. "We're out of money after South Carolina," McAuliffe told them, according to Carville. "Everybody said, 'What?' He says, 'Yeah, they spent it all.'" Later, Jonathan Mantz, who directed the fund-raising, was appalled when campaign officials blamed a lack of resources for the failure to fully contest some states. In an e-mail to Wolfson he called the assertion "bullshit."

Solis Doyle was adamant that Clinton knew the full state of the campaign's finances throughout the race. Never was there any attempt to hide the financial situation from the candidate, she said. Nor was it even possible. "Without question the idea that Hillary did not know about the financial situation is just ludicrous," Solis Doyle said after she left the campaign. "Totally and completely. Anybody who knows Hillary knows that she's an extraordinarily frugal person, worries about money, and she demands to know." Whatever the state of the finances, she said, Hillary Clinton knew at every turn how bad they were.

Late on the afternoon of the New Hampshire primary, Hillary Clinton knocked on Solis Doyle's hotel door. It was a very difficult discussion between two people who had been extraordinarily close until that moment. Solis Doyle joined the victory party that night. She was happy for Hillary, but personally felt as if she had been cast aside by a campaign looking for scapegoats.

The next day, as the entire Clinton campaign left New Hampshire early in the morning and returned to Washington for a chaotic day of meetings at their headquarters in suburban Virginia, Solis Doyle caught a later flight and returned by herself. Feeling abused and abandoned, she went home rather than to the headquarters.

The longtime Clinton friend and ally lasted another month before she was finally replaced. That too proved messy. After New Hampshire, Clinton brought a number of additional advisers into the campaign, Maggie Williams among them. But with Solis Doyle still there, Williams became frustrated and in early February announced she was returning to her consulting firm. To some in the campaign, it was an overt signal to Hillary Clinton that she had created an untenable environment inside her campaign and that it was time to choose between Williams and Solis Doyle.

Solis Doyle was equally frustrated by the lack of confidence shown her in those weeks. Once past Super Tuesday, she was planning to meet with Clinton on the morning of Sunday, February 10, to air her grievances, describe the low campaign morale, declare her intention to step down entirely, and urge again that something be done about Penn. At the last minute, she had to cancel because her babysitter could not look after her children that morning.

Clinton, under the stress of the campaign, reacted angrily to the apparent snub. She organized a conference call for that morning and announced that Williams would be taking over. The announcement of Solis Doyle's departure came later that night, as Clinton was losing the Maine caucuses. Solis Doyle left without talking to her. Four months later, when the primaries were over and Clinton was announcing the end of her losing campaign, Solis Doyle and Clinton still had not talked. Solis Doyle could not bring herself to go to Clinton's concession speech in person; she watched it on television. "I just didn't feel right about going," she said later. "But I saw it and I just could not stop sobbing uncontrollably. This is a woman I love and admire."*

---

* Solis Doyle later joined Obama's team for the general election.

CHAPTER ELEVEN

An Uncivil War

"Don't let them tell you we've got to wait. Our moment is now!"

—Obama in South Carolina

Cars began filling the parking lots around the University of South Carolina's Williams-Brice Stadium in Columbia early Sunday morning, December 9, 2007. People were standing three and four abreast near the entrances. Oprah Winfrey was in town, and Barack and Michelle Obama too. They would draw the largest crowd any candidate had seen to that point in the campaign. By early afternoon, when Obama took the stage, twenty-nine thousand people were inside the stadium, most of them African-American.

Echoes of the civil rights movement were powerful that day. "There are those who say that it's not his time, that he should wait his time," Winfrey said to cries of "No, no!" from the grandstand. "Think about where you would be in your life if you waited when the people told you to. . . . There are those who say that he should take a gradual approach to this presidential leadership. But . . . we have to respond to pressures and fortunes of history when the moment strikes in South Carolina. That moment is now. . . . Dr. King dreamed the dream. But we don't have to just dream the dream anymore. We get a chance to vote that dream into reality."

Obama linked his presidential campaign even more directly to the struggles of the sixties. "They stood up when it was risky," he said, his voice rising above the roar of the crowd. "They stood when it was hard. They stood up when it wasn't popular. They stood up and they went to jail. They sat down and then they stood up. They sat down when they weren't supposed to. The fire hoses came out. The dogs came out. But they kept on standing up. Because a few stood up, a few thousand stood up, and then a few million stood up. Standing up for courage and conviction, they changed the world."

Then, echoing Oprah, he said, "Don't let them tell you we've got to wait. Our moment is now!"

Political scientists have developed sophisticated models for predicting the winners of general elections, formulas that take into account economic conditions, presidential popularity, the public mood, and other fundamentals. But no one has yet devised a formula that with any reliability can anticipate how a truly competitive nominating contest will end. There are too few major differences on issues, too many players, too many contests, too many outside events, too many unpredictable developments. That was particularly true in the early weeks of the primary/caucus season of 2008.

South Carolina was the fourth state to vote in the Democratic nomination battle. The primary was marked by racial politics in which Bill Clinton's role became the centerpiece of smoldering resentments in both camps, igniting alarm throughout the Democratic Party. South Carolina produced the sharpest, nastiest debate of the campaign, provoking anger and grievances inside both campaigns. The state also became another powerful turning point in which the Obama campaign outmaneuvered the Clinton machine once again. When it was over, it was clear that Hillary Clinton had been lured into a trap—pushed into it by her husband might be more accurate—and had paid an enormous price for the mistake. Obama's victory not only cost her South Carolina, but also redrew the landscape heading into Super Tuesday on February 5. Most critical, South Carolina was where the Clintons lost the allegiance of much of the Democratic establishment, both black and white.

Bill Clinton provided Hillary with an asset no other candidate could employ. He was the ultimate surrogate, popular in virtually every corner of the Democratic Party, an obviously skilled campaigner who could double the reach of the campaign by assuring that the Clintons could be in twice as many places on any given day as Obama. He also was a strategist with few peers in presidential politics. There were limits on his powers, however. This was, after all, Hillary's campaign, not his, and her advisers talked at length about how to make maximum use of him without in any way allowing him to overshadow his wife. Behind the scenes, he was an influential voice on strategy but, as the experience of 2007 had shown, did not get his way on how much Obama should be attacked. When the campaign turned to South Carolina, however, he exerted himself.

Bill Clinton insisted that Hillary compete all out in South Carolina, against the advice of her top advisers. "I believe they felt that they could either win or come very close, and I know this from conversations with Bill Clinton himself and with her," said Don Fowler, a former Democratic Party chairman and one of Hillary Clinton's leading supporters in South Carolina. "I think that they believed that their loyalty in the African-American community would withstand the psychology of Obama's win in Iowa and at least they wouldn't get wiped away or embarrassed in the black community. I think that Bill Clinton wanted to demonstrate that he still had political force and influence within the African-American community."

There were eighteen days between New Hampshire and South Carolina, with an intervening contest in Nevada. Although Obama had the support of the Culinary Workers union in Nevada, the Clinton camp still believed she could win there. South Carolina was different. Through all of 2007, Clinton and Obama were almost even in the competition for the allegiance of African-Americans. The Clintons' deep connections with the black community and Obama's uncertain prospects kept those voters divided. Black women were especially conflicted over the choice between the first African-American with a serious chance to be president and the first woman. Clinton, whose multiple hairstyles had become a running joke when she was First Lady, took her campaign straight to the beauty salons of South Carolina. Her message included a pop-up brochure with photos of her many styles over the years and the words "Pay attention to your hair because everyone else will."

When Oprah Winfrey appeared with Obama in South Carolina in December 2007, polls showed that black women supported Clinton over Obama while black men were relatively evenly divided. Many African-Americans appeared to be holding back from saying they were for Obama because they doubted that white America would support him. Obama's team worked hard through the later months of 2007 to build support in the African-American community, working salons and barbershops as assiduously as they did the black churches. Largely white Iowa provided the proof. When Obama showed he could win among an electorate like that, the polls shifted almost overnight, with Obama now the overwhelming choice of African-Americans.

That reality changed the equation for Clinton in South Carolina. In the days after Iowa and New Hampshire, as the Clinton campaign was scrambling to set its strategy, South Carolina not only looked like a certain loser to Clinton's advisers but also appeared likely to be a huge drain on the time and resources of a campaign now badly strapped for money and needing its focus for Super Tuesday. Had Bill Clinton not intervened so forcefully, the campaign was set with what it thought was the ideal plan. She would debate Obama and spend a couple of days in the state. Bill Clinton would spend a day there but devote more time to fund-raising elsewhere. She would lose, but not so badly that it would cripple her campaign. "Bill Clinton decided, by God, we were going to do better with African-Americans," a senior Clinton adviser said. "The decision had been made not to do what we did—and we did it." Nobody foresaw the disaster ahead.

Part of Bill Clinton's response to the Iowa loss was understandable. He wanted his wife to win, truly believed she was the most fit to be president, and was prepared to fight as hard as he could to help her recover. But part of his reaction was destructive. He was convinced the caucuses had been manipulated in Iowa. He believed that Obama had gotten a free ride from the media, and he wanted to force a conversation about that. He believed Hillary's campaign had not been tough enough, and he took it upon himself to lead the attacks. It seemed for a time that his once certain political touch and instincts eluded him and the rest of the Clinton campaign.

The controversies had begun in New Hampshire, though they attracted attention only after Hillary Clinton won. First was Bill Clinton's finger-wagging effort to debunk Obama's antiwar credentials. "It is wrong," he said, eyes flashing at a young man who had dared challenge him, "that Senator Obama got to go through fifteen debates trumpeting his superior judgment and how he had been against the war in every year, enumerating the years, and never got asked one time—not once, 'Well, how could you say that when you said in 2004 you didn't know how you would have voted on the resolution? You said in 2004 there was no difference between you and George Bush on the war. And you took that speech you're now running on off your Web site in 2004. And there's no difference in your voting record and Hillary's ever since.' Give me a break. This whole thing is the biggest fairy tale I've ever seen."

Then came Hillary Clinton's comments about Martin Luther King Jr., Lyndon Johnson, and how civil rights became the law of the land. Fox

News correspondent Major Garrett asked her the night before the primary to react to something Obama had said that day. Obama had chastised her for suggesting during the New Hampshire debate that his campaign was an exercise in false hopes. "Dr. King's dream began to be realized," she told Garrett, "when President Lyndon Johnson passed the Civil Rights Act of 1964, when he was able to get through Congress something that President Kennedy was hopeful to do, presidents before had not even tried. But it took a president to get it done. That dream became a reality—the power of that dream became real in people's lives because we had a president who said we're going to do it and actually got it accomplished." Historically, she was entirely accurate about the role LBJ played in fulfilling King's dream after Selma. Politically, her words proved to be incendiary.

Many African-Americans were offended by Bill and Hillary's comments. Some took his "fairy tale" remark as a broad attack on Obama's message of hope and inspiration, though he insisted that was not his intent. Hillary had made similar comments in the past about Lyndon Johnson's central importance in passing civil rights legislation, but without the racially explosive connection to King that was taken by African-American critics as a denigration of King's role. Representative Jim Clyburn, South Carolina's most prominent black politician, rebuked Bill Clinton, saying the former president should "watch what and how he says it because there are a lot of people who see Barack Obama as their hopes and dreams. And they're going to feel like you're throwing cold water on their dream." Both Clintons sought to dampen the controversy that was hurting her candidacy in South Carolina. Then another incident brought new problems.

On the Sunday after New Hampshire, Hillary was campaigning in South Carolina with Robert Johnson, the billionaire founder of Black Entertainment Television. Johnson defended her King-LBJ comments, described Obama pejoratively as a kind of Sidney Poitier in *Guess Who's Coming to Dinner?* and then, inexplicably, invoked Obama's use of drugs as a teenager—which Obama had written candidly about in *Dreams from My Father*. "As an African-American," Johnson said, "I am frankly insulted that the Obama campaign would imply that we are so stupid that we would think Hillary and Bill Clinton, who have been deeply and emotionally involved in black issues since Barack Obama was doing something in the neighborhood—and I won't say what he was doing, but he said it in the book."

The Clinton campaign then allowed Johnson to issue a questionable denial on campaign letterhead. "My comments today were referring to

Barack Obama's time spent as a community organizer, and nothing else," he said in what the Obama campaign called a tortured explanation. "Any other suggestion is simply irresponsible and incorrect." Whatever Hillary Clinton was thinking as Johnson delivered those remarks, she did nothing to condemn them until she could no longer avoid it. It was not the first time she appeared reluctant to rebuke someone immediately in her campaign over questionable criticism of Obama.

A month earlier, her New Hampshire co-chairman, Billy Shaheen, had spoken openly about Obama's vulnerabilities as a general election candidate because of his past drug use. Shaheen told the *Washington Post's* Alec MacGillis that Republicans would jump on the issue if Obama were the nominee. "It'll be, 'When was the last time? Did you ever give drugs to anyone? Did you sell them to anyone?' There are so many openings for Republican dirty tricks." Clinton's staff were outraged by Shaheen's remarks and believed he should be dismissed. Clinton, according to one source with inside information, resisted. Only after her New Hampshire supporters insisted did she agree.

As the racial issue boiled over, yet another controversy erupted between Obama and Bill Clinton, triggered by what Obama said in Nevada. In an interview with the *Reno Gazette-Journal* editorial board, Obama was talking about the mood of the country and how Americans seemed ready for something different. "I don't want to present myself as some sort of singular figure," he said. "I think part of what's different are the times. I do think that, for example, that 1980 was different. I think Ronald Reagan changed the trajectory of America in a way that, you know, Richard Nixon did not and in a way that Bill Clinton did not. [Reagan] put us on a fundamentally different path because the country was ready for it. They felt like with all the excesses of the sixties and seventies and government had grown and grown but there wasn't much sense of accountability in terms of how it was operating. He tapped into what people were already feeling, which was, we want clarity, we want optimism, we want a return to that sense of dynamism and entrepreneurship that had been missing." Obama also said that Republicans have been "the party of ideas for a pretty long chunk of time there over the last ten, fifteen years, in the sense that they were challenging conventional wisdom."

Bill Clinton was enraged. In Nevada, he accused Obama of saying that, since 1992, "Republicans have had all the good ideas." In Buffalo, he claimed Obama had said, "President Reagan was the engine of innovation and did more, had a more lasting impact on America than I did. And then the next day he said, 'In the nineties, the good ideas came out from the Republicans.'" These were skillful distortions of what Obama had said by a master politician determined to defend his wife, but comments that led Clinton into a thicket of trouble.

On Saturday, January 19, Hillary Clinton won the Nevada caucuses (although because of the complex rules of the Democratic Party, Obama was awarded one more delegate than she was). Obama now had lost two contests in a row and was angry about what the Clintons—particularly Bill Clinton—were doing. By the time Obama got to South Carolina on Sunday afternoon, he and his advisers had had enough. "They had a surrogate unlike anybody else would ever have a surrogate," Gibbs said. "We were slow to recognize . . . that we had to respond." Obama's advisers realized that if anyone was going to call Bill Clinton to account, it would have to be Obama.

Axelrod, standing in the back of a room at Obama's Sunday night rally in Columbia, said of Bill Clinton, "It's disappointing, because I admire him as a former president, to see that. But he's out there on the battlefield. We're not going to stand by and allow Senator Obama's comments to be distorted by anybody. No one gets a pass when they're parsing words or truncating quotes or trying to mislead people."

On ABC's *Good Morning America*, Obama called the former president's remarks "troubling." It is time to stop, he added. "I understand him wanting to promote his wife's candidacy," Obama said. "She's got a record that she can run on. But I think it's important that we try to maintain some, you know, level of honesty and candor during the course of the campaign. If we don't, then we feed the cynicism that has led so many Americans to be turned off to politics."

The Clinton campaign quickly responded. "Everything the president has said is factual," Howard Wolfson said. "He's going to continue to campaign on behalf of his wife. Everywhere and anywhere."

Five days before the primary, Obama, Clinton, and Edwards met in Myrtle Beach for a debate that quickly became known as the "brawl on the beach." Obama arrived exhausted. In debate prep, he started to nod off. His advisers urged him to take a nap and come back when he was rested. They anticipated a tough debate and had prepared a series of pivot points—

scripted counterpunches in anticipation of a reprise from Hillary of the lines of attack Bill Clinton had been using. He was ready now. Obama had reached his own boiling point.

The audience was primed as well. They were a raucous, noisy crowd anticipating a fight. Within minutes, they got it. Asked about one of Hillary's criticisms of his programs, Obama said, "What she said wasn't true." Then, unprompted, he tried to knock down the other attacks from the Clintons. On whether his consistent opposition to the war was a fairy tale: "That simply is not true." On whether he had said Republicans had better economic policies since the 1980s: "That is not the case." Clinton then hammered back. "When it comes to a lot of the issues that are important in this race, it is sometimes difficult to understand what Senator Obama has said, because as soon as he is confronted on it, he says that's not what he meant," she said. "The facts are that he has said in the last week that he really liked the ideas of the Republicans over the last ten to fifteen years, and we can give you the exact quote. Now, I personally think they had ideas, but they were bad ideas. They were bad ideas for America."

When Obama retook the microphone, he returned to Reagan and the Republicans. "Now, let's talk about Ronald Reagan. What you just repeated here today is—" Clinton interrupted. "I did not say anything about Ronald Reagan," she said. "Hillary, we just had the tape," Obama responded. "You just said that I complimented the Republican ideas. That is not true. What I said—and I will provide you with a quote—what I said was that Ronald Reagan was a transformative political figure because he was able to get Democrats to vote against their economic interests to form a majority to push through their agenda, an agenda that I objected to. Because while I was working on those streets watching those folks see their jobs shift overseas, you were a corporate lawyer sitting on the board at Wal-Mart."

The Wal-Mart reference caught the audience by surprise and represented as personal an attack as Obama had ever made against her in a debate. She insisted again that she had never cited Reagan. Referring to Obama's interview with the *Reno Gazette-Journal*, she said, "You talked about Ronald Reagan being a transformative political leader. I did not mention his name."

"Your husband did," Obama interjected.

"Well, I'm here. He's not."

"Well, I can't tell who I'm running against sometimes," Obama complained.

The candidates were standing only a few feet apart, leaning toward one another. Their aides, watching from their holding rooms, couldn't believe what they were seeing. The debate was expected to be tough, but not like this. Wolfson's BlackBerry flashed with incoming messages from reporters. Have you ever seen anything like this? they asked. He was astonished by the tone of the debate, as were Obama's advisers.

Clinton still had the floor, determined to make her own point about who was fighting for Democratic Party values during the Reagan years. Obama's interview, she said, certainly sounded as if he were praising their Republican ideas. "Yes, they did have ideas, and they were bad ideas." Obama said he agreed, but Clinton kept talking. "Bad for America. And I was fighting against those ideas when you were practicing law and representing your contributor, Rezko, in his slum landlord business in inner-city Chicago."

The audience erupted at the reference to the developer Tony Rezko. He had been a major contributor to Obama, had entered into a questionable land sale with Obama, was under indictment, and became a major embarrassment once the presidential campaign was launched. All Obama could muster was, "No, no, no."

CNN's Wolf Blitzer, the debate moderator, finally turned to John Edwards, who had stood by awkwardly as Clinton and Obama exchanged insults. "I don't know if you want to get involved in this, Senator," Blitzer said.

Edwards, by now the odd man out in the presidential campaign, down to one last stand in the state where he was born and where he had won four years earlier, said in exasperation, "What I want to say first is, are there three people in this debate, not two?"

Everyone by then knew the answer.

Axelrod said much later, "There was this ugliness hanging over South Carolina." Neither Clinton nor Obama was particularly pleased with what happened in Myrtle Beach; later in the debate they seemed to go out of their way to be civil. But no temporary truce could undo the damage or the bitterness that would shape the final days of campaigning. Hillary Clinton left South Carolina the morning after the debate for three days out west. She was focusing on Super Tuesday states, a decision her South Carolina supporters believed was a major mistake. "I personally thought it was very costly and I raised hell to anybody I could find," Don Fowler said. With Hillary absent, Bill Clinton now took the lead role in the South Carolina campaign.

The morning after the debate, Bill Clinton was campaigning at the Lizard's Thicket, a restaurant in Columbia. He sparred with reporters over his role in the campaign. As he was leaving, *Time* magazine's Mark Halperin asked one of Clinton's companions, someone who had been with him since his Arkansas days, whether the former president was as good a politician now as he had been in 1992. "Better," the friend responded. Clinton interjected with a shake of his head. "He's rusty and old and creaky," he said of himself, though he didn't really mean it. But he was right; in those weeks, his words and actions showed him to be a politician who had lost his normally unerring instincts as a campaigner.

Neither did Obama seem at the top of his game. The battle against two Clintons was taking its toll. The day after the debate, the weather turned rainy and cold. Obama was on a rolling tour through the state, with his big stop of the day in Greenwood, a small town with a city councilwoman named Edith Childs, who had inspired Obama's chant of *Fired up? Ready to go!* that he used to close his rallies and who joined him there. As he was working the rope line after he and Childs led the crowd in the chant, Jeff Zeleny of the *New York Times*, who knew the candidate's moods and body language, shouted out, "Are you letting Bill Clinton get inside your head?" Obama looked irritated. "I am trying to make sure that his statements by him are answered. Don't you think that's important?" he shot back. As he walked away to shake hands with voters, Zeleny tried again. Obama had not answered his question, he observed. Obama turned, flashed a grin that seemed to hide his peevishness. "Don't try cheap stunts like that, Jeff," he said. "Come on, you're better than that." Zeleny persisted and Obama finally tried to shrug it off, saying, "My suspicion is that the other side must be rattled if they're continuing saying false things about us." But everyone could see how frustrated the normally unflappable Obama was.

All through the campaign, Obama benefited from a combination of preparation, organization—and luck. In South Carolina all came together in the last few days to turn an expected victory into an extraordinary one.

Obama had a key advantage that was not understood at the time. He had built an organization unlike anything that Democrats in the state had ever done before. Steve Hildebrand, the deputy campaign manager who oversaw operations in the early states, had come to South Carolina early in 2007 with the idea of building an organization from scratch. Traditional organizing called for candidates to graft themselves onto existing political networks, particularly in the black community. It was not only common; it was expected. As early as February 2007, Hildebrand learned about the normal terms of doing business when the Obama campaign lost out in the bidding for the support of an African-American legislator. His asking price in consulting fees was simply beyond what the campaign was prepared to pay. Obama's team decided they would not supply "walking-around money" to local political leaders. Hildebrand, a white midwesterner, recruited another young white organizer, Jeremy Bird, who believed the key to organizing the state lay in empowering volunteers, not just relying on paid staff. In mid-2007, the campaign helped organize two thousand house parties to recruit volunteers. "A huge percentage of those house meetings were held by African-American women," Hildebrand said. "It was really African-American women in South Carolina who built this from the ground up." On election day, the Obama campaign had thirteen thousand volunteers on the streets helping turn out the vote—eleven thousand of them from in-state. The Clinton campaign, in contrast, was no match. It was pitting an Obama F-16 jet fighter against a Clinton World War II P-51. "There are not enough superlatives to describe the Obama campaign," Fowler said later. "As good as the Obama campaign was at getting out the vote, the Clinton campaign was that bad."

A late poll helped shape perceptions of the race in ways that played to Obama's benefit. MSNBC and McClatchy newspapers released a poll two days out that showed a close race and an electorate polarized along racial lines, Obama leading Clinton by just eight points and winning just 10 percent of the white vote. If this poll was correct, Obama was in danger of coming out of South Carolina tagged as the black candidate with limited appeal to white voters. Obama's internal polling had him doing much better among whites, but his advisers let the media spin the story in what they believed was a false, but helpful, direction.

The Clinton campaign was now trapped between Bill Clinton's all-in approach to the primary and the impression that Hillary Clinton, spending time out of the state, was ducking it. Bill Clinton's controversial comments damaged his wife's candidacy and her absence discouraged some white voters who might otherwise have come out for her.

Everyone expected Obama to win, but no one anticipated the blowout that occurred. Clinton advisers believed Obama's margin might be as much as ten or twelve points, as narrow as single digits. He won 55 percent of the vote to Clinton's 27, with Edwards third at 18 percent. Obama won three-quarters of the black vote against a candidate whose husband had been called the first black president. He also won a quarter of the white vote, assembling a black-white majority that the polling had suggested two days earlier was beyond his grasp. South Carolina became a huge victory for Obama and, commentators said, a rejection of the tactics the Clintons had used against him.

Obama's team had learned from Iowa and New Hampshire that the results of any single contest could be fleeting, that he was in a battle against Clinton that would be long, difficult, and chancy. His victory speech that night was edgy and defiant, intended to declare he would not be intimidated by the battle ahead.

"We are looking for more than just a change of party in the White House," he said. "We are looking to fundamentally change the status quo in Washington. It's a status quo that extends beyond a particular party. And that status quo is fighting back with everything it's got, with the same old tactics that divide and distract us from solving the problems people face, whether the problems are health care that folks can't afford or a mort-gage they cannot pay. This will not be easy. Make no mistake about what we are up against."

Obama had told his speechwriters he did not want to make the speech a personal attack on the Clintons. But his meaning was clear. "Let me say this, South Carolina. With what we have seen in the last weeks, we are up against forces that are not the fault of any one campaign. They feed the habits that prevent us from being who we want to be as a nation. . . . So let me remind you tonight, change will not be easy. Change will take time. . . . This election is about the past versus the future. It's about whether we settle for the same division and distractions and drama that passes for politics today or whether we reach for politics of common sense, innovation, politics of shared sacrifice and shared prosperity."

Hillary Clinton left the state before the votes were tallied. Bill Clinton, on his way out, was asked why it took two Clintons to try to beat Obama in South Carolina. "Jesse Jackson won South Carolina twice, in '84 and '88," he said, though the reporter had not mentioned Jackson. "He ran a good campaign. And Senator Obama ran a good campaign here. He's run a good campaign everywhere." It was a parting shot from Clinton, a com-ment that seemed infused with racial implications and an apparent at-tempt to dismiss Obama's victory—and candidacy—as nothing more than an extension of the former civil rights leader's two losing efforts. But those were not his last words. Clinton also talked to Jim Clyburn in what a friend of the congressman's later described as a "red-faced rant." The former president was fuming over what had happened in South Carolina, to his wife and to himself—and for good reason. South Carolina was a huge event.

Long afterwards, we asked Obama whether he felt that Bill Clinton was playing the race card against him in South Carolina. He said he thought some criticisms of Clinton had been unfair. "I think when he said this is a fairy tale about my position on Iraq, I think he was factually wrong, but I don't think he was playing the race card. He was trying to make an argument that somehow this mythology of me being opposed to Iraq wasn't entirely true—which is a perfectly legitimate political attack. It wasn't backed up by the facts, but I don't think there was anything racial about it. I think some African-Americans took offense." The Jackson comments, he said, seemed as if what Clinton "was trying to do was be dismissive about the victory and discount it a little bit."

It was understandable, he said, why black voters took offense.

John Lewis was not offended by Bill Clinton's campaign in South Carolina, but Lewis's own role there underscored how devastating a defeat Hillary had sustained. It was much more than the loss of an early primary state. In the end, it was the irretrievable loss of the black leadership upon which the Clintons had counted. Nothing better demonstrated that than the defection of Lewis himself, for he had campaigned loyally for Hillary out of long devotion to and admiration for both Clintons. As he would tell us later, "I love Hillary. I love President Clinton. They are like family."

Of all the black civil rights leaders, John Lewis had emerged from the violent battles to end segregation as one of the movement's most admired and heroic figures. His skull had been fractured on that Bloody Sunday in Selma, and in the years since as a Georgia congressman he continued to win praise for his efforts to heal racial tensions and follow the tenets of Martin Luther King. He had long been a staunch supporter first of Bill, and, more than a decade later, of Hillary. He remembered having breakfast with the soon-to-be candidate from Arkansas, and how two of Lewis's staff members later said, "Congressman, Bill Clinton acts more like a brother than a lot of brothers." Lewis became one of the first major black politicians to endorse Clinton; later, he did the same for Hillary. Over the years, when he'd meet with either of them, he remembered how Bill "always said to me, 'I love you, John,' and I said, 'I love you.'" And Hillary, too. "Hillary would come to Atlanta from time to time and say, 'When I grow up I want to be just like John Lewis,'" he recalled. He became so admiring of her that he told Bill before she decided to run for president, "'Mr. President, Hillary is really smart, she's smarter than you. She'd be a great president.' Later I made the decision to endorse her because that was in my soul."

Lewis hadn't known Obama so well then, though he had linked arms with him and Hillary in Selma in commemoration of the march to freedom as the campaign was just beginning. But even before the South Carolina primary, he began to, as he put it, "sense something" about Obama's appeal. He particularly remembered being out of the country on a congressional fact-finding trip during the Iowa and New Hampshire contests, and how he and other congressmen had listened from Vietnam to both Hillary's and Barack's concession and victory speeches. When Lewis returned home, he felt even more strongly that "something's happening here." By South Carolina, where he began by campaigning for Hillary, he felt increasingly besieged by conflicting emotions. "I had what I call an executive session with myself. I said to myself, I want to be on the right side of history, and I can't let this moment pass me by." So he switched his endorsement to Obama. "It was hard, it was like turning my back on a member of my family."

Bill Clinton's role in South Carolina was not a factor in Lewis's decision. "The president," he told us later, "was so committed to seeing that his wife had a victory. In his heart, in his gut, he wanted her to win, because I think he felt it was her time, that she had sacrificed for him big-time, in a very big way, that he owed her, and also that his own history, his legacy, was at stake. Sometimes I think he was misunderstood, and she was misunderstood. I'm not sure whether the American people, or the media, read that stuff about racism right. That stuff about King was horrible, awful bullshit. I understood from day one what she was saying there about President Johnson and Martin Luther King Jr.: that it took [both of them] to see that the voting rights legislation was passed."

Lewis's most anguished moment came when he had to tell Hillary and Bill Clinton he was switching his support to Obama. Both were gracious, Hillary saying she understood, and that "we were friends before this campaign and we'll be friends after this campaign." Bill was equally friendly and understanding. Left unsaid was what the loss of someone so admired and politically important in the black community would mean for the outcome of the Clinton campaign.

CHAPTER TWELVE

Clash of Dynasties

"The votes you're going to have to cast [as senator], whether it's guns or . . . abortion or . . . any one of the hot-button items, finishes you as a national political leader in this country. You just can't do it. It's not possible."

—Senator Ted Kennedy's 2006 advice to Obama

In the fall of 2006, Ted Kennedy was looking for a candidate, a special kind of candidate who might inspire the country. The Massachusetts senator, leader of the liberals and the Democratic Party's most famous figure, saw potential in many candidates who were then looking to run: in Chris Dodd and Joe Biden, his friends; in Hillary Clinton, a solid legislator in her first term; and in the young and relatively untested Barack Obama. When Obama came to the Senate, Kennedy recruited him to the Committee on Health, Education, Labor, and Pensions. He admired the young senator's commitment to finding a compromise on immigration. He saw genuine leadership qualities in Obama, so when Obama talked to him privately about running for president, Kennedy was encouraging.

Kennedy believed the longer Obama stayed in the Senate, the less chance he would ever have to become president. According to a source familiar with their conversation, he told Obama, "The votes you're going to have to cast, whether it's guns or whether it's abortion or whether it's any one of the hot-button items, finishes you as a national political leader in this country. You just can't do it. It's not possible." Kennedy admired Clinton but felt she was wrong for the times. A successful candidacy in 2008 had to be an outside-Washington effort. You couldn't be a Washington insider to run, and Clinton appeared to be positioning herself in just the wrong way. Kennedy believed the time was right for Obama and that Clinton was, as an associate put it, "the past."

Kennedy was in no rush to make an early endorsement. He continued watching the race and the public's reaction to the candidates. In the summer of 2007, he was with Caroline Kennedy and her children on a boat in Tarpaulin Cove off Cape Cod. Earlier Caroline had taken her children to hear both Obama and Clinton at fund-raisers. As the children talked about the candidates, Kennedy was moved by their enthusiasm for Obama. He had not seen that kind of excitement in young people in a generation and was struck by how Obama's appeal to them was less about his policies and more about how he represented a dramatic break from the divisive politics of the present. Still, for much of 2007, as the race developed he held back from an endorsement.

In September, he ran into Clinton on the Senate floor and thought she looked very tired. She told him that if she got this nomination she wanted to start working with him right away on health care. When Obama came to see him about the same time, Kennedy remarked on the enthusiasm Obama's candidacy was generating among young people. My problem, Obama told him, is gravitas. Hillary's got it. Kennedy suggested Obama talk with Ted Sorensen, who had been President Kennedy's speechwriter. I talk to Ted all the time, Obama said. Obama asked what Kennedy's plans were for an endorsement. Kennedy said he had no plans to endorse. But he was still impressed with Obama's energy and charisma; if Obama became president, Kennedy thought, he could change the country. At the same time, he wondered whether Obama could build a campaign that could win the nomination and the presidency. Also in September, John and Elizabeth Edwards, in town for a fund-raiser, came to see Kennedy at his home in Northwest Washington. Edwards made a direct appeal. He knew Kennedy had friends in the race, he said, but urged him to do right for the country and the party. "I know you'll do that and when you do what's right for the party you will be with me," Edwards said, according to a Kennedy source. "It can make all the difference. We can win this. I'll win Iowa."

In the late fall, the phone calls intensified. Hillary Clinton was frank about her wanting his endorsement, though she understood how difficult it would be for him because of his close friendship with Dodd. Bill Clinton, with whom Kennedy had a stronger relationship than with Hillary, called regularly. At one point, Obama, obviously worried that Kennedy might endorse Dodd, said warily, "You could do me some damage in Iowa." Kennedy laughed it off. "Oh, I haven't been in Iowa for a long time," he said. To which Obama responded, "You still have some friends out there."

In late December, a 2003 tape recording of Obama made while he was still in the Illinois Senate became public. It was a comment on Kennedy's efforts to pass a prescription drug bill. Obama had described Kennedy as "getting old and getting tired" and said the backers of a strong prescription drug bill should get after him. Obama called Kennedy to make amends. "Well," Kennedy said when he picked up the phone, "you start the conversation." Obama began to grovel, but Kennedy stopped him. He would let Obama off the hook, he said gently, because he had once mangled Obama's name in a speech at the National Press Club the month Obama was sworn in as a senator, calling him "Osama bin Laden" before finally stammering out his right name.

The Kennedys and the Clintons were the royalty of the Democratic Party, their reigns stretching over half a century of national and party politics. Ted Kennedy never reached the White House, crushed by Jimmy Carter when he sought the Democratic nomination in 1980, but he was now an iconic figure, a supreme legislator and a giant in the Senate, the keeper of the Kennedy family flame, the leader of the party's liberal wing, the patriarch of a family that had seen glory, tragedy, and heartache. Now, at the age of seventy-six, Edward Moore Kennedy moved slowly, stooped as he walked, had the girth of an older man that contrasted with the slim young figure who had entered the Senate more than four decades ago, but his eyes were clear, his voice resonant, his broad Boston accent instantly identifiable, his political passions still burning.

Bill Clinton was as imposing a political figure, as popular within the party, and possessed of equally great political gifts and achievements that had made him the first Democrat since FDR to win back-to-back presidential terms. As a young politician, he had consciously tied his own political story to that of John F. Kennedy, linked by a memorable photograph taken in 1963 of the sixteen-year-old Clinton shaking hands with the young, handsome president in the White House Rose Garden. Later, he courted the Kennedy family. He and Hillary and their daughter, Chelsea, vacationed with them and were seen sailing with Jackie Kennedy and her children, and with Ted Kennedy and his family.

The lives of both men were the stuff of high drama and achievement, low melodrama and tawdry scandal. Both had overcome intensely publicized scandals that would have destroyed lesser politicians: Kennedy with the dead young aide, Mary Jo Kopechne, whose body was found inside an overturned car driven by Kennedy that had plunged from the Dike Bridge off

Martha's Vineyard into Poucha Pond of Chappaquiddick Island, resulting in Kennedy's arrest after he left the scene and failed to report the accident for more than twenty-four hours. Clinton's affair with the young White House intern Monica Lewinsky led to only the second presidential impeachment in American history and perhaps the longest-running melodrama in the current age of 24/7 cable TV scandal. Over the years, Clinton and Kennedy had developed a relationship of mutual respect.

Throughout the month of January 2008, as Obama and Hillary Clinton battled through the early states, Ted Kennedy and Bill Clinton were engaged in a behind-the-scenes struggle over Kennedy's endorsement that reached a crescendo just as Obama was winning South Carolina.

On the night of the Iowa caucuses, Kennedy had watched the television coverage from home. He was impressed with Obama's victory, how his appeal seemed to cut across all lines and all groups. With his wife, Vicki, he listened to Obama's victory speech. He thought it remarkable and inspirational, an uplifting message that defied the politics of divide-and-conquer. What hit him most, he told friends, was his feeling that Obama's message was "what the country both needs and that's what the country wants and he's saying it correctly." He began to see something of Jack and Bobby in the young senator from Illinois. But he was still not ready to get off the fence.

The day after Iowa, Bill Clinton called Kennedy. The former president believed he had been good to the Kennedys when he was in office, recalling to aides what he had done over the years. He had named Kennedy's sister, Jean Kennedy Smith, as ambassador to Ireland, and stood with her despite a State Department reprimand. He hosted an event for the Special Olympics, which Kennedy's sister Eunice Kennedy Shriver had helped to create. When Kennedy faced a tough reelection campaign against Mitt Romney in 1994, Clinton tried to steer federal funds into the state. When John F. Kennedy Jr.'s plane crashed on a flight to Martha's Vineyard in the summer of 1999, Clinton kept the Coast Guard out searching for the wreckage.

On the phone, the two men talked generally about three Kennedy cousins—Bobby and Ethel Kennedy's children Kathleen, Robert, and Kerry—who were campaigning for Hillary in Iowa and New Hampshire. Kennedy told Clinton that he had talked to Hillary the day before, the day of the caucuses, and that they had had a good conversation. He believed she would do well in New Hampshire because of her strong support in the greater Massachusetts area. Clinton then pressed Kennedy for an endorsement. He had not wanted to bother Kennedy as long as Chris Dodd and Joe Biden were in the race. But now, with their poor showings in Iowa, they were out; Clinton said he and Hillary very much wanted Kennedy's support. Kennedy was cool and noncommittal. He hoped to stay in touch, he told Clinton, but he would be very busy in the Senate in the coming weeks. In the course of the conversation, Clinton said something that deeply disturbed Kennedy. He never shared it publicly, but a veiled reference to it showed up days later in a column by Albert R. Hunt of Bloomberg News. Hunt said Clinton had "trashed" Obama.

Post-Iowa, Kennedy was still uncertain whether he should endorse anyone. He decided to watch the race develop as the candidates moved into New Hampshire and beyond, but he already was being drawn ever closer to Obama and more resistant to the Clintons.

Over the next ten days came the events that brought the race issue into the forefront of the Democratic campaign. Kennedy watched closely, and became increasingly disturbed at the tone and direction of the campaign. There was Hillary Clinton's comment about Martin Luther King and Lyndon Johnson. There was the retired teacher who introduced Hillary in New Hampshire the day before the primary, saying, "If you look back, some people have been comparing one of the candidates to JFK, and he was a wonderful leader, he gave us a lot of hope, but he was assassinated and Lyndon Baines Johnson actually did all his work and got the Republicans to pass those measures." There was an unnamed Clinton adviser who was quoted by Jonathan Freedland in the *Guardian* saying, "If you have a social need, you're with Hillary. If you want Obama to be your imaginary hip black friend and you're young and you have no social needs, then he's cool." There was New York attorney general Andrew Cuomo, another Clinton supporter, using the phrase "shuck and jive" in a way that seemed pointed at Obama, though Cuomo insisted afterwards it was not. There was Robert Johnson, with Hillary Clinton at his side, alluding to Obama's youthful drug use and Clinton's delay in distancing herself from it.

Kennedy was deeply offended by the cascading events. He believed the campaign was sliding into divisiveness, and held the Clintons principally responsible. He also believed that by invoking Martin Luther King in a comparison to Obama, Hillary was attempting to draw attention to the fact that Obama was black. He worried that the Clintons were trying to turn Obama into the black candidate—the Jesse Jackson of 2008.

On January 14, the day after Robert Johnson's appearance with Hillary, Bill Clinton called Kennedy. Kennedy decided not to call him back immediately, preferring to think about everything that had happened over the previous ten days before talking to him. But Kennedy did talk to Obama, discussing generally what was happening. For Kennedy, the injection of race into the campaign was hurting both candidates and was alienating to the party's African-American base. Obama said he was not personally bothered by what the Clintons had said, but he knew how much others had been. With his characteristic self-confidence, he told Kennedy he expected to win—not just South Carolina but the nomination—and again asked Kennedy for his endorsement. That's what you and your family are always about, Obama said, change and progress. Later, Kennedy, struck by Obama's confidence, told people close to him of his admiration for the way Obama was running his campaign. The Clintons, he said, were misrepresenting things for racial reasons. Kennedy understood that Obama did not want to dignify it by responding. He found it all very offensive.

That afternoon, Kennedy called Bill Clinton back, believing Clinton would try to explain away what had been said during the previous ten days. Clinton began by noting that their private conversation on January 4 had made its way into one of Al Hunt's columns. Kennedy brushed that aside and urged Clinton to get beyond the racial debate. "We have to move beyond it," he said. Clinton was furious, launching an attack on the Obama campaign for all they had done to attack his wife. He cited David Axelrod, saying Obama's strategist had suggested earlier that Hillary bore some of the responsibility for the assassination of Benazir Bhutto, the former prime minister of Pakistan. Kennedy accused Clinton of misrepresenting Axelrod's remarks. Clinton parried, arguing that his version was accurate. "Look," Kennedy said, "I've got the comment right here. You're distorting it."

Clinton then went after Obama for distorting Hillary's vote for the Iraq war resolution. That vote wasn't a vote for war, Clinton said. A Clinton associate said he cited the support for the resolution by Nebraska Senator Chuck Hagel, a Republican and sharp critic of the administration's policies. He urged Kennedy to examine some of Obama's comments in the summer of 2004, saying Obama had suggested then that there was little difference between his and Bush's positions on the war. The country needs a president who doesn't change his mind about whether he is for or against the war,

Clinton went on—thereby implying Obama had done exactly that. Kennedy, who had led the opposition to the war, was furious. "It *was* a vote for war," he said firmly. "I was there. I said it at the time. That resolution was a vote for war. Everybody understood it." Clinton continued his litany of the attacks the Obama campaign had launched against Hillary until Kennedy tried to cut him off. I don't know where I'm going to go, he told the former president, but I don't want to see this get into a pissing match on race.

Ted Kennedy believes that race in America is, as he sometimes puts it, "a-burning," by which he means that it bubbles just below the surface of the American psyche and it takes little to bring it out. Now he told Clinton, "You know it and I know it. It's a-burning. Let's get back and talk about health care. Let's get the hell off this thing."

Clinton would not let go of it. An associate of the former president said Clinton pressed Kennedy for examples and cited Hillary's support from African-American leaders, men and women, noting that many had been threatened with or had gotten primary opponents for their support of Hillary—from John Lewis on down. Clinton told Kennedy that others in the black community would vouch for him and Hillary. They were not racists. It was Obama who was exploiting the race issue, he insisted. The minute we attack Obama, he complained, everybody mentions racism. But Obama had attacked Hillary with seeming impunity from the press and public as the "senator from Punjab" over the money she had received from the Indian community in the United States.

As their conversation neared its tense conclusion, Clinton asked, How can we end this, what can we do? Kennedy said the Clintons should put out a statement saying it was time to get off the racial debate. Clinton said they intended to do that later in the day. But before they hung up, Clinton offered one more defiant comment. "We may get licked but we're not quitting," he said. "Clintons don't quit."

The Clintons were exasperated by what was happening, wounded by charges that they had raised the race issue after all they believed they had done on civil rights and for the African-American community and frustrated by their inability to attack Obama without being accused of racism. They believed that Obama, without openly running on a racial appeal, evoked emotions within the black community that worked to his benefit. They knew only one way to fight a campaign, which was as vigorously and directly as they could, but their playbook was badly out of date. As one prominent African-American Hillary supporter told us at the time, liberals don't know how to run against a black man like Obama.

That afternoon, the Clinton campaign issued a statement calling for a cease-fire over race. "We differ on a lot of things," Hillary said. "And it is critical to have the right kind of discussion on where we stand. But when it comes to civil rights and our commitment to diversity, when it comes to our heroes—President John F. Kennedy and Dr. King—Senator Obama and I are on the same side." The Obama campaign, seeming to anticipate a Clinton campaign truce, put out Obama's own statement just before hers was issued. "I think that Bill Clinton and Hillary have historically and consistently been on the right side of civil rights issues," Obama said. "I think that they care about the African-American community, they care about all Americans, and they want to see equal rights and equal justice in this country."

On January 22, three days after her victory in Nevada, Hillary Clinton and Kennedy spoke again. He was still troubled by the tone of the campaign. Over the previous week, Bill Clinton and Obama had been fighting another war of words—this time over Ronald Reagan's legacy. Kennedy was fed up. He told Hillary he had great respect for her but that the country needed to be lifted up and the current campaign was not achieving that. She told Kennedy the Republicans would eviscerate Obama in a general election. He had not been vetted, she insisted.

Bill Clinton also called Kennedy. He had been behaving himself since his "fairy tale" comment, he told Kennedy, but the purpose of the call was to amplify Hillary's arguments that Obama was vulnerable in the general election, a risk for the Democrats. Kennedy again said he was concerned by the negative tone of the campaign. He feared it could split the party and depress Democratic turnout in the fall, enough to endanger the party's chances of winning back the White House. Clinton said he was calling from South Carolina. He said Obama was likely to win, but told Kennedy, "We're giving it a battle."

Though Kennedy had ended his call with Hillary Clinton telling her he would get back to her before he did anything about an endorsement, the Clintons were now convinced he would not support her. The former president believed race trumped gender in Kennedy's endorsement calculus, although Kennedy associates said that was not the case. They said he was drawn to Obama because he believed Obama might be able to transcend race and move the country toward a less divisive politics. Kennedy associates soon began receiving calls and messages—prompted, they were certain, by the Clintons—from Democrats in Massachusetts, from donors, from members of the Massachusetts delegation, all urging Kennedy to remain neutral. But by then, Kennedy's mind was set. He told friends that, whether Obama won or lost in South Carolina, he would endorse him.

On Thursday, January 24, two days before the primary, he called Obama to say he was ready to endorse. He told Obama that at the beginning of the campaign he was looking for somebody to inspire the nation, and how impressed he had been by Obama's emphasis after his Iowa victory on the importance of ending the longtime divisions within the country. Obama's inspiration was what the country needed, he said, adding, "You're the man." But his endorsement came with conditions. Kennedy wanted a commitment from Obama that as president he would push for universal health care. He wanted it to be a first priority of an Obama administration. Obama agreed.

As Kennedy was reaching his final decision to endorse, his niece Caroline was planning to announce her support for Obama in a Sunday *New York Times* op-ed article. The news of Caroline's pending endorsement broke on the day of the South Carolina primary, just as Obama was being declared the winner. The timing, and her words, gave the endorsement far more power than any of Obama's advisers had anticipated. "Over the years, I've been deeply moved by the people who've told me they wished they could feel inspired and hopeful about America the way people did when my father was president," she began. "This sense is even more profound today. That is why I am supporting a presidential candidate in the Democratic primaries, Barack Obama."

She continued, "It isn't that the other candidates are not experienced or knowledgeable. But this year, that may not be enough. We need a change in the leadership of this country—just as we did in 1960. . . . Senator Obama is running a dignified and honest campaign. He has spoken eloquently about the role of faith in his life, and opened a window into his character in two compelling books. And when it comes to judgment, Barack Obama made the right call on the most important issue of our time by opposing the war in Iraq from the beginning. . . . I have never had a president who inspired me the way people tell me that my father inspired them. But for the first time, I believe I have found the man who could be that president—not just for me, but for a new generation of Americans."

The day that Caroline's endorsement was published, Ted Kennedy began to call members of his family to tell them of his plans. Almost instantly word of his decision to endorse Obama was leaked to the cable networks. Kennedy called Hillary but could not reach her. He did reach Bill Clinton. The call was brief. Then, minutes later, Bill Clinton called back, asking for a detailed explanation. Kennedy went through the reasons: how he had not seen someone in many, many years inspire people, particularly young people, the way Obama did; how it was not an endorsement against Hillary but only a statement of support for Obama and what he had tapped into and what that seemed to represent for the future of the country. Kennedy could hear the former president scribbling rapidly, apparently taking notes on the call. That made Kennedy nervous. His fear was that in some way Clinton loyalists might try to cast his endorsement as more racial politics in an effort to diminish its impact. Clinton was convinced that race was the reason Kennedy had sided with Obama.

The full story of those many phone calls may never be known. The two sides have sharply conflicting memories about some parts of the discussions, and the more time that elapses, the less each side wants to revisit them. But they had a profound impact on shaping the Democratic race at a pivotal moment.

The public endorsement came the next day at American University in Washington. When they met in the holding room before the rally, Obama and Kennedy initially exchanged no words, only a long and affectionate hug. Both Ted and Caroline Kennedy were at the rally with many members of the Kennedy family. As Roger Simon of *Politico* wrote that day, "It was not just an endorsement, it was a rebuke." Kennedy told the audience, "He is a fighter who cares passionately about the causes he believes in without demonizing those who hold a different view. He is tough-minded, but he also has an uncommon capacity to appeal to the better angels of our nature."

A Kennedy adviser remembered Obama saying, emotionally, that this was the greatest day of his life. That may have been an overstatement. But with his South Carolina victory and the blessing of the Kennedys, he was now far better positioned for the twenty-two-state mega-event on Super Tuesday, only eight days away.

CHAPTER THIRTEEN

King Caucus

*"By the time our first staffer landed in Idaho, Idahoans for Obama
had already figured out the caucus rules and put them together . . .
on how to caucus in Idaho."*

—Jon Carson, Obama's national field director

N o one understood the dangers and opportunities posed by Super
Tuesday better than David Plouffe. He had been worrying about
February 5th for months. Slight and intense, Plouffe ran the Obama operation from campaign headquarters in Chicago and was the yin to Axelrod's yang. Axelrod, who oversaw the Obama message and traveled with
him, attracted far more attention, but Plouffe was every bit his equal.

Like Obama, Plouffe was unflappable. Colleagues joked that his emotional range ran from A to B. He had come up through Dick Gephardt's
political operation, had run the Democratic Congressional Campaign Committee and later became a partner in Axelrod's consulting firm. When he was
drafted as campaign manager, he did not know Obama well, certainly not
the way Axelrod did, but his tenacity and belief in the power of organizing
fit ideally with Obama's "No Drama Obama" campaign. It was Plouffe who
authorized the ambitious organizing plan for Iowa, and Plouffe again who
set in motion the plans that would help Obama survive Super Tuesday.

At Obama headquarters, Super Tuesday had long been seen as the
most challenging day of the nomination battle, ready-made for Clinton's
candidacy—a virtual national primary where name recognition alone gave
her a huge head start. Plouffe knew that, because of the demands of the
four early states, Obama would have little time to devote to Super Tuesday
until just before voting began and feared a potential burying ground. Certainly the Clinton camp viewed it as *the* pivotal day. Many of her advisers
believed she could sew up the contest.

Later, Plouffe said, "As we began to figure out February 5th, it was clear that we had two goals: try to win as many states as we could, try to win as many delegates as we could." He had a third goal: "candidly, just survive it."

The stampede of states to the front of the nominating calendar created the single biggest day in the history of presidential politics. Every state wanted to play kingmaker by holding its contest as early as possible, and twenty-two (plus American Samoa) scheduled events for February 5th, including such megastates as California, New York, Illinois, and New Jersey. Together they accounted for 1,681 of the 3,253 pledged delegates at stake. Six of those states—mostly small ones—held caucuses: Alaska, Colorado, Idaho, Kansas, Minnesota, and North Dakota.

Ironically, the Democratic National Committee had spent a year trying in vain to avoid such a pileup. The effort to change the process grew out of long-standing complaints that Iowa and New Hampshire—two small and largely white states—had far too much influence in determining the nominee of a party as racially and economically diverse as the Democrats. In 2004 DNC officials created a commission to review the entire system. The awkwardly named Commission on Presidential Nomination Timing and Scheduling emerged with a messy compromise: Iowa and New Hampshire would continue to hold the first caucus and primary contests. To mollify critics, the commission authorized Nevada to hold a caucus between Iowa and New Hampshire, and South Carolina to hold a primary a week after New Hampshire. No contest could be held earlier than January 14, the commission recommended, and no other states would be authorized to hold one before February 5.

The goal was admirable, even if ultimately unmet: to reverse the trend toward earlier and earlier presidential campaigns, with earlier and earlier outcomes. That had meant nominations were sometimes settled before most states had a chance to vote. Critics recalled earlier election-year calendars that seemed more sensible, for both candidates and voters. The primaries and caucuses started later and stretched over a period of months. Now everything happened early—and all at once.

By the late spring of 2007, it became clear there was a mad dash among the states to schedule events on February 5, and all the campaigns were obsessed with the demands of Super Tuesday. The DNC schedule depended on the cooperation of individual states, where politicians had their own views about when to schedule their primaries. That was not to be the case. Florida wanted an even bigger voice for its primary and voted to move the date from February 5 to January 29. That triggered a chain reaction from South Carolina to Iowa to Michigan to New Hampshire, bringing even more chaos to the calendar and fears that Iowa or New Hampshire might leapfrog everyone to schedule their contest in December 2007. Iowa came close; it set January 3 for its caucuses.

Party officials looked the other way as Iowa and New Hampshire set earlier dates. But the decisions by Florida and Michigan to move their contests to January represented a serious challenge to the DNC's authority. To Plouffe, Florida's move was a real obstacle to Obama's winning the nomination. A Florida primary on February 5 was enough of a problem— one more populous state that would heighten Clinton's inherent advantages. But a January 29 primary was far worse. Plouffe liked the idea of South Carolina being the last contest before Super Tuesday. He believed Obama could win the state—narrowly—and that a victory there would provide Obama with modest momentum as the candidates turned toward February 5. Now Florida threatened that scenario.

With the Obama campaign cheering them on, DNC officials moved to sanction Florida and then Michigan. Plouffe wanted no halfway solutions. He and others in the campaign began pushing behind the scenes, talking to DNC officials, to members of the Rules and Bylaws Committee, to state party officials and others around the country. He wanted to make sure the two states were treated equally and severely. Plouffe was thrilled at the outcome. In his mind, South Carolina was always the contest that he believed could provide the boost Obama needed to get through Super Tuesday. But, as he explained, "We knew that if Florida was on the twenty-ninth and it was a real contest, South Carolina was going to be a blip. . . . So we spent weeks and weeks and hours and hours on this . . . work[ing] every angle we could to make sure that that argument on the rules committee was, you've got to have the full sanction, both for the clarity of the contest but also because there's all these other states lining up to move up." It was a case, as he candidly acknowledged, "where our own interest merged with the interest of the DNC to block other states from moving up."

On August 25, 2007, the DNC's Rules and Bylaws Committee, anxious to send a signal to other potential rule breakers, stripped Florida of its delegates to the national convention. Florida's January 29 primary would have no bearing on the nomination. The committee also signaled that it would do the same to Michigan if it moved its primary to January 15 (as it later did). Among those on the committee who voted for the stiff sanctions was Harold Ickes. Despite his position in the Clinton campaign, Ickes had a deeply held view that the nominating process was out of control. He believed the national party had to step in to prevent further chaos.

The party sanctions marked step one in a pair of events that locked in a calendar far less favorable to Clinton. The second step, initiated by politicians in the early states, was to get all the candidates to agree not to campaign or advertise in either Florida or Michigan. Richardson, Dodd, and Biden agreed immediately. They couldn't afford to spend time or money outside the early states anyway. The day before Labor Day, Edwards and Obama also signed on. Clinton initially resisted, but later that day said she would abide by the agreement. For her it was an agonizing decision. She knew that the other candidates were motivated by pure self-interest. They were out to deny her potentially easy victories. Wiping out Michigan and Florida would help the others, but could hurt her. Nevertheless, she accepted the argument from her advisers that, given her weaknesses in Iowa, she could not afford to anger the activists there.

The February 5th calendar was a giant puzzle, a mix of big and small states, primaries and caucuses. The Obama campaign concluded early on that investing in the caucus states could pay big dividends. Caucus states were generally smaller and had far fewer delegates than marquee states like California or New York, and except for Iowa, played a minor role in the nominating process. Turnout at these events was also traditionally low. But they could be organized for relatively small amounts of money.

Strategically, Obama's advisers anticipated that the four earliest contests might not produce a clear winner. Thus they should prepare for a campaign that extended into Super Tuesday and beyond. The nomination contest would then become a battle for delegates, and the first major test for Obama would be to prevent Clinton from amassing too many delegates on Super Tuesday.

Democratic rules were deliberately complex. The party allocated delegates in each state based on both the vote statewide and by congressional districts. The formulas for distributing delegates seemed confusing to outsiders but were clear to anyone who understood the system. Jeff Berman, a lawyer who oversaw Obama's delegate operations, had a shrewd understanding of how the delegate selection process worked. In the summer of 2007, he assembled a group of seventy-five lawyers to research the rules governing primaries and caucuses in all the states. To educate his colleagues, in meetings and memos, he cited two of Clinton's best Super Tuesday states, New Jersey and New York. Most congressional districts awarded three to six delegates. In New Jersey, ten districts awarded three delegates. Obama would need just 16.7 percent of the vote to win one delegate; to get the second delegate would mean winning 50.1 percent. A minimal effort in those districts would guarantee a third of the delegates. In New York, twenty-three of the twenty-nine districts awarded five delegates. Winning 30.1 percent of the vote assured Obama of two delegates, meaning he could win nearly 40 percent of the delegates in Clinton's home state by competing hard in New York. The rules assured a virtual stalemate between two evenly balanced candidates.

With this in mind, Plouffe began to implement what he hoped would be a survival strategy for February 5. That assumed a split decision coming out of Iowa, New Hampshire, Nevada, and South Carolina—as the results proved.

Clinton's senior campaign advisers' interpretation of the Democratic rules and the balance between primaries and caucuses plagued her disorganized team. As the campaign went into its tailspin in early 2008 and the sniping began, one story in particular became legendary. There was a meeting in the late summer at Mark Penn's house at which the electoral calendar was under discussion. Several inquiries by Penn about the potential impact of winning California suggested to Ickes that Penn believed a victory in the state would virtually lock up the nomination because it would mean such a large number of delegates. Ickes, who rarely made an effort to hide his contempt for Penn, spoke up. "Could it be that the vaunted chief strategist of the vaunted Clinton campaign does not understand proportional representation?" he asked mockingly.

Three people, including Ickes, said the story was true. Penn said, "The whole story is false." Whether or not Penn understood the rules, he and others in the Clinton campaign seemed oblivious to the Obama campaign's emerging delegate strategy. On September 27, Obama held a huge rally in New York, drawing twenty thousand or more people in Union Square. In a strategy memo dated September 29, Penn seemed bewildered by Obama's decision to spend time organizing such an event. "Why hold a 20,000 person rally and burn money in New York when you are losing Iowa and NH?" he wrote.

In fact, the Obama campaign, preparing for a prolonged struggle against Clinton, was far more advanced in its strategic planning, and well along in plotting a state-by-state, district-by-district battle. The huge New York rally was based on the delegate math strategy Berman and others were developing. Yes, they would concede, New York was Clinton territory, but there was also incredible enthusiasm for Obama in many places in the state. A big New York rally would help turn that enthusiasm into activism and prepare for a more organized effort to win as many delegates as possible there on February 5. Obama was not going to walk away from states that looked favorable to Clinton. "This is going to be more of a delegate fight than we've seen in a long time," Steve Hildebrand told us at the time. The Clinton campaign didn't get it.

Penn's September 29th internal memo is intriguing for one sentence. Written at the peak of Hillary Clinton's strength in the national polls, it was extraordinarily upbeat in tone. Penn saw few problems ahead for her—and plenty for Obama and the only other challenger of note at the time, John Edwards. But weighing Obama's chances, Penn wrote, "The biggest threat from Obama is not what we see, but what we don't see—if he is building a significant new type of organization."

His concern was that Obama might be assembling a movement of college students that would be invisible until caucus night in Iowa. But the Clinton campaign did not fully appreciate—and should have—how Obama was building organizations of activists and new voters not just in Iowa but across the country, aided by skillful exploitation of the tools and technology of the Internet, the cell phone, and social networking.

Just as critical was the shrewdness with which the Obama team captured the grassroots energy that was building around his candidacy. Jon Carson, who managed the Super Tuesday ground operation, liked to tell reporters that, to understand the Obama campaign, they had to go to my.barackobama.com. Without doing that, he said, covering the campaign was like trying to understand finance without looking at Wall Street. The potential power of the volunteers was evident from the beginning of the campaign. "We had a thousand grassroots volunteer groups created in the first twenty-four hours after he announced on February 10, 2007," said

Joe Rospars, who oversaw the new media operations. His team tapped into Facebook and MySpace, but through my.barackobama.com they could see what kind of activity was taking place around the country. What they found when they looked past the four early states was a preexisting base upon which to build their organization.

In the early fall of 2007, Obama's Chicago team began to dispatch organizers to the February 5 states for Super Tuesday, with particular attention to the caucus states. Their September budget memo was revealing. Fifteen new staff hires were recommended for California, but the far smaller caucus states were strongly staffed too: nine new hires recommended for Minnesota, eight for Colorado, five for Kansas, and two for tiny Idaho.

Idaho became the textbook study of the Obama strategy. Only a few thousand people had participated in the caucuses in 2004. Obama's advisers realized that with a relatively modest investment, they could probably win. What made Idaho even more attractive was the volunteer cadre already at work. "By the time our first staffer landed in Idaho at the beginning of October, the Idahoans for Obama had organized themselves," Carson told us. "They had an office ready to rent, had the phone lines already on order . . . and had already figured out the caucus rules and typed them up and put them together in sort of an easy-to-use here's how to caucus in Idaho."

The first young staffer who arrived there was Joey Bristol, who after graduating from Princeton's Woodrow Wilson School of Public and International Affairs volunteered for Obama. Later, after becoming a paid staffer, he was dispatched to Idaho. When he was leaving Chicago in October, he asked Carson for some last-minute advice. "Kick some ass out in Idaho," Carson told him. "We need it." It had been years—even decades— since a Democratic presidential candidate had put staff into Idaho. The local activists were thrilled.

Within two weeks, the grassroots organizers held a gala opening ceremony that attracted local and regional media attention and sparked new interest in Obama's campaign. "Most days at least one to two new faces would show up, poke their face in the door, and say, 'I just wanted to see if you guys really existed. I'll come back to volunteer now that I know it's real,'" Bristol said. A few supporters passing out Clinton buttons and bumper stickers was the only sign of her campaign.

The same enthusiasm was generated in other states, particularly those holding caucuses. In Colorado, Obama had such an energetic base of volunteers that Clinton allies warned Bill Clinton about the problem during one of his visits to the state. Clinton began sending staff to Colorado, but mostly the warnings went unheeded. By late fall, Obama had paid staff in sixteen of the twenty-two February 5th states. Clinton's team was invisible.

At that point the Clinton camp had no Super Tuesday strategy at all. They were entirely focused on Iowa. "Harold and I were both pushing very hard for more resources into the fifth and earlier decisions," said Guy Cecil, who had been put in charge of overseeing Super Tuesday. "And it just didn't happen. You can only set your hair on fire so many times."

Hillary and Bill Clinton bore a significant share of the responsibility. Because of their experiences in Iowa and Nevada, Bill Clinton had come to detest caucuses. He was persuaded that the Obama campaign had engaged in fraud in Nevada and still had questions about the legitimacy of the Iowa effort. Whenever either Bill or Hillary spoke about primaries and caucuses, they were dismissive of caucuses as favoring the kind of people likely to support Obama: liberal party activists, better-educated and wealthier Democrats who had flexible hours and were more likely to attend the caucuses. The caucuses also would draw the antiwar Democrats who were attracted to Obama and could not forgive Hillary Clinton for her 2002 vote.

No one in authority in the Clinton campaign ever offered a clear explanation of how the apparent decision to avoid the caucus states on Super Tuesday and the remainder of February happened—or accepted responsibility. One adviser said of her team, "It was malpractice what they did to her." Penn absolved himself of any responsibility, saying he was not invited to the meetings where the targeting decisions were made. Solis Doyle said it was preposterous to think that Penn as chief strategist did not have a major voice in where they would compete. Ickes agreed with Solis Doyle; Penn said Ickes cut money from the budget to poll the caucus states. Henry said there was no specific decision to ignore the caucus states, just a series of decisions that led them to concentrate their resources elsewhere. Money was tight at that point and forced them to make difficult decisions.

Late on the night of February 1, Obama's campaign touched down in Boise. It had been six days since his victory in South Carolina, four since the Kennedy endorsement rally. The Kennedy endorsement alone, Clinton's advisers later calculated, provided Obama with millions of dollars' worth of free advertising.

Edwards had quit the race days after his third-place finish in South Carolina, and Clinton and Obama had met the day before for their first one-on-one debate. Held in Los Angeles, it was a civil affair in contrast to the Myrtle Beach brawl, highlighting the historic reality that the Democrats' nominee would now shatter either the racial or the gender barrier. Instead of spending more time in California with its 370 delegates, Obama accepted his advisers' recommendation to travel to Idaho, which would award just eighteen delegates on Super Tuesday.

In Boise, Obama awoke to light snow that made the roads slick. His rally was scheduled for 9 a.m. at the Taco Bell Arena on the Boise State campus. Despite the weather, crowds started arriving hours before, with traffic snarled to a standstill and lines stretching half a mile from the arena. When Obama entered, an explosion of cheers greeted him from a crowd numbering more than fourteen thousand, nearly three times the number who had attended the Democratic caucuses in the entire state of Idaho four years earlier. Obama looked out at the crowd with a sense of awe. "So they told me there weren't any Democrats in Idaho," he teased them. They hooted and applauded even louder.

Plouffe's February 5th go-everywhere, play-everywhere strategy was now on full display. From Boise, Obama flew to Minnesota, where eighteen thousand people turned out to see him in a basketball arena. From there, it was on to St. Louis for a nighttime rally with twenty thousand people on the floor of the Rams' football stadium. In Delaware the next day he drew twenty thousand, and in Connecticut the day after, seventeen thousand more.

Clinton, who had long assumed February 5th would be the day she secured her nomination, could now sense the gathering momentum of Obama's candidacy. She was forced to scramble, and her voice was raspy from too little sleep and endless rallies. She was in St. Louis two days before Super Tuesday. It was Super Bowl Sunday—the New England Patriots against the New York Giants. "Somebody asked me today who I'm rooting for," she told a labor audience. "Please! You know, we've got two big contests coming up. We've got the Super Bowl tonight and Super Tuesday. I want the New York team to win both." She got half her wish.

After her loss in South Carolina, her advisers saw their projected Super Tuesday delegate estimates slip. Now the price of her pledge to support sanctions against Florida became painfully clear. Cecil said later, "There's no doubt that Florida would have been very helpful in stemming that tide and giving us something else to talk about: winning an election in a big state with delegates allocated to it." Her team earlier had anticipated that she would emerge from Super Tuesday with a lead in both pledged delegates and superdelegates. Their new calculations showed Obama gaining strength. Her strategy now looked extraordinarily shaky.

The media narrative had returned to one of Obama's momentum. The only question was, did he have enough time to overcome Clinton's lead in most of the states? Polls showed California closing. With that came talk about a possible Super Tuesday knockout blow to Clinton. But at Obama headquarters, Plouffe was still nervous. Surviving February 5 was still critical. Before South Carolina, Plouffe had feared Clinton might win a hundred more delegates on Super Tuesday. By the day of the voting, he was mildly pessimistic. "I did not think we were going to be ahead in delegates that day and I thought we'd be lucky to win more states," he said.

The Super Tuesday returns came cascading in. In the early evening, Clinton was the beneficiary of time zones and geography. She racked up a big and expected victory in New York and won New Jersey handily. She took Massachusetts, even though Obama had the support of the Kennedys, Governor Deval Patrick, and Senator John F. Kerry. The cable networks made much of that. At Obama headquarters, the staff pounded on the networks to show Obama's victory in the Kansas caucuses. But Clinton was winning Arizona, where Obama had the endorsement of Governor Janet Napolitano, and was ahead in New Mexico, seemingly further evidence of Obama's weakness among Latinos. And as midnight neared, she had a solid lead in California. Most viewers shut off their televisions. The story at that point appeared to be Clinton's success in blunting Obama's momentum. Plouffe knew otherwise. Late into the night the tide began to shift. By early morning it was clear at Obama campaign headquarters that he had managed to eke out a narrow victory in delegates and would capture a greater number of contests, even if they were the smaller caucus states. More important, the survival strategy he had been pursuing since the fall had worked even better than he had hoped—thanks to his momentum from South Carolina.

Two pairs of states tell that story. The first are New Jersey and Idaho. New Jersey was one of the four Clinton base states; Idaho, the prototypical caucus opportunity for Obama. New Jersey had 107 delegates at stake on

Super Tuesday, Idaho just eighteen. Clinton won New Jersey by ten points (54 percent to 44 percent) and won eleven more delegates than Obama. But Obama's investment in tiny Idaho neutralized the impact of New Jersey, as he won there by an astounding sixty-two points, more than 79 percent to Clinton's 17. With that margin, he gained twelve more delegates than Clinton. Plouffe had assumed that Obama would win the caucus states, but hardly by the margins achieved. The candidates' home states provide the other example of how Obama outmaneuvered Clinton. New York had 232 delegates at stake to 153 in Illinois. That should have meant she would come out of those states with more delegates. But Obama kept the race closer in New York than Clinton managed to do in Illinois, thanks to the decision to campaign on Clinton's home turf. Clinton, though she was born and raised in Illinois, had ignored her home state. The result was that Obama netted more delegates from Illinois than she did from delegate-rich New York.

Plouffe had calculated that if Obama could survive Super Tuesday by keeping the delegate count close and then do well for the rest of the month of February, the two campaigns might then be in a struggle that would last into the spring. But as he studied the results he came to a far more surprising conclusion—one not apparent to the expert commentators on television or in the press: "I really thought that night we were going to win the nomination," he said.

CHAPTER FOURTEEN

The Fighter

"This is like a great movie that's gone on about half an hour too long."

—Obama, after defeating Hillary in eleven straight contests

After Super Tuesday, Hillary Clinton lost eleven consecutive contests in fourteen days. She was trounced not only in caucus states like Washington, Nebraska, and Maine, but also in primaries in Virginia, Maryland, and Wisconsin, staggering losses that broke the morale at Clinton headquarters. The impact of her failure to compete fully in the caucuses was now devastatingly clear. With the conclusion of the February 19 Wisconsin primary, more than 2,200 delegates had been awarded—four-fifths in primaries, the remainder in caucuses. In the states with primaries, Obama had won just 27 more delegates than Clinton, but in the states with caucuses he had accumulated 138 more than she had. That meant that 80 percent of his lead came from caucuses, though they accounted for barely a fifth of the total delegates. Clinton's campaign had blown a critically important opportunity. Given the Democratic Party rules for allocating delegates, Obama now had what amounted to an insurmountable lead.

Obama drew enormous crowds and favorable press. He could see the finish line and was eager to cross it. Shortly after the Wisconsin primary he told Axelrod, "This is like a great movie that's gone on about half an hour too long." He was weary of the battle, as was his chief strategist. "I'm tired of fighting with my friends," Axelrod told us as he waited for Obama to speak before more than twenty thousand people in the shadow of the Texas Capitol on a chilly February evening.

Clinton's campaign was now in total disarray. "It was like acid inside," said a senior Clinton adviser. Reporters preparing expected postmortems found advisers eager to settle scores with one another publicly. With Solis Doyle gone soon after Super Tuesday, Penn became the prime target. He was criticized for his strategy of inevitability and incumbency in an election year dominated by change and attacked for his brusque and imperious manner.

As the campaign imploded in January and February, the long-running argument over how to present Clinton continued. Her advisers had long fought over whether they should attack Obama or try to show Hillary in a more appealing way. Now they argued over the message going forward. The disagreement resurfaced the day after New Hampshire at a meeting at the Clinton headquarters. Accounts describe a surreal gathering that began late in the day and went on until late in the night. Bill Clinton was there, as was Hillary. Advisers floated in and out, debating their opinions, disagreeing on what to do next. Penn came with a proposal to focus on the theme of community, an American community. It sounded like something Bill Clinton might have done in a series of speeches late in his presidency. No one liked the idea.

Mandy Grunwald argued that the template ought to focus on struggling families. She pointed to Hillary's moment in New Hampshire, when she welled up with tears as she was talking about fighting for people who themselves were struggling. All great campaigns that have fended off challenges, she said, have been about fighting for people—that was how Bill Clinton had defeated Paul Tsongas, how Walter Mondale had beaten Gary Hart, how Al Gore had stopped Bill Bradley. "Putting people first," the theme of Clinton's 1992 campaign, was still a model worth following, she said. Penn worried about anything that smacked of class warfare. Others were not sure it would work.

Days later, Roy Spence, who had been Mondale's ad maker in 1984 and was close to both Clintons, had a counterproposal: the "solutions business." Hillary should stress that she was about solving problems. For a time, the campaign tried that message—to little effect. It seemed contrived; it did not capture the mood of change; it was too detached from more passionate focus on working families. Hillary shifted to a message with more fire, and greater focus on hard-hit families.

Penn and Grunwald, often allies in the past, began to part ways over the message. They argued over ads. One exchange became so intense that Guy Cecil walked out in disgust. "You guys need to grow up," he snapped. "You're acting like kids." Penn continued his feud with Ickes. He disagreed with Wolfson over basic strategy. Critics said he was too powerful. Penn complained that he never had enough authority to do what he really wanted, to attack Obama relentlessly. Nerves were raw as the once mighty Clinton team absorbed the reality of Obama's now strong position. After an argument with Wolfson, Singer snapped, dropping a series of F-bombs before storming out of the headquarters. He stayed away the rest of the week, cooling down. "At that point, everybody had reached a breaking point with the press," said a senior Clinton adviser. "The press had reached their breaking point with us. And we all had reached our breaking point with each other."

Everyone understood the math. In addition to the 3,253 pledged delegates, there were approximately 800 superdelegates—Democratic elected officials and other party leaders—who were automatically given seats at the national convention. Under party rules, they were free to vote for any candidate of their choosing, regardless of which candidate had more pledged delegates. Harold Ickes and his deputy Lisa DiBartolomeo had prepared a memo on the eve of Super Tuesday that anticipated Obama would win more pledged delegates that day—and that Clinton could lose almost every subsequent contest for the remainder of the month. Her candidacy then depended on winning the support of superdelegates. Obama's advisers were making the case that the superdelegates should not override the popular will of Democratic voters, but Clinton was stressing that she would be the stronger nominee in November. The South Carolina primary, however, had damaged the relationship the Clintons had with much of the party establishment, which made her chances of winning over those superdelegates that much harder. "We are in for a real fight. . . . Given some breaks it is a fight that she can win," Ickes and DiBartolomeo wrote in the memo, which was later obtained by Josh Green of the *Atlantic*. "But it will be a fight." That was the rosy scenario.

Ahead on March 4 lay Ohio and Texas. Bill Clinton himself set expectations dangerously high for Hillary. An Obama victory in either state would knock Hillary out of the race, Bill suggested publicly while campaigning in Texas two days after Wisconsin. Even Hillary seemed resigned to losing, or so some thought on the night of February 21 when she and Obama met on the campus of the University of Texas for one of two debates before the March 4 primaries. As the session was ending, CNN's Campbell Brown asked both candidates to recall a moment in life that had tested them as a president is when confronted by crises. Obama gave a perfunctory and safe answer. Clinton created a stir with hers. "I think everybody here knows I've lived through some crises and some challenging moments in my life," she said in obvious reference to her husband's affair with Monica Lewinsky. She talked about the lives of people she had met and their struggles. "You know, the hits I've taken in life are nothing compared to what goes on every single day in the lives of people across our country," she said.

At this point she reached out to shake Obama's hand. In the press room, there was a collective "Where is this going?" moment. "I am honored, I am honored to be here with Barack Obama," she said. "I am absolutely honored. Whatever happens, we're going to be fine. You know, we have strong support from our families and our friends. I just hope that we'll be able to say the same thing about the American people, and that's what this election should be about."

Her words sounded like a valedictory, but as the coming days would show, they were not an exit from the stage.

Obama's team was determined to bring the nomination contest to a close on March 4. One day in February, Plouffe called Jon Carson and Larry Grisolano into a conference room at the Chicago headquarters. They were the field generals running two major departments in the campaign, Grisolano overseeing the media, polling, and research, and Carson directing the ground operations. By then Obama's victories were producing an avalanche of money (the campaign would take in a staggering $55 million in February alone) and Plouffe was ready to spend it to knock Clinton out of the race. He had a pool of between $15 and $20 million that he was budgeting for March 4 (which included Rhode Island and Vermont as well as Ohio and Texas). His instructions were straightforward. Spend the money, he told them. Let's end it.

But for all of Obama's advantages, neither Ohio nor Texas presented an easy victory. Clinton's Texas roots were deep. As a college student, she had gone there in 1972 to work for the Democratic National Committee while Bill Clinton was helping run George McGovern's Texas campaign. In 1992, the Clintons desperately wanted to win Texas, despite its growing red-state leanings. But Bush easily won the state. Even so, neither Clinton ever lost their affinity for Texas.

Their experiences then, and later during Bill's presidency, had left Hillary with ties to every possible community and constituency, from Ann Richards liberals to labor leaders in Houston to the moneyed crowd in Dallas, plus her connections to African-Americans and strong support from the state's large Hispanic community. Obama was a newcomer who hoped to appeal to a new generation of Texans, both Hispanics and Anglos. But he had little time to make his case. As Hidalgo County Judge J. D. Salinas told an Obama adviser who called seeking an endorsement, "It's too late."

Ohio was even more daunting. The state's economic woes made its electorate particularly receptive to Clinton's focus on bread-and-butter issues. Though Obama had begun his career as a community organizer, he had been slow to develop his voice on economic issues. Clinton might not be warm and fuzzy, but on economic issues voters trusted the Clinton name and record. Beyond that, blue-collar Ohio, southern Ohio, Appalachian Ohio appeared resistant to Obama. He constantly had to knock down mysterious e-mails and insidious Internet traffic falsely suggesting that he was Muslim. There were questions about his patriotism, stemming from a photo that seemed to suggest he refused to put his hand over his heart when he said the Pledge of Allegiance; the photo had actually been taken during the singing of the national anthem during the Tom Harkin steak fry in Iowa in September 2007 when, like millions of fans at sports contests, he stood with arms at his sides.

Just who was this man? voters wondered aloud as they shared their doubts with neighbors and reporters. Clinton benefited from the support of Ohio Governor Ted Strickland, who had led the Democratic resurgence there in 2006 and intuitively understood the conservative parts of southeastern Ohio. He devised a plan for the primary that would put both Clintons into the rural areas of the state during the final week of the primary campaign.

They were her last lifeline. She was counting on a strategy that would produce victories in the big states and thus persuade the superdelegates that Obama was not electable in the fall.

Clinton's generous words to Obama in Austin proved a fleeting moment of harmony in a contest that quickly turned bitter. If anyone thought she was preparing for a graceful exit, they did not understand her grit and determination. She was motivated by a belief that she would be the superior president and the more electable nominee against John McCain in November. She was also driven by a constitution and a work ethic that would not let her give up. Against the odds, she fought harder. Her message became more populist.

Two days after the Texas debate, she was handed a pair of Obama fliers that attacked her positions on health care and the North American Free

Trade Agreement. She responded with a withering denunciation of Obama during a press conference in Cincinnati. Obama's charges were "false and discredited," she said. She accused him of hypocrisy, of running a campaign of hope from his pedestal at big rallies while employing tactics "right out of Karl Rove's playbook." She called his campaign destructive and ended with a memorable challenge to her rival: "So shame on you, Barack Obama. It is time you ran a campaign that is consistent with your messages in public. That's what I expect from you. Meet me in Ohio. Let's have a debate about your tactics and your behavior in this campaign."

When that debate took place at Cleveland State University, Clinton was put on the defensive by moderators Brian Williams and Tim Russert of NBC News. She tried to fight back against Obama on health care, accusing him of putting forth a plan that fell short of the Democratic goal of universal coverage. But it was clear she was feeling the stress of her precarious situation. At one point she flared testily when she thought the moderators were not being evenhanded. "Could I just point out that, in the last several debates, I seem to get the first question all the time?" she complained. "And I don't mind. You know, I'll be happy to field them, but I do find it curious. And if anybody saw *Saturday Night Live*, you know, maybe we should ask Barack if he's comfortable and needs another pillow."

Days earlier, *SNL* had mocked the press over its fawning treatment of Obama; the Clinton campaign now was determined to embarrass the press into giving tougher coverage of Obama, who disparaged that attempt. "I am a little surprised that all the complaining about the refs has actually worked as well as it has for them," Obama told reporters. "This whole spin of how the press has just been so tough on them and not tough on us—I didn't expect that you guys would bite on that."

Five days before the primaries, she launched her toughest ad. Penn had finally gotten his way. The ad—his ad!—was titled "3 a.m." and showed sleeping children, a worried mother, and the sound of a phone ringing. When there is a crisis in the middle of the night, who do you want answering the phone in the White House? the ad asked. All you had to do was pose the question, and everybody knew the answer, Penn believed. The ad aired only in Texas, where Clinton's campaign was most worried and where economic issues alone were not enough to assure her victory, and it dominated coverage the final weekend, but Plouffe was dubious about its effect. Nevertheless he moved instantly to counter with an ad of his own. "Voters believe Barack Obama would be a strong commander in chief who would have the judgment and approach to handle a crisis," Plouffe said.

Despite the huge crowds, the momentum, and a sense of inevitability, Obama was once again losing his edge. His change message was becoming blurred and more conventional. Was he change or just another typical politician? He seized on NAFTA as a wedge issue to use against Clinton in Ohio, citing her support for the trade agreement while her husband was president. But then, in the closing days before the two primaries, reports surfaced about a meeting that one of his economic advisers, Austan Goolsbee of the University of Chicago, had convened at the Canadian consulate in Chicago. The reports said Goolsbee had assured the Canadians that Obama's tough anti-NAFTA stand was merely campaign rhetoric and not to be taken seriously. Obama denied the description of the meeting, but it dogged him nonetheless.

More distractions erupted on the eve of the primary. Tony Rezko, the Chicago developer who had been a significant Obama contributor and had sold Obama a small piece of property next to the Obama home in Hyde Park, went on trial for corruption charges. "I don't excuse myself for having made an error," Obama told reporters, "and I've said that repeatedly." Was there anything new, he asked in exasperation, other than the fact of the trial and the Clinton campaign's decision to make an issue of it? Nothing, the Clinton camp suggested, other than a possible vulnerability for Obama if he were to become the nominee.

For the first time since New Hampshire, the sure-footed instincts of Obama's operation broke down. He was campaigning at high altitude while Clinton was in the trenches. As in New Hampshire, she appeared to want victory more. Both were on the edge of exhaustion, but her days were longer and her perseverance greater. Then the Obama campaign made a key tactical error—the single biggest mistake of the nomination contest. Plouffe decided to have Obama split his time between Ohio and Texas in the final days. Later he concluded that had Obama focused exclusively on Texas he might have won the primary and ended the race. That was questionable hindsight, for in those final seventy-two hours, Hillary Clinton was the better candidate.

She also shuttled back and forth between the two states. From Texas she slipped away from her press corps and flew to New York for a surprise appearance on *Saturday Night Live*. The cast reenacted the Ohio debate, portraying Clinton as shrill and obnoxious and the moderators as fawning protectively over Obama. "Do I really laugh like that?" she asked after Amy Poehler mimicked what had become known as the candidate's cackle. Her campaign was cheered by the appearance—finally some humor from

Hillary. From there it was on to Ohio for a day that took her from the out-skirts of Columbus into some of the hardest-hit areas of the state, around Youngstown and Akron, before ending with an evening rally in Cleveland.

Her stump speech by then was a recitation of tales of woe: poignant stories of real people she had met or been told about along the campaign trail who were grappling with adversity—job losses, no health care coverage—and for whom there has been no happy ending. She wore their stories on her sleeve, and her audiences instantly responded in a way that said they knew the kinds of people she described. Campaigning through central Ohio days earlier, Bill Clinton asked those in his audiences to raise their hands if they knew someone without health insurance. All over the gymnasiums, hands shot up. Hillary's answer to all this hardship was not just to empathize with it but to show a fighting spirit. Ads featuring Strick-land repeatedly used the word "fighter" to describe her. The fight phraseol-ogy drowned out almost everything else coming from the campaign. An audience in a high school gymnasium in Westerville responded with foot-stomping approval when Clinton shouted, "One thing you know about me. I am not afraid to get into a fight on your behalf."

In New Hampshire, she had found her voice with a teary-eyed moment when her emotions got the best of her. In Ohio she found a different voice, one that took the vulnerabilities and problems of others and put them on her shoulders. This was the authentic Clinton, more so than the emotional Hil-lary in the New Hampshire diner. Her message to Ohio in the final hours was not uplifting, but it was direct and determined. She had become the embodiment of the voters who had the power to save her candidacy. She talked of the resilience of people in Ohio. What she hoped was that they would see the same strength in her and reward it with their votes.

Obama awaited the returns on the night of March 4 in San Antonio, where the chilly weather and small crowd seemed an ominous sign. Clinton cel-ebrated in Ohio, where the strains of Bruce Springsteen's "The Rising" expressed the metaphor that her campaign had been looking for since New Hampshire. The delegate numbers would eventually make the evening's results almost a wash. Clinton would win more in Ohio, but in Texas, with a split system of primary and caucus on the same day, Obama would even-tually come out ahead. But the popular vote was featured in the coverage and the analysis. In Texas, Clinton emerged with a narrow popular-vote victory. In Ohio, she won decisively.

Her campaign was in debt and still mired in internecine warfare. The delegate math still seemed impossible to overcome. But Clinton's victory provided the rationale to keep the race going. She vowed to keep fighting. "You know what they say: 'As Ohio goes, so goes the nation,'" she said. "Well, this nation's coming back and so is this campaign. We're going on, we're going strong, and we're going all the way." Obama insisted that her successes would not stop his march toward victory. "We know this," he said. "No matter what happens tonight, we have nearly the same delegate lead as we had this morning and we are on our way to winning this nomination."

On primary day, Obama was subdued. He had spent part of the day in his hotel suite. Michelle, Eric Whitaker, and Valerie Jarrett were there. Obama could not sit still. He paced the room as they watched a movie. He conferred with his advisers and looked at the numbers. He worked on his speech. They all ate a quiet dinner. By then the results were clear. His hopes of ending the nomination battle had evaporated. He knew the consequences. This was not a loss like New Hampshire, a defeat that truly threatened his candidacy. But in many ways it was more disheartening, because it meant there would be no early end to the battle. "New Hampshire was a gut check," he told us. "In New Hampshire, all our momentum from Iowa had been broken and we're looking at a bunch of contests. We could have lost [the nomination] after New Hampshire. After Ohio and Texas, my attitude was, we will win this thing but it will be painful."

The next morning, Obama had breakfast in the hotel before flying to Chicago. He was pensive as he thought about what the results meant. Efforts to cheer him fell flat. Michelle was eager to get back to Chicago and be with their daughters, and with the difficult assignment of telling them that their father would not be spending much time at home in the coming weeks. Obama said he wanted to meet with his staff, to hold an unscheduled gathering of the high command. The ride back was quiet. Barack and Michelle sat together and talked through part of the flight.

The staff was exhausted and dispirited. Axelrod, after seeming weary of the sniping, sounded newly pugnacious, telling reporters Obama would not sit idly by while under attack (though that had never been the case). "What's good for the goose is good for the gander," he told reporters. Gibbs said later, "We knew we were not going to have the luxury of winning this thing in March. We're not going to have the luxury of spending two months getting ready for the general election. We're not going to have all those things you wish you had. We're not going to get a week and a half off. At that point, all your batteries are dead because the truth is we've been running this marathon at a sprint pace for a really, really long time."

Obama was scheduled to take the rest of the day off. When he got back to Chicago, he went home, showered, and returned to the headquarters. He wasn't happy, but he took time to walk around the office, shaking hands with the young staffers, many of whom he barely knew. At the staff meeting, he had a notebook or piece of paper and Gibbs could see that the page was covered with jottings. Obama had written a series of lists: things he could have done better, things the staff could have done better. "He started off by saying, 'Look I'm not here to point fingers, because I can think of a dozen things I could have done better or more in the last couple of weeks. But plainly we didn't do well and we ought to figure out why and make sure we do better next time,'" Axelrod recalled.

Everyone sensed that Clinton had outcampaigned Obama in the final days of Ohio and Texas and that the style of their campaign needed to change. "She was campaigning close to the ground in a very visceral way," Axelrod said. "We were doing these iconic rallies which [gave a] sense of this cult-like following, but didn't give people the sense of closeness." Obama wanted smaller events where there was no separation between candidate and voters. He wanted to get back to being authentic, back to the message that had brought him into the race.

What made the day more difficult was the knowledge that Pennsylvania would likely be a repeat of Ohio. The Pennsylvania primary was then seven weeks away, seven weeks in which Obama would face repeated questions about why he couldn't win the big states, why he was struggling with white working-class voters, why this, why that. They would go through seven weeks and Clinton almost certainly would win another primary. The delegate math still favored him; she had few options and minimal hopes. The battle for the nomination might effectively be decided, but it was far from over. Obama's failures in Ohio and Texas were costly.

As he was leaving the meeting, Obama paused and looked back at his team. "Look, I'm not yelling at you guys," he said. He started to leave again and then stopped one more time. "Although after blowing through twenty million dollars in the last couple of weeks I could yell at you. But I'm not yelling at you." He laughed and left the room. The primary season was just two months old. Clinton's comeback meant three more hard months ahead.

CHAPTER FIFTEEN

Politics in Black and White

"God damn *America!"*

—The Reverend Jeremiah Wright Jr.

The losses in Ohio and Texas plunged Obama into two of his worst months. Almost overnight, the coverage changed. Before, he was the gifted, transformational politician leading a movement for change. For the next eight weeks, he was a candidate surrounded by question marks. He made mistakes, and events also moved against him.

Ten days after Ohio and Texas, the most serious threat to his candidacy appeared in the grainy videos of his pastor, the Reverend Jeremiah Wright, thundering, "God *damn* America!" from the pulpit of Trinity United Church of Christ. The preacher in the videos was not the benign and fatherly figure Obama had described as his spiritual adviser and inspiration for the title of his second best-selling book, *The Audacity of Hope*. This pastor was divisive and offensive, filled with resentment toward white America and the national government Obama was seeking to lead.

Days after the 9/11 attacks, Wright had been captured on video shouting, "We bombed Hiroshima. We bombed Nagasaki. And we nuked far more than the thousands in New York and the Pentagon—and we never batted an eye. We have supported state terrorism against the Palestinians and black South Africans and now we are indignant because the stuff we have done overseas is now brought right back into our own front yards." Then, pirouetting before the congregation, he roared, "America's chickens—are coming home—to roost!"

Race, the topic Obama had sought to transcend, now dominated the discussion about him. He wanted to be a post-racial candidate, not an extension of the civil rights generation, and suddenly he found himself at the center of a controversy that highlighted the gulf that still divided blacks and whites. "What you had was a moment where all the suspicions and misunderstandings that are embedded in our racial history were suddenly laid bare," he said during one of our interviews. He knew there was no way to dodge this crisis. "If we had not handled the Reverend Wright episode properly," he said, "I think we could have lost."

ABC News brought Jeremiah Wright to the public's attention after the network obtained videotapes of Wright's sermons that were sold at his church. During nearly four decades as senior pastor, Wright had built the church into a powerhouse of religious and social activity on Chicago's South Side and Wright had a reputation as one of the nation's leading African-American ministers. That he became an antagonist was no surprise to the Obama campaign. On the eve of announcing his presidential candidacy in February 2007, Obama had withdrawn his invitation for Wright to deliver the invocation. At that time, *Rolling Stone* was about to publish an article quoting Wright as saying America believed in "white supremacy and black inferiority," as well as using a vulgarity from the pulpit. Obama recalled for us his conversation with Wright then: "I said to him, 'You know what, you will end up being a center of attention, and I think potentially tagged unfairly, and we don't want a huge distraction.'" Although Wright's controversial sermons were readily available, no one on Obama's staff ordered up a thorough search of their content. "We were caught by surprise by those videos," Obama admitted to us. "It was just bad research on our part."

Obama had joined the church almost twenty years earlier as he was attempting to put down roots in his newly adopted home of Chicago. Wright married Barack and Michelle and baptized their daughters. While Obama considered Wright a provocative and fiery preacher, he claimed never to have seen or heard the most incendiary of his sermons. "Reverend Wright has a lot of fine qualities," Obama told us. "He's a great preacher . . . but Reverend Wright remained rooted in the rhetoric of the sixties. . . . What he was saying was not considered in any way exceptional in the African-American community for his generation. He never updated or refreshed that worldview to accommodate the changes that were taking place in America. And what you were seeing in Reverend Wright and those statements were not only offensive to everybody in many ways, but it also showed an anger and bitterness . . . that may be more acceptable in some circles in the African-American community but is never acceptable in mainstream America. And so you had that sudden, really volatile potential clash of visions."

The Wright story exploded on Friday, March 14. Obama returned to Chicago that afternoon already scheduled for interviews with the two Chicago papers about the controversy over his relationship with the corrupt Chicago developer Tony Rezko. But the Wright controversy demanded his immediate reaction. Obama's religious outreach adviser, Josh DuBois, had prepared a statement in Obama's name. After reading it, Obama decided to draft his own—eight paragraphs in which he described Wright's remarks as "inflammatory and appalling." Obama also decided he wanted to go on television that night. Some advisers questioned whether an on-camera interview was advisable. Wouldn't a strong statement suffice? No, Obama said. People are looking at Reverend Wright. They need to see me too. Valerie Jarrett remembered him saying, "I want them to look at me and I want them to hear and feel me. . . . It's not enough to just do a statement." That night on MSNBC, Obama condemned Wright's words but stepped gingerly around the man himself. "I have known him seventeen years," Obama said. "He helped bring me to Jesus and helped bring me to church. He's like an uncle who talked to me, not about political things and social views, but faith and God and family."

Obama's last order to his staff was to schedule a major speech on race as quickly as possible. As far back as Iowa, Obama had talked to his advisers about giving such a speech, but the right moment never came. Now was the time. "I want to deal with this squarely," he told his advisers. "I want to talk about this in a larger context. It's a huge thing that we have to confront."

Because Pennsylvania was his next primary, the speech was set for Philadelphia. Jon Favreau was told to draft something. Favreau balked. This is too personal a speech, he said. Before he started to write, he needed to hear from Obama, but Obama was campaigning. Not until 10:30 on Saturday night did they finally speak. Obama seemed resigned. Given his relationship with Wright and the church, he told Favreau, this would certainly be tough for him personally—that's a price of running for president, he added. For the next forty-five minutes, as Favreau typed into his computer, Obama dictated what he wanted to say—stream-of-consciousness thoughts about the themes of the speech and lawyerly precision about its structure.

While Obama filmed new campaign commercials on Sunday, Favreau worked on the draft, finishing it early that evening and sending it to Obama.

At home in Hyde Park, Obama began transforming the draft of what would be the most important speech of his campaign into his own words. Jarrett spoke to him around 11 p.m. "This is really complicated," he told her. The speech had been in his head for a long time; finding the right words still escaped him. Good luck, she said. "He had to do it himself. Every word had to be his word. The most important thing was that people knew he meant what he said. And the only way they were going to know what he means to say is if they were his words."

Obama worked far into the night, spent Monday campaigning, and then hunkered down in his hotel in Philadelphia to finish his draft. He e-mailed it to his advisers at 2 a.m. the morning of the speech.

"I think it's good," Obama told friends that morning. They had come to Philadelphia to offer support. That was Michelle's idea. She was there, as were Jarrett, Marty Nesbitt and Eric Holder. Jarrett's nerves were raw after a weekend of watching the video of Wright. "We all appreciated the painful irony of a person with whom he had had a relationship being responsible for potentially derailing his campaign," Jarrett said. Obama talked basketball as he waited to go onstage.

His text was the Constitution, his theme "A More Perfect Union." His most urgent goal was to explain his relationship to a minister whose words were so at odds with the tone and message of his own campaign. But he also wanted to speak frankly about the grievances and resentments that continued to divide black and white America.

Obama said Wright had expressed a "profoundly distorted view of this country—a view that sees white racism as endemic, and that elevates what is wrong with America above all that we know is right with America." While condemning Wright's words, Obama again declined to abandon his pastor. "I can no more disown him than I can disown the black community," he said. "I can no more disown him than I can my white grandmother." A grandmother, he added, who more than once uttered racial stereotypes "that made me cringe."

The rest of his speech set the controversy in a broader context, one that reflected "the complexities of race in this country that we've never really worked through—a part of our union that we have yet to perfect." He spoke of anger in the black community toward white Americans, resentment in white America toward black Americans, and the need for each side to understand the other. "This union may never be perfect," he said.

"But generation after generation has shown that it can always be perfected."

There were tears among his friends as he finished. Holder told everyone he wished his father had lived to see the moment. "I said what I wanted to say," Obama told his friends. "Let's see whether they understood what I was trying to say." Later, he told us, "I thought it was very important at that point for me to help translate the experiences both of Reverend Wright but also how the ordinary white American might feel in hearing Reverend Wright and how both sets of experiences were an outgrowth of our history and had to be acknowledged and dealt with instead of just papered over or reduced to a caricature. And I think that the speech in Philadelphia succeeded in doing that." His speech, he told us, "was one of my prouder moments of the campaign."

The question remained how it would be received. Axelrod told us a few minutes after the speech, "We were going to have this issue sometime. It might as well be now."

On March 21, Bill Richardson endorsed Obama at a critical time, helping to show that Reverend Wright had not frightened away high-profile Democrats. Given Richardson's ties to the Clintons—he served as United Nations ambassador and secretary of energy in the Clinton administration—the decision to back Obama was seen as a rejection of Hillary that came despite intensive efforts by both Clintons to win Richardson's support. Both Bill and Hillary had made repeated calls to him asking for his support. Former administration officials also pressured him, saying he owed the Clintons. "That's uncalled for," he said he told one caller. "I don't owe them anything. I served well. In fact I was always very loyal to President Clinton."

In a highly public moment of courtship, Bill Clinton had come to Santa Fe to watch the Super Bowl with Richardson. Clinton was still fuming over the way he had been treated during South Carolina. "We talked about the campaign," Richardson said. "He did feel the press had given him a bad rap: 'How can they call me a racist? Look what I did with African-Americans and Hispanics. The press is really after me and they're giving Obama a free ride.'" After the game, Richardson spoke to Hillary by phone. "She said, 'Bill, we need you, I need you to endorse me before Texas. Please consider. I hear you two ate everything at the Super Bowl. . . . I hear you smoked those terrible cigars of yours.' I said, 'Well, Senator, we'll be in touch.'"

Richardson was drawn to Obama, whose calls, he said, were always gracious. "This is Barack. Obama," he would say, with a short pause between his first and last names. He called Richardson regularly. As Richardson said, they were "gentle, elegant calls asking for an endorsement. 'Hey man, we can make history, let's make some history together, you, me, and Teddy.'" Richardson was also struck by Obama's casual elegance. One day, when they were together on Obama's bus, someone brought out some fruit. "Obama says, 'Where's the silverware?'" Richardson recalled. "So they bring in the silverware. He gets a little plate out and he starts like cutting the orange and then takes it and offers it to me. And I thought to myself, just grab the goddamn orange."

When Richardson finally decided to back Obama, his wife, Barbara, told him, "I'm behind you, but there's going to be fury on the other side." Before going public, he called Hillary. "I said, 'Senator, I just wanted you to know that tomorrow I'm going to endorse Senator Obama and it was a real tough decision for me,'" he told us. "And Hillary said, 'Bill, why, why?' And I said I think there's something special about this guy, something good. And I've gotten to know him and I think he's somebody that comes once in a generation. I really feel that. And I think you've run a great campaign. I love you both." He said Hillary responded, "But Bill, he can't win. He can't win. He can't win." She kept repeating that, Richardson said, and told him he was making a big mistake. "I could feel sort of the iciness on the other side," he said.

His call to Bill Clinton was not returned. James Carville publicly branded Richardson a traitor for endorsing Obama.

For the next two weeks, Obama appeared to be recovering. Immediately after the Wright videos appeared, Clinton's lead had widened, but after a few weeks, Obama was again gaining ground in Pennsylvania. Then came what Obama later told Matt Bai of the *New York Times Magazine* was "my biggest bonehead move" of the campaign.

On Sunday, April 6, Obama finished his campaigning with an evening fund-raiser in San Francisco. Most of his aides had returned to Chicago. On his own, in front of a friendly audience, Obama gave critics fresh evidence that he was out of touch with the real America. Because economic issues were now at the forefront of the campaign, Obama was trying to prove he could attract white working-class voters and appeal to those most affected by the downturn. In parts of Pennsylvania, that meant people who had been battered for years by the decline of the steel industry in the Mahoning Valley and by the contraction in the manufacturing sector. These voters saw little hope for the future and were skeptical of politicians who promised help. What he now said in San Francisco seemed to denigrate the very people he was struggling to win.

"You go into some of these small towns in Pennsylvania, and like a lot of small towns in the Midwest, the jobs have been gone now for twenty-five years and nothing's replaced them," Obama told his donors. "Each successive administration has said that somehow these communities are gonna regenerate and they have not. So it's not surprising then that they get bitter, they cling to guns or religion or antipathy to people who aren't like them or anti-immigrant sentiment or antitrade sentiment as a way to explain their frustrations."

The fund raiser was closed to the press. No one from the Obama campaign even had a recording of the comments. No one flagged headquarters that he had said something potentially controversial. But among those in the room was Mayhill Fowler, sixty-one, an Obama supporter and donor who was part of the *Huffington Post*'s "Off the Bus" reporting team of citizen journalists. The following Friday, after considerable soul-searching, she posted the remarks online. Within hours there were fifty thousand hits.

The Clinton team quickly mounted an attack to keep the controversy alive, organizing events and preparing statements for surrogates to heighten doubts about Obama. Since Ohio, Hillary had argued that she was the real champion of the beleaguered middle class, while Obama was the darling of the latte-drinkers. Now they had a vivid example and were determined to push it.

Not that they needed much help. Coming after Wright, Obama's comments provided prime material for cable TV, raising new questions about who he was and what he believed. Was he really as elitist as his comments in San Francisco sounded? Was he so out of touch with ordinary Americans that he would dismiss their faith and culture so insensitively? The next morning, we had breakfast with Axelrod in Chicago. He was wearing sweats under his jacket. He was clearly worried, while hoping that this would prove to be a passing tempest. "You can't assess these things as they're happening," he said. "But understanding this was not a helpful thing and we've got to dig ourselves out." After the primaries were over, he offered this assessment: "It was mildly damaging. But it came in the same period as the Reverend Wright stuff, which I think was much more damaging. At the end of the day . . . I think he fought his way through it and I think they overplayed it."

After Wright and "bitter," as his San Francisco comments were abbreviated by the media, Hillary Clinton was on the attack and would not let up. "I was taken aback by the demeaning remarks Senator Obama made about people in small-town America," she said in Indianapolis on April 12. "Senator Obama's remarks are elitist and out of touch. They are not reflective of the values and beliefs of Americans, certainly not the Americans that I know. . . . Americans who believe in the Second Amendment believe it's a matter of a constitutional right, Americans who believe in God believe it's a matter of personal faith." Obama tried to backpedal. "Obviously, if I worded things in a way that made people offended, I deeply regret that," he told a North Carolina newspaper.

Clinton repeated her criticisms at every stop. Irritated, Obama said that she was beginning to sound like Annie Oakley with all her appeals to gun owners. "Hillary Clinton's out there like she's on the duck blind every Sunday. She's packing a six-shooter. Come on, she knows better." But he continued to apologize. At a forum on faith and compassion, he described his words as "clumsy."

The controversy came amid new problems for Clinton. The first involved Hillary's embellishments about a trip to Bosnia she had made as First Lady. On the campaign trail, she described a harrowing arrival in Tuzla under sniper fire. Only when videos showed her being greeted on the tarmac by children did she recant and apologize. Later, Bill Clinton offered a spirited but inaccurate defense, which prompted Hillary to tell him to keep quiet.

Then she was forced to demote Mark Penn as chief strategist after the *Wall Street Journal* reported that, as CEO of Burson Marsteller, the giant public relations and lobbying firm, he had recently met with the Colombian ambassador. The Colombians were seeking to win passage of a free trade agreement that Clinton publicly opposed. Geoff Garin, who had been advising part-time, was named as co–chief strategist with communications director Howard Wolfson. The Penn demotion had both practical and symbolic significance. Symbolically, it removed the most visible antagonist from atop the campaign's management structure. Practically, the decision meant that Penn would never again play as central a role as he had before. He remained on the campaign team and continued to conduct polls (as did Garin) and offer advice. But other advisers found it far easier to ignore his ideas on strategy and message. The campaign became more collegial and, under the management of Maggie Williams and Cheryl Mills, operated with greater efficiency.

Despite Clinton's mishaps, Obama remained the focus of criticism and could not escape the charge that he wasn't connecting with white working-class voters. In Pennsylvania he adjusted his campaign style, scaling back on his big rallies in favor of roundtable discussions and informal stops at cafés or ice-cream shops. Clinton had the support of Governor Ed Rendell, the most prominent Pennsylvania Democrat, but Obama got the endorsement of Senator Bob Casey, whose pro-life father had been a popular governor. Casey was popular with the working-class voters Obama was trying to win, and the two campaigned by bus across the state. One day they stopped at a bowling alley for a photo opportunity. Obama, trying his hand on the lanes, embarrassed himself by rolling a thirty-seven. It was one more small indignity on top of more than a month of trouble.

A third bad moment for Obama came on April 16, when Obama and Hillary debated for the last time at the National Constitution Center in Philadelphia, where Obama had delivered his race speech. Obama now put forth one of the worst debate performances of his campaign.

He was in a foul mood before the debate. "I never felt surer that we were heading into a disaster as I did heading into that Philadelphia debate," Axelrod said later. "He had gotten word on his BlackBerry heading into the debate that Wright was going on a tour. He was preoccupied with that. He was completely distracted. He was on his BlackBerry through the debate prep. He just didn't want to do the debate. He was frankly just sick of debating Hillary Clinton." Obama took a long break during debate prep. Sometimes that helped. This time it did not. He was still unenthusiastic as the debate was ready to begin. "It was just a dreary day that yielded to a dreary night," Axelrod said.

ABC News hosted the debate, with anchor Charles Gibson and Sunday morning host George Stephanopoulos as moderators. Clinton was asked about her Bosnia exaggeration, but Obama drew tougher questions about his "bitter" comment and about Reverend Wright.

Obama called his "bitter" comment "mangled," saying it was neither the first nor last time he would make a mistake. Clinton went right at Obama. She spoke about her father and grandfather, who had grown up in Scranton. "I don't believe that my grandfather or my father or the many people whom I have had the privilege of knowing and meeting across Pennsylvania over many years cling to religion when Washington is not listening to them," she said. Asked whether Obama could beat John McCain, she danced around the question until Stephanopoulos pressed her. "Yes. Yes. Yes," she said. It was the most positive she had been about his November prospects, but she added, "I think I can do a better job."

Obama had gotten through earlier debates without too many embarrassing questions. Not this time. The moderators showed a video question from Nash McCabe of Latrobe. "I want to know if you believe in the American flag. I am not questioning your patriotism, but all our servicemen, policemen, and EMS wear the flag. I want to know why you don't." Obama, frustrated, responded, "I have never said that I don't wear flag pins or refuse to wear flag pins. This is the kind of manufactured issue that our politics has become obsessed with and, once again, distracts us from what should be my job when I'm commander in chief, which is going to be figuring out how we get our troops out of Iraq and how we actually make our economy better for the American people."

Stephanopoulos followed with a question about Obama's association with William Ayers, an issue that had been bubbling but had never been given a full airing in a debate. During the sixties and seventies Ayers was a member of the radical Weather Underground that had planted bombs at the Capitol and elsewhere. Decades later, he had worked with Obama on an education foundation board in Chicago. "This is a guy who lives in my neighborhood, who's a professor of English in Chicago who I know and who I have not received some official endorsement from," Obama said. "He's not somebody who I exchange ideas from on a regular basis. And the notion that somehow as a consequence of me knowing somebody who engaged in detestable acts forty years ago, when I was eight years old, somehow reflects on me and my values doesn't make much sense, George."

The moderators drew considerable criticism for their questions, especially from Obama's network of supporters around the country. But Obama suffered most from his performance.

Given the state's demographics and the solid working-class voters Clinton continued to attract, Obama was almost destined to lose Pennsylvania. But after the Wright controversy and the damage from his "bitter" comments, the debate slowed his movement and turned the primary wholly in Clinton's favor.

Obama's goal had been to keep her victory margin well below the ten points by which she had won Ohio. He failed. She won Pennsylvania by just over nine points, taking the white vote by twenty-six points (compared to thirty in Ohio). Obama attracted less support in the Philadelphia suburbs—a critically important area for Democratic candidates—than he had hoped. After revamping his campaign style, devoting most of seven weeks to Pennsylvania, and spending a record $11 million on television ads, Obama had made no real progress with white voters.

Obama and his advisers did not accept the analysis that he had a problem with white working-class voters. The press might have been obsessed with this, he told us, but "we were always just much more sanguine about it. Our view was never that we had a white working-class problem. Our view was that we had an age problem. Sixty-five and over was always our worst group; eighteen to twenty-nine was always our best group and it followed almost perfectly on graphs."

Despite these figures, Obama faced a critical question being raised both by the Clinton team and his critics: Why could he not win the major states, and how seriously would that affect his chances in a general election? No Democrat had ever won the nomination after losing primaries in Pennsylvania, Ohio, New York, New Jersey and California.

The Pennsylvania loss put new pressure on Obama as he headed toward the May 6 Indiana and North Carolina primaries. He was now certain he would be the Democratic nominee and believed that Clinton also knew that was so. But she was in the race to the end, determined to continue making the case that she would be the stronger general election candidate. Another five weeks of combat would prevent him from preparing for the fall campaign, threatening to damage him by exposing his weaknesses. "She was helping do the work of the Republicans by just beating up on him in pretty significant ways," an Obama adviser said.

The day after Pennsylvania, an unhappy Obama made a round of calls seeking advice and then convened his senior staff for a lengthy discussion. He felt his campaign had underperformed in Pennsylvania, and wanted to refocus his operation. "There was a clear message from the candidate that he did not want to win the nomination limping across the finish line," Anita Dunn, his communications director, said.

Then Reverend Wright reappeared. He was interviewed by Bill Moyers on PBS on April 25, feted at an NAACP dinner in Detroit two days later, and on Monday, April 28, spoke to a breakfast gathering at the National Press Club, where he declined to take back his most controversial comments about how the United States brought the 9/11 attacks on itself, praised the Nation of Islam leader the Reverend Louis Farrakhan, saying, "He didn't put me in chains," and, in a final thrust, dismissed Obama as a typical politician. Even though Wright's performance reinforced his image as a self-obsessed minister determined to salve his own damaged ego, his latest appearance could not have been worse for Obama. Yet Obama was slow to react. He was campaigning when he learned of Wright's latest barrage. How bad is it? he asked Jarrett by telephone. Not good, she said, but struggled to describe just how bad. You have to watch it. Under pressure to say something, Obama issued a tepid statement rebuking Wright, but it fell far short of what many of his friends and outside advisers believed was necessary. The best Obama could muster was "He does not speak for me."

The new eruption caused Obama real anguish. "The second one was in some ways more painful because I felt that was a personal breach on the part of Reverend Wright," he told us.

Obama and the senior staff conferred by phone. The question, as one adviser bluntly put it, was "How are we going to elect someone president of the United States who has this person as pastor?" Obama and his team agreed he would need a much stronger statement to mark his full break with Wright. It came the next day: "His comments were not only divisive and destructive, but I believe that they end up giving comfort to those who prey on hate, and I believe that they do not portray accurately the perspective of the black church," Obama said. "They certainly don't portray accurately my values and beliefs." He described Wright's comments as "outrageous" and "ridiculous."

After Wright's reappearance, Obama's numbers plummeted in Indiana. A CBS News/*New York Times* poll showed doubt about Obama's ability to win the nomination. And doubts about his values and his patriotism had grown, adding to concerns about whether he could win the general election. But the polls also showed that Clinton had been weakened by her combat with Obama. Geoff Garin told reporters that he saw two important shifts that favored Clinton over Obama in the fall. The economy was now the most important issue in the election, eclipsing Iraq, and Clinton did consistently better than Obama among voters who felt the economy was the most important issue.

With the Wright issue threatening his candidacy anew, Obama decided to make a major issue out of Clinton's support for a summer holiday from gasoline taxes. The dispute captured fundamental differences in their campaigns. He claimed she was practicing the old politics of pander; she argued that she was more willing to take whatever steps she could to help working families. Obama pushed the gas tax debate hard not just because of the clear philosophical difference with Clinton. By focusing voters on a substantive dispute, he hoped to divert attention from Reverend Wright.

Clinton, gambling that she would win Indiana easily, shifted more of her focus to North Carolina. If she could hold down Obama's margin there and decisively defeat him in Indiana, she would strengthen her argument to superdelegates that she would be stronger against McCain in November. As she began the final weekend of that campaign, she knew the script by heart: Once again her back was against the wall. Her slim hopes depended on her victories and on mistakes by Obama. If she couldn't emerge from the primaries with more delegates, she needed to overtake him in the popular vote. Only then might superdelegates start swinging back toward her.

She had found a groove, pushing forward relentlessly, demonstrating with each stop that she would not yield until she was defeated once and for all. The time was short and so her days were long. Most began very early in the morning and almost always stretched late into the night. Rallies. Town hall meetings. Small gatherings. Rope lines. Local interviews. Network heavies. Hotel arrivals after midnight. It was an endless rotation, repeated over and over again.

She throttled back on some of the hot rhetoric that had marked her closing days before the Ohio primary. She was less the pure fighter than in Ohio. But she was as resilient. North Carolina Governor Mike Easley, a supporter, told an audience in rural Kinston that she was "as tough as a lighter knot," a regionalism that refers to the hardest spots on a piece of pinewood. That brought a smile from the candidate. Her core message was "jobs, jobs, jobs." Her secondary message: "When I tell you I'll do something I'll do it, or move heaven and earth" trying.

She was looser, liberated from the constraints of being the inevitable front-runner. She attacked the rope lines with more gusto than even her husband. She signed endless autographs on everything imaginable—placards, scraps of paper, photos, books, boxing gloves. "Ha Ha! Hillary," she scrawled in large letters on the T-shirt of a young man in Terre

Haute. She roared when someone asked her to sign a placard that read, "I've got a crush on Hillary." She laughed even harder over a T-shirt worn by another man with Bill Clinton's likeness superimposed over a painting of Jesus. Before Kentucky Derby weekend, she told supporters in Louisville, "I want everybody to place a little money on the filly."

As the votes in Indiana and North Carolina neared, Obama's pace nearly equaled Clinton's. For several nights in a row he had only a few hours of sleep as the staff piled on extra events and flights. "We just had to dig deep," Obama told us later. "[We] probably worked as hard during that week as we did at any time in the election."

The night before Indiana, the campaign staged a big rally with Stevie Wonder in Indianapolis. When it was over, Obama had some time to relax before a late-night visit to a factory. As was often the case in moments of stress or relaxation, he was joined by friends Eric Whitaker, Valerie Jarrett, and Marty Nesbitt. Jarrett remembers Obama despondent. He told us, "We had lost Pennsylvania and now we're going into a couple of pretty tough states. We [were] just getting our groove back and suddenly this [Wright] thing pops up again. And you felt like, well maybe we're just not going to survive this. Maybe people are just going to feel too skittish or just feel that I was mortally wounded and that I wouldn't be able to survive a general election and that could start changing how delegates think."

Jarrett said she had never seen Obama as down as he was that night. "That was the worst night," she said. "There've been other tough nights, certainly, but for me there was no worse night. He was saying you know there's so many people who've worked so hard on this campaign, just how devastating it would be to lose because of Reverend Wright, somebody who's supposed to be on his side," Jarrett said. "It was a conversation where he was just so troubled by the whole episode. It was so bad we were just trying to, like, make jokes about it because, you know how some situations are just beyond the pale, and this one was way beyond the pale and we spent an hour trying to get him to laugh and he just wouldn't laugh. Finally Marty said something completely ridiculous and started to get a little bit of a response out of him."

At that point, Axelrod came into the room. He did not know how grim the mood had been earlier. He only saw Obama and his close friends laughing and smiling. I have some bad news, he told Obama. The final night of tracking in Indiana showed Clinton ahead by twelve points. Public polls showed the race far closer and Axelrod had been warned by pollster Paul Harstad that the numbers might simply reflect a bad one-night sample. But the poll appeared to confirm Obama's fears. He told the group: Whatever happens is going to happen.

CHAPTER SIXTEEN

Over the Top

"We now know who the Democratic nominee is going to be."

—Tim Russert, May 6, 2008

On the night of May 6, Clinton's staff settled into the war room at the campaign's Virginia headquarters. Mexican food, as always, had been ordered. Clinton was in Indianapolis awaiting the returns. Everyone anticipated another good night. Hillary and Bill were optimistic, believing she would win Indiana and come close in North Carolina. They had dipped once again into their personal fortune, lending her campaign more than a million dollars in the week before those votes. But that night, nothing went according to plan. The networks called North Carolina for Obama early—a double-digit victory. Then, as the Indiana returns dribbled in, for hours the TV analysts offered increasingly pessimistic commentary about her candidacy. Even after she finally narrowly won Indiana, their negative drumbeat continued.

Around midnight, NBC's Tim Russert declared, almost matter-of-factly, "We now know who the Democratic nominee is going to be and no one's going to dispute it." At Clinton headquarters, as one adviser recalled, after Russert's statement, "The air came out of the room."*

For weeks, Clinton's team had grasped at anything to keep alive the hope she might still defeat Obama. Now that hope had died. Obama's lead in pledged delegates was too large to overcome in the remaining contests. Short of a last act of defiance on her part that would risk shattering the Democratic Party and lessen its chances in November, she could not make the case she'd be able to accumulate enough delegates to win the nomination. Against great odds, after setbacks that might have destroyed weaker

---

* Tim Russert died of a heart attack on June 13, 2008.

candidates, Obama had prevailed. "He survived . . . six weeks that would have taken most other candidates down the drain, given the strength of Hillary Clinton," Harold Ickes later said. There was still another month to go before the last primary. But for Hillary Clinton, after a campaign of near-deaths and premature obits, her dream of becoming the first female president was over.

A week later, Clinton won West Virginia by forty-one points. The next week she won Kentucky by thirty-six points. Those two lopsided Clinton victories again raised doubts about whether Obama could win white working-class voters.* But on the day of Kentucky, Obama took Oregon handily. On June 1, Clinton won Puerto Rico. Then, on June 3, the final day of the long primary process, the two rivals split the results: Obama won Montana, Hillary won South Dakota. On that last day, Obama gained the support of enough superdelegates to assure his nomination. They came to his side in a rush. When the returns were finally in on the last night, he had enough delegates to claim the nomination. Barack Obama had neither limped nor sprinted across the finish line. Hillary Clinton had never given up.

The final chapter of her campaign could be said to have been the best time of her candidacy. In the face of near hopeless political odds, she displayed her greatest talent as a campaigner. She had begun the race as the inevitable nominee, and by the end found herself fighting off repeated calls to quit. "She could accept losing," one adviser said. "She could not accept quitting." After earlier months of turmoil and bitter internal strife, her campaign staff had functioned effectively and, mostly in the final two months, collegially. Most important, in that final period Hillary had found her voice, and her most effective campaign style. Axelrod described her in those days as "frighteningly good."

Her success came too late. In the crucial months of January and February, Obama had outplayed her. After Ohio and Texas, her strategy of necessity was focused on convincing uncommitted superdelegates that she would be the stronger nominee. Mark Penn believed brute force was needed to attract them. Obama's delegate team knew from their private conversations that that would never work (as did Clinton's delegate team).

---

* Talk that Obama could not win white working-class voters prompted John Edwards to endorse Obama. He called Obama the night of West Virginia to give him the news. Obama wanted to do it immediately. Edwards asked for time to put his thoughts together. He said Obama offered to get him talking points. The endorsement went ahead the next day. Edwards tried to call Hillary. She later told Elizabeth Edwards she was so upset she couldn't bring herself to call him back.

They had secured private pledges from many of the superdelegates, who were, they knew, risk-averse by nature. They preferred to avoid going public as long as possible. But the Obama team was confident they would never swing in Clinton's direction. We asked Garin why the Clinton campaign could never crack those superdelegates, many of whom had started out on her side. He said, "I think it's a mystery and an irony, and an irony in the sense that Hillary was seen as inevitable when it didn't matter and Obama was seen as inevitable when it did."

The popular vote ended in a near tie and amid competing estimates of the actual counts. The Web site Real Clear Politics estimated the popular vote from the primaries and caucuses, using official and unofficial sources, and found Obama had won 152,000 more than Clinton. His total was 17,822,145. Hers was 17,717,698.*

Obama's achievement was remarkable. He had toppled the mighty machine that everyone thought was invincible. On the night of Tuesday, June 3, he celebrated his victory in St. Paul, the site of the upcoming Republican National Convention. "Tonight we mark the end of one historic journey with the beginning of another—a journey that will bring a new and better day to America," he said. "Because of you, tonight I can stand before you and say that I will be the Democratic nominee for president of the United States of America." Of Clinton he said, "She has made history not just because she's a woman who has done what no woman has done before, but because she is a leader who inspires millions of Americans with her strength, her courage, and her commitment to the causes that brought us here tonight."

On the flight back to Chicago, Jim Margolis, Obama's media adviser, asked Obama to join him in a beer to celebrate. "I said, 'Hey, you just became essentially the nominee, how about a beer?' And he starts to say yeah, and then says, 'I've got [a speech to] AIPAC in the morning at 7:30.'"

Clinton appeared that night in New York in a grimy basement gymnasium at Baruch College. On the Monday flight from South Dakota back to New York, the *Washington Post's* Anne Kornblut reported that she had sat

---

* Part of the confusion stemmed from the way caucus states reported results. Four states with caucuses did not release official popular vote totals. Real Clear Politics made estimates of the popular vote in those states, but also calculated that if those four states were not included, Obama's lead would have been a mere 41,662, or one-tenth of one percent. If the results from Michigan's disputed primary—where Obama's name was not on the ballot but Clinton's was—were included, Clinton had a margin of 176,465 over Obama, according to Real Clear Politics estimates.

quietly with her husband as reporters and even aides kept their distance. The next day, with the polls still open, she came under intense pressure to announce her withdrawal from the race that night. She resisted, choosing instead to highlight the achievements of her campaign. "So many people said this race was over five months ago in Iowa," she said, "but we had faith in each other. And you brought me back in New Hampshire, and on Super Tuesday, and in Ohio, and in Pennsylvania and Texas and Indiana, West Virginia, Kentucky, Puerto Rico, and South Dakota. I will carry your stories and your dreams with me every day for the rest of my life."

She continued, "Now the question is, where do we go from here? And where do we need to go as a party? It's a question I don't take lightly. This has been a long campaign, and I will be making no decisions tonight." From her cheering section came chants of "*Denver. Denver.*" Her most die-hard supporters wanted her to take the fight all the way to the convention.

On Wednesday, her advisers talked about the next steps. Virtually everyone wanted her to get out and endorse Obama quickly. Penn believed she shouldn't quit, though he did not favor active campaigning. He also suggested they try to negotiate with Obama over the price of her withdrawal. "Make him grovel," he said.

Later Clinton met with her team: Penn, Howard Wolfson, Maggie Williams, Geoff Garin, Cheryl Mills, Tina Flournoy, Mandy Grunwald, and Huma Abedin. Penn again made his arguments for negotiations, but Clinton quickly decided it was time to end the campaign and endorse Obama. She canvassed her advisers. Can Obama win? she asked them. Flournoy, who played a key role during the final months, said, "Yes—with your support." Penn said no, Obama could not win. He believed Obama would face a far more serious vetting in the general election and would not survive it. Clinton then left for a conference call with the New York delegation. It was later reported that she was forced out of the race because Representative Charles Rangel and others told her it was time to quit. In fact, according to those in the room that day, her mind was made up before the call with the New Yorkers.

Her official exit came on June 7 at the Pension Building in Washington. The speechwriters had labored over the text; there were more than twenty drafts, but by Friday night it was in good shape. By Saturday morning, the word "endorse" had been removed from the speech, one last sign of the divisions in her campaign. This time it proved to be only a minor problem; the endorsement was quickly reinserted. In her speech, Clinton urged her supporters to turn their energies to electing Obama president. "When you hear people saying, or think to yourself, 'if only' or 'what if,' I say—please don't go there," Clinton said. She pledged to "work my heart out to make sure that Senator Obama is our next president, and I hope and pray that all of you will join me in that effort."

In the most memorable line of the speech, she spoke of what her campaign had achieved: "Although we weren't able to shatter that highest, hardest glass ceiling this time, thanks to you, it's got about eighteen million cracks in it. And the light is shining through like never before, filling us all with the hope and the sure knowledge that the path will be a little easier next time."

Many of her supporters believed the opposite: that she had been hampered in her campaign because of lingering sexism in society.

In the aftermath of the Obama-Clinton battle, what Churchill called "the terrible Ifs" of history could be found everywhere. What if the Clinton campaign had followed Mike Henry's advice and skipped Iowa? What if a state other than Iowa had started the process? What if Obama had won South Carolina by nine points rather than twenty-nine? What if John Edwards's affair had been exposed, forcing him from the race and possibly changing the outcome of the race? What if Florida and Michigan had not been penalized—especially Florida? Plouffe told a forum at Harvard's Kennedy School after the election, "If that Florida primary, coming three days after South Carolina, happened, it might have mitigated all the momentum we got from South Carolina. In fact, we might not be the nominee." There were many ways to second-guess the Clinton campaign for its strategic and tactical decisions: from positioning her as the ultimate insider in a year of change, to failing to compete harder in the caucuses; from never adequately addressing questions about her character, to the role Bill Clinton played.

Given the mistakes Clinton made, it was easy to understate the significance of what Obama and his team accomplished—perhaps the most dramatic victory in the history of presidential nomination battles. In early 2007, few people gave Obama a chance to defeat Clinton. His was anything but a smooth ride to the nomination. When it was over, Axelrod looked back and counted up the false starts and missteps the Obama campaign had made, from its slow start-up to taking New Hampshire for granted—"We looked like a rock star taking victory laps," he said—to mistakes in message and resource allocation that resulted in Clinton winning both Texas and Ohio. That alone cost the campaign $40 million and three months of time.

What they did right, Axelrod believed, was to understand the shadow that George W. Bush cast over the election and to take advantage of the fact that Obama represented the cleanest break with the status quo. In his estimation, the turning points came in January starting with Iowa and ending with South Carolina and the Kennedys. "The three most important days in this campaign other than the Iowa caucuses were the South Carolina primary, Caroline Kennedy writing her piece in the *New York Times* the next day, and Teddy doing his thing on Monday," he said. "You can scope out whether Kennedy helped us or hurt us in this state or that state but it gave an emotional lift to this campaign that I think was the gas that fueled us through the month of February. It really propelled us to a new height."

Obama had what other winning candidates have always had: a message that matched the mood of the electorate, an instinct for where the country wanted to go, the discipline to learn from mistakes and improve with time, the patience to weather setbacks. Obama understood better than Clinton how to tap into the public's desire for change, however defined, and to project himself as the kind of president who could deliver it. He also had something that the other candidates never had, an organization as large, as innovative, and as effective as anything ever put together in presidential politics. Finally, and perhaps most important, Obama's campaign understood that the nomination battle was a fight for delegates, not for popular votes or success in this or that primary. They never lost sight of that. Plouffe's focus on delegates—in finding ways to accumulate them and in repeatedly forcing the focus and the narrative of the Obama-Clinton battle back to that reality—kept Obama moving forward even during times of trouble.

By the end, both Barack Obama and Hillary Clinton were superb candidates. But Obama found, at almost every critical turn, the combination of message, strategy, innovation, and discipline to prevail. He was a high-altitude candidate who rose to big moments. Hillary inspired great passion among her supporters, especially women—a reality often overlooked during the campaign. But Obama inspired more, and not just among young voters, who were consistently his strongest supporters. He married new technology and new media to produce dollars and volunteers that her campaign could not match. Obama also ran an operation that was in many respects the opposite of Clinton's in its collegiality and sense of mutual respect.

Long after the election, we asked two chief strategists of the Clinton campaign, Geoff Garin and Mark Penn, why Obama had won and why Clinton had lost. They offered strikingly different answers.

Garin said, "There was nothing about this election that was traditional or that followed form. And in any other circumstance Obama would have been a counterintuitive candidate to say the least. But I think we were at a moment in America when people, including Democrats, were not just truly angry but worried about the future. They thought the government had come to a standstill and were looking for someone with leadership qualities to lift the country up . . . move the country forward. And Obama's genuine skills were closely related to what voters thought was required to do that. As you got to the end of 2007, I think he figured out how to articulate the case that he had the leadership qualities that America needed at the moment. . . . Obama's ability to sort of seize the moment to me was the most important factor. It took them a while to get there. But that JJ [Jefferson Jackson Dinner] speech in Iowa, it was like curtain up and lights on. . . . He made all of the right connections. People were much more interested in leadership than experience. . . . I didn't feel at the beginning that just talking about change took him far enough. He needed to make a more specific case about why he had the right qualities to do that. . . . Position papers saying change [were not] going to get him elected. At the beginning, aspects of his campaign were more like a Senate campaign than a presidential campaign. But in Iowa he hit the nerve."

Garin also believed the Clinton campaign's miscalculations contributed to Obama's success. Long before he joined her campaign, he had worked for Mark Warner, the former Virginia governor who after a year of exploration decided not to run in 2008. Garin was struck then by how many Democrats were willing to look past Clinton for another candidate. They admired her but that admiration was intellectual. "There was no emotional connection at all," he said. "The reasons for people to hold back were abundantly clear. They worried that she would be polarizing, not just as a candidate . . . but also as a president. People were always dying to know what made Hillary tick. . . . Just as experience was Obama's unique burden, the question of what makes Hillary tick was her burden. Obama faced up to his; the Clinton campaign never faced up to hers."

Still, he said, Clinton ended on a high note. "One of the not fully told stories of the 2008 campaign is the transformation of Hillary Clinton from former First Lady to someone who is a great political candidate and leader in her own right. But it took too long for that to happen."

Penn offered a counterview on what happened, though he agreed with Garin that Obama had run a strong race. In a lengthy e-mail, Penn wrote, "The Obama campaign was a formidable and superb effort—its strength was that it did what it had to do when it had to do it—often freed from the Washington insider model. They got young people to show up in Iowa, they secured the African-American voters when they needed them, they attacked Hillary when she was strong and seemed to be on the verge of winning. . . . They perfected the mass event . . . and they successfully used the Internet to raise money like it had never been raised before, at the same time building a unique coalition of richer progressive voters combined with the African-American vote. At the end of the day, Obama was a once-in-a-generation leader atop a national movement."

Penn argued that Obama benefited mightily from a favorable press. "It was so obvious that *Saturday Night Live* struck a national nerve highlighting the press bias. Hillary had to get her message through without the aid of a single consistently favorable columnist or writer. Not one."

Clinton, he said, despite her many advantages, faced big challenges. She had to overcome doubts among some voters about a woman's ability to serve as president. She carried baggage from her husband's impeachment and her role in the Clinton administration's failed health care attempt. And she had no history or connection with voters in Iowa, "a state that did not take to Hillary and sure wasn't Hillary's favorite place to campaign in."

Penn defended himself against the criticism that he had misunderstood the big changes under way in the country and had orchestrated a campaign message that prized experience over change, turning Clinton into an incumbent in a year when people wanted an outsider. "The message of her campaign was never simple experience—that was the opposition's reframing of her message," he wrote. "It was an argument that it takes experience to make change happen and when people saw the two candidates side by side responding to tough questions, in all but one of the debates, Hillary came off as the one you knew both would turn around the country from George Bush's policies and yet also was ready to handle anything the presidency could throw at her."

He then addressed the internal divisions in the Clinton campaign over how to present her. "Some believed that she should have shown a softer side as the key to showing her sincerity. I believed that the only way for her to win was to show a combination of strength and leadership. . . . The more she came out fighting for people and the more she took him on directly on experience, on economics, on his 'bitter' comments, the more she seemed both a stronger candidate and the more she won."

The errors, he said, included "not going to Iowa in earlier years, not having the organization to play early enough in the other caucus states, not fighting to keep Florida and Michigan in, not successfully budgeting 2007 resources, not having an extended press operation to deal with the bias, and I take my share of the blame and responsibility for them."

But the biggest failure, he argued, was not attacking Obama early. "There is only one thing that could have made a clear early game-changing difference—and that would have been to take on Barack Obama early on directly and forcefully. . . . Imagine if she had branded him out of touch in Iowa when Obama said 'has anyone seen the price of arugula lately at Whole Foods?' We did not take the offensive until too late in the game."

The other mistake was not competing vigorously for the support of progressive Democrats. "Hillary was a progressive seen by the right as too far to the left. And by the left as too far to the center," he said. "She had voted for the war and she did take money from lobbyists. Obama success-fully exploited this with his emphasis on his 2002 speech and his 'no funds from lobbyists' policies. She was not going to win progressive voters over without challenging him on these issues—Obama's follow-through on the 2002 speech was open to question and he took millions from lobbyists right on through the start of the presidential race—facts that never got out there strongly enough to give pause to his progressive supporters. To win we needed to take him on and take the heat for taking him on. We needed to break through the Washington chatter and do what we needed to do—as the Obama campaign did when it faced tough problems. And we also had to reach out more and earlier to college campuses and young people, es-pecially younger women."

Because Obama had solid support among African-Americans, Clinton needed to win a bigger share of younger voters and of older progressives. Penn wrote, "That is where the extra several hundred thousand votes were to win this election, and once we did not take him on early with them, his edge in these groups produced his solid wins from Super Tuesday through Wisconsin."

When the nomination campaign was over, we asked Obama about his competition with Hillary. "After February 5th, we win eleven contests in a row, by huge margins," he said. "I mean, we're winning by fifteen, eighteen, seventeen, and she's just still going." He started to chuckle. "And you're thinking to yourself, my goodness! I give her enormous credit. The tenacity she showed was remarkable. We had great debates in Texas and Ohio. At that point, I knew how to debate and we were on our game. I was givin' as good as I was gettin'. And yet she just kept hammerin' away. After Ohio and Texas, the sense that, man, this is an endurance contest. . . . You're just grinding it out."

After he won the nomination, aides in his Chicago headquarters had plastered the pillars in the press area with front pages of newspapers from around the country marking his victory as the Democratic nominee. Every one of them had the word "history" in the headlines. We asked whether, on the night of June 3 as he claimed the nomination, he felt caught up in the emotion of making history. He told us, "I am very glad that there are people who have been inspired by this race. But I did not begin this race to run a symbolic contest. I ran to win. And what I thought, and this is the honest truth—I said this to Axelrod—having won against a very formidable opponent, my main thought was, I'd better win the general election. Because this should be a Democratic year and I beat somebody who would have been a good general election candidate, so we'd better get our act together now."

BOOK FOUR

THE REPUBLICANS

CHAPTER SEVENTEEN

Looking for Reagan

"For more than twenty years every conservative I know has been looking for Ronald Reagan. Is he down the hall, around the corner, down the street?"

—Richard Viguerie, conservative activist

When they gathered for their first debate at the Ronald Reagan Presidential Library on May 3, 2007, eleven Republican candidates were on the stage with a twelfth in the wings: four former governors, three members of the House, two senators, a former senator, and a former mayor.* The party was shrinking, thanks to President Bush's unpopularity. Independents had shifted dramatically toward the Democrats in the 2006 midterms and were holding there. Pollsters found that fewer Americans were willing to identify themselves as Republicans. The party was reduced to a smaller, more conservative core—to which all the candidates were appealing.

Most in the field had no hope of winning the nomination and knew it. Even among those few who did—at the time that seemed to be only John McCain, Mitt Romney, and Rudy Giuliani—there was no dominant frontrunner, certainly no one like Hillary Clinton, who then was the odds-on favorite in the Democratic race. Even experts in the party were stumped. A prominent Republican governor told us privately that it was easier to explain why each of the leading candidates could never win the nomination than to describe how any of them might win it.

---

* They were former governors Mitt Romney of Massachusetts, Mike Huckabee of Arkansas, Tommy Thompson of Wisconsin, James Gilmore of Virginia, Senators John McCain and Sam Brownback, former senator Fred Thompson, former New York mayor Rudy Giuliani, and Representatives Duncan Hunter, Ron Paul, and Tom Tancredo. A twelfth, former House Speaker Newt Gingrich, had not formally ruled out running at that time.

For the first time in memory, the party of royalists, which always seemed to have a designated heir apparent, had no obvious successor to George W. Bush. Nor was there a consensus candidate for conservatives. Vice President Cheney had chosen not to run, the first time in decades that a sitting vice president had shown no interest in succeeding the outgoing president, though had he tried his own unpopularity would have made his candidacy problematic. One sitting governor might have filled the void: Jeb Bush of Florida had carved out a record of distinction as a state executive and his conservative pedigree was without question. But his brother's low national esteem disqualified him. McCain came closer than anyone to being the heir apparent, and that fact alone underscored why Republicans were in such a funk, given his many battles with others in his party over the years.

The candidates were on a high stage close to the fuselage of the former Air Force One that had flown Reagan around the world and was now part of the library's permanent display. Nancy Reagan was in the front row of the audience. Moderator Chris Matthews of MSNBC asked the candidates, "How do we get back to Ronald Reagan's 'morning in America'?" Through the rest of the debate, each candidate vied to identify his candidacy with the former president. "We need leadership that's strong," Mitt Romney said. "Ronald Reagan was a president of strength. His philosophy was the philosophy of strength—the strong military, the strong economy, and strong families." Rudy Giuliani cited Reagan's sunny confidence. "What we can borrow from Ronald Reagan, since we are in his library, is that great sense of optimism that he had." Mike Huckabee said, "It's important to remember that what Ronald Reagan did was to give us a vision for this country, a morning in America, a city on a hill." McCain attached himself to Reagan's desire—ultimately frustrated—to shrink government, saying if he had been president the previous six years, he would have vetoed one pork-laden spending bill after another "in the tradition of President Reagan."

The debate symbolized the plight of a Republican Party that had fallen on hard times and was now looking back to one of its greatest heroes for inspiration. But none of the candidates could seem to find the keys to Reagan's kingdom. As the campaign opened, Republicans, especially ardent Reagan disciples, were deeply discouraged. "I was with hundreds of conservatives last night at two different functions," Richard Viguerie told us.

"Nobody is excited about this election. They're just down about it. Partly that's because of the field [of candidates] out there, but it's also because in the last ten, twelve years we've seen the Washington politicians abandon the conservative cause—the Reagan revolution, the Gingrich revolution of '94. Putting everything together, conservatives are very, very discouraged."

They had every reason to feel down. The conservative movement had been in ascendance in America for nearly thirty years. Now, after transforming American politics from liberal to conservative, the movement struggled. Just as FDR's liberal New Deal had shaped the modern U.S. political state until the collapse of Lyndon Johnson's Great Society, so the conservative movement that had affected everything now labored to reclaim its leadership position.

Viguerie spoke for an older generation of Republicans. They had thrilled to the conservative intellectual leadership of Russell Kirk and William F. Buckley Jr., whose *National Review*, founded in 1955, declared its mission to be one that "stands athwart of history, yelling Stop." Viguerie remembered the excitement as conservatives rallied behind Barry Goldwater, and shared the anticommunist views of Joe McCarthy and the John Birch Society warning of "un-American" dangers of liberalism, socialism, "the left-wing press," and the Warren Court. Finally, after Goldwater's crushing defeat in 1964, he and other conservatives found their leader in Ronald Reagan. "When Reagan was elected in 1980," Viguerie recalled, "we were off the wall, off the wall."

Fourteen years later, Newt Gingrich's 1994 "Contract with America" campaign led the party to one of its greatest triumphs in modern political history—and sparked another, younger generation of conservatives to action. In Bill Clinton's first midterm election, Republicans rode their anti-government rhetoric to victory. They captured both houses of Congress for the first time in forty years, sweeping Democratic barons on Capitol Hill from power. Six years later, George W. Bush added the presidency, and for a time Republicans controlled all the levers of power in Washington and held a majority of the governorships, stirring dreams of a durable conservative majority long into the future.

Bush's descent brought an end to those aspirations. Republicans were adrift and pessimistic about the future of their party. "Now," as Viguerie said, "Republicans are very unhappy with the Republican president. They're not going to get involved; they're just going to sit on the sideline and grumble." That was why, as Viguerie said, "for more than twenty years every conservative I know has been looking for Ronald Reagan. Is he down the hall, around the corner, down the street?"

There was no shortage of aspirants to the Reagan mantle. So eager were Republicans to begin their search for a nominee that the first cattle call and straw poll for the candidates was held in March 2006 in Memphis. The winner of that straw poll, then Senate Republican Leader Bill Frist, never made it to the starting line, however. Another Republican who attracted considerable attention at the Memphis gathering, Virginia Senator George Allen, also fell by the wayside by year's end, a casualty of the Democratic takeover of the Senate and self-inflicted wounds.

Still, the field of candidates filled out quickly. However much they differed in personality, experience, and background, from the southern governor (Huckabee) to the northern governor (Romney), from the big-city mayor (Giuliani) to the border state senator turned actor (Fred Thompson) to the independent-minded senator (McCain), each Republican candidate sought to wrap himself in Reagan. They became conservatism's best defenders. They all had pieces of Reagan but none was the complete package. The problem was how best to position themselves at a time when the old Reagan coalition was no longer large enough or vibrant enough to elect a president. What, exactly, did it mean to be a conservative in 2008?

The confusion and disappointment among Republican voters looking for a nominee illustrated the depth of the party's difficulties. As the campaign began, William Galston, a Brookings Institution scholar and political scientist who had been White House domestic policy adviser to Bill Clinton, said American politics was either nearing or at the end of the decades-long conservative cycle. "You can just see the wind going out of the sails of one ship and filling the sails of the other," Galston said. "Everything I know about American politics tells me that once these large impressions are formed they're not easily squashed." For candidates hoping to win the White House, the calculus was exceedingly difficult. Was America still a conservative country? Was it still center-right or was it becoming center-left? Or was the balance of power in the electorate lodged somewhere in the middle, motivated more by practicality than by ideology? What message would stir conservatives *and* attract Independents?

Attack on government was at the heart of Reagan's message. Government, he would say, was not the solution. It was the problem. He lashed out at the bureaucracy ("puzzle palaces on the Potomac"), invoked memories of the Founding Fathers, and, mixing historical fact and fiction, declared, "They knew that governments don't control things. . . . They also knew, those Founding Fathers, that outside of its legitimate functions, government does nothing as well or as economically as the private sector of the economy." At the time of his political emergence, Reagan's views represented a minority of American opinion. Sixteen years later, in 1980, they became the majority. His conservative themes shaped every winning Republican presidential campaign from 1980 through 2004: lower taxes, smaller government, faith in free markets, less regulation, promotion of cultural conservatism, and a strong national defense.

Over those decades, the Republicans successfully enlarged their coalition, attracting disaffected Democrats—Reagan Democrats—who were loosed from their traditional moorings. They were drawn to the conservative message of family values, law and order, and lower taxes. Race and civil rights helped shatter the Democrats' hold on the South, beginning at the presidential level in the 1960s, and over the next thirty years the shift in the party balance trickled down to other offices.

Republicans also mobilized Christian conservatives, who after many years on the sidelines of politics became the most loyal constituency in the party. This began with the emergence of televangelists like Pat Robertson and Jerry Falwell, preaching a conservative message and forming the Moral Majority and then the Christian Coalition. Eventually, social and religious conservatives became a grassroots army that aided in the consolidation of Republican power in the South, which was the key to taking control of Congress in the Gingrich-led victories of 1994. Their coalition of economic, national security, and social conservatives, while difficult to manage at times, proved large enough to keep the party in power.

By the time of Bush's election in 2000, religious conservatives were fully integrated into the party structure. They became precinct chairmen and county chairmen and dominated the apparatus of the party in states across the country. Their influence within the party reached a high point during Bush's presidency, symbolized by Bush's assiduous courtship of them and by the confirmation of two Supreme Court justices in 2005, Chief Justice John Roberts and Justice Samuel Alito, whom they strongly supported. Another moment that spring illustrated the power of the religious right, but in a way that would cost the Republicans. Congress passed legislation ordering federal courts to intervene in the case of Terri Schiavo, a brain-damaged woman, after state courts had authorized doctors to remove her feeding tube. If the Roberts and Alito nominations showed the long-lasting influence of the religious right on the country's politics, the Schiavo episode showed the dangers of overreaching. The Schiavo measure subverted conservative principles, putting federal authority ahead of state authority. Public reaction to Washington's intervention in a family dispute was extremely negative. Inside the Republican coalition, other conservatives complained that the religious right had become too powerful for the party's good.

Democrats were quick to say that Republicans had prospered over the years through a relentless attack on government and by mastering the art of negative politics. Both were true. Republicans successfully attacked Michael Dukakis in 1988 for the furlough program that let Willie Horton out of jail to kill again and for a veto of legislation that would have punished teachers who did not lead their students in the Pledge of Allegiance. Republicans accused Democratic candidates of being soft on crime and soft on communism. The Gingrich coalition of the 1990s consistently attacked the Democrats as corrupt and railed against the federal government and its defenders. In 2002, Republicans attacked Georgia Senator Max Cleland, a triple amputee from Vietnam wounds, as soft on terrorism for opposing the creation of the Department of Homeland Security because of a dispute over the organizing rights of federal workers. The Swift Boat Veterans for Truth successfully attacked John Kerry in 2004, despite his decorations for valor in Vietnam. But the conservative ascendance was built on more than attack ads and hardball politics. Republicans prospered in the battle of ideas, capitalizing on public antipathy over the excesses of the New Deal and the Great Society and the sense that Democrats had become the party of cultural elites out of touch with the values of Main Street America. Bill Clinton's winning 1992 campaign was shaped in reaction to those trends as he sought to move the Democrats back toward the center, but his presidency failed to bring about the lasting turn for which many Democrats had hoped. When historian Sean Wilentz published his history of the period from 1974 to 2004, he entitled his book *The Age of Reagan*.

Where Republicans had faltered, where they had crippled themselves, was in their inability to translate their antigovernment message into a governing philosophy. Gingrich's revolution cratered over a budget fight that led to a government shutdown and over the GOP's push to impeach Clinton for his affair with Monica Lewinsky. Bush's presidency was arguably one of the most conservative in modern times, and yet when the party controlled Congress and the White House, government spending rose more rapidly than at any time since the Great Society. Republicans could not reconcile their message with the requirements of power. Bush's policies proved too conservative and controversial for many moderates and Independents, but not sufficiently effective in exercising stronger control of the federal government to satisfy many in the Republican base.

By the beginning of the 2008 campaign, the Reagan coalition was splintering. Republicans appeared exhausted, out of ideas, lacking clear leaders, and in disagreement over their future. The Republican Party that had celebrated Bush's second inauguration as the beginning of a long era in power was a party in disarray. In the 2006 midterm elections, Republicans lost both houses of Congress. They reeled from self-inflicted wounds. GOP legislators and lobbyists went to prison on corruption charges. A House Republican was forced to resign over a sex scandal. A Republican senator attracted wide press coverage after an embarrassing incident in a men's airport bathroom. The country's changing demographics left the largely white Republican Party in a weakened position. Young voters were defecting to the Democrats. Hispanics, America's fastest-growing demographic group, were shifting back to the Democrats after inroads by Bush.

Republican presidential candidates were struggling to replicate Bush's success in consolidating the party's conservative base while facing a broader electorate that had lost faith in the party's leadership. And while the nation faced immense challenges and hungered for a new direction, the Republican Party was failing to offer clear political choices. Even from within its own ranks, critics complained that their party and the conservative cause were out of ideas.

"I think the Republican Party has no particular focus at the present time," Robert S. Walker, who had been a key Gingrich lieutenant and Pennsylvania congressman, told us. As he watched the campaign unfold, Walker was bluntly critical of his party. "During the Reagan era, we knew we were for economic growth through reducing the amount of government impact on the economy. So taxes were lowered and we cut back on regulations. We were for strong national security, defined as winning the Cold War. Then something else began during the Reagan era. That was the advent of social conservatives of the Christian right that became an essential part of the coalition that drove the social agenda of the party." He too viewed the legacy of George W. Bush as a negative for Republicans in

2008. Polls showed Bush was defined by major mistakes: mismanagement of the war in Iraq and mismanagement of the aftermath of Hurricane Katrina. Walker focused in particular on the effects of Katrina. "What I think Katrina proved more than anything else is that government, at all levels, has become dysfunctional," Walker said. "People lost faith in Bush's ability to manage: 'Oh, he can't even handle a storm in New Orleans.'"

Republican candidates had to make the case that the unpopular record of their party, and their president, would not keep them from winning in 2008. That required attracting more than movement conservatives "looking for Reagan." It meant demonstrating the Reagan magic could still create a new majority coalition. If they could do that, despite their long odds, they just might win one more for the Gipper.

CHAPTER EIGHTEEN

Prisoner of War

"I would much rather lose a campaign than lose a war."

—McCain, on the threat his support for the Iraq
war posed to his candidacy

In a party struggling for its identity, John McCain was always an uncomfortable front-runner. He was fit neither by constitution, temperament, nor instinct to run at the head of the pack. McCain had always seemed more suited to the maverick role of 2000, a politician who relished bumping up against the power of President Bush and the Republican establishment. "In 2000 it was a necessity," he told us in the spring of 2008. "We were the outsider. We didn't have the financial base. We didn't have the political base. Everybody thinks I chose to be a maverick. I didn't have a choice. By the time we got into [the campaign in] 1999, Governor Bush had done a masterful job, along with [Karl] Rove and his team, of basically sewing up the Republican establishment. Of course [mine] was an outsider kind of campaign. And I think I was suited to it. But it wasn't 'Hey I think I'll run as an outsider.' I competed for those establishment folks. Most of them had signed on to President Bush."

In 2008 he needed a wholly different approach. As his friend Lindsey Graham, the senator from South Carolina, often said, McCain had to learn to make the transition from being the leader of a movement to the leader of his party. Though he had quarreled frequently with the president, cooperated regularly with the Democrats, and often irritated his conservative colleagues in the Senate and House, John McCain would now try to become the candidate of the Republican establishment. "We started [going after] the establishment and planning on raising a lot of money and running that kind of campaign which is generally successful," McCain told us.

John Weaver, his chief strategist at the time, described the game plan as one that every successful candidate had used since Richard Nixon launched his comeback in 1966: "Move him around the country, raise money, do everything you can for the party first. Meet as many of the key donors and bundlers that the president had that we had little relationship with. Meet and develop as allies as many of the top operatives and volunteer leadership around the country that the president had and governors and whatnot. That was our goal . . . and I think we were very successful."

Resistance to a McCain candidacy among establishment Republicans began to soften with every tick down in Bush's approval ratings. McCain began his courtship of the party establishment at a time when Bush was riding high. But rising unhappiness over the war in Iraq, signs of economic distress, and a backlash over the administration's handling of Hurricane Katrina encouraged a reassessment of McCain among those who had viewed him with great skepticism. He seemed to be the only Republican who might be able to defeat Hillary Clinton. A prominent conservative Republican governor said privately, "If my party believes we're going to lose this presidential election because of the dynamics, because of incumbency, because of Iraq, because of the economy, we have a hole card and that's John McCain. We may not like McCain-Feingold, we may not like his view on this or this, but if we want to win the election for the good of the country, John McCain's the guy. He can beat her."

As McCain courted Bush fund-raisers and key supporters around the country, his advisers began to lock down experienced Republican operatives who had guided Bush's campaigns. Almost every week, Weaver lunched with somebody from Bush's 2004 team, gathering intelligence on how they had operated or trying to recruit them to join McCain's campaign. Through those months, the McCain team gained a greater appreciation of the machinery and particularly the discipline that had made Bush successful in his campaigns. "It firmed up our view of how disciplined a campaign they had run—which is so totally alien to our world," Weaver said. "Our goal was to try to bring some of that discipline to John's world."

Though McCain was considered the nominal front-runner, he actually trailed Rudy Giuliani in national polls of Republicans. Giuliani was a rare superstar within the party, "America's Mayor," as he liked to be called, a hero to many for his response to the 9/11 attacks. *Time* magazine had named him "Person of the Year" over President Bush, and that celebrity status helped push him to the top of the Republican field. But if McCain was an unlikely front-runner, given his strained relations with the Republican base, Giuliani was an even more implausible nominee—a socially liberal New Yorker seeking to take over a party dominated by southerners and evangelical Christians. Giuliani was a true conservative in many respects. His economic philosophy tilted sharply toward supply-side theories. His years as a mob-busting prosecutor and his crackdown on crime as mayor earned him a reputation as a law-and-order politician. On national security, no one in the field, save possibly McCain, was so outspoken about the need to stay on offense—or talked more about the damage to the country's security that could occur if a Democrat were elected in 2008. Democrats in power, he said, would "wave the white flag" in Iraq, strip back the Patriot Act, reduce electronic surveillance, and soften the administration's interrogation policy. "We're going to cut back, cut back, cut back, and we'll be back in our pre–September 11 mentality of being on defense," he told a New Hampshire audience. A Democratic president would mean a prolonged war on terror that likely would cost the country the lives of many more of its own citizens. But even with that message there were doubts that he could overcome resistance to his support for abortion rights, gay rights, and gun control. The polls notwithstanding, Republican insiders were doubtful.

For months Giuliani seemed ambivalent about running for president. As other candidates recruited their teams and reached out in the early states, Giuliani spent much of 2006 running in place. He campaigned for other Republican candidates but took few of the necessary steps to build on his attributes. McCain advisers worried less about Giuliani than other potential foes. "Frankly I didn't care if Rudy ran or not," John Weaver told us. "We thought he might but we didn't know for sure." McCain and Giuliani admired one another and considered each other friends. Weaver said, "At one point in '06 McCain and I had dinner with Rudy and Judy [Giuliani's wife] and Tony Carbonetti [one of Giuliani's closest confidants] here in Washington at Mr. K's just to make sure of the line of communication. Both sides were playing a little bit of chicken with the other."

Behind the scenes, Giuliani was moving steadily toward a candidacy, evidenced by a detailed strategy memo prepared in the fall of 2006 that fell into the possession of the New York Daily News. The document outlined plans to try to raise $100 million in 2007. Giuliani recruited as his campaign manager Mike DuHaime, who had served as political director at the Republican National Committee. He signed up the Tarrance Group, one of the party's leading polling firms. The firm's lead partner, Ed Goeas, described a path to the nomination predicated on an analysis that in all the early states there were enough Republicans who did not see Giuliani's abortion position as disqualifying. On February 5, 2007, to quell the doubters, Giuliani filed his declaration of candidacy and appeared on Sean Hannity's Fox News program. "I'm in this to win," he said, in words almost identical to the other prominent New Yorker in the presidential race, Hillary Clinton.

The only other prospective candidate who had done anything comparable to McCain in trying to build a campaign was Mitt Romney, and he approached the task with the same single-mindedness that had marked his business career. He was highly regarded because of his success in the business world and for salvaging the scandal-tainted 2002 Salt Lake City Olympics. His assets included good looks, a large and handsome family, a tremendous work ethic, the energy to outhustle his opponents, and a résumé that could be employed to sell him as a fresh face at a time the country wanted change.

Romney's father, George, also had been a successful businessman turned politician. He served ably as governor of Michigan and in 1968 sought the Republican presidential nomination. His campaign faltered when he said he had been brainwashed by the generals in Vietnam, but his reputation as a devoted public servant survived. So the younger Romney had politics in his blood. He challenged Ted Kennedy for the Senate in 1994 and ran a spirited race, until Kennedy demolished him in one of their debates. He came back eight years later to run for governor, this time successfully.

By the middle of his first term, he concluded that a reelection campaign and the burdens of executive office could diminish rather than enhance his prospects for winning the Republican nomination. He decided to forgo a second term in Massachusetts in favor of a full-time run for the White House. While still in office, he used the chairmanship of the Republican Governors Association as a platform to travel around the country, meet prominent Republican officials and donors, and begin to build a national political network. Through much of 2006, he and McCain competed fiercely for talent as they constructed political teams in Iowa, New Hampshire, South Carolina, and Florida.

Though Romney attracted considerable attention from the press and from a small circle of Republicans, he was little-known nationally. As Giuliani and McCain topped the polls, he languished in single digits. To demonstrate his potential—to show he belonged in the top tier with the other two—he decided to show his strength financially. In early January 2007 he staged a day of national fund-raising in Boston, calling in wealthy friends like eBay's Meg Whitman to contact their wealthy friends. By the end of the day, he had $6.5 million in donations and pledges.

Romney began the race with a balance sheet that included liabilities almost as great as his assets. He was a one-term governor from one of the most liberal states in the nation. He was a devout Mormon in a party whose evangelical wing viewed the Mormon religion with something between skepticism and hostility. He had taken positions in Massachusetts that were anathema to the conservative base, particularly on abortion and gay rights. Running against Kennedy in 1994, Romney had declared himself a supporter of a woman's right to choose on abortion and claimed he would do more for gay rights than Kennedy. Then he changed positions on abortion. A year before he launched his presidential candidacy, he tried to explain his evolving views to several *Washington Post* reporters. Columnist Ruth Marcus, who had grilled him that day, later described his explanations as "baroque circumlocutions."

The McCain campaign, sensing an opportunity to stop Romney even before he could get launched, stoked the story line that Romney was an opportunist and a flip-flopper. A video of Romney from 1994 surfaced that showed him defending abortion rights. The nascent Romney campaign was overwhelmed by the barrage of criticism and bungled its efforts to counter it. Campaign manager Beth Myers told us later, "At the beginning of the campaign, people didn't know much about Mitt Romney. But if they did know him, that's what they knew about him. Our challenge was to make sure they got to know more." It was not a good place from which to launch a candidacy.

Romney formally announced in February at the Henry Ford Museum in Michigan, rather than in Massachusetts. He cast himself as a doer, not just a dreamer, who had managed large enterprises, and as an outsider who would shake up the capital. "I do not believe Washington can be transformed from within by a lifelong politician," he said. "There have been too many deals, too many favors, too many entanglements, and too little real-world experience managing, guiding, leading." If Republicans wanted competence, he would be that candidate.

One issue above all symbolized the difficulty McCain would face as he tried to hold his old supporters among the Independents and moderates while attempting to mollify, if not consolidate, the establishment

conservatives. That was Iraq. McCain had managed to find the most politically uncomfortable position imaginable, and his discomfort was plain
whenever he talked about the war.

McCain had charted his own course. He was one of the strongest advocates for going after Saddam Hussein when Bush launched the invasion in March 2003. But only months after U.S. forces toppled the Iraqi
dictator and his regime, McCain became a critic of what he believed was
gross mishandling of the aftermath—and the lack of troops necessary to
finish the job. Before the Council on Foreign Relations in November
2003, he said, "President Bush speaks frequently of the need to take the
offensive—in the war on terror—but in Iraq we too often appear to be
playing defense. The simple truth is that we do not have sufficient forces
in Iraq to meet our military objectives."

In the spring of 2004, when the scandal over the Abu Ghraib prison
broke, McCain excoriated Donald Rumsfeld in public hearings before the
Armed Services Committee, demanding explanations. After campaigning
coast-to-coast for the president's reelection, he renewed his attacks on the
defense secretary. In an interview with the Associated Press, he was asked
whether he had confidence in Rumsfeld's leadership. "My answer is still
no. No confidence," he said. He stopped short of calling for Rumsfeld's
resignation, saying that decision was a presidential prerogative. But he
never flagged in his advocacy of a policy of stay the course. "We cannot
afford to lose," he said.

By late 2006, McCain faced a wholly different political reality, as the
country turned against Bush and the war and support for withdrawing
troops increased. One scene vividly captured his predicament. Ten days
before the midterm elections, he came to Connecticut to campaign for two
Republican House members in difficult races. One was Christopher Shays,
who had supported the Iraq war and still did. But in the face of a serious
challenge, he spent the autumn voicing public reservations to a constituency that had soured on the president's policies. McCain had just spoken
at a fund-raiser for Shays and now they were on their way to a public rally.
McCain sat motionless in the front passenger seat, sunglasses covering his
eyes. Shays sat directly behind him, hunched forward and talking rapidly
into McCain's ear, trying futilely to explain his now tortured stance on
the war. "I just want you to know my position," Shays said plaintively.
McCain was unresponsive as Shays chattered on, until finally, with a tone
of exasperation, he ended the conversation: "Like I said, there are no good

options."* Flying back to Washington that evening, he acknowledged that the war put his political aspirations at risk. "There's nothing I can do about it," he told us.

The day after the midterm elections, Bush dismissed Rumsfeld. In his place he nominated Robert Gates, a veteran of his father's administration. On December 5, Gates appeared on Capitol Hill for his confirmation hearings. Asked whether the United States was winning the war, he replied, "No, sir." The United States was neither losing nor winning, he said; the next year or two would be critical in determining the outcome.

A day later, the ten-member Iraq Study Group, headed by former secretary of state James A. Baker III and former Indiana congressman Lee Hamilton, issued its long-awaited report. The bipartisan panel proposed a new policy that was seen as a repudiation of the president. The report was interpreted as a triumph of the foreign policy realists over the neocons and ideologues around Bush. The group said a short-term infusion of troops might be needed, but what captured the headlines was a call for a timetable for withdrawal. "The primary mission of U.S. forces in Iraq should evolve to one of supporting the Iraqi army, which would take over primary responsibility for combat operations. By the first quarter of 2008, subject to unexpected developments in the security situation on the ground, all combat brigades not necessary for force protection could be out of Iraq."

Praise for the report seemed to offer Bush cover for a retreat from a war policy widely judged a failure. McCain, a lone voice in opposition, sharply criticized the panel's findings. Once again he called for more troops to be sent into battle. "There's only one thing worse than an overstressed Army and Marine Corps, and that's a defeated Army and Marine Corps," he said. "We saw that in 1973 [in Vietnam]. And I believe that this is a recipe that will lead to, sooner or later, our defeat in Iraq."

Over the next month, as it became clear Bush was moving toward ordering the troop surge, McCain became the most visible supporter of the new policy. In mid-December he visited Iraq and said he found "a steadily deteriorating situation," which urgently required more troops. In early January he and Democratic Senator Joseph Lieberman spoke at the American Enterprise Institute in Washington, where he argued, "To be of value the surge must be substantial and it must be sustained."

McCain's passionate support for sending in more troops drew attacks

---

* Shays narrowly won reelection in 2006 but was defeated in 2008.

from his potential Democratic presidential rivals. Rather than going after Bush, they gleefully aimed at McCain, the likely GOP presidential front-runner. John Edwards, appearing on ABC's *This Week*, labeled the troop surge "the McCain doctrine." "I think he's dead wrong about this," Edwards said.

McCain remained steadfast. One prospective recruit for his presidential campaign remembers what McCain told him when he came to interview for a job. "He said, 'You can't change my mind on Iraq, don't even try. I'm not going to change my mind.'" Still, McCain talked frequently about the political impact, said Lindsey Graham, the South Carolina senator who was as close to McCain as anyone in Congress. "This I'll always remember," Graham told us. "We were coming back from Iraq on one of these early trips and it was just me and him sitting over dinner somewhere on the plane, and when you've got fifteen hours you've got a lot to talk about. And he said, 'Lindsey, my boy, this one may get us.'"

Bush announced the new policy on national television from the White House library on January 10, 2007. He conceded that there had been too few troops in and around Baghdad and warned of additional U.S. casualties in the months ahead. But, he said, "to step back now would force a collapse of the Iraqi government."

A *Washington Post*/ABC News overnight poll found 61 percent of Americans opposed to the troop surge, most of them strongly opposed. A bare majority of the public said they would like to see the new Democratic majorities in Congress block the plan. Even some military commanders opposed the plan. McCain remained one of Bush's few allies. When asked by CNN's Larry King how the war might affect his presidential candidacy, McCain said, "I would much rather lose a campaign than lose a war."

The risk at that moment was that both might be lost.

The day after the president's speech, McCain sat for an interview in his Senate office.* He was subdued. It was late in the afternoon and outside dusk had fallen. The light in his office was low, adding to the somber mood. The surge policy appeared to fit neither of McCain's standards for success: that it be substantial and sustained. The president had asked for about twenty thousand additional troops; McCain had recommended as many as fifty thousand. Some administration officials were already talking about a

---

* The interview was conducted by co-author Dan Balz and Shailagh Murray of the *Washington Post*.

short stay for the additional forces. McCain said he had been assured by the president that morning the new forces would stay as long as needed. "I think it can succeed and I cannot guarantee success, but I can guarantee failure if we don't adopt this new strategy," he said.

We debated back and forth whether Democratic victories in the midterm elections of November signaled a mandate for the start of a troop withdrawal, rather than a surge. "It's very important for us to be able to convince Americans that we can succeed," he said. "I admit that this is a challenge to us. But I can make the counterargument that withdrawal means defeat and chaos. . . . I believe this is our only chance of success. I can't elaborate much more than that, except to remind you that it's been my position for more than three years."

In interviews, McCain speaks quietly, particularly when the subject matter is difficult. And on this afternoon he was especially reserved. He seemed in conflict—not over the new policy but over the mess the administration had created. He said the war "will go down as one of the worst" blunders in the history of the American military.

His anguish was apparent as he talked about the damage the war had done. "Many things that have happened in the world that are unfavorable to the United States are the result of our weakness in the Iraqi conflict," he said. Later in the hour he said, "One of the most frustrating things that's ever happened in my political life is watching this train wreck. I saw it. Every hearing, every opportunity that I had—I said this is not going right, you've got to get more people on the ground here."

He talked about the emotions he felt when he started to read *Fiasco*, the best-selling book by journalist Thomas E. Ricks. "I had to put it down," he said. We asked why. "Because it's so sad and it makes me remember the things that happened. We very appropriately grieve and mourn the loss of American lives. They're our citizens. But think of what this has done to the average Iraqi, the families displaced, guys grabbed off the street and tortured and shot, bodies thrown on the sidewalk. It's terrible. It's heart-wrenching."

He was asked about becoming the object of attacks from Democratic presidential candidates. Would he accept that the surge policy represented the McCain doctrine? "No, but I am willing to accept it as a McCain principle," he said. "That is when I sign up, when I raise my hand and vote to go to war, that I want to see the completion of the mission."

McCain advisers wanted him at least to express some differences with the White House over the size of the force—to put some distance between himself and the president. "I can remember a conversation when I said, ah-ha, this is your opening," Graham said. "Get on the record now and say I'm not so sure this will work because we don't have enough troops. Right idea, just not enough people. So you cover yourself basically. And he did say, I'm not so sure this is enough but this is all we got, this is what we'll do."

Three years of criticism of the Pentagon and Rumsfeld, three years of trying to be his own man on Iraq, were washed away with his embrace of the surge. He was once again a prisoner of war, hostage to the president's plan and its success. McCain was still judged the most likely nominee in a field where no one stood out the way Clinton and Obama did in the Democratic race. But he was a man weighed down by the most important policy dispute in the country and by a campaign structure built for a different kind of politician and for a different campaign. McCain was the leader of the pack, but he was alone and unhappy.

The winter months brought little to cheer about. McCain went to Iowa in mid-February—three stops on a wintry Saturday. The crowds were decent and far from hostile. But even the conservative audiences seemed skeptical about the surge in Iraq. Flying across the state that afternoon, McCain told several reporters, "Looking around at the faces, I thought most of the people were willing to listen to what I had to say. But I also saw a lot of faces that hadn't bought in to it. I didn't see a lot of vigorous nodding."

Early the next month, he decided to skip CPAC (Conservative Political Action Conference), the annual gathering of conservatives in Washington. His two major rivals, Romney and Giuliani, did appear. Romney especially seemed to strike a chord. McCain's absence drew fresh criticism from the wing of the party that had always viewed him with suspicion. His political position was increasingly precarious. Moderates who had once enthusiastically supported him now were backing away over Iraq and Jerry Falwell. But conservatives still did not trust him fully.

In mid-March he rolled out the Straight Talk Express for a tour through Iowa and New Hampshire amid stories critical of his campaign. "Everybody says, 'We just want you to be like last time,'" he told reporters. "Last time we lost!" He took every question reporters threw at him in the back of the bus. "Well, what else?" he asked when their inquiries flagged. For a moment, it was easy to overlook his problems.

He visited Iraq and immediately created a controversy by offering an overly rosy description of conditions there. Before leaving the United States, he said in a radio interview, "There are neighborhoods in Baghdad where you and I could walk . . . today." In Baghdad, an incredulous reporter asked him about that claim. "Yeah, I just came from one," McCain said. He had visited the Shorja market, but rather than a leisurely stroll, he was backed by heavy security—including a hundred armed U.S. soldiers, ten armored Humvees, two Apache attack helicopters overhead, and snipers overlooking the scene. Under questioning by Scott Pelley of CBS's *60 Minutes*, he offered a tepid apology for overstating things. "Of course I am going to misspeak and I've done it on numerous occasions and I'll probably do it in the future. I regret that when I divert attention, but you know that's just life and I'm happy frankly with the way I operate. Otherwise it would be a lot less fun." No one saw the humor.

McCain made his formal announcement on April 25, 2007, in New Hampshire. The day was gray, the crowd modest, the excitement minimal. He stood on the banks of the Piscataqua River overlooking the Portsmouth Naval Ship Yard and presented himself as a commonsense conservative. He tried to separate himself from the president. He said he wanted to change Washington and hoped for a mandate decisive enough to prove that Americans wanted an end to partisan gridlock in Washington. "I'm not the youngest candidate. But I am the most experienced," he said. "I know how the military works, what it can do, what it can do better, and what it should not do. I know how Congress works, and how to make it work for the country and not just the reelection of its members. I know how the world works. I know the good and the evil in it. I know how to work with leaders who share our dreams of a freer, safer, and more prosperous world, and how to stand up to those who don't. I know how to fight and I know how to make peace. I know who I am and what I want to do."

But McCain hardly knew himself or his campaign at that point. All the coverage of him was negative. Iraq was his albatross and, to the exclusion of everything else, now defined his candidacy—which greatly worried his advisers. "It showed principle on his part but there was a sense it was killing us," one senior adviser said later. His efforts to reach out to conservatives like Jerry Falwell had been judged by the right as halfhearted, a case study in how not to do it, as one conservative told us that week. He trailed Rudy Giuliani in national polls; on the ground Mitt Romney was digging into Iowa and New Hampshire at his expense. McCain's announcement day was more than a formal launching of the campaign; it was the opportunity for a badly needed fresh start.

McCain read his speech to cheers from the crowd. Afterwards he tried to hold a short press conference, but there was no stage, no microphone, and no sound system. He and Cindy were pressed up against the door of his campaign bus, with reporters chaotically trying to shout questions and straining to hear the answers. From Portsmouth, McCain's entourage motored to Concord for television interviews, including one with Larry King in which McCain called for the resignation of Alberto Gonzales, Bush's weakened attorney general. From there the campaign moved on to Manchester. Throughout the day, he rotated groups of reporters onto the Straight Talk Express campaign bus, as he had always done. But instead of the easy give-and-take of 2000, the atmosphere was more adversarial. Reporters, crammed into the tiny cubicle in the back that was McCain's rolling lair, peppered him with questions about the war, about fund-raising, about the shaky state of his campaign. In Manchester, his last stop of the day, he arrived to a steady rain. An aide held an umbrella over him as he read the same speech he had given that morning. He spoke with little emotion while peering into a big flat-screen monitor behind the audience that served as a teleprompter. Backstage his advisers openly griped about the staging, which they did not think suited the candidate.

McCain had built a huge battleship of a campaign and now, almost four months into the new year, his discomfort was visible. He was not accustomed to being a front-runner and even less comfortable as the establishment candidate. He had agreed with his advisers that he needed to start early and do everything that past winners had done, but now they could see he was unhappy. "The campaign was not forced upon him early," Weaver said later. "But he so dreaded it. He so dreaded it. I think he dreaded the pressure of being the front-runner. I think he dreaded the politicization of his position on the war. . . . I didn't see him upbeat one day. And that's not his general nature."

CHAPTER NINETEEN

The Implosion

"This guy's dead, nails in his coffin . . . fifth in a four-person race."

—Senator Lindsey Graham on John McCain, July 2007

When the first-quarter fund-raising numbers were released in early April, Mitt Romney dominated the list of Republican candidates with $21 million. That put Romney almost in the same league as Barack Obama and Hillary Clinton and gave his candidacy a fresh burst of credibility. Rudy Giuliani was a distant second, with barely $15 million. McCain, who had spent almost two years building a fund-raising network, raised just $12.5 million. In previous years, that would have been respectable. But given all the hype and all the expectations, and a budget plan that had called for tens of millions more, it was a political debacle.

The campaign's financial problems had surfaced months earlier. Terry Nelson took over as campaign manager in December 2006 and discovered there was no fund-raising plan. There were only a handful of major fund-raisers scheduled for January or February. Budget projections that called for McCain to raise $48 million in the first quarter were built on sand. In early January, Nelson went to Paris with his wife to celebrate their wedding anniversary. A few days after their arrival, he got a call from a campaign official overseeing the accounts. "We're in the red," he was told. From that day until summer, the campaign was never in the black. "We managed our budget against a deficit the entire time," Nelson said.

Throughout January, the situation worsened. The political team was spending freely, only to be told by the fund-raising department that quarterly receipts likely would fall to no more than $36 million. Then, over a period of weeks, the estimates shrank repeatedly to less than $20 million. With each diminished projection, Nelson said he attempted to cut the operating budget but couldn't do it fast enough. The first cut took it from $154 million to $137 million. In early February, it was cut again to $100 million. At the end of the first quarter, it stood at $78 million, half of the original projection. The bold plan of December was now inoperative. "We were slower getting started than we ever should have been," finance director Carla Eudy said later. "We didn't do as many events in the first quarter as we should have done. In some people's minds it was going to be easier than it was. . . . I think basically we started the campaign from the expenditure side as a general election campaign and that was a mistake. . . . We should have seen what our fund-raising was going to be in the first quarter before we built up such an expenditure level that we couldn't support it."

The first-quarter shortfall forced drastic action. McCain asked his friend Tom Loeffler to oversee the fund-raising operation. Loeffler, a former Texas congressman and successful lobbyist, had supported Bush in 2000 and 2004 but was loyal to McCain. He once said he would "wash bottles and change tires on the Straight Talk Express," if that's what McCain asked. Steve Schmidt, a veteran of the Bush 2004 reelection who had just finished running Arnold Schwarzenegger's reelection campaign and was a consultant to the McCain campaign, was called in to review the books. It was worse than he had feared, almost irretrievably so. McCain yielded to Weaver and Nelson and replaced finance director Eudy with Mary Kate Johnson, who was part of the Bush '04 team. "To be completely honest, there was a sense of relief," Eudy told us. "I just didn't feel like the campaign was going in the direction it should go. I didn't feel like there was a team effort or a team that had one thing in mind and that was John McCain only. It became my head on the chopping block and I was happy to take responsibility." Campaign officials engaged in a pointed debate over why the shortfall had happened: Was it a failure of the fund-raising team to meet projections, or a failure of the political team to eliminate wasteful and extravagant expenditures when fund-raising slackened?

McCain said he was always dubious about the rosy projections. "I thought, Well, you know maybe we're just a little slow getting started," he later told us. "You kind of think, well, maybe we can catch up. . . . I was worried, but obviously not worried enough to take the decisive action. And I did put the brakes on some things and demanded certain reductions, but obviously not nearly enough to adjust to the realities of the situation." Weaver's explanation was more direct: "We believed our own bullshit."

Shortly before the campaign was due to report its dismal fund-raising numbers, the McCain top advisers met at the Phoenix Park Hotel to devise a strategy to deal with the coming public relations blow. The group included Weaver, Nelson, Salter, Loeffler, Schmidt, media adviser Russ Schriefer, and communications director Brian Jones. They settled on a damage control plan designed to show that the campaign's financial woes were not slowing McCain down. He would give a major speech on Iraq at Virginia Military Institute after his trip to Iraq. Other speeches were planned. They would gear up for the formal announcement tour. They also prepared talking points for reporters for the day the numbers went out. Nelson called us the day the numbers were released. It was a painful conversation. "I'm going to give you a monologue," he said as he laid out the grim numbers. "We obviously had hoped to do better. . . . We would like to place some things in context. . . . Hope is not a plan. . . . We have instituted a couple of steps and will institute more. . . . It's something we've been focused on here for many weeks." It was hardly a persuasive performance.

By now the campaign was under severe stress internally. The operation was not working and was beset with infighting. McCain had created not so much a team of rivals, as Hillary Clinton had done, but a clash of cultures. The effort to meld together McCain 2000 and Bush 2004 created a huge gulf within the organization. Some longtime McCain aides jealously guarded their memories of that first campaign and, still bitter over what had happened, treated some of the new recruits as hostile outsiders. Campaign manager Terry Nelson said later, "I remember sitting down with [finance director] Carla Eudy in December and said are we going to do the Ranger and Pioneer thing [terms used for people who raised the most money for Bush] and she said no. And I say, 'What?' and she said, 'That's the Bush way and we're not going to do that.' There was this sense that folks who were not part of the McCain 2000 team you weren't there for the right reasons or you didn't really care about the McCains or you were a hired guy." Eudy said later she did not remember the conversation.

There were four people atop the campaign: John Weaver, Mark Salter, Rick Davis and Terry Nelson. Weaver served as chief strategist. Tall and thin, he had spent years in Texas, where he had feuded with Karl Rove, before going national. He was shrewd and tough, overseeing all of McCain's political operations. After the 2000 campaign, he was so bitterly disappointed that he briefly defected to the Democrats. He was a fierce competitor, impulsive in the way McCain could be. He had a keen understanding of the strengths and weaknesses of McCain's 2000 campaign and no one had done more to put McCain in position to start the 2008 race as the leading candidate. Salter was McCain's alter ego and, like a brother, had an unbreakable emotional bond with his boss. He had been with the senator since the late 1980s, an almost accidental hire who rose to become McCain's top aide in the Senate office. He wrote all of McCain's speeches as well as the best-selling books that bore both their names and, in a sign of McCain's generosity and friendship, shared fully in the proceeds. He thought like McCain and knew his voice perfectly. Nobody spoke more authentically for McCain than Salter. He could anticipate McCain's moods and reactions faster than the candidate. Salter reflected those moods too, both good and bad, and he was quick to defend his boss against what he saw as niggling and unfair criticism in the press.

Davis had been with McCain for many years. He had managerial skills and a bubbly personality that sometimes disguised what a canny inside player he was. Davis had built a successful lobbying firm in Washington, one that had dealt with some unsavory foreign leaders. More than anyone, he was a survivor. One senior official new to McCain's world was told when he joined the campaign, "Make friends with Rick Davis; you don't know how things will work out." Davis maintained tight relations with the candidate, with Cindy McCain, and with major fund-raisers. Nelson was the newcomer. A low-key midwesterner, he had served as political director of Bush's campaign, where he earned the affection and loyalty of other Bush staffers. Nelson was recruited because he knew what a big political enterprise needed. If McCain wanted to replicate his live-off-the-land campaign of 2000, Nelson told people, he was ill-suited for that role. If McCain intended to run a version of the Bush reelection campaign, a large and robust operation designed to go the distance, Nelson believed he had the skills to do it. What he lacked was a close relationship with the candidate.

The lines of authority were never clear. McCain preferred a lean and nimble operation. He often acted precipitately and preferred a campaign structure with no hierarchy or bureaucracy—a pirate ship rather than a battleship, as his advisers often joked. But that style was incompatible with the structure he had authorized. "Every bad internal management decision was a derivative ultimately of us not addressing the structure of the campaign," Weaver said. Davis coexisted with Weaver and Salter, but tensely so in the early going. They operated in "independent silos," as one adviser put it. As the campaign was gearing up, Weaver and Salter convinced McCain to bring in Nelson as campaign manager, the title Davis had held in 2000. Davis did not fight the move and said he would take the title of

CEO. Later the trio urged McCain to strip Davis of his CEO title, fearing conflicts between Davis's campaign role and his work with outside companies doing business with the campaign. McCain agreed, but the decision was soon reversed. The dispute lasted only a few weeks. In McCain's world, that was typical; decisions like that rarely stuck.

At the Phoenix Park meeting, the political team had discussed what to do about Davis. There was agreement that it would be best if Davis left the campaign entirely. Salter, who knew McCain and had no personal grudge against Davis, offered a more realistic view. According to an account by Robert Draper in *Gentleman's Quarterly*, Salter told the others, "It's not like we can just put Rick in a corner and give him a fucking banana."

Despite the changes at the beginning of the second quarter, the problems inside the campaign persisted.

In the spring, Romney began airing television commercials in the early states. The expenditure seemed a classic waste of money: Would anyone pay attention to political ads so early? But for Romney, money was never a source of concern. Not only had he raised more than $20 million, he was prepared to dip into his personal fortune to make up for any shortfalls.

Romney's strategy for winning the nomination was tried and true: Win early and run on momentum. He tried what other lesser-known candidates had done, which was to focus his energies and resources on Iowa and New Hampshire in the hope of besting McCain or Giuliani in one or both. If he could win these states, he believed he might ride those victories through the other early contests. He could then seal his nomination on February 5th, when nearly two dozen states would vote. That early-state strategy had worked for Democrats John Kerry in 2004 and Al Gore in 2000 (both had won Iowa and New Hampshire and were never seriously challenged thereafter), but no Republican in the modern era had won both states' contests.

Romney had rapidly built a large and impressive campaign team, hiring many of the best operatives in the Republican Party. He had an inner circle that included campaign manager Beth Myers, trusted business associate Bob White, and fund-raiser Spencer Zwick. He recruited older veterans like Ron Kaufman, Ben Ginsberg, and Tom Rath, who had experience in past presidential campaigns, and hired young, up-and-coming operatives like Matt Rhoades, who ran communications, and Kevin Madden, the press secretary. Alex Castellanos was the lead voice on advertising early in the campaign. Alex Gage, one of the party's experts on microtargeting, helped Myers manage the operation. Carl Forti, a hard-nosed strategist who had worked at the National Republican Congressional Committee, ran the political shop.

The Romney team assumed he would never move up dramatically in the national polls until he demonstrated support in the early states. By sinking millions into early ads, he began to be taken more seriously. With McCain hobbled by fund-raising problems and Giuliani following an uncertain strategy, Romney soon led the polls in both Iowa and New Hampshire. Romney's media adviser Castellanos said, "When you put Mitt Romney on TV, good things happen."

Giuliani continued to lead in national polls but otherwise appeared far less ready for a national campaign. He enjoyed playing the celebrity and the attention and adulation that went with it, but he seemed ill-equipped for the style of politics convincing to voters in Iowa and New Hampshire. He did not devote time to town meetings like McCain or Romney. He didn't always appear versed in local politics. "He never really sat down and interacted," a McCain supporter from New Hampshire later told us. "He was sort of doing it New York style and people were going, 'When's he going to sit down and let me ask him three follow-ups?' Probably in New York that's how you do it. You put out a press release you're going to the deli. You go in and shake a few hands. You come out, you talk to the press, you get in the cars and take off." Beyond that, he did not have a clear strategy.

On social issues, he was forced to play defense. In the first Republican debate at the Reagan Library, moderator Chris Matthews asked all the candidates, "Would the day that *Roe v. Wade* is repealed be a good day for Americans?" Romney: "Absolutely." Sam Brownback: "Be a glorious day of human liberty and freedom." Mike Huckabee: "Most certainly." On down the line of candidates until it was Giuliani's turn. "It would be okay," he said. "Okay to repeal?" Matthews asked incredulously. "It would be okay to repeal," Giuliani replied. "Or it would be okay also if a strict constructionist judge viewed it as precedent, and I think a judge has to make that decision."

Later he tried to clarify his position. In a speech in Texas, he called abortion "morally wrong" but nonetheless said he believed the choice should be left to the woman. "I am open to seeking ways of limiting abortions and I am open to decreasing abortions," he said. "But I believe you have to respect [women's] viewpoint and give them a level of choice. I would grant women the right to make that choice." The speech left all sides unhappy. Social conservatives saw a pro-abortion liberal. His former abortion rights allies in New York saw a turncoat. "I'm ashamed of him," said Fran Reiter, who had been a deputy mayor under Giuliani and had run his 1997 reelection campaign.

On May 17, at Lindsey Graham's urging, McCain broke off the campaign to return to Washington. There he stood with a bipartisan group of senators, including Edward M. Kennedy, to announce support for a compromise immigration reform package. It came a year after he and many of the same senators had tried, with the president's help, to enact legislation, only to see it blocked by Republicans. With the Democrats now in control of the House and Senate, and the president still behind the bill, the prospects for passage looked marginally better. But on June 28 the effort collapsed, once again sunk by the opposition of Republican lawmakers and a grassroots uprising fueled by talk radio and conservative constituencies around the country.

Immigration, like health care and energy policy, was an example of how difficult it is to achieve public consensus on a controversial issue. In the country, the issue was a flashpoint, blocking compromise in Washington. As Doris Meissner, former U.S. Immigration and Naturalization commissioner, told us during the campaign, "Regardless of who wins the presidential election, the way the immigration issue is being handled makes it significantly more difficult to do some of the things we need to do once the election is over. It's not like you can say, 'Oh, this is one of those toxic eruptions and then you put it back in the bottle.' We can't put these things back in the bottle. Who wants to touch this thing after it has become the third rail of politics?"

She added, "We have to have immigration for our long-term future. Until the last ten or fifteen years, immigration was basically an issue that affected five or six large states and the big cities in them. Now immigration is happening in very large ways in almost every state in the country— almost every state! The states that are particularly dramatic are so unlikely. South Carolina and Tennessee, Nevada and Iowa. When your foreign population [keeps increasing at such a rate] it is shocking. It's all happening because of jobs, because these are all places that would be dying without new immigration and these communities are not set up to deal with it. And this is intensified by the fact that in all of these new growth areas, more than half, and sometimes seventy to eighty percent, of the people are illegal."

At this point, Meissner sat back and threw up her hands. "It makes me feel helpless," she said. "I'll be very honest with you. I feel like I have a responsibility to do something to combat this, and I don't know what to do. This issue has completely run amok. It feels like anarchy." Immigration, she said, "touches on everything, and goes everywhere. We could be setting the stage for these changes in our political campaign, but we're doing exactly the opposite. Instead, nothing. Nothing! Not only nothing, but opening up a Pandora's box and taking the lock off all the others. Now the creepy-crawlies are really out there."

McCain's campaign sank further with the bill's demise. Support in Iowa, tepid to begin with, collapsed. McCain recalled a town hall meeting he attended in Marshalltown, Iowa, where there had been a rapid influx of immigrants. "After my spiel a woman said why do we have to dial 1 for English?" he told us. "[She said] 'These Mexicans are destroying our culture. Why can't you make them all learn English?' I mean it wasn't even 'our borders are broken,' it was a genuine concern bordering on fear."

In New Hampshire, the morning of a Republican debate in early June, McCain warmed up with a town hall meeting at the fire station in Guilford but was hit repeatedly with immigration questions. That night, he found himself isolated as Romney, Giuliani, and several other rivals attacked him for supporting a bill they said would give amnesty to twelve million illegal immigrants living in the United States. McCain argued that doing nothing on immigration was worse and amounted to de facto amnesty.

McCain said reaction to his candidacy on talk radio turned even more negative, with the hosts denouncing McCain's bill as amnesty. "I remember being on talk shows and the host wouldn't let me get a word in," he said. "Then listening to the talk shows in the car: 'Amnesty John' and 'Lindsey Gomez' [a reference to Senator Lindsey Graham]. It became pretty apparent that the depth of the emotion on this issue was quite significant."

Tucker Bounds, a press spokesman, recalled "a half-empty fund-raiser in Sacramento. There were four or five gentlemen at a table that were outwardly confrontational with the candidate. And they had paid a thousand dollars to be there. They were argumentative with him about immigration policy inside his own fund-raiser in Sacramento. That was the point I realized we had a real problem on our hands."

Immigration savaged McCain's fund-raising efforts. The campaign had raised little money in April, as the new finance team took hold, but still believed they could raise as much as $18 or $20 million in the second quarter, enough to erase questions about his political viability. Instead, they went into financial freefall. Fund-raising events were canceled because of lack of interest. Events projected to raise $200,000 pulled in half that amount or less. A bundler in California who had told Nelson he had pledges in April and early May for $100,000 couldn't deliver 50 percent. "People were literally saying that they couldn't do it, wouldn't do it, didn't want to do it," Nelson said. "[They] were going to wait to see what happened. That's what you would hear."

Inside McCain headquarters, a grim reality now took hold. The campaign could no longer afford the superstructure that McCain's team had constructed. McCain was hearing from others that the budgetary situation was dire. Greg Wendt, a wealthy mutual fund manager from San Francisco and McCain fund-raiser, said he began sounding alarms in March and April. Cindy McCain took a close look at the books and she too told her husband he had to act. "Cindy is a good business person," Graham said. "She got into the books and showed John how some of this money was just quite frankly wasted." McCain told us, "She became very alarmed at the fiscal status."

Nelson said that by mid-June he knew there would have to be major cuts in the staff. He told communications director Jones to come back with staff reductions for his department. Jones offered a list of three people. Nelson told him that wasn't enough; his entire department had to be cut to three people.

In early June, Nelson said, he laid out the details for McCain, who wanted to start cutting staff and expenses immediately. Nelson said, "You know what, if we do that, we'll really impact our fund-raising, that there's real downside risk in doing it. [I said] we're going to save a couple hundred grand by laying some people off but we could lose some seven-figure number and we would take a hit in our fund-raising."

McCain reluctantly agreed but he was still terribly unhappy.

On the weekend of June 30th, McCain hosted a gathering at his cabin in Sedona, Arizona. Many of the top fund-raisers were there. Nelson and

Loeffler briefed them on the cuts that were coming. But there was considerable disagreement about what should be done to right the campaign. Before the meeting, Weaver and Cindy McCain had gotten into an argument on the phone. She complained about the influence of the Bush network inside the campaign; Weaver said that the young staffers who would lose their jobs the next week had given their heart and soul to McCain and deserved better. They ended on an angry note.

Throughout these days, McCain was continuing to hear from some of the fund-raisers that he needed to take more drastic steps, that he should get rid of Nelson and bring Davis back in as campaign manager. Weaver was tipped to these problems by Phil Gramm, the former Texas senator who was a friend and an economic adviser to McCain, before the Sedona meeting; in Arizona, Loeffler warned Nelson that McCain was in a bad mood.

When McCain returned to Washington on Sunday, Salter came to his condominium for what others said was an emotional meeting. Salter told his boss that Nelson was thinking of tendering his resignation. McCain said he did not want that to happen. McCain was preparing for a trip to Iraq over the July Fourth holiday. On Monday, the day before his departure, Nelson and McCain met alone in McCain's Senate office to review the staff cuts that would be announced on Tuesday. McCain made some minor changes in the plan and Nelson returned to the campaign headquarters in Crystal City, Virginia, to begin to slash the staff. He was neither asked to resign nor did he volunteer to do so.

Nelson, Weaver, and Salter delivered the bad news to the staff. "They just looked exhausted," said Tucker Bounds. "I think they all realized, or believed at that point in time, that this was the beginning of a certain end to this campaign. That was the look on their faces, like this is the first part of how you put down a campaign. It's a horse with a broken leg."

On Tuesday, Nelson and Weaver held a conference call with reporters to announce that the campaign had raised just $11.2 million in the second quarter and that cash on hand was just $2 million, pitifully low. In oblique terms they described the restructuring of the campaign, but offered no hint of the extent to which the reductions would decimate the operation. Nelson said the campaign was now considering applying for federal matching funds—a step that, if McCain were to win the nomination, would leave him financially crippled through the spring and summer of 2008 because of spending limits to which he would have to agree to get the federal money. Nelson told reporters, "We confronted reality and we dealt with it in the best way that we could, so that we can move forward with this campaign."

The trip to Iraq deepened McCain's commitment to make more changes. Lindsey Graham, who was also on the trip, recalled his mood. "This guy's dead, nails in his coffin. He felt pretty bad I can tell you. We were out of money; we were fifth in a four-person race. He had lost confidence in his campaign team and he hadn't made decisions about how to change yet, but he was thinking about it." McCain could not understand how he had fallen so fast. "He's a human being. You can just tell it on his face. You can hear it in his voice," Graham said.

In Iraq, McCain and Graham attended a reenlistment ceremony and a naturalization ceremony. McCain was so moved by the spirit of the troops that he told Graham he was determined to take back his campaign and keep going. Graham said, "We were all on the plane and he says, you know, if these guys can do this, we can get this campaign back on track. If they're willing to reenlist for another term we're going to get this campaign back." He returned back from Iraq, said one of his advisers, "and his mind was set."

On the flight, McCain called Weaver and said he wanted to meet on Monday. Salter, who was in Maine that weekend, spoke to McCain by phone on Sunday. McCain was very cool. The next morning, Weaver and Nelson met McCain in his Senate office. They believed the agenda was Iraq. For weeks they had been working to revise McCain's Iraq message away from the surge, hoping to make Iraq a less central focus of his daily stump speech. They were working on a document that laid out the details of the new message and assumed McCain wanted to review where they were. Instead, McCain asked to see the budget. Nelson said he had not brought the budget but could be back within the hour. Then the meeting quickly deteriorated into an argument about the state of the campaign's finances. Weaver recalled, "He looked at me and said, 'John, how did we end up in this situation?'"

Weaver was irritated at having to relitigate the entire matter. He complained that the structure of the campaign had impeded sensible decision-making. He said his resignation had been on the table for two weeks and McCain could exercise it whenever he wanted. He then left the room. "At that point, I knew it was over," he told us. Nelson stayed behind briefly. He told McCain he was prepared to resign whenever the candidate wanted. He left and caught up with Weaver. "I said [to Weaver] he doesn't have confidence anymore," Nelson told us. "You can't stick around if he doesn't have confidence." Weaver had one more conversation with McCain that night. "I said I don't want to have any more arguments with you," Weaver recalled. "If you want to make a change, I urge you to consider the ramifications internally. If you make it precipitously, you're going to greatly damage your campaign and your candidacy. People will walk out the door."

The next morning, Nelson and Weaver resigned. When word first leaked, there was a press frenzy. Reaction was spontaneous and unanimous. The departures were seen as a crippling blow to McCain's campaign. Other resignations followed. Davis pleaded with the remaining advisers not to quit. Civil war erupted, with the warring camps using the media to tell their stories.

Davis's side weighed in through a Robert Novak column that trashed Weaver and Nelson for mismanagement and extravagant spending. Three members of the communications team—Brian Jones, Danny Diaz, and Matt David—were considering leaving but had been asked to stay on long enough to see McCain through a trip to New Hampshire. The column infuriated Jones. He would not stay to be part of an effort to tar Weaver and Nelson. Salter begged them not to leave. Jones agreed but was alarmed by the almost tribal nature of the infighting.

McCain was terribly distraught—"It was as ugly as it could get," a McCain confidant told us later—and briefly talked about shutting down the entire campaign. Salter told others of his concerns that McCain might drop out, but later insisted to us that McCain never seriously considered it. Quitting was simply not in his nature.

Determined to show the campaign was alive and well, McCain went to New Hampshire that weekend. There he uttered his memorable line that "contracting a fatal disease" was the only thing he could think of that might prevent him from being a candidate at the time of the New Hampshire primary, then six months into the future. He spent the night in Vermont, reminiscing with Salter, Jones, his son Jimmy, who was soon to ship off to Iraq with the Marines, and several reporters. He talked about his escapades in the Navy, of meeting Lucky Luciano in a bar in Rome, of seeing Elizabeth Taylor and Richard Burton in Paris, of a brief fling with a former Miss Brazil. It was all captured brilliantly by GQ's national correspondent Robert Draper. "This was the McCain he wanted us to know," Draper wrote. "A man brave enough to lose it all. The kind of man who never seems to win anymore."

The next morning he held a town hall meeting at an American Legion post in Claremont, New Hampshire. The small second-floor room was stained with smoke and packed with people. Salter hung out in the back, pacing nervously as the candidate fielded questions. Months later Salter told us that he believed reporters were on a death watch that weekend, like "vultures on a . . . wire. Is he actually going to clutch his chest and drop dead of a heart attack right here, right before our very eyes and cameras?"

The second questioner asked McCain about the state of the campaign. He had watched television the night before and the pundits were sounding the death knell. What did the candidate have to say about all that? McCain showed he hadn't lost his sense of humor. "I should have called on your wife," he quipped. He took off his blazer and set it aside. "Look," he said in a serious tone, "I've had tough times in my life. This is a day at the beach compared to that."

The room erupted in applause. In the back, Salter applauded the loudest.

CHAPTER TWENTY

No Surrender

"We believe . . . we have a superior product to market."

—Rick Davis, McCain's campaign manager

John McCain was no longer master of his fate. Once his campaign collapsed, he was dependent on the shortcomings of his opponents to find a way back. Had any of them seized command of the race, he would not have had a chance. Mark McKinnon, his campaign's media adviser, said, "He had to draw to an inside straight over and over and over again. A hundred things had to happen, most of them improbable."

In the immediate aftermath of the implosion, McCain's advisers had only one goal: to preserve his dignity and salvage his reputation. They anticipated an almost certain end to his candidacy, exactly when they did not know, but their belief was that his second campaign for the nomination would end as had the first, in defeat and disappointment. They were determined that it not end in humiliation. One adviser who remained in the campaign then said, "Part of sticking around was just to help restore his honor, just help the old soldier get his medals back." Another adviser said, "Our first concern was, get this guy's reputation as an effective campaigner back, as a guy with stature in the politics of this country. So if he returned to the Senate he'd still be a person of influence, a dealmaker and all the things he had become." McCain sought a respectable end as well, win or lose. "There was one part of it that aroused my competitive spirit," he later told us. "Since I never considered dropping out, I just said we'll do the best we can and we'll run an honorable campaign and one that we can look back on and say even if we lost we ran an honorable campaign."

On the trip to Iraq, McCain and Graham had talked through the options. "I said okay let's go down the list," Graham said. "Name somebody here we can't beat. And we went through each one of them as to how we could beat them." Mitt Romney was beginning to take hold in Iowa and New Hampshire, but conservatives still doubted his reliability. Mike Huckabee was not yet a factor. Fred Thompson was still in the exploratory stages and all talk. Rudy Giuliani led the polls but his liberal views on abortion and gay rights still left him at odds with the base—far more so than McCain. "My line was we're the most reliable conservative who can win in November," Graham said.

The question was how to get to the general election. For advice, McCain turned to Charlie Black, a veteran Republican strategist who had been a young operative in Reagan's 1980 campaign and later built a lucrative lobbying and consulting business in Washington while advising many Republican candidates. Black was the campaign's most experienced senior adviser and McCain asked him for his best judgment, knowing Black would give him an unvarnished assessment. Was it possible for him to win the nomination, given the campaign's financial problems? Black came back to McCain and said yes, he had as good a chance as anyone else in the field and told McCain he had a sophisticated strategy to get there. "What is it?" McCain asked. Black said he told him, "Be the last man standing."

McCain's implosion opened the way for four other candidates to take control: Mitt Romney, Rudy Giuliani, Mike Huckabee, and Fred Thompson. Each had a profoundly different strategy for winning the nomination, and from early July to the eve of the Iowa caucuses, they all sought to prove they were ready to lead the party.

First up was Romney, who was moving quickly even before McCain's collapse. For years, Iowa Republicans had staged a straw poll in Ames for presidential candidates in the summer before the caucuses. Over the years, the straw poll had become a significant, and expensive, early test of the Republican field, a daylong political carnival with consequences. Candidates who didn't meet expectations were often driven to the sidelines.

In June, sensing Romney's organizational advantage in Iowa and determined to avoid embarrassment, McCain and Giuliani announced they would not participate. That left Romney with an unfortunate choice. He had decided earlier that he would participate in any event that measured the candidates against one another: debates, forums, straw polls. But competing in Ames meant spending a million or two million dollars to rent buses for supporters, buy their tickets, feed them barbecue, provide entertainment, and handle logistics. Romney's team had seen the straw poll as an opportunity to beat McCain and Giuliani and vault him securely into the top tier. Now his advisers worried that with those two out, he would be expected to win easily. A victory would produce limited payoff while gobbling up valuable resources. But to drop out would risk demoralizing his Iowa team, offend party activists, and possibly hurt his chances to win the caucuses in January. Committed to his early-state strategy, he decided to compete all out.

August 11 was warm and sunny, perfect for a daylong political picnic, and thousands turned out in Ames. Romney told supporters, "Change begins in Iowa and change begins today." He won easily with 32 percent of the votes. Giuliani ran eighth with 1 percent and McCain tenth with less than 1 percent. But the real story was that, in a battle for religious conservatives, little-known Mike Huckabee had defeated the better-known Sam Brownback for second. Romney's advisers tried to ignore Huckabee, spinning his victory as evidence that he was the true conservative in the GOP race, in contrast to Giuliani or McCain. Huckabee claimed he was *the* conservative candidate in a state where Christian conservatives had major influence in the caucuses.

That day, Romney's advisers talked over their post-Ames options. Should they spend heavily to win Iowa if McCain and Giuliani were not likely to campaign actively there? Should they focus more heavily on New Hampshire? "We should have pulled the plug on Iowa," Romney adviser Ron Kaufman said later. He did not mean quit Iowa entirely but that Romney should scale back the operation significantly. "Knock back the TV. Don't spend time in Iowa. Don't have two fronts. Go to New Hampshire and take on McCain." Instead they decided to stay. Winning Iowa, even under changed circumstances, would start the slingshot strategy designed to propel him to the nomination. Kaufman regretted that he did not make that case forcefully once Romney had won the straw poll.

At that time, however, Romney's advisers worried little about McCain causing problems in New Hampshire. If anything, they anticipated a battle there with Giuliani. They saw little chance for McCain to rise again. One staffer argued vigorously for attacking McCain after his campaign imploded. "He's not dead yet, let's stomp on him," Myers said this staffer argued. She and Romney disagreed. She said, "Mitt said no. Rudy was getting bigger and bigger. . . . We had other fish to fry."

Romney's straw poll victory, coupled with McCain's apparent demise, changed the dynamic of the race in a way that proved detrimental to Romney's strategy. In Ames, his advisers began to argue that the Republican race was now a two-person contest between a real conservative (Romney) and a faux conservative (Giuliani). But they badly misjudged the new post-McCain dynamic. In fact, the race was quickly becoming everybody against Mitt.

McCain plotted his comeback by taking a leaf from Barack Obama. He would be audacious. Instead of steering away from the divisive Iraq issue, as his advisers had been urging for months, he would make Iraq the central pillar of his campaign. He would salvage his nomination by campaigning all-out for the surge.

A new member of his inner circle was the principal architect of this strategy. Steve Schmidt, built like a linebacker with a shaved head, had run Bush's rapid-response reelection operation with such tenacity that Karl Rove dubbed him "Bullet." After that he joined Vice President Cheney's staff, later helped a beleaguered Arnold Schwarzenegger win reelection as California's governor, then became a consultant to McCain's campaign, where he and McCain developed a close relationship. He could be terse and abrasive. During a phone call in the summer of 2007, after McCain returned from Iraq, Schmidt grilled McCain like a prosecutor: Are we winning? he asked. Yes, McCain said. You believe that? Yes. What happens if we leave? We lose. So it's de facto surrender if we leave? Yes. You have to say that, Schmidt told him. McCain said that's what he was saying every day. Schmidt disagreed. "You're telling people things are a little bit better," he recalled telling McCain. "You've got to say what you believe on this. If you believe we're winning there because of a new strategy, then you need to say that."

In September, Army General David Petraeus, the commander of U.S. forces in Iraq, and Ryan Crocker, the U.S. ambassador to Iraq, were scheduled to testify before Congress about the surge. The hearings gave McCain a platform to reinvigorate his candidacy. Schmidt told him, "What I think you should do [is] take every dime this campaign has, get all your veteran buddies together, start in California and drive across the country to New Hampshire and then down to Washington saying, 'We're not going to surrender. . . .' He got it immediately."

Thus was born the "No Surrender" tour and the strategy to force McCain back into contention for the nomination. In August, on one of his trips to New Hampshire, McCain held a town hall meeting in tiny Wolfeboro. Lynn Savage, whose twenty-two-year-old son, Matthew Stanley, had been killed in Iraq on his second tour of duty, asked McCain if he would wear a bracelet with her son's name on it. McCain said he would wear the bracelet every day. Stanley's mother asked him to make one more pledge: Do everything in your power to make sure my son did not die in vain.

Few people were paying attention to McCain. To the political community, September loomed as the month Fred Thompson would announce his candidacy and potentially reshape the Republican race. McCain's advisers were determined to make September the moment he once again became a viable candidate. For that he needed three things: a successful debate in New Hampshire; positive testimony from Petraeus; and a No Surrender tour that solidified his message on the war and kept Iraq at the center of his comeback strategy.

On September 5, Republican candidates debated at the University of New Hampshire. Charlie Black had said McCain's only path to victory was to win the New Hampshire primary. The rest of the country might not be paying attention to this debate, but New Hampshire voters, those McCain needed most, were. McCain had disappeared for most of the summer, ignored by the press and his competitors. The debate would be his moment to reemerge, and for once he knew what he wanted to accomplish. The opportunity came when Romney said, "The surge is apparently working." McCain jumped him. "Governor, the surge *is* working," he said. "The surge is working, sir. It is working." Romney protested, "That's just what I said." McCain kept up the attack. "No, not *apparently*—it's working!"

That night, in Burbank, California, Thompson announced his candidacy on *The Tonight Show with Jay Leno*. It seemed a clever way to take attention away from the other candidates.

The next week Petraeus gave a cautiously upbeat report on the surge, blunting Democratic efforts to force Bush to accept a timetable for withdrawing troops. General Petraeus had given surge supporters like McCain a boost in credibility, permitting them to argue that they had been right from the start.

The No Surrender tour followed. McCain visited VFW and American Legion halls, accompanied by Vietnam and Iraq war veterans. He attacked the liberal group MoveOn.org, which had sponsored a scurrilous newspaper ad calling Petraeus "General Betray Us." He criticized Hillary Clinton, who had told Petraeus his assessment of the situation in Iraq required "the willing suspension of disbelief." McCain said acidly, "It's a willing suspension of disbelief that Senator Clinton thinks she knows more than General Petraeus."

September marked a turning point for McCain. Not that he registered big gains in the polls. Not that his rivals suddenly began worrying about him. But it helped restore his confidence. When he looked back, McCain pinpointed that debate as the beginning of his comeback. "We didn't see an immediate response in the polls," he told us, "but what we did see was a little uptick in town hall meetings and people saying, 'You know, I think I'll give this old guy a second look.' And I think that started us at a very slow but very steady path back up in New Hampshire."

As the other candidates focused on each other, McCain bided his time. He used the debates to remind Republican voters that he not only was still in the race but that he remained the party's strongest candidate against the likely candidate, Hillary Clinton. In Orlando on October 21, Chris Wallace of Fox News asked McCain whether he could defeat Clinton in a general election, given public opinion on the war. "Let me just say that I know and respect Senator Clinton," McCain said, as he began to turn the question to his advantage. "The debate that I have between me and her will be based on national security, on fiscal conservatism, and on social conservatism. It will be a respectful debate. That's what the American people want." Then he began his pivot. "Now, one of them will be spending. I have fought against out-of-control, disgraceful spending that's been going on, and I have saved the American people as much as two billion dollars at one stroke." He looked down at his notes. "In case you missed it," he continued, "a few days ago Senator Clinton tried to spend one million dollars on the Woodstock Concert Museum. Now, my friends, I wasn't there. I'm sure it was a cultural and pharmaceutical event." The audience laughed, as McCain went on. "I was tied up at the time." More laughter, along with applause. Then, as the audience got the full impact of his words referring to his torture in Vietnam, they rose and gave him a sustained ovation. The other Republican candidates on the stage joined in the applause.

Giuliani was expert at playing president. In the fall of 2007, he went to London, where he met with Margaret Thatcher, Tony Blair, and Prime Minister Gordon Brown. After meeting with Brown, Giuliani said rather patronizingly that he was "very, very heartened by how seriously" the new prime minister saw the Iranian threat, as if he were on a trip to shore up an ally's resolve. He portrayed himself as already a world leader. "I'm probably one of the four or five best-known Americans in the world," he told reporters. But the images impressed Republicans back home. A Republican strategist marveled, saying Giuliani's trip gave GOP voters the first image of "the post-Bush era with another Republican standing on the world stage."

Giuliani's strategy for winning the nomination was the opposite of Romney's. His was a late-state strategy. He would downplay Iowa and New Hampshire to focus his resources on Florida and the Super Tuesday states of February 5th. It was a risky strategy, one never tried before and adopted out of weakness rather than the strength he tried to project. He was simply too liberal for Iowa's electorate. He was better suited to New Hampshire, but McCain and Romney had clear advantages there at the start of the campaign. Giuliani's advisers concluded his best hope was to capitalize on Florida and February 5th.

The arithmetic behind a late-state strategy made some sense, given the rules of the Republican Party. Many states were winner-take-all, the same rules that apply in calculating votes in the Electoral College. Others were winner-take-all by congressional district. Giuliani's team foresaw the possibility of a huge delegate haul on February 5th. They assumed he would easily win New York, New Jersey, Connecticut, and Delaware, all winner-take-all states with a combined delegate count of about 200. They expected him to win the majority of California's 170 delegates, which were awarded by congressional district. And he counted on winning all of Florida's delegates on January 29. That, they calculated, would put him well ahead of anyone else in the field after Super Tuesday, in pursuit of the 1,191 delegates needed for the nomination. The question was whether Giuliani could stay alive until Florida without success in one of the early states.

Giuliani's late-state strategy always came with an asterisk. His real hope was to exceed expectations in New Hampshire and give himself a boost heading to Florida. As his campaign manager, Mike DuHaime, later explained, "It was more intended to be a New Hampshire, Florida, February 5th strategy, rather than simply a late-state strategy, but unfortunately that is not how it worked out."

In November, Giuliani began his move in New Hampshire, airing television commercials and booking more campaign time. We caught up with him on Thanksgiving weekend, aboard his bus, as he traveled from the lakes district to Concord. Are you here to win? we asked. Giuliani laughed. "Sure I'm here to win," he said. "What else would we be doing here, but to win? That's the whole idea of it. Romney spent seven or eight million to get where he is and has stayed pretty much where he's been, so we think we can catch him and get ahead of him."

Already, however, his candidacy was experiencing problems. Early in November, Bernard B. Kerik, the former Giuliani driver, New York police commissioner, and business partner, whom Giuliani had pushed to become secretary of homeland security in the Bush administration, was indicted on corruption charges. Giuliani was forced to acknowledge that he had failed to check Kerik out. But damning new evidence in the *New York Times* showed that Giuliani had been briefed about Kerik's possible problems in December 2004 and still ignored the warnings.

Politico reporter Ben Smith then published a story detailing how Giuliani, as mayor, had "billed obscure city agencies for tens of thousands of dollars in security expenses amassed during the time when he was beginning an extramarital relationship with future wife Judith Nathan in the Hamptons." The exposé created a major problem nationally for Giuliani. In New Hampshire, the conservative *Manchester Union Leader*, no friend of Giuliani's, gave the story huge play.

A third setback disrupted Giuliani's plans. He was counting on an endorsement from Florida Governor Charlie Crist. According to three Giuliani advisers, Crist had gone to see Giuliani in the Hamptons in July and told the mayor he would back his candidacy. On October 9, the day the Republican candidates debated in Michigan, Crist called Giuliani's closest confidant, Tony Carbonetti. "I'm in," he told Carbonetti, according to an official familiar with the conversation. Giuliani's team penciled in mid-November for an announcement and planned a series of events around it, starting in Florida and then going to New Hampshire. Then, inexplicably, Crist backed out, leaving Giuliani without the credibility boost he badly needed.

Despite his spending several million on his New Hampshire advertising blitz, Giuliani's poll numbers began to drop as the scandal stories took root. The candidate and his staff suddenly drew back, pulling down their ads and effectively abandoning the state. Giuliani's decision to pull out of New Hampshire proved to be an unexpected gift to his friend John McCain. McCain pollster Bill McInturff said later, "They left open the one piece of real estate John McCain could win." Beth Myers later said at an Institute of Politics conference at Harvard, "When Rudy stopped advertising in New Hampshire, that was one of the worst days in our campaign. . . . He went down and McCain went right up."

The Giuliani team saw it differently. They were desperate to keep the race as fluid as possible until Florida. Because they still regarded Romney as their biggest threat and believing he would win Iowa, they were determined to do what they could to prevent him from winning New Hampshire. If Giuliani couldn't win, perhaps McCain could. "We knew by the middle of December we could not win New Hampshire," the Giuliani adviser said. "But we knew if we stayed full throttle, Romney would win [because McCain and Giuliani would divide the moderate vote]. We were not trying to hurt Romney. We were trying to help ourselves. We were trying to stretch the election out another month."

CHAPTER TWENTY-ONE

Can Anybody Play This Game?

The most trustworthy, competent, and conservative of all those seeking the nomination.

—*Manchester Union Leader* endorsement of McCain

For much of 2007, no one took Mike Huckabee very seriously. His role seemed to be chief comic in the Republican field. Not that his résumé was anything to scoff at. He had served as governor of Arkansas for a decade. He had chaired the National Governors Association and earned a reputation as a conservative who could work with his Democratic counterparts. He was quick and engaging, deeply conservative but with a beguiling personality that disarmed those with whom he disagreed.

His personal story was compelling. He grew up in a family with little money. His spare-the-rod-and-spoil-the-child father was a fireman and his mother worked as a clerk. He was a Baptist minister who also played bass guitar in a band called "Capitol Offense." He told one reporter he would like the Rolling Stones to play at his inaugural. When a doctor told him his health was threatened by obesity, he lost 110 pounds, completed a marathon, and wrote a book about his experience. He had a quick sense of humor. "I'm from the small town of Hope," he said once. "You may have heard of it. [It was also Bill Clinton's hometown.] All I ask you is, give us one more chance."

Since he lacked money or a big name, debates became his route to prominence. Because he was an ordained minister who was openly seeking the support of Christian conservatives and because he was lightly regarded as a possible nominee, Huckabee drew questions about the Bible, theology, and the intersection of church and state. His deft responses to these delicate questions made him an early standout. In a debate co-sponsored by YouTube, which featured questions from around the country, he was asked about Jesus and the death penalty. "What would Jesus do?" the video inquisitor asked. Without hesitating, Huckabee quipped, "Jesus was too smart ever to run for public office."

In New Hampshire, CNN's Wolf Blitzer asked Huckabee, "At a previous debate, you and two of your colleagues indicated that you do not believe in evolution. You're an ordained minister. What do you believe? Is it the story of creation as it is reported in the Bible?"

"It's interesting that that question would even be asked of somebody running for president," Huckabee began. "I'm not planning on writing the curriculum for an eighth-grade science book. I'm asking for the opportunity to be president of the United States. But you've raised the question, so let me answer it. 'In the beginning, God created the heavens and the Earth.' To me it's pretty simple, a person either believes that God created this process or believes that it was an accident and that it just happened all on its own. . . . Let me be very clear: I believe there is a God. I believe there is a God who was active in the creation process. Now, how did he do it, and when did he do it, and how long did he take? I don't honestly know, and I don't think knowing that would make me a better or a worse president."

When the candidates debated in Michigan on October 9, 2007, and some offered upbeat assessments of the economy, he dissented. "A lot of people are going to be watching this debate. They're going to hear Republicans on this stage talk about how great the economy is," he said. "And frankly, when they hear that, they're going to probably reach for the dial. I want to make sure people understand that for many people on this stage the economy's doing terrifically well, but for a lot of Americans it's not doing so well."

He offered contrary views on trade and stood up for an Arkansas program that allowed the children of illegal immigrants to apply for college scholarships. When Romney attacked the program, Huckabee cut him down. "I'm standing here tonight on this stage because I got an education. If I hadn't had the education, I wouldn't be standing on this stage. I might be picking lettuce. . . . In all due respect, we're a better country than to punish children for what their parents did."

Huckabee's political strategy was narrowly focused on locking in conservative Christian and pro-life activists in Iowa. If Romney had an early-state strategy and Giuliani had a late-state strategy, Huckabee had a one-state strategy: Iowa. Support from religious conservatives would not be enough to win the nomination, but if he could consolidate the Christian right in Iowa, Huckabee knew he could win there. He would take his chances after that.

Surprisingly, Huckabee opposed participating in the Ames straw poll, particularly after McCain and Giuliani dropped out. "He thought it was a waste of time and money if the other people didn't do it," campaign manager Chip Saltsman recalled. Huckabee saw it as high risk. "I knew that if we played and did poorly, it was over for us," he later wrote. Saltsman told Huckabee that he had to compete and had to do well. Ducking Ames would have the same impact as doing poorly: There wouldn't be enough money to survive until January.

His second-place showing gave him an immediate boost, at least in publicity and recognition. His next major goal was to deepen his appeal as the candidate of the religious right by impressing the participants at the October "Values Voters" conference in Washington hosted by the conservative Family Research Council. "I come today not as one who comes to you, but as one who comes from you," he said. Speaking shortly after Giuliani had addressed the crowd, he urged the audience not to be influenced by questions of electability. Better to support candidates who "sing from their hearts" than to follow those who "just lip-synch the lyrics from our songs." His strongest response came when he said, "Let us never sacrifice our principles for anybody's politics. Not now. Not ever."

By then, Huckabee was beginning to move in Iowa, boosted by networks of evangelical churches and the community of homeschool advocates. He made ever more direct appeals to Christian voters. As the caucuses neared, he aired a television commercial that opened with the words "Christian leader" on the screen. At the end of December, he put on a beautifully produced Christmas commercial. He wore a red sweater. There was a Christmas tree to one side and "Silent Night" played softly on the soundtrack. In the background, as the camera panned slowly, light reflected off the bookshelves to form the image of a white cross. "Are you about worn out of all the television commercials you're seeing, mostly about politics? I don't blame you," he said. "At this time of year, sometimes it's nice to pull aside from all of that and just remember that what really matters is the celebration of the birth of Christ and being with our family and our friends. I hope that you and your family will have a magnificent Christmas season."

The ad drew criticism for its overtly Christian appeal, but that was of little concern to Huckabee. The polls showed he was now the front-runner in Iowa.

No one loomed larger at the time of McCain's implosion than Fred Thompson. The former Tennessee senator, veteran movie actor, and star of NBC's *Law and Order* started sending out signals in the spring that he was interested in running. Big and ruggedly handsome, a natural in front of the camera, he seemed to fit what many disgruntled Republicans were looking for: someone with a Reaganesque style, an appealing demeanor, and conservative values.

His campaign went through three phases: anticipation, hype, and disappointment. He initially surrounded himself with a team that had little experience in modern presidential campaigns. They convinced him that new media offered a way around the rigors of the campaign trail, which appealed to a man with a reputation in Republican circles as a not particularly hard worker. When left-wing moviemaker Michael Moore released *Sicko*, a documentary that compared Cuba's health care system favorably to America's, a cigar-chomping Thompson cut a quick video offering a sarcastic response. It became an instant hit on YouTube. His advisers pointed to it as the template for the Internet-age campaign he could run.

"Fred was sold a bill of goods about what it took to run for president," communications director Todd Harris later told us. "He was given the distinct impression by people who have never even worked on a presidential campaign, much less mapped one out, that in 2008 all you needed to do was have a heavy blog presence, appear regularly on Fox News and specifically on *Hannity & Colmes*, and from time to time go out and have an event."

As McCain foundered, Thompson dithered. June turned to July and July to August without any real campaign structure in place. His initial fund-raising fell short of his advisers' expectations. His wife, Jeri, a powerful behind-the-scenes force, warred with some of the senior talent he had recruited. Staff upheaval began long before there was even a plan for an announcement. Tom Collamore, who was brought in to put the campaign together, was pushed out. Other staffers left or were forced out. Bickering and leaks permeated the campaign. It was as if the wheels were coming off the wagon before it even left the assembly line.

The last weekend in July, Thompson called Bill Lacy, who had run his successful 1994 campaign for the Senate and was then the director of the Robert C. Dole Institute at the University of Kansas. "I need your help," Thompson told him. Lacy asked a few questions and requested basic information about the campaign: the basic strategy document, polling data, the budget and fund-raising plan, an organizational chart, opposition research. "He stopped me," Lacy recalled later. "[He said], 'Bill, I don't believe we have any of those things.'" The two met the following week at Thompson's home in McLean, Virginia. "He took me back into the study, just the two of us," Lacy said. "He said, 'Bill, I am desperate. I would like to be president. But this is a mess and I need you to come in and fix it.'"

From there on, Lacy was running a triage operation. A staff already shaken by upheaval went through another round of changes. Five months before the Iowa caucuses, there was no infrastructure in place, no plan for an announcement, no draft of a speech. Worse, the finance department envisioned raising only half of what the campaign team had budgeted to spend.

Thompson often said that while he wanted to be president, he never really wanted to run for president. He proved that once he became a candidate by doing things that seemed ingenious but in fact were politically detrimental. By announcing his candidacy on Jay Leno's *Tonight Show* on the evening of the Republican debate in New Hampshire, he simultaneously snubbed his rivals and offended the constituency of an important early state.

His path to the nomination was obvious, though difficult. He was the southern candidate the field had lacked after Tennessee's Bill Frist and Virginia's George Allen forfeited their chances of running. (Like others, he underestimated Huckabee.) He needed to win South Carolina; to get that far, he would have to finish a strong second in Iowa. Instead, he ran a no-state strategy, a campaign marked by lack of energy or clear commitment on his part.

Bob Haus, a veteran Iowa Republican operative who was part of the Thompson team, recalled his frustration when Thompson abruptly canceled a long-scheduled hunting trip in Iowa with members of the National Rifle Association board that had been set up as an ideal photo-op. He said Jeri Thompson and others did not want Thompson worn out before a big speech that night. Later that weekend, Jeri told Haus that she objected to some of the questions she and Thompson had gotten at a meeting with activists. She said her husband intended to run a different kind of campaign. Haus said he told her, "This is what all candidates have to do. I summarized by saying, 'Mrs. Thompson, you and the senator have to submit yourself to this process or this process will humble you.' It was the last time she ever spoke to me directly."

E-mails from inside the campaign, provided by Thompson staffers after the campaign ended, show the degree of frustration many of them felt trying to get Thompson to do even the most basic campaign activities. In the late fall, a staffer at headquarters e-mailed a staffer in Iowa, noting that Huckabee was doing six events the next day and Ron Paul three. The reply read, "We? Are doing 0. Zeeerooooh. Nada. Zilch. Nuttin." On New Year's Day, CNN was eager to book an interview with Thompson, but he wouldn't budge. With the caucuses two days away, all the other candidates were running at full speed. Thompson had set aside the day to watch college football, then took a nap, according to two of his aides. His lone event was a half-hour stop at a home for veterans. There was an internal squabble over how far he would have to go to get to the CNN satellite truck for the appearance. The frustrated press staffer told his colleagues that CNN "thinks I'm an idiot."

Thompson resisted making phone calls to donors or even responding to developments on the campaign trail. For a campaign built on the concept of exploiting the new media, he was slow to grasp the demands of a 24/7 news cycle. When campaign advisers wanted to respond to breaking developments, one adviser said, "Fred's response often would be, 'Now hold on, they're not going to dictate to us when we respond to things.'" Decisions that should have taken hours took days. The staff sometimes had to send proposed responses to the road and then wait for the candidate's approval. One frustrated adviser said, "Literally something would happen on a Monday and we'd send the statement out to the road and like on Wednesday get an e-mail. The best is we'd get back a hard copy of it, 'Approved.'"

Toward the end of the Iowa campaign, Thompson was persuaded by a few old hands that the way to turn his candidacy around was to take a page out of Ronald Reagan's 1976 campaign playbook and deliver a twenty-minute talk (actual time was seventeen minutes) straight to camera. Lacy protested and thought he had stopped it. But a film crew was flown to Iowa to produce the video and a staffer delivered it to a television station. Other staffers frantically e-mailed one another trying to figure out whether the video had been killed. Lacy later told us, "Reagan was Reagan. Fred is incredible but there's no other Reagan. It's a different era. I just thought it was a total waste of time and it was."

When Thompson announced his candidacy, he surged to near the front of the pack. From there to the end, he experienced a slow but steady decline in his support, due in large measure to his own performance. His closest advisers argued later that he eventually became an effective candidate, but by then he had been written off. The coverage of his early trips left an indelible impression that his heart was not in the game. Adam Nagourney of the *New York Times* described Thompson speaking for twenty-four minutes in a small restaurant in Nevada, Iowa. When he finished, no one stirred. "Can I have a round of applause?" he asked plaintively.

In late summer, *Newsweek* ran a cover story about Thompson with the headline "Lazy Like a Fox?" The message: Watch out for the wily Thompson. Months later, *Politico's* Roger Simon wrote a column under the headline "Thompson, Lazy as Charged."

Lacy later concluded the campaign was doomed almost from the beginning, that few of the late mistakes mattered much. "He hadn't been out on the trail for ten years and it took him a while to get back in the game," one adviser said. "He needed time to get back in the groove again." Thompson had promised a campaign of bold ideas, but they were smothered by the fact that he was not prepared to fight for the nomination. "We did not meet expectations from the beginning and we steadily declined," Lacy said. "I think that's because over time the voters didn't think we measured up either as a candidate or a campaign."

Had Thompson been ready to enter the race when McCain stumbled, he might have found an audience and become a force. Instead, his lackluster campaign removed one more potential obstacle in the path of McCain's resurrection.

McCain was blessed by his opposition. In one way or another, all his opponents had made strategic or tactical decisions that helped McCain put himself back into the thick of the Republican race. McCain no longer pretended to be running a national campaign. Now every decision was made with one objective: Does it help or hurt his chances of winning New Hampshire? When Lindsey Graham begged for money for South Carolina, Salter told him, "The only thing that will cure McCain's problems there is winning New Hampshire."

McCain doggedly continued to conduct town hall meetings and visited every newspaper editorial board possible—dailies and weeklies—in hope of winning their endorsements. With the help of Mike Dennehy, a New

Hampshire–based staffer, he courted Joseph W. McQuaid, publisher of the *Manchester Union Leader*. The paper no longer possessed the power of earlier decades—a power often recklessly used to reward allies and punish opponents—but it remained the most important voice of conservatism in the state and a force in Republican presidential primaries. The newspaper had not endorsed McCain in 2000; his maverick conservative politics were at odds with its philosophy. But now, on December 2, in a front-page editorial signed by McQuaid, the *Union Leader* wrote, "We don't agree with him on every issue. . . . What is most compelling about McCain, however, is that his record, his character, and his courage show him to be the most trustworthy, competent, and conservative of all those seeking the nomination." The editorial also said, "Simply put, McCain can be trusted to make informed decisions based on the best interests of his country, come hell or high water."

By that time, McCain was beginning to move up in New Hampshire polls. In early December, Romney's internal polling showed him at 34 percent in New Hampshire, with Giuliani second at 17 percent, and McCain third at 14 percent. Although Giuliani was beginning to fade, Romney's advisers were not worried. His vote appeared solid; they doubted Giuliani would truly collapse. But by mid-December, the daily tracks showed a clear pattern. "All of a sudden, McCain comes back," Alex Gage remembered. "The Phoenix rises." Romney advisers decided to attack McCain. McCain stormed back, airing a television ad quoting the *Concord Monitor*, which had written a devastating editorial saying Romney should never be president and calling him a "phony."

The Romney campaign was now suffering from internal strife. His message was fuzzy. He did not seem authentic as a candidate and was still struggling to find a message. Was he running as a true conservative, an outsider, a Mr. Fixit ready to reform Washington? It was never clear. One conservative strategist volunteered to us late in the year that the more he saw of Romney, the less he liked him.

Romney's advertising team was split into dueling camps. He had started out with Alex Castellanos as his main media adviser. When McCain's campaign collapsed in the summer, Romney successfully wooed McCain's media duo, Russ Schriefer and Stuart Stevens, who also had produced ads for Bush's two campaigns. The effort at creative tension backfired, as the ad makers squabbled repeatedly about message and commercials. "It created a very difficult environment to manage the strategy and tactics. . . . They spent hours arguing," Alex Gage later complained.

The day after Christmas, Romney's polls showed McCain had taken the lead. Giuliani had collapsed, and was heading toward single digits. "The environment got very good for McCain," Gage said. "People in New Hampshire that had written him off, all of a sudden [saw it was coming] back together for him."

CHAPTER TWENTY-TWO

Phoenix Rising

*"I'm past the age when I can claim the noun 'kid,' no matter what
adjective precedes it. But tonight, we sure showed them what a
comeback looks like."*

—John McCain after winning New Hampshire

T he New Year opened with the nomination battle almost as confused
as it had been at the start of 2007, although the landscape was more
favorable than McCain could have dreamed when his campaign blew up
six months earlier. All his rivals were struggling. Romney was in trouble in
New Hampshire and pinned down in Iowa in a nasty fight with Huckabee.
Huckabee had no clear path after Iowa. Giuliani had abandoned New
Hampshire and the other early states and was staking everything on
Florida; he was an increasingly irrelevant factor. Thompson had never gotten off the ground and could get no attention.

Most of the media attention was focused on the Democratic race in
Iowa, with Clinton, Obama, and Edwards rallying their supporters in the
first days of January. But even as a sideshow, the Republican race provided
fireworks and unexpected twists.

Huckabee, now leading in Iowa, was weathering some of the toughest
weeks of his campaign. He drew a rebuke from Secretary of State Condo-
leezza Rice after describing the Bush administration's foreign policy as
having an "arrogant bunker mentality." He made a churlish comment about
Romney's Mormon religion, for which he apologized. There were new
questions about gifts he had taken as governor of Arkansas and other eth-
ical issues. But his supporters remained enthusiastic about a candidate
whose message emphasized conservative values, economic populism, and
a call to change the Republican Party. "You have an opportunity to do
something completely different that would utterly confound the political

ruling class in this country," he told one audience a week before the caucuses.

Romney, desperate to avoid defeat, lashed out at Huckabee. Ed Rollins, who had run Reagan's 1984 reelection campaign and was Huckabee's new national chairman, urged his candidate to fight back. Rollins, a former boxer, enjoyed a good political brawl. On December 30, Huckabee flew back to Little Rock aboard a chartered airplane, accompanied by Rollins, Chip Saltsman, and ad maker Bob Wicker. They filmed a commercial and prepared for a rollout the next day. The plan included a radio ad and new direct-mail brochure hitting Romney.

The campaign had scheduled a press conference for noon at the Marriott Hotel in downtown Des Moines, where it would draw a big media crowd. That morning, unbeknownst to his advisers, Huckabee had a change of mind. Barely an hour before the press conference, he announced he did not want to put the ad on television. Saltsman and Rollins were shocked. Huckabee told them, Saltsman recalled, "We started positive and I want to stay positive." But he would go ahead with his press conference and, in a bizarre decision, show the ad to reporters. Huckabee stood against a backdrop that said, "Enough is Enough," and announced his decision. "It's never too late to do the right thing," he said solemnly. Then, to derisive laughter, he proceeded to show the ad to the reporters. He left Des Moines to spend New Year's Eve on *The Tonight Show with Jay Leno*.

The national press hammered Huckabee that day, but in Iowa, particularly among Huckabee's supporters, the decision not to succumb to negative campaigning proved popular. The next night he appeared at the Val Air Ballroom in Des Moines for an exuberant rally that featured the actor Chuck Norris, Huckabee's leading surrogate, and a rock and roll band that Huckabee and MSNBC host Joe Scarborough joined for several songs. It was clear that he was the Republican candidate with the energy in Iowa.

McCain continued to make cameo appearances in Iowa. He flew in two days after Christmas, having won the endorsement of the *Des Moines Register*. Speaking with reporters, he played down expectations for the caucuses but said he felt good about his campaign. "The Comeback Kid is always uppermost in my mind," he said. "I look forward to that name." He left immediately for New Hampshire, but returned on the eve of the caucuses, traveling with three senators: Sam Brownback of Kansas, John Thune of South Dakota, and Lindsey Graham of South Carolina. Though not a factor in the race in Iowa, McCain hoped his last-minute appearance might enable him to steal third place against the slumping Thompson.* It was bitterly cold, but his headquarters office was overflowing and overheated as supporters waited for him to arrive. Graham offered testimonials, telling the audience, "Send him out of here with as much momentum as you can, and John, when you get to South Carolina this time, we're going to close the deal."

McCain's hopes depended on Huckabee's ability to pull off an upset in Iowa. Romney had a talented Iowa team and was extremely well organized. But Huckabee once again proved that even in a caucus state, momentum trumps organization. On caucus night 120,000 people turned out for the Republican caucuses, exceeding everyone's expectations. Sixty percent of those who turned out said they were evangelical Christians—far above anything Romney's team had estimated. Huckabee won almost half of those voters while Romney managed barely a fifth, and Huckabee won the caucuses with 34 percent to Romney's 25. McCain's hopes for third fell short; he was edged out by Thompson. It didn't matter. Huckabee's stunning victory was overshadowed that night by Obama's shocking Democratic triumph, but it damaged the only candidate, Romney, with a chance to defeat McCain in New Hampshire. Huckabee was jubilant. So was McCain. When McCain called to offer his congratulations, Huckabee thanked him and said, "Now it's your turn to kick his butt."

After Iowa, Romney retooled his message. Piggybacking on Obama's Iowa victory, he now presented himself as the change candidate, a Republican outsider who could shake up Washington. But he ran into a wall of opposition in New Hampshire.

Over months of campaigning Romney had managed to offend most of his rivals. Now, at a debate at Saint Anselm College three days before the primary, they gleefully ganged up on him. Thompson took a shot, as did Huckabee, who accused Romney of supporting a timetable for withdrawal in Iraq. "Governor, don't try to characterize my position," Romney replied testily. "Which one?" Huckabee asked. Stung, Romney said, "You know, we're wise to talk about policies and not to make personal attacks."

McCain delivered a sarcastic slap: "We disagree on a lot of issues," he told Romney. "But I agree. You are the candidate of change." The audience

---

* Thompson's campaign team was angrily denying a report that he was about to drop out of the race and endorse McCain.

howled at the obvious reference to Romney as a flip-flopper. The next day, McCain offered no regrets for his rough handling of Romney. "We've had a flood of e-mails and calls saying, 'Way to go,' because there has been an inaccurate portrayal of my positions on issues in mass mailings and others, and, I mean, you've got to respond and I responded," he said in an interview.

By now, McCain was cautiously optimistic about his prospects. "Tempered confidence," he told reporters. His aides were, as Mark Salter later put it, "cocky confident" about victory. "McCain was totally on his game, [the voters] were totally into him," Salter said. McCain was in his element, touring the state on what was called the "Mac Is Back" tour. He drew overflow crowds. In some places fire marshals had to shut the doors. John McCain was loose and freewheeling, bantering with reporters as if it were 2000 again.

Romney's team openly rooted for Obama to attract a heavy Independent vote—still the core of McCain's appeal in New Hampshire—to diminish their influence in the Republican primary and preserve his hopes of winning. But to no avail. On primary night, Hillary Clinton's upset victory of Obama was the story that captured most of the attention, but no less remarkable, given all he had been through the previous six months, was McCain's triumph in the Republican primary. McCain and Romney split the Republican vote, but McCain won Independents running away. With that showing, he achieved something that had seemed almost impossible when he held his post-implosion press conference in Concord the previous July. Aides could see the sense of satisfaction, the spirit of the survivor, in their candidate that night. "I'm past the age when I can claim the noun 'kid,' no matter what adjective precedes it," an ebullient McCain said at his victory rally. "But tonight, we sure showed them what a comeback looks like."

The next contest was in Michigan. McCain had won there in 2000, but Michigan was Romney's home state, and after two disappointing second-place finishes, he began to show his mettle as a campaigner. He and his wife were glum the night of New Hampshire, deeply disappointed by his failure to win either of the first two states. But they were not ready to give up; the Republican race was, in their estimation, still too unpredictable. Michigan's battered economy dominated the campaign there and fit Romney's profile. McCain, never comfortable talking about the economy, stumbled when he told voters that many of the jobs that had been lost would never come back, a realistic assessment that nonetheless sounded too pessimistic. Romney's victory taught the McCain campaign a lesson. They regretted making such a strong stand in Michigan, because they enhanced Romney's victory. They vowed to be more disciplined in their decisions.

In almost every other way, however, events were conspiring in McCain's favor. Romney, focused on Michigan, cut back his spending in South Carolina, where he was the only candidate with money enough to run a negative campaign against McCain. Huckabee inexplicably decided to compete actively in Michigan instead of going straight to South Carolina. "We spent precious time and resources in Michigan," Chip Saltsman said later. Huckabee's detour to Michigan gave Fred Thompson an opening for one last stand in South Carolina. Giuliani, meanwhile, continued to sink into obscurity.

The Republican dynamic was strikingly different than that of the Democratic race, which had quickly devolved to a fierce two-person contest between Clinton and Obama and a succession of head-to-head, state-by-state contests. The Republican race reflected the continuing sense of fragmentation within the party, with a series of contests in which the main competitors varied week by week and gamesmanship became an important element in each candidate's strategy.

After three contests, the Republicans now had three winners. McCain was in a stronger position than any of the others, but still a precarious front-runner. Victory in South Carolina was critical for him, but at least he was now in a better position than the other candidates. Had one of his opponents been able to beat him in South Carolina, as Bush had done eight years earlier, his hopes for the nomination might again have vanished. Instead, his rivals were more worried about their ability to survive to compete in Florida and the Super Tuesday states than in slowing McCain before he gained unstoppable momentum.

South Carolina was an emotionally fraught contest. McCain remained scarred by what had happened to him there eight years ago; Cindy McCain even more so because of the scurrilous attacks on their adopted daughter from Bangladesh. The day of the primary, ice and snow coated parts of the state. Early in the evening, as McCain awaited the returns with a coterie of advisers, his team was alerted that the Associated Press was about to call the race for him. Then nothing happened. The vote showed a tight race, with McCain narrowly trailing Huckabee; some counties had ballot problems that delayed returns. McCain appeared tense as he watched the numbers come in, saying little to his advisers. Finally a pattern emerged: Huckabee was underperforming in the upstate region around Greenville and Spartanburg, where the religious conservative vote was especially strong; McCain was getting his share, and Thompson was clearly helping hold down Huckabee's vote. Meanwhile, McCain was rolling up big margins in the more moderate coastal counties.

When Horry County finally reported a big McCain margin, it was over. McCain had edged Huckabee by three points, 33 percent to 30 percent. Thompson, with 16 percent, had drained enough votes from Huckabee to keep him from winning. McCain is given to few public displays of emotion, but those who know him best could see how this victory affected him. Not only had it compensated for his 2000 defeat, but it also proved to him and to all the doubters who had declared his candidacy dead six months earlier that he was tougher, more resilient, and more dogged than all the rest of his rivals.

In his victory speech, he told a cheering crowd, "It took us a while, but what's eight years among friends?" He smiled widely. "I am aware that for the last twenty-eight years, the winner of the South Carolina primary has been the nominee of our party," he said. "We have a ways to go, of course. There are some tough contests ahead, starting tomorrow in the state of Florida. But, my friends, we are well on our way tonight."

McCain was again the front-runner, but not in the classic sense. He had won the two most important primaries to date, but had yet to prove he was the clear choice of Republican voters. Without the Independent vote, neither victory would have been assured. He was doing no better than splitting the Republican vote with his closest competitor. The exit polls showed that he was the candidate of the disgruntled: He was winning voters who were least likely to approve of Bush's performance, least happy with the war in Iraq, and most pessimistic about the economy. Though he was on a path to winning the nomination, McCain still had to prove his conservative credentials.

The Republican race now moved to Florida for the decisive primary. McCain was in the strongest position, but he needed to ratify his South Carolina success—and Florida's primary, unlike those in New Hampshire and South Carolina, was closed to Independents.

Giuliani's late-state strategy had backfired. In New Hampshire, Michigan, and South Carolina, he had finished sixth, fourth, and sixth. "What has happened to your candidacy?" NBC anchor Brian Williams asked him at a debate in Boca Raton on January 24, five days before the primary. "I believe that I'm going to have the same faith that the New York Giants had last week [in their Super Bowl victory] and we're going to come from behind and surprise everyone," he gamely replied. "We have them all lulled into a very false sense of security now." The audience laughed, but it was an empty show of bravado. He was sinking, to the dismay of Romney's advisers. Romney needed a healthy Giuliani to maintain his hopes of winning Florida. Because McCain and Giuliani still appealed to many of the same voters, a Giuliani collapse would open up a part of the electorate for McCain that Romney likely couldn't get.

Romney poured money and energy into Florida and focused his message on the economy in a state devastated by the subprime mortgage crisis. Less than a week before the primary, he had climbed into a tie with McCain in private tracking polls. The longer the campaign stayed on economic issues, the better it was for Romney. McCain decided to force the debate back to Iraq and national security. Earlier in the year, Romney had made a fuzzy statement suggesting that the military prepare "a private timetable" for troop presence in Iraq. Charlie Black told us later, "Salter and I both had literally been carrying the thing around in our pocket for months waiting for a spot to use it. We needed to change the subject, so that's what we did that Saturday morning before the primary, and of course, he took the bait."

On January 26, at a rally in Fort Myers, McCain blistered Romney. "If we surrender and wave a white flag, like Senator Clinton wants to do, and withdraw, as Governor Romney wanted to do, then there will be chaos, genocide, and the cost of American blood and treasure would be dramatically higher," he said. It was a questionable charge based on flimsy evidence, but it created the diversion McCain wanted. Romney's team foolishly took the bait. Romney called the attack dishonest and demanded an apology. McCain responded, "The apology is owed to the young men and women serving this nation in uniform."

McCain won two decisive endorsements in the final days, first from Senator Mel Martinez and then from Governor Charlie Crist. Martinez had given clear indications he would remain neutral, so his endorsement stung the Romney team. Crist had once pledged his support to Giuliani, then seemed resigned to remaining neutral. His last-minute support for

McCain came unexpectedly, and without any warning to either the Giuliani or Romney campaigns.

The endorsements and McCain's attack on Romney over an Iraq time-table stopped Romney's surge. McCain's victory in Florida provided the momentum that carried him to the nomination. Giuliani immediately dropped out, flew to California, and endorsed McCain. He never looked happier than in announcing his support for his friend. McCain still had to weather Super Tuesday and a challenge from Romney in California. Two days after Super Tuesday, Romney quit the race and endorsed McCain. McCain clinched the nomination on March 4 with victories in Ohio and Texas. Huckabee, who had refused to quit to the annoyance of McCain's advisers, then ended his candidacy.

Against all odds, McCain was now the leader of the Republican Party. But it was still a demoralized and disgruntled party. His victory marked the triumph of his singular personality, and that alone was one of the most remarkable achievements of the 2008 campaign. But it was not one that, by itself, reunified his party, nor necessarily made the country feel better about Republican leadership. Conservatives still viewed him with suspicion—Rush Limbaugh continued to attack him and Ann Coulter said she would vote for Hillary over McCain. When McCain had been introduced at the CPAC conference after Super Tuesday, he was roundly booed.

On March 5th, McCain went to the White House to receive Bush's endorsement, a symbolic passing of the torch between the two rivals. The punctual president was in a jovial mood and did a little soft-shoe dance for reporters as he waited on the steps of the North Portico for the late-arriving McCain. McCain thanked the president for his support. The president, who remained a huge drag on Republican hopes in November, said he would help in any way he could. "If my showing up and endorsing him helps him, or if I'm against him and it helps him, either way, I want him to win," he said. McCain said he would welcome the president on the campaign trail. "I intend to have as much possible campaigning events together as is in keeping with the president's heavy schedule."

Bush and McCain went inside for a celebratory lunch of hot dogs. It was the last time the two appeared in public together for the rest of the campaign.

BOOK FIVE

THE ELECTION

CHAPTER TWENTY-THREE

America: Decision Time

Asked to raise their hands if they thought Obama was a Muslim, seven of twelve Independent voters did.

—From a Peter Hart focus group three months before the Democratic convention

M ore than a year had passed since Peter Hart convened his first group of voters. Now, as the primaries were ending late in May, the politics of 2008 had become even more uncertain.

Barack Obama already had made history by defeating Hillary Clinton. He was on his way to nomination by the Democrats in Denver at the end of August, backed by a passionate band of supporters. His problem, as Hart concluded after listening to voters composed entirely of Independents, was that while Obama's supporters were shouting, "Yes, We Can!" others were increasingly asking, "Who Are You?"

These doubts among Independent voters presented Obama with a challenge as daunting as his primary battle with Clinton. Based on what these Independents were saying, Obama had largely been defined by his controversial association with Reverend Wright and by what they believed about his personal background. That made them uneasy about him and uncertain as to what kind of president he would be.

Obama faced two great tests as he turned toward the general election against John McCain: First, he had to define the stakes that faced the nation in 2008; but second, and more important, he had to introduce himself convincingly to a larger number of American voters, particularly to those Independents who were crucial to the election of a president. And McCain had always done well with such voters. Hart had assembled twelve voters for his Charlottesville, Virginia, session: six men and six women, ranging in age from twenty-four to seventy-two. Eleven were white and seven of the twelve had voted for George W. Bush in 2004. Though none of them had voted in either the Republican or Democratic primaries, they all were certain they would vote in November.

Obama had a long way to go to reassure them. Their concerns were not about his policy proposals but rather arose from their limited, often shocking misinformation about him—who he was, where he came from, what his values were. Even among those who were attracted by his message and personality, the negative images of an angry Jeremiah Wright shouting, "God *damn* America!" were engraved in their minds as a symbol of the campaign.

Asked to recall any two memories of the campaign, seven of the twelve voters cited Wright by name. One said Obama's catchphrase was "change," but "it also means that [Obama] changed his mind about Reverend Wright, because at first he was very much defending the man, but then after he saw that public opinion was going against Reverend Wright, all of a sudden now it's like 'Oh, yeah, he's a bad person.'"

Their discussion became "truly chilling," as Hart later put it, when they elaborated on what they understood to be Obama's background. One voter said Obama "is Muslim." No one contradicted him. Someone else mentioned Obama's "Muslim background"—again without protest or qualification from the others. When asked to raise their hands if they thought Obama was a Muslim, seven of the twelve voters did, including two who were supporting him over McCain. One voter had heard something about Obama and the Pledge of Allegiance. Another believed he had placed his hand on the Koran when he was sworn in as a senator. "He is representing a minority in more than one case," a male voter said. "He is African-American and he is Muslim. And in light of that, . . . it does feel like we're being judged or pounded on because we want to carry a gun or we want to wear the American flag pin." Another voiced her uncertainty. "I'm a little concerned," she said. "I don't know enough about his Muslim background and their beliefs and how he views everything. I need to check into his background."

These voters all wanted change, passionately. As Hart said, the word was first and foremost in everyone's thoughts, regardless of political views or ideology. They were even angrier about America's condition and direction than those in Hart's focus groups during 2007. Their quick characterizations of the state of the nation were uniformly negative, even despairing:

"Declining."

"Depressing."

"In the toilet."

"Downslide."

They were equally scathing when they talked about the economy. Rising gas prices, food prices, the housing market—all created a feeling that things were dangerously out of control, and getting worse. Heightening their bleak mood was their harsh assessment of George W. Bush's presidency:

"Worthless."

"Misleading."

"Disappointed."

"Misinformed."

"Warmonger."

"Gullible."

"Expected more."

"Not very smart."

And three-fourths of them had voted for Bush the last time! These attitudes were more than a snapshot of a carefully selected, if small and unscientific, demographic group. They matched the latest national opinion surveys revealing overwhelmingly negative feelings about the state of the nation and the performance of the president. At that point, 85 percent of voters believed the country was headed seriously in the wrong direction, while Bush's favorability rating was at an all-time low.

The Charlottesville Independents were split: half for Obama, half for McCain. They were doubtful about Obama, worried he might be too "soft-minded" or too "gullible" to lead America in a time of trouble. But they were even more doubtful about John McCain. Though they respected his military record and political experience, many of them believed he was tied too closely to the Bush administration's record, making his presidency "a third Bush term." McCain had another problem: in the year since Hart began his series of focus groups, McCain's standing among voters had neither broadened nor improved. Thus November's presidential election was shaping up as a choice between the uncertainty of a Barack Obama presidency and the undesirability of a John McCain one.

In that test, Obama had the edge. Given the choice between a change candidate and one seen as status quo, voters of all political backgrounds were signaling they wanted change. Three of every four voters were telling national pollsters they wanted a president who would take the country in a direction different from Bush. Seven in ten thought McCain would take them in the same direction as Bush. This presented an exceedingly difficult challenge for McCain, and a great opportunity for Obama—but only if he reassured Americans about who he was, what he stood for, and removed many of the doubts that still surrounded him. That required Obama to deal with the way voters felt about such complex issues as race and religion and, as Hart said, "most fundamentally, comfort" about himself. He had to persuade voters to take a chance for change and gather behind him to unite the country. In Hart's analogy, it was for Obama like the children's game of chutes and ladders. As he climbed the ladder to a new plateau, there was a new chute that sent him back to the beginning.

Obama understood the problem. In a midsummer interview, he told us, "With change comes some risk, and I combine two things. One is an insistence that we move in a new direction, which takes some time for people to process. . . . The other thing is that my biography involves a pretty significant change that takes time for people to process. And it's not just the issue of race. I think it's much more the fact that I haven't been on the national scene. . . . They're going to keep their powder dry and get as much information as they can the next three months, without leaping into it, but [I think] that ultimately when they compare my policy agenda to John McCain's, when they conclude that I can execute on that policy agenda, I think we'll be in good shape."

For Hillary Clinton, the endless primaries had decisively clarified the way voters felt about her candidacy. Among voters we tracked over those months, attitudes of three of them explained why her presidential attempt had failed after such high expectations.

Fay Citerone was the IT professional we had been following since that first Hart focus group more than a year before. At that time Citerone, a liberal Democrat, was leaning toward Hillary, but had doubts. Clinton struck her as "shrill." Obama was intriguing, but still, as she put it, "a question mark." Citerone was paying close attention to the campaign, believed it "extremely important" because as a country "we just have a lot of repairs to make." But she also said of McCain's candidacy, "I have lots of respect for him. He seems very authentic. I don't think it's just because of his POW experience. He comes off as very intelligent and thoughtful, a straightforward sort of person." She could see him as president.

She was following the campaign even more avidly when we spoke again months later. "This has been a fascinating political season," she said. "I'm trying to think about any other presidential campaign like this one. Four years ago, none of the candidates, Democrat or Republican, made you think, 'Gee, I want to go to the polls and vote.' This time it's so different." It made her presidential choice even more difficult.

That was where she stood as the primary voting began in early 2008. By then, she liked Hillary more than before. Hillary would make progress with health care reform and had the ability "to right the wrongs that have happened with the Republican administration." Most important, Citerone wanted to see a woman in the White House. "We're overdue," she said. "England's had Thatcher, and that was quite a while ago. Other countries had female leaders, and it seems the U.S., being a significant power, should step up and have a female president. I just hope she's the right one." As for Obama, she still thought him appealing, "but I'm feeling less certain that he has the experience and the assertiveness to handle this job at this point. He's a young man, relatively young. In the future he might be the right president, but maybe not now."

When we spoke to her again, after Iowa, New Hampshire, and Super Tuesday, she had experienced a complete change. As the time approached to cast her own primary vote in Maryland in mid-February, she struggled with her choice, studied the candidates' records, watched even more debates, asked friends what they were thinking, how they were deciding. "Most of those I spoke to are registered Democrats—well, a couple are Republicans—and a lot of those I talked to are leaning toward Obama," she said. "But my friends are saying he has a lot of charisma. They find that attractive, and I do too. I decided myself that I would vote for him."

She explained her decision to shift from Clinton to Obama this way: "What turned the tide for me was the negative campaigning that President Clinton did a few weeks back [in South Carolina]. That struck me. I tried to weigh it. Did it really matter? Someone said, 'Oh, that's the way politicians are. They get down and dirty. And that happens.' So at first I thought, well, grin and bear it. But through all that negative campaigning I didn't learn anything about Obama that I didn't like. Then a few people like Ted Kennedy came out and said to the Clintons, 'Why don't you stop? That doesn't look good.' I thought that's interesting that someone so powerful has to step in. And that turned the tide for me."

The Hillary equation, and what it said about the internal divisions within the Democratic Party, was even more striking, and complicated, for Karen Kaplowitz and her husband Alan Cohen of affluent Bucks County, Pennsylvania. Both are ardent Democrats, both lawyers who have a marketing consulting business, and both began as Hillary supporters. When we spoke, on the eve of the Pennsylvania primary in April, they had just cast their absentee ballots.

Karen Kaplowitz voted for Clinton, but was unsure how her husband voted. "If you don't tell her, I can tell you," Alan told us. "I voted for Obama because I want Hillary to be out now and I want it to be over."

Splitting their vote did not mean they disagreed about Hillary's abilities, or on how they viewed Obama and the stakes for the country. "If I didn't have a wife to answer to," Alan said, "I would've been an Obama supporter earlier, but I didn't have a problem joining her in supporting Hillary. I think she'd make a wonderful president." As for Karen, she said, "I see Hillary as one of the great women of our generation, enormously competent." Karen was a lifelong feminist, had campaigned for Bobby Kennedy while a student at Columbia. Then, in law school, she moved from civil rights to women's rights. Though she admired Obama and would be happy for him to be president, she said, "I adore Hillary Clinton. That's just how it comes out."

As for the election, "I'd say the stakes are as great as they've ever been. And the idea of there being four more years of a Bush-like administration is chilling to me."

By the time she voted in the primary, Karen had become increasingly troubled by Bill Clinton's campaign role and was forced, reluctantly, to rethink her support for Hillary. "During the first phase of the campaign, when [Bill] seemed to be helping Hillary, I certainly wasn't upset. But of late, it's more upsetting to see him do things that diminish her. . . . Frankly, I think it's been uphill for Hillary since Iowa. I don't think she's done a bad job. I just think Obama swept in on the strength of her clearing that path."

So despite her ardent enthusiasm for Hillary, she concluded Hillary could not be nominated. "I'm hugely impressed with her tenacity, relentlessness, fight, capability to get up every time she's knocked down," she said. "But at this point it's enough already. I'd love to see Hillary be president. I think she'd be spectacular. But I'm okay with Obama being president. I just can't stand four more Bush-like years. We need closure."

As for Obama, the more she watched the campaign, the more impressed she became; he was, she said, "a person of enormous capability, enormous intelligence. But I do worry about whether he's electable. I worry about whether there are people who won't vote for him because he's black. I worry about the Republican attack machine." In the end, if Obama were nominated would she support him? "Totally. Enthusiastically. I'd walk precincts for him. Raise money for him. Donate money to him. Do whatever it takes to elect a Democrat this November."

In this, she and her husband Alan were in agreement. He too had been troubled by Bill Clinton. "For a guy who is extremely smart, the best speaker since Martin Luther King, and now you have to put Obama in there, I don't understand why he's been so off. I have concerns about having him back in the White House: his personal self-control. That's a risk for turning the presidency again into a circus."

He had no reservations about Obama, and believed he had the ability "to rally the populace to refuse to put up with the business as usual that we've seen over the past few years." It was a point he was making regularly with friends and neighbors, many of them Republicans. "I have a neighbor across the street I walk with regularly, a staunch Republican who says he's sleeping better at night because the Democrats are beating each other up," he said. "I keep telling him, 'Don't sleep too much. McCain is not that strong a candidate.'"

The neighbor, Bob Macauley, a sixty-nine-year-old investment banker, started out as a Democrat, then turned to the Republicans after what he viewed as the disastrous Jimmy Carter presidency. That "entire calculus changed with Ronald Reagan." At that time, Macauley was serving on Philadelphia's economic development committee as a Democrat. "I saw the total dissipation of taxpayer funds into programs that amounted to absolutely nothing," he recalled. "I said, 'This is not someone else's money being thrown down a rat hole. It was my wife's money and my money.' So I voted for Reagan and switched to the Republican Party. When Reagan reduced the capital gains rate from forty-five to twenty-eight percent, it turned our life around. I've voted straight Republican since that time."

When the election year began, Macauley was pessimistic about GOP chances. He voted twice for George W. Bush ("a monumental mistake") and thought Republicans "truly deserved to lose."

But to him, John McCain was "an outlaw among Republicans. He works with people on both sides of the aisle, and I like that. And half of the Republican leadership can't stand him. The fact that he doesn't get along with all of them is fine by me. With a president who can work both sides of the aisle, it will be similar to Eisenhower and the Democratic Congress, which was a work of art."

As he watched the campaign unfold, with bitterness dividing the Clinton and Obama camps, Macauley was even more optimistic about McCain's chances. "I torment Alan," he said, "by saying it will be a brokered

convention and at the second or third ballot it will be Albert Arnold Gore."
To that, "Alan of course brings up [McCain's] age. I point out that his mom
is ninety-five and plays tennis."

Still, Macauley recognized McCain's age could be a problem. His greatest worry about McCain's electability was that "he doesn't make a disastrous-
type Republican pick for VP. On the contrary, the Democrats do a pretty
good job of picking vice presidents beginning with Truman. Why are Republicans so abysmal?"

All the more reason, he went on, why the vice presidential choice this
year was "going to be critical for McCain."

The age issue—if elected, he would be the oldest president entering a first
term—was only one of John McCain's problems. Voters we encountered
during focus groups and in our individual interviews in primary states not
only were negative about George W. Bush's presidency, but equally negative about the Republican Party itself. "I keep looking at McCain and I fear
that, well, it's four more years," said a male voter in the Charlottesville
group. "I think with any Republican in there, I would feel the same way."
A woman voter agreed: "I think John McCain is set in his ways, and I think
it would be . . . just another Republican presidency. I don't think it really
matters at this point what Republican we put there. It's going to be the
same thing."

These were tremendous obstacles for the McCain candidacy and for
Republicans in general, obstacles that kept resurfacing in our talks with
voters. While they were doubtful about Obama, their doubts about McCain
and his party were greater. A telling example: In the 2000 election, the
NBC News/*Wall Street Journal* survey showed Democrats holding a five-
point advantage over Republicans. By 2008, the same survey revealed a
twelve-point advantage for the Democrats. "That is an enormous difference," said Peter Hart, who conducted many of those NBC/*Journal* surveys
with Republican pollster Bill McInturff, "equivalent to having to carry a
fifty-pound sack of potatoes and a one-hundred-twenty-pound sack of potatoes. One individual can carry the first sack, but for the second sack, one
needs some kind of assistance."

In the end, attitudes about the political parties, or even the candidates,
were not the most crucial aspect of the election.

Peter Hart summed up where things stood nationally after his Charlottesville session. "The mood is not only negative, spilling into disgust and

rejection of the Bush administration," he said, "but it reflects a more nervous and uncertain time. It is as though one era is ending, but few seem to know what the next era is going to look like. It is the nervousness people feel when seventy percent say the next generation will be worse off than this one. The public knows the fundamentals are wrong and something must be changed, but exactly how one achieves the right kind of change is what the country is grappling with right now. There is a wish and a desire for an 'easy button' to solve our problems, but we all know this is not possible."

In our travels across the country throughout 2007 and 2008, conversations with voters in Ohio's Mahoning Valley around Youngstown stand out as most memorable. The valley, once one of the great steel-producing places in the world, was known as America's Ruhr. Older residents recalled that when the steel mills were booming no one worried about soot that landed everywhere, on sidewalks, on windowsills, on floors. As one person told us, "We knew that was money landing there. And everybody had jobs. You'll hear the stories, if you haven't already, about how women didn't even mind if the soot came down when they put their laundry out to dry."

The valley enjoyed such a mixture of pride and prosperity that it came to embody the best of the American story. It boasted high homeownership. It had multicultural neighborhoods with Romanians and Ukrainians living amid Serbs and Croatians, Greeks and Italians. Its churches epitomized the strength of the country: Jewish synagogues, Ukrainian Byzantine and Ukrainian Orthodox, Russian Orthodox, even Italian Protestant churches. It had the aluminum industry, as well as the steel industry, major rubber and concrete enterprises, one of the nation's largest commercial furniture businesses.

Progress continued into the early seventies; then danger signals began flashing in the face of competition from Japan, Taiwan, and China. As Harry Meshell, a political and economic leader of Youngstown, and a former Democratic state senator, told us, "In the Far East, they were smart enough to learn how to do things, how to make every damn thing in the world that we ever made."

In 1979, Meshell led a regional delegation to a steel area in China similar to the Mahoning Valley. A friendship agreement was signed, economic delegations were exchanged. Ten years later, he went back to find tremendous growth. "You know, virtually everything you buy in the store comes from there. That led to the economic downfall in many parts of this country, because we didn't do very much about it. We were not keeping up.

"Those of us in office tried to do whatever we could to create an environment in which growth could occur. We put money in the university. Every time I had a chance, I just pumped another five million, two million, whatever, into Youngstown State. Thank God for that, because it created jobs. We tried to find a way to use state and federal funds to help build the economies, help build stability, and try to create a future for the state. But you can only catch up so much, because other forces were working against us. With high unemployment comes a lot of poverty. And with poverty comes crime. Then you have the housing stock going to hell. All these factors are working against you."

Without meaning to, Harry Meshell had framed the issues confronting the nation as the people approached their time of decision in 2008.

CHAPTER TWENTY-FOUR

Citizen of the World

"Americans . . . don't want to elect the president of Europe."

—Republican Vin Weber, on Obama's global tour

The e-mail went out from Obama headquarters at 3:35 a.m. on July 19, under the name of Robert Gibbs. It read, "At approximately 3:15 AM Eastern/2:15 AM Central, I received a phone call telling me that Senator Obama had landed at the airport in Kabul, Afghanistan." Gibbs's predawn message was the official announcement that Obama had begun the opening phase of one of the most ambitious ventures of the campaign.

Obama departed Chicago around noon on July 17 in a Gulfstream III executive jet, which took him to Washington's Reagan National Airport. From there he was transported by motorcade to Andrews Air Force Base in suburban Maryland. Waiting at Andrews were his traveling companions, Democratic Senator Jack Reed of Rhode Island and Republican Senator Chuck Hagel of Nebraska; one of his foreign policy advisers, Mark Lippert, who had recently completed a tour of duty in Iraq; and several other congressional aides. At about 3 p.m., he boarded an unmarked Boeing C-40 aircraft and under strict security and a news blackout was flown to Kuwait and later to Afghanistan.

No presidential candidate had ever attempted a foreign trip of such magnitude. Obama's itinerary would cover eight countries in ten days. The trappings were identical to those of a presidential trip abroad, but because he was a presidential candidate on what was considered a political trip, Obama's team had to undertake the mission without the support of the State Department or the U.S. embassies in the countries he would visit once he left the war zone. The trip was actually two in one. The first portion, covering Kuwait, Afghanistan, and Iraq, was under the auspices of the Defense Department. The rest of the trip would be run by his campaign, using the candidate's chartered aircraft, his own advance teams, and his Secret Service detail. The second part of the itinerary included Jordan, Israel, Germany, France, and Great Britain, and a huge media contingent—including network anchors—would join him, along with a large retinue of foreign policy and political advisers. Security was so tight on the opening legs of the trip that the Secret Service would not allow the campaign even to say when Obama would be visiting Iraq and Afghanistan. Only when he was safely inside each country would they make any public announcement of his movements.

Obama's foreign trip was both a gamble and a necessity. His advisers had learned from research at the end of the primaries that fixing the economy was a far more important issue in the minds of most voters—especially those considered up for grabs—than the question of which candidate would make a better commander in chief. What Obama's advisers concluded was that as long as he cleared a minimum threshold in this area, he could be elected. One way to do that was to demonstrate his comfort on a world stage, standing shoulder to shoulder with foreign leaders. The risks were obvious, however. Any misstep, any hesitation, any garbled statement, any sign of unfamiliarity, any slips on names or places would be magnified into a major gaffe. Any logistical snarls—chronic lateness, lost baggage, poor briefings—would receive worldwide coverage and undermine the main message of the trip.

His foreign policy advisers—Denis McDonough, Greg Craig, Phil Gordon, Susan Rice, and others—had long talked about the desirability of a trip abroad. Planning became more serious later in 2007, and on a conference call in the fall, Craig made the case that a foreign trip would "change the way the world looks at the United States . . . that it would be a transformational moment for the United States." He also said that Obama could draw crowds in places like Berlin or Paris or London that no other candidate could attract. "We can probably get as many as five thousand people," he said.

Obama himself and his main political advisers, focused then on Iowa and New Hampshire, were wary. Obama recommended delaying the trip. No presidential candidate had ever done anything like this; the sheer logistical demands were overwhelming. "Let's wait until I get the nomination," he said. "I'll do it after the nomination and we'll have thirty thousand people."

Obama's foreign journey came at the end of a discouraging opening to the general election. Nothing in the early weeks suggested that either candidate was prepared to rise to the challenge presented by an election of enormous significance, at a time of deepening problems and growing anxiety. The contrasts between Obama and McCain on the issues—Iraq, the economy, and health care—were sizable. And both had records that suggested they might be able to move the country to a better style of politics. Yet everything about the opening weeks of the general election reinforced old politics and deepening polarization.

Obama and McCain tried in some of their speeches to outline their differences, but they were often drowned out by the snarling putdowns and taunting e-mails that flowed from both headquarters. A McCain surrogate responded to something Obama had said about the rights of terrorist detainees—a topic on which reasonable people could differ—as "delusional." An Obama surrogate described as "stupid" the positions McCain had taken on the Iraq war, though it was clearly arguable at that point that the surge strategy was working. It was a depressing start to a historic choice for the country.

McCain had the advantage of wrapping up his nomination in March, while Obama was still tied down fighting off a revived Hillary Clinton for three more months. So he was free to start running his general election campaign, but he squandered the spring. McCain went abroad, where he got little attention. He took a "biographical tour" to places in the United States that illustrated how his character had been formed. The press ignored him. He went to "forgotten places"—the Lower Ninth Ward in New Orleans and coal mining country in Appalachia—as a way to assert that he was not a stereotypical Republican. They remained forgotten, swamped by the focus on the Democratic race.

McCain needed to turn the skeletal operation that had seen him through to the nomination into a strong general election campaign. But the first steps, including an ill-advised structure of regional campaign managers that created management headaches, were poorly thought out and eventually had to be jettisoned. The most visible mistake came on June 3, the final night of the primaries. As Obama was getting ready to claim the nomination at a huge rally in St. Paul, McCain delivered a toughly worded speech in New Orleans that was designed to make the case that he was the true change agent. He said of Obama, "He is an impressive man, who makes a great first impression. But he hasn't been willing to make the tough calls, to challenge his party, to risk criticism from his supporters to bring real change to Washington. I have." But that night, the sharp rhetoric was overshadowed by the images. Against a garish green backdrop, McCain looked old and tired, in contrast to his youthful opponent.

For Republicans, the appearance symbolized a McCain on the wrong side of a "change" election, and it touched off a new round of hand-wringing: His campaign structure wasn't working. His message was inconsistent. McCain seemed angry rather than inspiring. He projected disdain rather than respect for his rival. Relations with the press deteriorated. McCain and his advisers felt reporters were more interested in gotcha journalism than engaging with McCain in the combination of banter and serious inquiry that had marked the old Straight Talk Express. Ultimately they would sharply limit press access, leading to more complaints that the McCain of 2000 had disappeared. Other Republicans said that was a weak excuse for the slow start. "They've run a schizophrenic campaign," a Republican who knew McCain well told us at the time.

Staffing was one of the issues. Rick Davis was overloaded, as even he was quick to admit. "I basically told McCain I was dying, that I was shouldering an inordinate burden for the growth of the campaign," he told us. "Through a series of meetings and discussions, it was determined that Steve [Schmidt] had the flexibility and frankly the background to be the most help to me." Schmidt was brought in to bring discipline to the message and order to the campaign and to oversee the operations of the road show. In a related move, Mike DuHaime, Giuliani's former campaign manager, was recruited to oversee the political operation. Schmidt's elevation sparked another round of stories about a campaign in disarray and, in essence, that a hostile takeover at the top had taken place. Neither Schmidt nor Davis would describe it that way in after-action interviews. "It obviously didn't roll out that well," Davis said. "It was like this huge coup that Steve was coming in to take over the campaign. It was something McCain, Schmidt, and I had designed." Still, the change underscored that McCain's campaign still wasn't running smoothly, despite four months of general election preparation.

Obama's problem was his sheer exhaustion, the fatigue of his top advisers, and his late start, owing to the long nomination battle. What hopes Plouffe and Axelrod had of shifting their focus to the general election kept getting derailed. When the time came to take on McCain, the campaign was weeks behind where Obama's advisers had hoped to be. Planning followed two tracks: readjustment in messaging to reflect Obama's new opponent, and the development of an electoral map strategy designed to break the mold of the previous two elections.

That Plouffe was still at the helm as the general election began was another untold story of the Obama campaign. In April, Plouffe let Obama know he wanted to step down after the primaries. He was worn out, having managed the campaign from the first day and on through the most rigorous nomination battle ever. Of more concern, his wife was pregnant, due to deliver their second child days before the election. She would be returning to Washington in the summer so their son could enroll in school in the fall, and to oversee the renovation of their house. Plouffe, a private person, felt an obligation to his family. Staying in Chicago would have meant "abandoning my very pregnant wife and son in very tough circumstances," he said later.

Plouffe had hoped the nomination battle would be wrapped up by late spring, giving his successor time to make a smooth transition for the general election. Obama implored him to stay. No one had contributed more to the success of the campaign and Obama didn't want to lose him. Axelrod said, "He was just dissipated by the end of the primary season and he made some attempt to quit and Obama wouldn't accept his decision." After the primaries, the Obama campaign was behind both in the vice presidential selection process and in convention planning. Plouffe felt he couldn't leave. To ease his burden, Jim Messina was hired as chief of staff to take over some of his responsibilities.

Obama's team ordered up a crash research project. They quickly conducted polls on the economy, domestic issues, and national security. They polled Spanish-speaking voters. They looked at the potential impact of young voters on the general election. They studied the racial contours of the election. They looked closely at how voters perceived McCain and Obama.

From the research, they drew several conclusions that shaped Obama's strategy. The first and most important conclusion was the most obvious: The economy was now the key issue. Obama would attempt to own it. "All Roads Lead to the Economy," read the first page of the domestic policy survey presented to him at one meeting. The second conclusion was counterintuitive. The campaign's assumption that voters saw McCain as a man who went his own way as a maverick and a reformer did not hold up. Joel Benenson, Obama's lead pollster, told us later, "People in America had no knowledge of McCain as a maverick, as a force for change, as any more bipartisan than Barack Obama." Instead, voters worried that he would merely be an extension of Bush. McCain had failed to use the spring months to distance himself effectively from the president. Dan Pfeiffer, Obama's deputy communications director, said, "Our message was basically to tie him to Bush, particularly on the economy, and we did it every day."

The final issue was how to deal with the question voters had about Barack Obama. The problems revealed in Peter Hart's focus group of Independent voters were well-known inside the campaign. As one senior adviser observed at the time, "We're asking them [voters] to embrace a guy who is four years out of the Illinois state senate and who's black, whose name is Barack Hussein Obama, and make him president of the United States. . . . That's a big, big lift." The problem was not strictly racially based. Communications director Anita Dunn said, "It was much more that he had an exotic name, a different background. It was a proxy for 'He's weird,' for the 'otherness.'"

The campaign attacked the problem with rhetoric and imagery. They employed Obama's family, hoping that the images of a strong and loving family would convey values with which all Americans could identify. On June 30th, Obama gave a widely covered speech about patriotism in Independence, Missouri. Declaring his love of country, he said, "At certain times over the last sixteen months, I have found, for the first time, my patriotism challenged—at times as a result of my own carelessness, more often as a result of the desire by some to score political points and raise fears about who I am and what I stand for." He offered his own story, told so vividly in *Dreams from My Father*, as evidence that, adrift as a youth, he had found himself in the narrative of America. "For a young man of mixed race," he said, "without firm anchor in any particular community, without even a father's steadying hand, it is this essential American idea—that we are not constrained by the accident of birth but can make of our lives what we will—that has defined my life, just as it has defined the life of so many other Americans."

There were also questions about where Obama really stood ideologically. He talked like a centrist, a pragmatist, someone who would work actively with Republicans. But his agenda—a big health care package, higher taxes on the rich, an aggressive alternative energy plan—sounded conventionally liberal. At that point his agenda lacked focus or priorities that a president would need to be successful.

Plouffe was determined not to leave his candidate in the predicament that befell Al Gore and John Kerry. In 2000 and 2004, their path to the

White House depended on winning Florida or Ohio, both Republican-leaning states. Plouffe vowed that Obama's electoral map options would not be so constricted. As deputy campaign manager Steve Hildebrand told us after the primaries, "We would be perfectly happy to win the presidency based on an electoral strategy that included Ohio and Florida, but we don't want that to be the only pathway."

For two elections in a row, the electoral outcome had been extremely close. In 2000 Bush won with 271 electoral votes, one more than needed. He lost the popular vote to Gore, Bush winning just under 50.5 million for 47.8 percent of the vote to Gore's nearly 51 million popular votes, or 48.4 percent of the tally. Gore got 266 electoral votes. In his reelection four years later, Bush won 286 electoral votes with just over 60 million votes, or 50.7 percent of the ballots, as opposed to Kerry's 252 electoral votes and slightly more than 59 million votes, for 48.3 percent of the ballots. Between 2000 and 2004, only three states switched from one party to another: Iowa and New Mexico from Democrat to Republican; New Hampshire from Republican to Democrat. Red and blue America became the shorthand for describing the polarized politics of Bush's presidency.

By the summer of 2008, however, it was clear the electoral map was changing. Fewer Americans called themselves Republicans. Many Independents acted more like Democrats. The nation's ever-shifting demographics were creating greater competition in some regions, particularly the Rocky Mountain West with its increasing Latino population. Obama's unique candidacy, and the enthusiasm of African-Americans, added to the fluidity of the electoral map, particularly in some southern states. These conditions created irresistible opportunities for the Obama team to try to change the electoral calculus.

Obama's advisers made several crucial decisions that departed from orthodoxy. First, there would be no halfway efforts in the targeted states. "If we were in, we put in the resources needed to win," said Jon Carson, who oversaw the field operations. "There were no feints going on, which was an expensive proposition." The campaign planned a massive ground game to go along with an expensive advertising budget, and when they came up with a list of possible targets—traditional battlegrounds and new opportunities—they quickly realized that even their cash-rich campaign could not afford to play in all of them. This led to a second decision, controversial at the time, not to expend resources in some nominally blue states that had been real battlegrounds in the past. These included Oregon, Washington, Maine, and Minnesota. Plouffe's team gambled that by

November, all would be safely in Obama's column, though they were not at the start of the general election.

Their final list still surprised many political analysts. The targets included long-established battleground states, such as Ohio, Florida, Pennsylvania, Michigan, Missouri, Wisconsin, Iowa, and New Mexico. To these Plouffe added Colorado, Nevada, and Virginia, all emerging purple states that both campaigns knew would be competitive. Then Obama's team added North Carolina, Indiana, Alaska, Montana, North Dakota, and Georgia. Some of these states had not voted for a Democratic nominee since Lyndon Johnson in 1964. Others had voted consistently Republican with an occasional deviation for either Jimmy Carter or Bill Clinton. Plouffe was a major advocate for Indiana. He referred to it as "my dog"—everyone liked to kick it, but it was always there. "How's my dog doing?" he would ask his staff.

Plouffe assumed Obama would hold all of Kerry's 252 electoral votes and likely add Iowa's seven, given his success there during the caucuses. That would leave him eleven short of the 270 necessary for election. Carrying either Florida or Ohio would easily get him to the White House. So would any of the following combinations of two or three other states: Iowa, New Mexico, and Colorado; Iowa and North Carolina; Colorado and Indiana; or North Carolina and Nevada. As Plouffe intended, there were multiple combinations.

Yet the campaign was hardly crisp at the start. Obama was caught flat-footed when McCain, recognizing the growing concerns about four-dollar-a-gallon gasoline, proposed ending the ban on offshore drilling. Obama's first instinct was to cling to traditional Democratic orthodoxy, which saw the issue through the prism of environmentalists. He was forced, awkwardly, to yield by making clear he would accept offshore drilling as part of a more comprehensive energy package. Axelrod later regarded the campaign's handling of the drilling issue a serious mistake.

On July 20, the day after Obama had landed in Afghanistan, we met up with Axelrod over lunch in downtown Chicago. Later in the day, he would join the rest of the Obama staff and the traveling press corps for the flight from Chicago to Amman, Jordan, there to meet up with Obama for the second leg of the foreign trip.

The coverage of Obama in Kuwait and Afghanistan was positive, but Axelrod worried that over the previous month the campaign had been ground down in tactical wars and that the incessant back-and-forth with McCain had diminished Obama's strongest attributes. He had just finished a memo for the campaign. "Here's my admonition to everybody," he said. "I don't think any president in our lifetime will have the confluence of challenges that the next president's going to face. And if they're handled wrong, we could dig ourselves into a hole that'll be very hard to get out of. . . . We got into this because this was an election about big things . . . and when we live up there, when it's about big things, we're at our best."

Axelrod was pleased about the timing of the foreign trip. "This is a big moment in history and this is not a time to play small ball," he said. "The trip came at a propitious time in that regard."

Every successful politician is also a lucky politician, and Barack Obama was blessed by good fortune as the trip began. In Kuwait, in a gymnasium packed with U.S. troops, he grabbed a basketball, did a few quick stretching motions, and turned to the crowd. "I may not make the first one," he said. Then he let fly from the edge of the three-point line. The ball curled softly into the hoop to an eruption of cheers.

Something far more significant happened while he was in Afghanistan. The German magazine *Der Spiegel* published an interview with Iraqi Prime Minister Nouri al-Maliki, who said he looked favorably upon Obama's sixteen-month timetable for withdrawing U.S. forces from Iraq. The interview caught the White House by surprise. Though U.S. and Iraqi officials had just announced agreement on the need to set a timetable—vague as it might be—Maliki's statement went far beyond anything he had said publicly. When Obama met with Maliki two days later, the prime minister reiterated his belief that U.S. forces should be gone from Iraq by 2010. The debate over U.S. policy suddenly appeared to be moving toward Obama's position—an unexpected gift for the Democratic candidate in the opening days of his trip.

Obama's Iraq itinerary included a lengthy meeting with General David Petraeus, the commander of U.S. forces in Iraq, and U.S. ambassador Ryan Crocker. Petraeus believed troop withdrawals should be based on conditions on the ground, not a timetable. In the meeting, Petraeus, according to an account by author Steve Coll in the *New Yorker*, carefully made his case for the success of the surge that Obama had opposed and for a more flexible policy on troop withdrawal. Obama held his ground, saying that if he became commander in chief, he would need to think about Iraq in a broader context that also included a growing need for more troops in Afghanistan to defeat al-Qaeda and a resurgent Taliban. Obama and Petraeus did not settle their differences but were careful not to let their disagreement cloud what both knew could be a critically important relationship within a matter of months. They were photographed together in a helicopter, Obama in sunglasses, both smiling broadly.

Obama left Iraq on the afternoon of Tuesday, July 22, arriving in Amman to begin the next phase of his trip. Joined by Hagel and Reed, he held a press conference at the Citadel, whose most notable feature is the ancient Temple of Hercules, a stunning setting for the first public event of his journey. Asked about his meeting with Petraeus and their disagreement about a withdrawal timetable, Obama said, "The notion is that either I do exactly what my military commanders tell me to do or I'm ignoring their advice. No. I'm factoring in their advice but placing it in this broader strategic . . . framework." That night, in an interview conducted earlier in Iraq with Terry Moran of ABC's *Nightline*, Obama said he would have opposed the surge in January 2007, even if he had known then what it was accomplishing.

His answers raised questions that would follow him through the campaign, but his trip was off to a smashing start. Newspapers put his movements in Afghanistan and Iraq on the front page and the images on television showed a confident politician mingling with troops and dealing with government and military leaders. Newspaper Web sites updated his movements throughout the days. Obama's advisers, led by spokesman Bill Burton, pulled off a coup by choreographing a series of one-on-one interviews with network anchors and key correspondents as he moved from country to country, guaranteeing such visibility that the press quickly again came under attack for favoritism.

After his press conference in Amman, Obama sat down with CBS anchor Katie Couric and then had dinner with King Abdullah and others. When dinner ended, the king insisted on personally driving Obama to the airport in his Mercedes in a motorcade at high speed from the palace to the foot of the stairs of Obama's plane. Obama was exhausted by the time he reached the King David Hotel in Jerusalem late that night. He had been traveling hard for five days and had not adjusted well to the time zone changes. When he began his first meeting the next morning, Likud Party leader Binyamin Netanyahu asked him how he was holding up. Obama said, "I could fall asleep standing up."

The day in Israel presented the most diplomatically challenging itinerary of the remainder of the trip. Obama was seen as suspect by some American Jews, who worried that because of some of his past statements and friendships, he would tilt American policy toward the Palestinians. He was anxious to allay those fears, reassuring Israeli leaders on Iran while telling both sides he would make peace talks a high priority as president. His schedule was packed with meetings with all the important Israeli and Palestinian officials and symbolic stops for the cameras.

Late in the afternoon, he took a helicopter ride across the narrow country to the town of Sderot, which sat just miles from the Hamas-controlled Gaza Strip. Against a backdrop of spent rockets and missiles that had been launched on the town, Obama vowed his commitment to Israel's security. "The first job of any nation-state is to protect its citizens," he said. "And so I can assure you that if—I don't even care if I was a politician. If somebody was sending rockets into my house, where my two daughters sleep at night, I'm going to do everything in my power to stop that. And I would expect Israelis to do the same thing."

After he left, several people said the response was "very Israeli," one of his advisers recalled. "And they meant it as a compliment."

With the war zone and the Middle East portions of the trip over, Obama now turned his sights on Europe and the one big public event of the week, an outdoor speech on the night of July 25 in the heart of Berlin. In each country, preparations were carried out smoothly, save for Berlin. When word leaked that Obama's team was eyeing the Brandenburg Gate as the site of his public speech, German Chancellor Angela Merkel protested.

For three decades, the famous pillars stood behind the Berlin Wall, symbolizing Europe's divisions during the Cold War. John F. Kennedy had come to view the wall from a site near the Brandenburg Gate in 1963, when he said, "Ich bin ein Berliner." It was in the shadow of the Brandenburg Gate that Ronald Reagan had declared, "Mr. Gorbachev, tear down this wall." Obama told his senior advisers he opposed the site, though by the time he weighed in, his team in Berlin had already crossed it off. They chose instead Tiergarten Park. Obama would speak from a stage erected at the base of the Victory Column, which commemorated German military victories of the nineteenth century. The Brandenburg Gate would be captured in the pictures, a mile or so off in the distance.

On the flight from Israel to Berlin that morning, Obama's aides briefed him on the plans for the speech. "I did not know that they had set up the space that accommodated five hundred thousand people, and I did not hear that until we were leaving Israel," Obama told us a day later. "I said, 'What!' We were sort of walking the tightrope without a net there." Were his aides certain they could fill enough of the space to make it look good? His arrival into Berlin resolved that question. Foreign press lined the sidewalk outside his hotel, the Adlon, and the streets were filled with spectators eager to get their first look at this young American, who was treated more like a rock star than a politician.

Obama conducted a series of meetings and then taped an interview with NBC's Brian Williams. When he returned to his hotel, he said to advisers, "My work day is done." He planned a trip to the gym and some rest. "Got to give a speech tonight," he added. "I'm in great shape."

It was a soft summer evening, with a near-cloudless sky and warm temperatures. In Tiergarten a festive atmosphere reigned, part rock concert, part political rally, with two hundred thousand people stretching from the base of the Victory Column along the Strasse des 17 Juni almost to the Brandenburg Gate. Television crews and still photographers were packed to capacity on an enormous riser. The campaign set up a crane so photographers could take in the whole sweep of the scene. Obama was scheduled to speak at 7:30. When he was introduced he came from the back of the column to confront the sea of humanity that now seemed to surge to greet him. Jonathan Freedland of the *Guardian* said Obama "almost floated into view, walking to the podium on a raised, blue-carpeted runway as if he were somehow, magically, walking on water."

Obama called his speech "A World That Stands as One." "Tonight I speak to you not as a candidate for president but as a citizen—a proud citizen of the United States, and a fellow citizen of the world." The address was sober and substantive; a call for a renewal of transatlantic cooperation and a tribute to the struggles Berliners had overcome during the depths of the Cold War. "People of the world," he said, "look at Berlin!" His words were strong, but far more memorable were the visuals of flag-waving Europeans cheering an American politician.

His only blemish in Germany came over canceling a visit to the Landstuhl Regional Medical Center to visit with wounded troops. That came after the Pentagon told his team he could not take any campaign staff with him. Obama said he decided not to go in order to keep wounded soldiers from being drawn into a political controversy. But the decision created controversy back home. McCain's campaign accused him of stiffing the troops. McCain said that, if it had been him, he would have gone to see them alone to show his respect

By now Obama's team was eager to get home, though he still had stops in France and Great Britain, where he would receive more adulation, particularly from French President Nicolas Sarkozy, whose enthusiasm seemed unbridled. The trip had been enormously successful at home and abroad. Nevertheless, Obama and his advisers worried that ten days away from the campaign trail could cost him among voters. "I don't think that we'll see a bump in the polls," he told us the day before he returned to the United States. "I think we might even lose some points. People back home are worried about gas prices, they're worried about jobs." He knew voters cared less about what the Europeans thought of him than their own well-being. As Republican Vin Weber put it, "Americans would like the president to be more popular in the world, but they don't want to elect the president of Europe."

The scorekeepers back home tallied the week as a rout for Obama. "McCain lost the week badly, let's be honest," said John Weaver, McCain's former chief strategist, as Obama was nearing the end of the trip. "John is still in striking distance, thanks to his own character, biography, and memories of the McCain of previous election cycles. But he cannot afford another week like this one."

McCain's campaign was staggering in the face of the coverage of Obama's foreign trip and stumbled in responding. The day before Obama's departure, Jill Hazelbaker, the communications director, had dismissed Obama's trip as a "first-of-its-kind campaign rally overseas." Her remarks were part of a plan approved by McCain to counter Obama's favorable publicity. But when reporters confronted McCain, who had long urged Obama to go to Iraq, McCain disassociated himself from her remarks. "I will talk to her," McCain said. "The fact is that I'm glad he is going to Iraq. I am glad he is going to Afghanistan. It's long, long overdue if you want to lead this nation."

Hazelbaker, who began the campaign as McCain's communications director in New Hampshire and ascended to the bigger job when the campaign imploded in July 2007, was angry. She had been one of his most loyal staffers, and now, in public view, he was rebuking her. She called McCain: What are you doing? He apologized and later in the day tried to soften his remarks, saying the scheduled rally in Berlin certainly could be seen as a campaign event. Hazelbaker, frustrated by what happened, did not come into the office the next day. McCain advisers had been working for nearly a week on the new communications plan and McCain had signed off on it. Now he seemed to have forgotten. They wondered, does he really want to win?

McCain's advisers had anticipated blanket coverage of the trip, but even they were taken aback by what they saw as the frenzy of the media. The networks, responding to criticism, offered interviews to McCain, but there was little he could do to stem the story of a triumphal tour. He hammered Obama over Iraq, saying his opponent had been "completely wrong" about the policy, pointing to the success of the surge that Obama opposed.

While Obama was in Berlin, McCain went to a German restaurant in Ohio. He would love to give a speech in Germany, he said, but would prefer to do it as president. At an event with Tour de France cycling champion Lance Armstrong, McCain jabbed at the media's favorable coverage of his rival. "My opponent, of course, is traveling in Europe, and tomorrow his tour takes him to France," he said. "In a scene Lance would recognize, a throng of adoring fans awaits Senator Obama in Paris—and that's just the American press."

Schmidt worried that Obama was attempting to put the election away before the conventions. Obama would come back from Europe in the lead and would hold the first convention, destined to give him another bounce in the polls. The Republican convention would follow with a first-night schedule likely to include appearances by the unpopular President Bush and Vice President Cheney. Schmidt feared that, by the second night of the Republican convention, McCain could be down by twenty points. He told others they needed to break Obama's stride. "He's on his way to running away with this in August," he said.

On July 27, McCain's top advisers met in Phoenix to decide what to do. Schmidt laid out a hypothesis. Measured by the amount of favorable coverage he was receiving, Obama was now operating at a higher altitude than any previous politician. If Bill Clinton in 1992 or John McCain in 2000 had topped out at fifteen thousand feet, Obama was at thirty thousand. Pulling him back to earth would not work, Schmidt argued. It was like trying to hit somebody on the roof of a tall building with a bunch of rocks. "You can't throw a rock that high, no matter how hard you try," he said. "So you can't engage with him." The only way to bring him down was to force him even higher and hope for an "Icarus effect," so high that he couldn't sustain himself. McCain's team decided to try to turn what they regarded as Obama's greatest asset, his celebrity, into a liability.

The result was the most famous ad of McCain's campaign, unveiled days after Obama's return to the United States. The thirty-second spot opened with scenes of Obama in Berlin, and then, as images of Britney Spears and Paris Hilton flashed quickly across the screen, a narrator said, "He's the biggest celebrity in the world, but is he ready to lead?"

The ad was mocked as petty, a diversion, and the latest example of how far McCain had strayed from the kind of campaign he ran eight years earlier. Obama's campaign tested the spot and concluded it had little resonance with voters. "People thought it was trivial. They didn't like it," Joel Benenson said. The election was too important to let it get sidetracked by ads featuring Paris Hilton. And yet the commercial worked: It put McCain on offense and, despite the public's apparent dismissal of the ad, threw the Obama team off its stride.

Obama's advisers were sensitive to the charge that Obama was too lofty, too elitist—something they had worried about since the primaries—and knew he still had not overcome doubts about him. Whether it was fatigue after the foreign trip or the distraction of preparing for the Democratic convention now only weeks away, the celebrity ad spooked Obama's team. They did exactly the opposite of what Axelrod had recommended before the foreign trip, scaling back on the size of his events and taking much of the energy out of his campaign. "We went very small," Axelrod said. Gibbs said, "We got inside our own heads too much."

Obama went to Hawaii for vacation in the middle of August, unhappy with the state of things. "He knew that we were out of synch and I think more than anything what he felt was like we were in the doldrums," Axelrod said. At a meeting on August 12, Obama pollster Joel Benenson presented the findings from new data. "We began this race by running against Washington and the broken politics that have blocked progress and we can, and must, reclaim that territory and block McCain from encroaching on it," the opening slide of his PowerPoint presentation said. McCain's team, surprisingly, had bought time to regroup and devise a real plan for winning the election. For both campaigns, the coming conventions would be critical opportunities to reenergize and reframe the election.

CHAPTER TWENTY-FIVE

Mile High in Denver

"Barack Obama is my candidate. And he must be our president."
—Hillary Clinton, addressing the Democratic convention

In 1908, when Democrats had last selected the "Mile High City" for their national convention, the *Denver Post*, in a burst of boosterism, hailed the news as "the greatest thing to ever happen to the city. It will bring in millions and millions of dollars." The sardonic Damon Runyon, one of the horde of journalists covering that convention, watched as a troop of dancing Apaches hired by the city whooped and mingled with the delegates and wrote that it was hard to distinguish between Indians and delegates except that the delegates were wearing badges and shouting all the time. That year for the third time the Democrats picked William Jennings Bryan, the Great Commoner, as their nominee, and for the third time Bryan lost, even more disastrously than in 1896 and 1900.

A century later, in August 2008, the Democrats were back in Denver, badges, funny hats, shouts, and all, and once again visions of convention money danced before city leaders. But this time, the Democrats were poised to make history and nominate an African-American as their presidential candidate. Finally, they believed, they were on the way to winning back the White House.

As the Democrats gathered, however, another narrative competed for attention in the media, focused on Obama and the Clintons and asking whether there could ever be true peace between them. Certainly there were lingering resentments between supporters of Obama and Clinton. Her advisers did not believe he had done enough to help retire her campaign debt. His supporters believed the Clintons were still not convinced that Obama could defeat McCain. Could they come together in Denver?

The vice presidential selection created more hard feelings among her loyalists. Early in June, immediately after she ended her campaign and endorsed Obama, her supporters—not Clinton herself, who repeatedly praised Obama in her public appearances—began lobbying for him to choose her as his vice president. It was never to be. As one Obama adviser put it later, "You can't have two alpha dogs on the ticket." Still, when Obama picked Biden as his vice president on the eve of the convention, it was reported that Clinton had not even been vetted. Her supporters took that as the ultimate snub.

Two days after the primaries ended, Obama and Clinton met alone in the Washington home of California Senator Dianne Feinstein. Their meeting had all the trappings of a cloak-and-dagger operation. Obama had just finished an event that Saturday in nearby Virginia and was supposed to fly back to Chicago. When reporters traveling with him boarded the plane at Dulles, Obama wasn't there. No one on his staff told them why, or where he was. At Feinstein's home he and Clinton talked for an hour in an upstairs room, then left. After the press found out, Obama's staff said it was a "productive meeting" to discuss Democratic Party unity as they approached the fall campaign. Obama, according to one of his most senior advisers, indicated to Clinton that while she was more than qualified, there were mitigating circumstances that might make it difficult for him to select her. Clinton said that while she was willing to be considered, she did not want to go through the exhaustive vetting process unless there was a high likelihood she would be chosen.

Their relationship had been strained by the nomination battle and Obama could see that she still had not worked her way through what had happened. But that was not the last time he thought about her as a running mate. Gradually the relationship improved, and he would occasionally raise her name when talking about possible running mates. "Through the process he'd always come back and say what about Hillary?" one adviser said. "She's smart, she's tough, she certainly is qualified." But Biden was always the front-runner, and just before the convention, Obama tapped him. End of story—but not for elements in the media that remained focused on how bitterness between the rival camps could explode in Denver and tear apart the party.

Talk of tensions between the Clintons and Obama persisted into the opening of the convention, in part because there were real grievances. *New York Times* columnist Maureen Dowd perfectly captured the underlying emotions of a convention that "has a vibe so at odds with the thrilling, fairy dust feel of the Obama revolution" that she asked a noted political strategist, "What is that feeling in the air?" He replied: "Submerged hate."

But both the Clinton and Obama teams were determined not to let rancor and distrust disrupt the convention. Whatever her feelings, Clinton would be "blowing up those balloons herself, hanging them in the net," if that's what it took to produce a harmonious convention, an aide joked. The overwhelming majority of Democrats wanted exactly that; they had had enough of losing elections. They did not want internecine warfare to doom their prospects again. As Democratic strategist William Galston told us before the convention, "The Democratic Party is like a mule. If you hit it over the head with a two-by-four often enough it finally gets the message."

There *was* cause for concern, but party disunity wasn't the main problem. It was what came after the balloons popped: whether Obama could actually beat McCain. Some governors—notably Pennsylvania's Ed Rendell, a staunch Hillary backer—openly expressed doubts about Obama. Some supporters were troubled because he still had not found an effective message for dealing with the worsening economic conditions. Despite overwhelming evidence that voters wanted change, as the convention began that Monday, August 25th, the daily Gallup presidential tracking poll showed Obama and McCain dead even. For the second day in a row, Gallup had them tied at 45 percent. Other polls showed them running neck and neck: McCain, up by four in Florida; Obama, up by seven in Pennsylvania; both even in Ohio, though one survey there had McCain ahead by one. For Democrats, all this was evidence that it was crucial to unite behind Obama—and for Obama to step up.

By 2008, the national political convention had become a charade, robbed of suspense, its outcome determined well in advance. Tedious, boring, too long. All these elements were present for the Democrats in Denver. But three dramas will be remembered in a convention that *did* create history.

The first came at the opening session when Senator Ted Kennedy haltingly mounted the podium that night to address the delegates.

Two months before, Kennedy was operated on at the Duke University Medical Center to remove a malignant glioma, a fast-growing tumor, in his brain. Home from the hospital, he let family and friends know that he wanted to address the Democrats in person, not by way of a videotaped tribute. Since his operation he received daily radiation therapy, followed by chemotherapy. For three weeks before the convention, despite his failing health, he rehearsed his speech. On the Sunday before the convention opened, he made a long flight by private jet to Denver. He arrived in excruciating pain. At first doctors feared the pain was connected to his cancer, then determined he was suffering from notoriously painful kidney stones.

Kennedy remained in a University of Colorado Hospital room, enduring a sleepless night and morning pain, until less than two hours before he was scheduled to speak. "There was nothing that was going to keep him away," his niece Caroline Kennedy later told the *Boston Globe*. With a doctor, paramedics, his wife, Vicki, and Caroline, he left his hospital bed, was driven to the convention center, then transported by golf cart into the Pepsi Center. With Caroline and Vicki at his side, he walked laboriously, limping slightly, to the podium and faced the delegates. An intravenous tube, implanted to administer pain medication, could be seen sticking from an Ace bandage on his left hand.

The Ted Kennedy who stood before the delegates in Denver was seventy-six years old and in his forty-sixth year in the Senate. He was the last link to his assassinated brothers—and to the time when the Democratic Party stood supreme as the nation's majority party. He was the unquestioned leader of the liberals, and of course the man whose endorsement gave Barack Obama his greatest boost with Democrats and helped him defeat Hillary Clinton.

As he began to speak, there were tears throughout the hall as the last of the Kennedy brothers—the "lion in winter," he was now being called—delivered the speech that might well be his last hurrah. It wasn't great oratory, but that didn't matter. His familiar voice, if huskier and at times halting, struck deep chords. In calling for the election of Obama as a harbinger of "a season of hope," he evoked the memory of his slain brothers. He was passing the torch, and everyone in the hall knew it. As John Lewis, the Georgia civil rights leader and congressman, who had been close to Robert Kennedy, said afterward, the speech was a signal that Obama was about to inherit the Kennedy family legacy. JFK's daughter, Caroline, said later, "On many levels, it was a very difficult thing to do—logistically, medically, emotionally. It was really inspiring to all of us." Whatever breach had existed among Democrats before Kennedy spoke was being closed as the convention began.

The next moment came on Tuesday when Hillary took the stage in prime time. From her opening words, she left no question about where she stood:

"I am honored to be here tonight. A proud mother. A proud Democrat. A proud American. And a proud supporter of Barack Obama." Applause and cheers. Speaking to both her supporters and Obama's, she said, "Whether you voted for me or voted for Barack, the time is now to unite as a single party with a single purpose. We are on the same team, and none of us can sit on the sidelines." More applause. She hadn't spent thirty-five years in the trenches, fighting for children, for universal health care, for women's rights, "to see another Republican in the White House squander the promise of our country and the hopes of our people." Then, in a line that drew even louder applause, she said, "No way. No how. No McCain."

Lest anyone listening fail to get her message, she added, "Barack Obama is my candidate. And he must be our president," as the sound of cheering again echoed throughout the hall. She drove the point harder. "Before we can keep going, we have to get going by electing Barack Obama president. We don't have a moment to lose or a vote to spare. Nothing less than the fate of our nation and the future of our children hang in the balance."

Whatever resentment or recrimination remained from the long primary battles, however deep her supporters' disappointment at her not being picked as Obama's vice president, everyone watching had to know she was a team player. The reaction of a Hillary supporter, Kelly Friendly from Wellesley, Massachusetts, where Hillary attended college, summed up the new feeling of party harmony. Would she vote for Obama? Friendly was asked after Hillary's speech. "Absolutely," she told the *New York Times*. "She just told us to, didn't she?" Mark Smith, a Texas delegate, told *USA Today*, "When Barack became her candidate, he became mine. He's my No. 1 now."

Hillary had one more dramatic role to play on Wednesday afternoon, during the roll call of the states when the delegations begin announcing their votes. Earlier, Hillary had wanted her name put in nomination in recognition of her historic candidacy, but two-thirds of the way through the roll call, an elaborately planned series of handoffs began to unfold. New Mexico yielded to Illinois, which yielded to New York. The cameras zeroed in on Hillary moving across the convention floor amid cheers from the delegates. Taking the microphone where her New York State delegation was seated, she said, "In the spirit of unity, with the goal of victory, let's declare together in one voice, right here, right now, that Barack Obama is our candidate and he will be our president." She moved that the convention stop the roll call and nominate Obama by acclamation. Thunderous applause. The motion quickly passed, setting off a jubilant floor demonstration. Delegates danced in the aisles to the strains of "Love Train," then began chanting, *Yes, we can! Yes, we can!* Speaker Pelosi gaveled the roll call to an end. The long battle was over. Obama was the candidate.

That night it was Bill's turn. He grabbed the stage and supplied the convention with its third memorable moment.

The applause that greeted him as he took the podium grew louder and louder, drowning out his repeated words of thanks and his imploring them to be seated. The ovation continued. Now they were shouting, *Bill! Bill! Bill!* "Please stop. Sit down. Sit down. Thank you," Clinton repeated, to no avail. *Bill! Bill! Bill!* they shouted. "Please sit, please sit," he repeated, with a smile and wave. "You know, I love this, and I thank you, but we have important work to do tonight. I am here first to support Barack Obama"—again his words were drowned by applause, even louder this time—"and second," he continued, "I'm here to warm up the crowd for Joe Biden"—more applause—"though as you'll soon see, he doesn't need any help from me."

The hall rang with laughter. He had them. "I love Joe Biden, and America will too." He went on, "What a year we Democrats have had. The primary began with an all-star lineup. And it came down to two remarkable Americans locked in a hard-fought contest right to the very end. That campaign generated so much heat, it increased global warming." More laughter. "Now, in the end, my candidate didn't win. But I'm really proud of the campaign she ran." Greater applause. "I am proud that she never quit on the people she stood up for . . . and I'm grateful for the chance Chelsea and I had to go all over America to tell people about the person we know and love." A pause, a broad grin, then: "Now, I'm not so grateful for the chance to speak in the wake of Hillary's magnificent speech night." Laughter. "But I'll do the best I can." Applause. "Last night, Hillary told us in no uncertain terms that she is going to do everything she can to elect Barack Obama." Even greater applause, eclipsed by his next words: "That makes two of us." Another pause, another grin, then: "Actually that makes eighteen million of us"—referring to the number who voted for Hillary in the primaries—"because, like Hillary, I want all of you who supported her to vote for Barack Obama in November."

Silence filled the hall; the Democrats listened intently: "Our nation is in trouble on two fronts. The American dream is under siege at home, and America's leadership in the world has been weakened." Then Clinton said the job of the next president was to rebuild the American dream and restore American leadership in the world. "And here's what I have to say about that," he continued. "Everything I learned in my eight years as president, and in the work I have done since in America and across the globe, has convinced me that Barack Obama is the man for this job."

The Democrats went wild. From then on, they interrupted virtually every sentence with applause. Clinton praised Obama for his choice of Biden: "In his first presidential decision, the selection of a running mate, he hit it out of the park." With that line, Clinton bound the Democrats together. "With Joe Biden's experience and wisdom, supporting Barack Obama's proven understanding instincts and insight, Americans have the national security leadership we need." He paused dramatically, gazed out over the delegates, and, his voice rising, said, "And so, my fellow Democrats, I say to you Barack Obama is ready to lead America and to restore American leadership in the world." Applause. "Barack Obama is ready to honor the oath to preserve, protect, and defend the Constitution of the United States." Applause. "Barack Obama is ready to be president of the United States."

They all knew readiness had been Hillary's strongest attack on Obama: *He* was untested, *she* was ready to be president on "day one." They all got it, and understood too that the Clintons had offered the strongest possible call for party unity. That was the message the Democrats hungered to hear.

Bill Clinton had been harmful to the party during the primaries, often negative and divisive, but on this night it was the old charming, teasing Comeback Kid who occupied the stage—and, speaking with the authority of a former president, issued a command for the party to come together. For the rest of his speech, he played with the audience. They responded with applause and shouts and with loud boos whenever he mentioned the name of Republicans and the Republican disasters from Iraq to Katrina to cronyism to the assault on science and the defense of torture. Then he said, "My fellow Democrats, America can do better than that, and Barack Obama will do better than . . ." His words were lost amid the sound of cheering delegates. When he tried to continue, they burst into the chant: *Yes, we can! Yes, we can! Yes, we can! Yes, we can! Yes, we can!* Nine times, louder and louder, the chant rising until Clinton delivered his ultimate political challenge: "Yes, *he* can, but first, we have to elect him."

The Clintons, following in Kennedy's path, had set the stage for Obama. Together, they presented the gift of a unified Democratic Party. Now it was up to him to deliver.

Obama and his aides knew well how crucial his Thursday night acceptance speech would be. Their private focus group findings and the polls that showed a dead-even race spelled out the challenge: He had to reassure voters still harboring doubts about him, make them feel comfortable about him as commander in chief of a country in deep trouble, and deliver the strongest, most forceful case against George W. Bush and the Republicans who had controlled Washington for much of the past eight years—and particularly against John McCain.

They knew his speech had to take on McCain directly. Normally presidential nominees let others attack their opponent, but Obama had to show his toughness to members of his own party. He had another challenge: He would be speaking on the forty-fifth anniversary of Martin Luther King's great "I Have a Dream" address from the steps of the Lincoln Memorial that paved the way for the achievements of the civil rights movement, of which Obama was an heir.

Obama arrived in Denver Wednesday afternoon and immediately began huddling with key aides about the next night's speech. He had read other nomination acceptance speeches, and found three particularly memorable: John Kennedy's, short but effective in 1960; Ronald Reagan's, even tighter in 1980; Bill Clinton's, too long but a speech that powerfully appealed to Americans with its theme of putting people first, in 1992.

Though there had been numerous discussions over many weeks about the speech, with drafts prepared and exchanged by Obama and others, not until eleven o'clock Thursday morning, after hours of labor over the address, did Obama say this draft is the one. I like it. Hours later, after Obama's meetings ended, he, David Axelrod, and speechwriter Jon Favreau met late in the afternoon in a room at the Westin Hotel, for his first chance to rehearse his speech before them. They had only three or four hours until his address.

No sooner had Obama begun the tense speech rehearsal than a knock on the suite door interrupted them. Obama, closest to the door, opened it to find a room service waiter with a silver tray. He was delivering an order for a chicken Caesar salad. That would be mine, Axelrod said sheepishly. Obama took the tray, carried it to Axelrod, and said, Ax, I'm sorry to interrupt your lunch for my speech prep for the convention speech tonight. That broke the tension and nervousness over the rehearsal. All three began laughing. The rehearsal continued.

It went smoothly until almost the end. Obama had reached the point when he was going to refer to King's historic speech forty-five years ago that day. Suddenly, the ever-cool Barack Obama stopped, visibly choked up. Hang on a second, guys. I'm sorry, but this is hitting me. This is really a big deal. He paced the room, talking about how many people had suffered and sacrificed to enable him to give this speech that night. Then, still clearly moved, he asked them to give him a few minutes. "I started reading it and I got to the section right at the end when it talks about, you know, this young preacher from Georgia. And . . . I had to stop. I choked up," Obama later told us. He went into the bathroom and closed the door. When he returned, it was the cool, composed Obama who resumed his speech rehearsal.

While he was rehearsing, workmen were putting the final touches on transforming Invesco Field, home of the Denver Broncos, into the setting for Obama's acceptance speech.

Not since 1960, when Kennedy moved his acceptance speech outdoors to the Los Angeles Coliseum, had such a convention shift been made. In Denver, hundreds of crew members had been working around the clock. On the fifty-yard line they built a stage resembling a miniature Greek temple. Fake marble columns, painted off-white and looking like those of the U.S. Capitol or the White House, formed a backdrop for the temple. Two hundred spotlights would bathe the scene in a sea of soft light. And when Obama finished his address, confetti would rain down on him and fireworks would explode into the heavens.

This latest example of an age of excess, of mass Super Bowl and rock concert extravaganzas, was instantly mocked. McCain's campaign described the massive neoclassical set as the "Barackopolis," suggesting delegates should don togas as did the ancient Greeks. The conservative *New York Post* reported that Democrats would be kneeling before the "Temple of Obama" when he spoke, and added that a "Rocky Mountain coronation was not lofty enough. Obama will aim for Mount Olympus." During the week, Axelrod, aware of criticism of the stage setting, asked media adviser Jim Margolis to make sure the site was not too over-the-top. The columns, he thought, were fine, but other features were not. It looked like a set from *Deal or No Deal*, he told the *New Yorker's* Ryan Lizza. Margolis ordered some of it toned down, but not the Greek columns.

For hours people stood in lines to witness this moment of political history, and by the time Obama spoke, more than eighty thousand had filled the stadium. Once again, he did not disappoint them.

First he saluted Hillary, "a champion for working Americans and an inspiration to my daughters and to yours," then "President Clinton, who last night made the case for change as only he can do it," and finally Ted Kennedy, "who embodies the spirit of service." Then, as planned, he told his story: of "the brief union between a young man from Kenya and a young woman from Kansas who weren't well-off or well-known but shared a belief that in America their son could achieve whatever he set his mind to. That promise has always set this country apart."

Then he spoke of the challenge confronting the nation, telling the crowd that America stands at one of its "defining moments—a moment when our nation is at war, our economy is in turmoil, and the American promise has been threatened once more."

These challenges, he continued, "are not all of government's making. But the failure to respond is a direct result of a broken politics in Washington and the failed policies of George W. Bush. America, we are better than these last eight years. We are a better country than this." He saluted John McCain's heroism and military service, but said, "The record's clear: John McCain has voted with George Bush ninety percent of the time. Senator McCain likes to talk about judgment, but really, what does it say about your judgment when you think George Bush has been right more than ninety percent of the time?" The problem was not that he "doesn't care" about what was happening to ordinary American. The problem was he just "doesn't get it."

Then Obama laid out the theme on which he and his speech advisers had worked so hard: his determination to recapture the American promise for the people. He said, "Our government should work for us, not against us. It should help us, not hurt us. It should ensure opportunity not just for those with the most money and influence, but for every American who's willing to work. That's the promise of America."

In the end, he sounded his message of change and hope. "I realize that I am not the likeliest candidate for this office," he said. "I don't fit the typical pedigree, and I haven't spent my career in the halls of Washington. . . . But this election has never been about me. It's been about you. For eighteen long months, you have stood up . . . and said enough to the politics of the past. . . . You have shown what history teaches us—that at defining moments like this one, the change we need doesn't come from Washington. Change happens because the American people demand it—because they rise up and insist on new ideas and new leadership, a new politics for a new time."

By every measure, Obama's speech was a success. The public was enthusiastic, the critics positive, the polls registered an immediate turn in his favor. From dead even, he was now six points ahead. Democrats, all talk of disunity gone, were confident that victory awaited them in November. Republicans, about to convene the following Monday in St. Paul, were reported to be despondent. As euphoric Democrats were departing from Denver, the Republican delegates nervously awaited the news about the choice of McCain's running mate to be announced that same Friday.

CHAPTER TWENTY-SIX

Palinmania

*"You know . . . the difference between a hockey mom and a pit
bull? Lipstick!"*

—Sarah Palin at the Republican convention

S hortly before 1 p.m. on Wednesday, August 27, a black car carrying
Alaska Governor Sarah Palin pulled up next to the stairs of a Learjet
35A at the executive terminal at the Ted Stevens Anchorage International
Airport. Palin had just finished an appearance in town and was driven to
the airport by her husband, Todd. She bade him goodbye and, along with
aide Kris Perry, boarded quickly, lest anyone notice her leaving. In minutes
she was airborne. All arrangements had been handled in strict confidence.
Twenty minutes into the flight she was handed a phone-book-sized packet
of materials by Davis White, John McCain's director of advance, who had
slipped into Alaska late Monday night to oversee the secret journey. The
packet contained her reading for the long flight south: McCain's speeches,
a schedule, and other background on the campaign. White explained two
possible outcomes. They would fly to Boeing Field in Seattle to refuel, and
then on to Flagstaff, Arizona. She would meet with McCain on Thursday
morning. If all went well, she would become his vice presidential running
mate and not see Alaska for many days. If not, she faced a quick trip home
and a return to relative obscurity.

Palin was not well-known outside of Alaska, but to those conservatives
who had met her or followed her rise to power, she was already something
of a folk hero: a down-to-earth mother of five, staunchly pro-life, pro-gun,
an avid hunter, a runner, a beauty queen, a gutsy politician who champi-
oned limited government and individual liberty. She had risen from the
PTA to the city council to mayor of the small town of Wasilla (population
at the time, less than ten thousand) to a state energy board. In 2006, she

challenged the deeply unpopular governor, Frank Murkowski, in the Republican primary, winning the three-way contest on her charm, straightforward demeanor, and a message of reform. She then beat a former governor, Democrat Tony Knowles, in the general election.

In a bleak Republican year, Sarah Palin was one of the few bright spots. She came to office on a pledge to build a long-stalled natural gas pipeline and break up the old-boy politics in Juneau. She was not afraid to tangle with two of Alaska's most powerful Republicans, Senator Ted Stevens—principal advocate of the infamous Bridge to Nowhere—and Representative Don Young.

As governor, Palin had attracted favorable notices in prominent conservative publications. Six months into her term, she hosted an informal lunch for the *Weekly Standard*'s William Kristol and Fred Barnes, and former White House speechwriter Michael Gerson, who were on a magazine-sponsored cruise of Alaska's Inside Passage. Barnes later wrote a glowing piece that, noting her approval rating of around 90 percent, called her a Republican star with a record of "eye-popping integrity." That same summer she met another group of conservative thinkers who were on a cruise sponsored by *National Review* and drew more flattering notices. Still she was so little-known that the *Weekly Standard* felt the need to tell how to pronounce her name: "pale-in."

Outside conservative circles, Palin remained a dark horse candidate whose inexperience made her a highly risky choice for the Republican ticket. She had been in office less than twenty months and though popular at home had remained out of the national debates. But as her plane headed south to Arizona, she now had the inside track to win the job as McCain's running mate.

McCain believed he needed someone dramatic to transform the presidential race. Though he had knocked Obama back in early August with the ads featuring Britney Spears and Paris Hilton, everyone around him knew that was merely a summertime diversion, a tactical exercise that would quickly be overwhelmed by Obama's convention. The McCain team may have mocked Obama's Greek temple setting in Denver, but they needed a real strategy, propelled by a bold choice for vice president, to preserve any hope of winning in November.

As McCain approached his convention, his advisers saw the challenges as overwhelming—and contradictory. First, he needed to distance himself decisively from the president. Second, he needed to cut into Obama's advantage among women voters. Despite the bitterness of the primary race, and some of the mutinous talk among Clinton's most vocal holdouts, the polls showed Obama consolidating most of the Clinton vote. By mid-summer, this had become an acute problem for McCain. Third, he needed to energize the lethargic Republican base. While polling showed McCain now winning roughly the same level of support among Republicans as Obama was receiving among Democrats, McCain enjoyed little enthusiasm among conservatives. They might turn out to vote for him—might—but would they staff local offices, make phone calls, knock on doors, contribute money, and rally friends and neighbors as they had done for Bush four years earlier? Fourth, and perhaps most important, McCain had to regain the one advantage he had always counted on: his identity as a reformer. As Steve Schmidt put it, "We had to get that reform mojo back."

Obama had gone the safe route in his selection of Joe Biden, a do-no-harm pick that followed the classic vice presidential manual. McCain did not have such a luxury—or so argued some of his closest advisers. Schmidt and campaign manager Rick Davis believed McCain's only hope of winning was to make an out-of-the-box choice. If we pick a traditional candidate and run a really good race, Schmidt told Mark Salter late one night, we still lose.

Palin's plane landed after dark in Flagstaff. Christian Ferry, McCain's deputy campaign manager, met the plane and drove the group to the home of Robert Delgado, the CEO of Hensley & Co., the large beer distributorship started by Cindy McCain's father. Though it was late, Palin still had a long night ahead of her. Waiting there to see her were Schmidt and Salter. Waiting back in Washington to talk to her by telephone was A. B. Culvahouse, a former White House counsel under Ronald Reagan who was in charge of the vetting process and needed to conduct the all-important personal interview. Waiting in Sedona was McCain, who was scheduled to leave around 10 a.m. the next morning after his running mate had been chosen.

McCain's team now had barely twelve hours to complete the vetting process, take a face-to-face measure of their leading candidate, decide whether McCain and Palin had the chemistry to coexist as a ticket, and make a judgment about whether she was ready for the rigors of a national campaign.

McCain's search for a vice president had started in the spring with about two dozen names. Palin was not a serious candidate. One person said she wasn't even on the initial list; others said she was—barely. It was only later in the summer, when the campaign team became alarmed at the size of Obama's lead among women, that she was added to the list of genuine contenders. "Toward the end of the process, in July, we started taking a look at, like okay, who are we missing? Let's take a sharper look at women candidates and try that one more time," Davis said. "That's when Palin came on." Palin, he added, "stood out significantly from the rest of that list."

Eventually, McCain narrowed his choices to six finalists. In addition to Palin, they were Independent-Democratic Senator Joseph Lieberman, McCain's former rival Mitt Romney, Minnesota Governor Tim Pawlenty, New York Mayor Michael Bloomberg, and Florida Governor Charlie Crist. Louisiana Governor Bobby Jindal might have been a finalist had he not taken himself out of contention.

Until days before McCain's deadline, Lieberman appeared to be the leading contender, although one top official later told us it was never as clear-cut as that. "If you characterize this as yes or no on Lieberman and then someone else [became the top contender], that's not it at all," he said. "Was he the romantic pick? Yes."

Certainly none of the others enjoyed the kind of relationship with McCain that Lieberman did. The Connecticut senator ran for vice president with Al Gore in 2000, but broke with his party over the war in Iraq. In August 2006, he lost his primary race to antiwar businessman Ned Lamont, who attracted enthusiastic support from liberal bloggers furious over Lieberman's support of Bush's war policies. Defeated in the primary, Lieberman ran as an Independent and was reelected. McCain and Lieberman shared almost identical views on the war. If anything, McCain was a more vocal critic of Bush's policies, but both strongly opposed withdrawal timetables and believed victory could be achieved. They were steadfast in their views when public opinion on the war was running strongly in the other direction.

Beyond that, they simply enjoyed each other's company. Lieberman and Lindsey Graham traveled regularly with McCain. It was often said that Graham was Robin to McCain's Batman, a youthful sidekick who had a quick sense of humor, was loyal to the older man, and shared with him a willingness to criticize his own party. Lieberman was different, more an equal than a sidekick. McCain loved him. He admired his probity, enjoyed his corny Borscht Belt humor, and most of all trusted his judgment. They differed on many aspects of domestic policy, but they saw a dangerous world through the same prism.

Advisers thought picking Lieberman would shake up the race, particularly if coupled with the move McCain was seriously considering: a pledge to serve just one term. Virtually all his top advisers favored the idea. A one-term pledge had long been talked about inside the campaign. At the time of McCain's announcement in April 2007, the draft of his speech included a statement that he would serve only one term. But Davis strongly opposed the idea, and McCain was dubious, believing that it would unnecessarily limit his power. The pledge was removed less than twenty-four hours before the speech, according to two advisers, but resurfaced seriously as part of plans for a possible McCain-Lieberman ticket.

The appeal of picking Lieberman was that it would send a powerful signal that a McCain administration would represent an attempt to break out of partisan politics in Washington, that as president he would actively seek to build a governing consensus at the center of the electorate. The one-term pledge would add an exclamation point to this message, allowing McCain to argue that his administration would have but one goal: to clean up a toxic political system in Washington and take on the most intractable issues that had resisted solution without having to worry about how it might affect his reelection. By now, even Davis had softened in his opposition. "My opposition to it in the primary was that it really was a cheap way to try to win the primary," he later told us. "It wasn't worth making that sacrifice for a primary win. . . . That being said, I understood the need for a device like that if you were going to sell Lieberman because Lieberman was going to be a hard sell."

Both Davis and Culvahouse raised the one-term pledge directly with Lieberman. "My answer to both of them was, hey guys, I didn't expect to be considered for vice president at all," Lieberman told us. "I still think it's a long shot, so you're asking if it happens would I agree to do it for only four years, that's an easy question. Of course I would." Even McCain had come around, according to his most senior advisers. "There would have to be a one-term pledge," one said. "McCain knew that."

McCain's team knew there would be conservative opposition to Lieberman because of his pro-choice views on abortion and his support for gay rights. They developed a plan to reach out to delegates before the convention, with Charlie Black dispatched to St. Paul early for that purpose. As late as the third week of August, the vetting team was still working hard to finish

Lieberman's background checks, questionnaire, and personal interview with Culvahouse. Lieberman joked to Culvahouse that the questionnaire was so personally intrusive that the only thing he had not been asked was "whether I had had sexual relations with an animal."* Ironically, Lindsey Graham, one of Lieberman's main advocates, hurt Lieberman's chances by talking openly about his possible selection, allowing conservative opposition to intensify. "Lindsey was out talking to people before he should have and the story got ahead of us," one McCain adviser said.

McCain's team had circled the three days between the Democratic and Republican conventions as the time to announce their vice presidential choice and scheduled big rallies on all three days to give McCain flexibility to make his decision. But they preferred Friday, August 29, the day after the Democratic convention, as the best way to stop Obama's momentum after Denver.

On Sunday morning, August 24, McCain's senior staff met at the Ritz-Carlton in Phoenix to review their options. The group included Rick Davis, Schmidt, Charlie Black, pollster Bill McInturff, media adviser Fred Davis, and senior adviser Greg Strimple, although only Rick Davis, Schmidt, and Black had been privy to the inside details of the selection process. During the meeting, McInturff went through the results of his latest polling and analysis. He argued that McCain's position had improved since early July, particularly in battleground states. But much work remained. McCain needed to reinforce his maverick label; a Republican would have trouble winning in November but a maverick McCain might. Given the political climate, McCain would need an unconventional and unorthodox campaign and message.

But McInturff raised serious questions about picking Lieberman, or anyone who was pro-choice, as a vice presidential running mate. That included Mayor Bloomberg and former Pennsylvania governor Tom Ridge. Days earlier, McInturff tested pro-choice attitudes in a poll. Forty percent of McCain's core supporters said they would be less likely to support him if he selected a pro-choice running mate.

McInturff sketched out a possible doomsday scenario. First, he said, there was no way anyone could predict or control how the selection of a pro-choice running mate would be covered by the press. Would the story

---

* Culvahouse's team found one potentially serious problem with a Lieberman pick for vice president. Laws in some states prohibited a candidate from running for office from one party or another unless they had been registered with that party for a specified period of time. No one really wanted another *Bush v. Gore* to sully the 2008 election.

line be "McCain the maverick"—as everyone hoped—or would it be "McCain shatters the Republican coalition"? Second, he asked, had anyone read the rules of the convention? Majorities of just four state delegations could force a roll call on the vice presidential nomination. Picking a pro-choice running mate virtually guaranteed a divisive floor fight over abortion. While McCain might be able to impose his choice in St. Paul, the damage would be too costly. The story in September would be about a divided Republican Party, not about McCain's position on the economy or the war or his criticisms of Obama. Others in the campaign later said McInturff's analysis ended any realistic chance of Lieberman becoming vice president, although one senior official said McCain had not totally ruled out Lieberman at that point.

The group briefed McCain that afternoon. McInturff shared his findings and repeated his assessment of what could happen in St. Paul. McCain listened, but "John was very inscrutable," one person who attended the meeting recalled. "He was in his quiet, subdued, shoulder-hunched listening mode. . . . We said to each other after the meeting, 'From that conversation, we have no clue.'"

At that point, there seemed to be only two realistic finalists: Pawlenty and Palin, although press speculation focused mostly on Pawlenty and Mitt Romney. Romney's star had risen over the summer. He was not a Washington insider and could talk about the economy in ways McCain could not. Furthermore, his relationship with McCain had warmed considerably since the primaries. McCain was impressed at how hard Romney was willing to work to get him elected. Romney's prospects may have ended after a McCain gaffe the previous week. In an interview with *Politico*, McCain said he couldn't remember how many homes he and Cindy owned, making him sound badly out of touch with the lives of ordinary Americans. Romney owned four homes. Amid such economic hardship, Republicans could not present voters with nominees who between them owned nearly a dozen homes.

Pawlenty was young and vigorous, a conservative who had grown up in a blue-collar family—his father was a truck driver—and he was pro-life. He had won reelection in the Democratic year of 2006 and was seen as a future leader of the party, an advocate of modernizing the GOP without abandoning its conservative principles. Though not particularly flashy, he was seen as a more than credible choice, a running mate who might keep the Upper Midwest competitive. He was the safe choice if Palin faltered.

That night, Davis and Schmidt went alone to see McCain at his apartment in Phoenix. They urged him to take a serious look at Palin. Davis had been talking with her regularly all through August as part of a confidential plan designed to keep secret the fact that she was even under serious consideration. That weekend, Davis checked with Culvahouse to ask if he could complete a thorough vetting of Palin in the short time remaining. Culvahouse said he could. With that reassurance, McCain called Palin, who was at the Alaska State Fair, and invited her to come to Arizona to meet with him.

By the time Palin arrived at Delgado's house on Wednesday night, Culvahouse's team already knew much about her. They had scoured the public record. They had looked closely at an investigation that came to be known as Troopergate, into whether Palin had pressured and then fired the state public safety commissioner, Walter Monegan, after he refused to fire her former brother-in-law, who was in a divorce and child custody fight with her younger sister. They examined her tax returns and other financial records. Nothing appeared amiss. They did turn up a small blemish: Palin had once been fined for fishing without a valid license.

Culvahouse did not send Palin the lengthy questionnaire that all finalists were asked to complete until McCain invited her to Arizona. The questionnaire ran to seventy questions. Some were highly intrusive, the kind once saved for a personal interview: Did you ever fail to pay taxes for household help? Have you ever filed for bankruptcy? Have you undergone treatment for drug or alcohol abuse? Have you ever downloaded porn from the Internet? Have you ever paid for sex? Have you ever been unfaithful? Palin's questionnaire turned up one new piece of information: Her husband had once been arrested for driving while intoxicated. The questionnaire also asked if there was anything particularly sensitive that a prospective candidate preferred to discuss verbally. Palin indicated there was.

At the Delgado house, Palin spoke with Culvahouse. It was now well after 10 p.m. Phoenix time, and their interview lasted between ninety minutes and three hours. She was direct and cooperative, according to officials privy to the conversation, and revealed that her unmarried teenage daughter Bristol was pregnant. When Culvahouse finished, he gave Rick Davis a readout of the conversation.

In the days after her selection, Palin's vetting became a major question, with top officials insisting that nothing of significance had surfaced after her selection. Although they didn't learn of her daughter's pregnancy until she was about to meet McCain, they agreed that it should not be disqualifying. The appearance of haste in choosing her fueled speculation that McCain had acted impulsively. But if there was a breakdown it appears not to have been in the vetting but rather in a decision made without a deeper understanding of whether Palin would be judged ready to sit a heartbeat away from the presidency. As one person close to the campaign put it, Palin may have received a thorough legal vetting, but what she didn't receive was a thorough political vetting. Those closest to the decision claimed that in the weeks before the choice they discussed with McCain the pros and cons of picking Palin as much as they talked about other finalists. They believed the potential reward outweighed the risk.

While Palin talked with Culvahouse, Schmidt and Salter waited impatiently. They approached the decision from different perspectives. Schmidt was more committed. Like Davis, he believed she was the best remaining hope to change the dynamic of the campaign. One of his business partners worked in Alaska; through those contacts, he had become aware of Palin. He checked her with people he knew; the reviews were positive. She represented a risk, but one Schmidt believed worth taking. Salter was more skeptical, but he was open to the possibility. And he was utterly loyal to McCain.

The two advisers spent an hour or more with Palin, impressing on her the degree to which her life would be turned upside down. Nothing she had ever experienced would prepare her for the scrutiny, the intensity, and the outright brutality of a presidential campaign. Schmidt did most of the talking. You're going to be very far from home, he told her. You will have executive and constitutional duties in Alaska, but short of an emergency in the state, you're not likely to be going back. This is incredibly demanding and rigorous. Your advisers and people with opinions back in Alaska will not have a seat at the table. Your job in this race, should this project go forward, is to perform at your highest level of ability every day.

Palin, unruffled and self-confident, said she got it. Salter asked her about her statements in support of creationism. Did she disbelieve the theory of evolution? "No," she told them. "My father's a science teacher." Salter later told author Robert Draper, "The sense you immediately get is how tough-minded and self-assured she is." On the ride back to their hotel, Schmidt told Salter he still believed they needed a game-changing pick, meaning Palin was worth the risk. Salter still liked Pawlenty.

Early Thursday morning, the group set off for Sedona. The campaign had taken every precaution to preserve secrecy about Palin. Their next challenge was getting her to Sedona without being recognized. Christian Ferry bought baby shields to cover the windows of the SUV. The advance team asked the Secret Service to withdraw to an outer perimeter around McCain's compound. The group arrived without incident at around 8:30 a.m. McCain greeted Palin, offered her coffee, and then took her down to a bend in the creek where he often liked to sit and watch a hawk's nest in the tree above.

While Palin was being driven to Sedona, McCain spoke to Culvahouse by telephone about the previous night's interview. Culvahouse gave a positive report. She had knocked some of the broader questions* out of the park, he told McCain. She would not necessarily be ready on January 20, 2009, to be vice president, but in his estimation few candidates ever are. Culvahouse believed she had a lot of capacity. "What's your bottom line?" McCain asked. Culvahouse responded, "John, high risk, high reward." McCain then replied, "You shouldn't have told me that. I've been a risk-taker all of my life."

Palin's biography appealed to McCain. He liked her spunk and the fact that she had tangled with Stevens and Young—as had he. Yet he didn't really know her, certainly not the way he knew Lieberman or even Pawlenty. The previous February, he had met Palin in Washington when he hosted several governors during the National Governors Association meeting. She had impressed him during a discussion of energy policy. Palin also attended a reception McCain hosted for all Republican governors and they spent a few more minutes talking that night.

Now they talked for about an hour down by the creek and were joined toward the end by Cindy McCain. That was the extent of McCain's personal interview with the woman whom he was about to thrust into the national spotlight. When they finished their conversation, McCain took a short walk with Cindy. He then huddled with Schmidt and Salter, who by prior arrangement argued the case for and against her. Schmidt restated his case: McCain needed to shake up the race; Palin's profile would reestablish his reform image; Pawlenty was credible and acceptable, but once the convention was over he would disappear. Salter argued that Palin was untested nationally and a high risk. He also said that, for all the talk about "country first" in his campaign, McCain could be accused of making a

---

* These questions, asked of the final contenders, included whether she was prepared to use nuclear weapons to defend the United States and whether, if told that Osama bin Laden had been located, she would authorize taking him out even though that would result in civilian casualties.

political choice designed only to help him win the election, not enhance his ability to govern. Pawlenty, he argued, was solid, had an attractive biography, and could talk to both the Republican base and swing voters.

Their conversation over, McCain returned to the deck of his cabin and offered Palin the job. After pictures were taken, McCain and Cindy left. He would see his running mate again the next morning in Dayton, Ohio.

Advisers later said the decision was McCain's, that he was in no way forced to take Palin against his better judgment. Because McCain is a gambler, the decision was described in the press as a roll of the dice. There was no disputing that. But one person who knows McCain well offered a different interpretation. Remember, he said, McCain is an ex–Navy pilot. Fighter pilots do things routinely that normal people wouldn't have the guts to do. They undertake risky maneuvers and feel they are in control at all times. And, he said, if they are losing, they will go to the very limits of what is possible, first to stay alive and then to win. That does not necessarily make them unsteady or unreliable; they simply live with a level of risk and danger that most people cannot tolerate, physically or emotionally.

What persuaded McCain? In part he believed that, in Palin, he had found a fellow reformer who would help him transform the special-interest-dominated culture of Washington. But there was more to it than that, as Rick Davis later explained to us. "I think he realized that everything that was an indicator of success in the campaign was pointing down for us," Davis said. That included the economy, the country's pessimistic mood, the president's unpopularity, and McCain's belief that the press was in Obama's corner. "When you looked at everyone else, they all were good solid selections in their own right, but who was really going to help us try and push back all these signals that said we were going to lose? Sixty days wasn't enough time to crawl our way back into the election." Nor did McCain's advisers worry about seeming to give away the experience argument he had been using all summer against Obama; they did not believe that alone could win it for McCain, any more than it had for Clinton. "We couldn't win with experience," Davis said. "McInturff, when he came back on payroll, said experience will get you to forty-seven [percent]. Well, good luck."

If that were true, however, they had wasted weeks making the case. It was an example of the campaign's inability to settle on a message, emblematic of larger disorganization.

After the McCains departed, Palin and the others waited until they were certain that no reporters remained in the area, then she was driven back to Flagstaff for the flight to Ohio. En route her plane touched down in Amarillo, Texas, to refuel—and to refile the flight plan to make tracking the aircraft more difficult for reporters trying to learn the name of McCain's running mate.

McCain's team was determined not to let the choice leak that night, partly out of deference to Obama, who was to give his acceptance speech in Denver. McCain did not want to be accused of sabotaging that event. But his team also wanted the element of surprise to dramatize their choice. Their goal was to keep Palin under wraps until the moment she stepped onto the stage in Dayton.

Earlier in the week, the campaign had put in motion a stealthy plan designed to get Palin and her family to Ohio without anyone knowing. Davis White had called Tom Yeilding, a close friend in Alabama who had once done advance work for Vice President Cheney. "I need you to get on a flight to Cincinnati today," White told him. Yeilding, who worked for a company called CraneWorks, protested, saying he was on a construction site. "You're the only one who can do this," White implored him. Yeilding walked off the site and headed for Ohio. His role, as White later put it, was to "catch the package" there on Thursday night. The plan called for Palin and the others to stay at the Manchester Inn in Middletown, thirty miles south of Dayton. Yeilding made reservations for them under the name of the Uptons (Yeilding's bosses). The cover story for airport workers, who might wonder why jets were arriving from Arizona and Anchorage, was they were part of a family fishing trip in Alaska. Meanwhile, Schmidt had sent his colleague Jonathan Berrier to Alaska to assist in getting Palin's family to Ohio.

Palin arrived early in the evening and was taken to her hotel. Next to arrive were Nicolle Wallace, the former White House communications director who served as spokeswoman for McCain, and Matthew Scully, a former Bush White House speechwriter who would be writing Palin's speech. Schmidt led them to room 508. "I'm about to introduce you to our nominee," he said. No BlackBerry communications, no calls to family. When they walked in and saw Palin, they were astonished. Wallace remembers Palin that night as "super mellow . . . really calm."

Davis White drove to Dayton at midnight to check out the event site.

He found one problem: The lectern was set up for a tall person—the assumption among the advance team was that Romney was the choice. "When I told them to lower it for someone who was five-seven, they thought it was Bloomberg," White said.

The secret held until morning and then exploded across the country, provoking a sense of disbelief. McCain called Lieberman, who was vacationing on Long Island, to give him the news before it was confirmed publicly. Lieberman was stunned. "I said, 'No kidding!'" he told us. "I was surprised. I said, 'Gee, I don't know much about her.'" He then watched with amusement as the cable networks went through a process of elimination before declaring Palin the choice, at one point speculating that it might be Lieberman because he had issued no public statement saying it was not him, as had some of the other presumed finalists.*

Axelrod told Obama of the pick as he was about to leave Denver. "Wow, that's surprising," Obama said. "Why do you think he did that?" Joe Biden, in the front cabin of Obama's plane, drew a blank. "Who's Sarah Palin?" he asked. In Denver, David Plouffe woke up campaign chief of staff Jim Messina. "Get your ass up here. They picked Palin," he said. Messina was in charge of assembling material on McCain's possible choices so the campaign would be ready to respond. He was dumbfounded. He knew Palin was a possibility, but on the basis of the Troopergate investigation alone he believed she was a non-starter. On his vice presidential charts, "Palin never left the third tier."

Palin joined McCain in Dayton for the rollout at a rally that drew between ten and fifteen thousand people, the biggest crowd of his campaign. McCain appeared pleased with his history-making pick—the first woman chosen for a Republican ticket—and by the surprise he had pulled off. Not even Palin's staffers in Alaska knew where she was that morning. In his remarks, he emphasized Palin's credentials as a reformer as he tried to seize the change message from Obama. McCain said, "I found someone with an outstanding reputation for standing up to special interests and entrenched bureaucracies; someone who has fought against corruption and the failed policies of the past. . . . She's exactly who this country needs to help me fight the same old Washington politics of me first and country second."

Palin was poised and confident, delivering her speech with no sign of

---

* The *Washington Post's* Michael D. Shear had two confirmations early that morning, but reporters and editors were still skeptical that Palin was the choice and delayed posting the news on the Web.

nervousness, as if she had long been ready for this day. She praised the man who had selected her, saying, "There is only one candidate who has truly fought for America, and that man is John McCain." She paid tribute to Democrat Geraldine Ferraro, the first woman nominated for vice president, and to Hillary Clinton for the "grace and determination" she showed in her battle against Obama. "It was rightly noted in Denver this week that Hillary left eighteen million cracks in the highest, hardest glass ceiling in America," Palin said in the line that drew the most attention. "But it turns out the women of America aren't finished yet, and we can shatter that glass ceiling once and for all."

Palin's selection created a frenzy. Reporters scrambled to confirm the choice, then to explain who she was and why she was picked. Few people knew anything about her background or record, including those in the McCain campaign now charged with helping introduce her to the country. Scully—who thought McCain had made a bold choice—had spent part of the night on the Internet gathering information about Palin to include in her speech.

At McCain headquarters in Virginia, the communications team was caught unawares. No one had given them the advance word they needed to prepare background material. Inundated by press calls trying to confirm the choice, they were helpless, some of them not sure how to pronounce her name. One staffer was frantically trying to download information about Palin when the overloaded Alaska state government Web site crashed. Unable to get answers to basic questions, the campaign gave out inaccurate information, telling one news organization she had been to Iraq when she had only been near the border on a visit to Kuwait. "It was horrific," one campaign official said. "It was a disaster. It was a huge disaster."

The choice of Palin generated mixed signals from the Obama campaign. Their first statement was a harsh putdown. "Today, John McCain put the former mayor of a town of nine thousand with zero foreign policy experience a heartbeat away from the presidency," spokesman Bill Burton said. When Obama saw those words, he ordered the campaign to back off and issued a more gracious statement in his and Biden's names.*

Obama advisers argued with one another about whether Palin was a real threat. Steve Murphy, a member of the media team, had worked on the Knowles gubernatorial campaign in 2006 against Palin. He believed

---

* Obama also ordered the campaign not to air a new commercial timed for McCain's seventy-second birthday that day, believing it was a cheap shot about his age.

she had natural political talents and could pose problems. Axelrod disagreed, strongly. The campaign should take a deep breath, he e-mailed others. She is not ready for the national stage. Murphy pushed back, and so did the normally mild-mannered Axelrod. "There was just an awesome fight between Axelrod and Murphy," Messina recalled. Axelrod said later, "My initial reaction was that they'd just blown up their message, that they'd spent the whole summer talking about celebrity, inexperience, and that John McCain was always going to put country first. And now they'd picked a candidate who was incredibly inexperienced. They made her an immediate celebrity and McCain didn't look like a guy who had put the country first because he had picked someone who was plainly suspect in terms of her preparedness."

Nevertheless, in the short run, Palin's selection stopped any momentum Obama had hoped to gain coming out of his convention and breathed life into the Republican base beyond anything McCain's campaign had anticipated. The element of surprise, the impact of having a woman on the ticket, the fact that she was strongly pro-life and had an infant son with Down syndrome, and her debut performance in Dayton turned Palin into an instant star, from her good looks and designer glasses to her easy ability to connect with people. Within twenty-four hours, McCain's campaign raised $7 million (although Obama's campaign raised huge amounts in that time as well). The campaign Web site saw a sevenfold increase in traffic. At McCain offices around the country, volunteers signed up to help at a rate faster than anything the campaign had yet experienced. Davis called the reaction "seismic." That weekend he told us only half-jokingly, "I wish [McCain] hadn't committed to the public money [for the general election]."

Almost as quickly came the backlash, criticizing McCain's judgment, questioning her background, fueled by Democratic attacks and by rumors. The media pack was in full pursuit. Reporters were digging into the Troopergate scandal, her record as mayor of Wasilla, her views on abortion, her religious beliefs. Then came ugly rumors that little Trig was not Palin's baby. The Internet was awash with stories and blog chatter questioning the circumstances of Palin's pregnancy and the birth. By the time she arrived in Minneapolis–St. Paul on Sunday to prepare for her convention speech, the McCain team was in crisis mode. One adviser with long experience in crisis communications was appalled. "It was the ease with which a really disgusting rumor could live in the blogosphere and just jump into the body politic through mainstream sources," the official said. "When I get an e-mail from a *Washington Post* e-mail address asking me to comment on the parentage of the governor's baby, it strikes me that we've reached a new low and it did not portend well for our country, much less this campaign."

When Schmidt did an interview with one organization, he was asked to supply proof that the baby was hers. Told by campaign officials about the repeated inquiries about whether Trig was her baby, Palin responded, "What do they want me to do, show them my stretch marks?" To kill the rumors about Trig, the campaign revealed that Bristol was pregnant and therefore could not be Trig's mother, though they had hoped to get through the convention without having to confirm the daughter's pregnancy. When on Monday morning Steve Holland of Reuters flashed an exclusive story on the wire revealing Bristol Palin's pregnancy, the news created another firestorm.

Conventional wisdom gyrated wildly in those opening days. Republicans in St. Paul were ecstatic about their new vice presidential candidate, but each day brought new questions or rumors about her. Not all of them were accurate, but enough were to keep alive questions about McCain's judgment. "Sarah Who?" had been replaced by "Who is Sarah?" "What was John McCain thinking?" had been replaced by "What did John McCain know?" Fighting inaccurate information was only part of the challenge. Shaping her image became crucial. "We're letting you guys paint the picture [of Palin] before we even get into the game," campaign manager Davis grumbled to a group of reporters.

With the convention about to open, the mood inside the McCain camp had gone from euphoria over the immediate reaction to Palin's selection to apprehension as the questions about her mushroomed. McCain's team was spread thin, dealing with multiple problems. Davis was scrambling to rewrite the convention schedule as Hurricane Gustav bore down on the Gulf Coast. Republicans wanted no Katrina reruns; they did not want to be seen celebrating in St. Paul while people were suffering in the aftermath of another devastating storm.* Monday night's opening session was scrubbed, which had the side benefit of keeping Bush and Cheney from speaking, but the schedule was still a work in progress.

---

* Obama's campaign also took note of Hurricane Gustav and decided to encourage those on their extensive e-mail list to contribute to the Red Cross. Jim Messina contacted the Red Cross and asked if they could handle a potential crush of online donations. The Red Cross representative assured him they had plenty of capacity and not to worry. "We crashed their Web site in twenty-three minutes after we sent the e-mail to our people," Messina told us later. "Our people just went out and shut down the Red Cross Web site."

Schmidt was busy running the crisis communications operation on Palin. Salter was working on McCain's acceptance speech. Palin was in her hotel, sequestered away from reporters and photographers, working with Matthew Scully and Nicolle Wallace on her speech and going through briefings with foreign policy advisers.

There was other activity as well. Palin was acquiring a new wardrobe to see her through the convention and the campaign weeks after. She left Anchorage on Wednesday with only a small bag of clothes. A campaign official had called Wallace over the weekend. Could she pick out some outfits? "I said, you want me to go shopping? I can't do that, I'm leaving for Minneapolis in the morning," Wallace recalled. "They said, no, just find someone. I made a few calls. There are personal shoppers who do that for people who are too busy to shop, and then the campaign entered into a contract with them. I made one call to Kris Perry, her assistant, to find out what she liked. . . . So I had one more conversation on the front end with the shoppers and said she's petite, she looked great at her announcement, that's her signature look." Now there were racks of clothes in the suite and a seamstress was making sewing machine alterations to the garments. There were several sizes of the same outfit being tried on and fitted, and many pairs of shoes from which to choose. At one point someone said to no one in particular, Do you realize how much there was? Another person guessed tens of thousands of dollars' worth. But there were too many other pressing matters to worry about the clothes.

Despite the disorder, Palin concentrated on her convention speech and on prepping for the campaign trail. "She had an ability to focus that's un-believable," Wallace said. Scully was working from a template: a speech draft written in advance without knowing whom McCain would pick. After a conversation with her the day after her rollout, he delivered a new draft on Monday afternoon. Palin liked what she read, including some of the tough lines of attack. Wallace helped her with her delivery. The campaign had also hired a speech coach, Priscilla Shanks, to help modulate Palin's sometimes grating voice.

Palin's practices began on Tuesday night in a specially equipped room in the convention center. Her delivery was workmanlike but not exceptional. She was the kind of politician who fed off the energy of her audience. "There was never a delivery of the speech in prep as powerful as her delivery in the hall," one official recalled.

By the night of her speech, Wednesday, September 3, the stakes were extraordinarily high. Shortly before she took the stage, a McCain loyalist sent us a message. "Frankly, it's all or nothing. She'll either float the boat or sink it," he said. "It's classic McCain."

The Palin who appeared on the stage at the Xcel Energy Center that night bore no resemblance to the negative caricatures of her in the press. Poised, charming, and combative, she roused the Republican audience with a speech that took on Barack Obama, the Democrats, and her critics in the press. "I've learned quickly these past few days that, if you're not a member in good standing of the Washington elite, then some in the media consider a candidate unqualified for that reason alone," she said. "But here's a little news flash for all those reporters and commentators: I'm not going to Washington to seek their good opinion—I'm going to Washington to serve the people of this country." When Palin described herself as "just your average hockey mom" from a small town, the audience began to chant, *"Hockey moms! Hockey moms!"* She paused for a moment, then responded, "I love those hockey moms. You know, they say the difference between a hockey mom and a pit bull?"—and here she paused theatrically—"Lipstick!" It was a line that had not appeared in any of the drafts of the speech.

Palin's speech electrified the convention. Overnight, opinion turned in her favor. On Thursday, McCain followed with an acceptance speech that included a description of his time in a North Vietnamese prison camp, which in his first campaign he had avoided talking about, and ended with a rousing call to arms. "Stand up, stand up, stand up and fight!" he shouted over sustained applause. "Nothing is inevitable here. We're Americans, and we never give up. We never quit. We never hide from history. We make history."

The Republicans left St. Paul united and energized. McCain's team loved the chaos their Palin choice had created and remained on offense. The Democrats attacked McCain and accused his team of dishonesty in their ads, but Gallup's tracking polls showed a reversal in the race. The weekly average on the eve of the Democratic convention showed the race tied. The weekend after Denver, Obama held a six-point lead. By the end of the Republican convention, Obama was ahead by just two points. By the end of the next week, McCain was ahead by two points.

Obama's team now felt the heat from second-guessers from within their own party. Obama said to his top advisers that, based on his own incoming BlackBerry traffic, they must be deluged with criticism. "I remember the ten days after Sarah Palin got picked was the roughest ten days of the general election," Messina said. "In D.C., there was panic." Messina participated in a weekly conference call with Democrats in Congress. Normally he would make an opening statement and then answer questions. The week after the Republican convention, he said, "I got two words out of my mouth and people began shouting at me."

Obama told his advisers during one of their nightly calls to hold firm. "We have a plan. We know what we're doing. We're going to execute the plan." Still, his advisers were irritated by the lack of confidence from Democrats outside the campaign. Plouffe deliberately let his frustrations show when he told the *New York Times*, "We're familiar with this. And I'm sure between now and November 4 there will be another period of hand-wringing and bed-wetting. It comes with the territory."

For all their outward calm, Obama's team was rapidly making adjustments. Having been intimidated by the celebrity ads in early August, they began to recognize their mistake. McCain and Palin were now drawing huge and enthusiastic crowds while Obama was doing small events—and losing the edge in intensity that had been so much a part of his primary campaign. His advisers decided to resume the big rallies. They needed an infusion of energy. Whatever they thought of the long-term effect of the Palin pick, they recognized that she had taken over the campaign.

Palin was now a huge celebrity, at least the equal of Obama's star-quality status, and a cultural phenomenon. Tina Fey returned to *Saturday Night Live* with a dead-on caricature of Palin's windshield-wiping waves, her designer glasses, pursed lips, and winks. "I can see Russia from my house," Fey-as-Palin said with a twinkle. Palin was perhaps the only politician in America who could simultaneously energize the Republican base and give a jolt to *SNL*'s ratings. But she remained a work in progress, as her advisers were well aware. The week after the convention she returned to Alaska to see her son Track deploy to Iraq and to conduct her first interview with a network anchor. The session with ABC's Charlie Gibson was no home run, but neither was it the disaster that some of her critics had predicted. She was still providing lift to McCain's candidacy.

Ten days after the Republican convention, on the night of September 14, Obama met with his senior advisers at the offices of Axelrod's firm. Plouffe and Gibbs were there. On the phone were communications director Anita Dunn, pollster Joel Benenson, and media adviser Jim Margolis. Obama was not looking for a discussion that night as much as he wanted to deliver a message—as he had done in July 2007 when his campaign was flagging. He was worried that the campaign had become too reactive. "He thought we needed to get back on our game," Dunn recalled. "His basic thing was we're in the stretch here. We've got three debates, a limited number of days. We're slightly ahead or tied and we need to go win this thing."

At that moment, his Palin gamble had achieved what McCain hoped. He had shaken up the campaign to keep the election within reach, despite the very tough climate.

CHAPTER TWENTY-SEVEN

Collapse

"If we don't act boldly, Mr. President, we could be in a depression greater than the Great Depression."

—Treasury Secretary Henry Paulson and Fed Chairman
Ben Bernanke to Bush in the White House

Six weeks before the election, panic was spreading throughout America's financial markets and around the world. It was against that background on Wednesday, September 24, that George W. Bush invited John McCain, Barack Obama, and congressional leaders for a White House meeting the next day. The subject: the urgent need to pass an emergency financial bailout plan providing more than $700 billion to calm the markets and stem the economic chaos.

For weeks Fed Chairman Ben Bernanke and Treasury Secretary Henry Paulson had been warning the president about the danger of imminent economic collapse. In March, Bear Stearns, the fifth largest investment bank and a global powerhouse with some $350 billion in assets, had declared bankruptcy after its stock plummeted to an almost unbelievable low of two dollars a share. A last-minute bailout of U.S. taxpayer funds failed to save it. Bear Stearns, which had survived the 1929 crash, was swallowed up in a merger with J. P. Morgan Chase. Since then, there had been one shock wave after another, forcing some of the most venerated financial players either to merge or go out of business.

On Sunday, September 7th, came the stunning news that the federal government had seized the mortgage giants Fannie Mae and Freddie Mac, putting a liability of more than $5 trillion of mortgages on the backs of U.S. taxpayers. Over the weekend of September 13th, Lehman Brothers, whose history dated back to 1850, was forced into bankruptcy after desperate attempts to rescue it through mergers had failed. When the administration decided to let Lehman go and no U.S. bailout funds were offered, the bank ceased to exist. At the same time, the insurance giant AIG (American International Group) was teetering on bankruptcy, a prospect so alarming that on September 16 the Federal Reserve announced it was lending AIG $85 billion in exchange for nearly 80 percent of its stock. (Three weeks later, that immense bailout hadn't achieved its goal; the Fed was forced to increase its AIG loans to nearly $123 billion.)* In the meantime, banks were refusing to lend to each other or to customers, the price of insuring against bankruptcy was soaring to levels never previously seen, panicked investors were withdrawing funds from stocks, bonds, and money market accounts and putting them in U.S. Treasury bills, considered the safest investment in the world. Retirement funds, college endowments, foundation assets were being slashed by a third or half.

These were the catastrophic events that led Paulson and Bernanke to warn Bush in the Roosevelt Room across from the Oval Office that the U.S. capital markets were "just so frozen" that stronger government action would be required to avert another Great Depression—or worse. They would have to ask Congress to take extraordinary action to create instant bailout/rescue funds of historic proportions, perhaps as high as a trillion dollars.

It was John McCain who precipitated Bush's summons for him and Obama to join congressional leaders to "come together at a time of crisis" as they had after 9/11. McCain publicly urged the president to convene that crisis meeting, saying in a New York statement on Wednesday, September 24, "if we do not act . . . every corner of our country will be impacted. We cannot allow that to happen." After hearing from McCain, Bush called Obama that day to issue his invitation to the crisis meeting. The president sounded almost apologetic, a senior Obama aide told us, adding that he was not sure the meeting was needed, but McCain was insistent.†

---

* This was not the end of AIG's problems. In a confidential draft for government officials on February 26, 2009, it asked for more help from the Treasury Department and Federal Reserve to prevent "potentially catastrophic unforeseen consequences," warning that without more funds an AIG failure would cause a "chain reaction of enormous proportions." Days later, AIG got $30 billion more in bailout funds. At the same time it posted the largest loss in U.S. corporate history, $61.7 billion. Not long after, the revelation that AIG used public bailout money to pay bonuses to top employees ignited a national firestorm of outrage. Bonuses totaling $33.6 million were paid to 418 employees, including fifty-two who had left the firm. Bonuses of more than $1 million each went to seventy-three people, nearly all in the unit responsible for AIG's near collapse.

† A month after the election, in a December 3 "exit interview," Bush told ABC's Charles Gibson that hearing Bernanke and Paulson say "we could be in a depression greater than the Great Depression" was an 'uh-oh moment.'" Two weeks later, on December 18th, in a speech before the American Enterprise Institute in Washington, D.C., he recalled having "quipped" while at his Texas ranch that "Wall Street got drunk and we got a hangover."

These dramatic events began earlier that day when Obama phoned McCain at 8:30 that morning to propose that they issue a joint statement of support for the bailout. Hours later, when they spoke again, McCain told him that, because of the emergency, he believed they should both go back to Washington. Obama wasn't sure. Robert Gibbs, who was with him, recalled, "Obama says let's work through that but the first thing to do is let's get this statement done." McCain told Obama to have their staffs talk. Shortly after that, McCain went on TV with a dramatic announcement. He was going to "set politics aside," suspend his campaign, pull down his television ads, cancel an appearance on the Letterman show, and return to Washington the next morning to deal with the economic crisis. He also said he would not participate in his long-scheduled, long-anticipated nationally televised first debate with Obama just two days away. Obama was dumbfounded when he heard the news. Other than McCain's proposal that they both return to Washington, McCain had said nothing about suspending his campaign and bailing out of the first debate.

For John McCain's presidential hopes, his decision came at a critical moment. The week before, while markets were crashing and fear was spreading, he repeated what he had said before: "The fundamentals of our economy are strong." That comment was seen as one of the biggest blunders of his campaign, recognized instantly as such by both the Obama and the McCain teams, and it forced McCain to begin backpedaling at his next stop. Then when he offered a sharply contradictory warning that the same fundamentals "are at great risk," he appeared uncertain about what he really thought. Throughout the week, McCain had scrambled to find the right message to deal with an economy in crisis. Obama, who was in close touch with Treasury Secretary Henry Paulson and Federal Reserve Chairman Ben Bernanke, awaited further developments. McCain was suddenly taking a huge gamble in returning to Washington. He hoped he would be seen as having put aside political considerations to help fashion the bailout legislation. But he also risked being portrayed as reckless in the face of a crisis—or exploiting it in an ill-considered publicity stunt.

Newt Gingrich hailed his action, likening it to Eisenhower's dramatic "I shall go to Korea" statement during his 1952 presidential campaign, which was credited with paving the way for the end of that war—and also electing Ike. McCain, the warrior, like Eisenhower, the great commander, was demonstrating his instinct for bold action.

Rick Davis, McCain's campaign manager, later told us the decision to suspend (though not to go back to Washington) was "the worst example of group think you'll ever see." Everywhere McCain turned for allies, he was shunned. On that day, having read of a plan proposed by Hillary Clinton, he had unsuccessfully tried to entice her into joining him for a public discussion of the housing crisis. Next he met with leading Wall Street executives and economic advisers, where gloom and doom pervaded their discussion. McCain and his advisers then caucused, fearful that the downward spiral of the economy would be blamed on Bush and the Republicans. Davis said, "You know John. He's a man of the moment. He came out of there like, this is the most important thing we have to worry about. Honestly, we just got each other all jacked up. One minute it's go back to Washington. The next minute it's suspend the campaign, next minute it's like cancel Letterman, the next minute it's like take our TV ads down. And the coup de grace was, oh, and we won't go to the debate if this is not done by then, thinking that's a nice way to put pressure on House Republicans. . . . It was just one of the ratcheting-up things that occur when you get excited. And we got excited. It was an unprofessional thing to have done, but we had gotten taken in by the moment."

The next day, Thursday, September 25, was crucial. After meeting for hours behind closed doors, the top congressional leaders emerged shortly before 1 p.m. They had reached broad agreement on the rescue bailout. "I now expect we will indeed have a plan that can pass the House, pass the Senate, and bring a sense of certainty to this crisis that is still roiling in the markets," said Senator Robert F. Bennett, a respected conservative Republican from Utah and a veteran member of the banking committee. Their meeting, he stressed, "was one of the most productive sessions in that regard that I have participated in since I have been in the Senate."

Three hours later, flush with a feeling of bipartisan cooperation, Bush convened his Cabinet Room meeting with the congressional leaders, his economic advisers, and the two presidential candidates. It was a disaster. After hearing Bush warn that "this sucker could go down"—meaning the entire American economy—without passage of the bailout, the meeting degenerated into partisan bickering. The leading House Republican, John Boehner, suddenly offered a totally different bailout plan that the solid GOP conservative House members had overwhelmingly privately backed earlier—more a free-market plan, steering away from a government intervention in the markets that they believed was a path toward socialism. Swiftly, optimism turned to despair. The meeting degenerated into a display of anger, bitterness, and recrimination eclipsing even what a polarized nation's capital had witnessed in recent years. Shortly after the meeting ended, a melodramatic scene took place in the Roosevelt Room. There, Paulson knelt on one knee before Speaker Pelosi. He appealed to her not to "blow it up" by withdrawing Democratic support from the rescue plan. "It's not me blowing this up," said the Speaker, who felt betrayed, "it's the Republicans." During the forty-minute meeting with the president, participants inside the room, who quickly reported to the press, observed that John McCain was mainly silent, with virtually nothing to offer, while Barack Obama had asked a series of sharp questions. McCain had not saved the day. His rescue was not triumphal.

And then he shifted again. The next morning he said he would, after all, participate in the first presidential debate that Friday night—another sudden change in course that brought him harsh new criticism. Some critics compared his race to Washington, and then his retreat, as a desperate "Hail Mary pass" that had failed. Others said that "what at first had looked like a brilliant political gambit had turned into a nightmare."

The stakes could not have been higher for both candidates as they took the stage at the University of Mississippi in Oxford. For McCain, it was an opportunity to calm doubts he was impulsive, even erratic. His test was to persuade those watching about his leadership qualities after two weeks of zigs and zags over the economy. For Obama it was a chance to reassure voters that he had the strength and temperament to be commander in chief. In order to win he had to make voters feel comfortable about him.

The Friday night debate proved to be a turning point. For ninety minutes, more than fifty-three million people were able to form strong impressions about which candidate might make the best president. What viewers saw was a cool, composed Barack Obama, in command of facts and seemingly at ease on the stage. In John McCain they saw someone who repeatedly dismissed his opponent. "I honestly don't believe that Senator Obama has the knowledge or experience" to be president, he said at one point. Most disconcertingly, McCain was unwilling even to look into Obama's eyes. When the debate was over, nearly all polls gave Obama a decisive edge, USA Today/Gallup by 52 to 35 percent. CNN gave Obama a 51 percent to 38 percent lead. It wasn't a knockout, but it seemed to signal the moment when Obama crossed the threshold to answer the "is he ready" question.

Meanwhile, in Washington more frantic meetings were being held to rebuild support for the rescue plan, now scheduled for a crucial House vote Monday. Sunday night, Bush put more of his presidential prestige on the line. "This plan sends a strong signal to markets around the world that the United States is serious about restoring confidence and stability to our financial system," he said. "Without this rescue plan, the costs to the American economy could be disastrous."

At that point, it was widely reported that the bipartisan forces would prevail in Monday's House vote. The consequences of rejection were too dreadful to contemplate, or so it was believed.

But the rejection came. By a vote of 228 to 205 the bailout lost. Not a single Republican voted for it, and when their leaders met reporters afterward, they seemed to blame Pelosi for having delivered a partisan speech in the closing moments of the debate. On Tuesday morning, September 30, 2008, spread across the front page of the *Wall Street Journal* were two bold eight-column headlines:

BAILOUT PLAN REJECTED, MARKETS PLUNGE, FORCING NEW SCRAMBLE TO SOLVE CRISIS

and its lead story:

> WASHINGTON—The House of Representatives defeated the White House's historic $700 billion financial rescue package—a stunning turn of events that sent the stock market into a tailspin and added to concerns that the U.S. faces a prolonged recession if the legislation isn't revived.

By the time the markets closed on the day of the vote, the Dow Jones Industrial Average had sustained its biggest point drop in history.

In another page one headline that day, the *Washington Post* offered a glimpse at the trauma the financial meltdown was causing Americans everywhere:

RETIREMENT SAVINGS LOST $2 TRILLION IN 15 MONTHS

The economic crisis was spiraling. The country was in shock. Global markets tumbled. The International Monetary Fund warned the spreading crisis could push several advanced economies into recession. For the first time since the Great Depression, the Federal Reserve said it would bypass ailing banks and lend directly to American corporations. Repeatedly,

President Bush appeared before the TV cameras—twenty times in all during those September days, according to a CBS tally—to try to calm the markets. Each time they ignored him and continued their downward plunge. Finally, on October 3, the $700 billion bailout bill passed Congress—but by then more than confidence was shaken. Global markets fell further. The president of the World Bank, Robert B. Zoellick, warned that the global system might have reached "a tipping point," a moment when crisis mushrooms into "a full-blown meltdown and becomes extremely difficult for governments to contain."

Economic conditions were becoming even more dire. Financial historians, with longer memories, compared the unfolding panic to great collapses of the past: the Dutch tulip mania of the 1630s, the South Sea Bubble of 1720, the panics of 1825 and 1907, the crashes of 1929 and 1987. By the end of the first week in October, history had been made. Over those five days, the Dow recorded the biggest weekly percentage drop in its 112-year history, surpassing the record set during the Great Depression for the week ending July 22, 1933.

Of many analyses produced during this critical period, one deserves special notice—a *Wall Street Journal* op-ed column by Daniel Henninger on Thursday, October 16th, three weeks before the election. Henninger is a true-blue conservative and deputy editorial page editor of the most influential conservative paper in America.

If John McCain loses the election, Henninger wrote, he can trace it to the six days starting September 24, when he suspended his campaign, to September 29th when the House GOP defeated the first Paulson plan to rescue the American financial system. "Neither Mr. McCain nor the GOP is likely to recover from those dramatic days," he wrote. "Call it the Katrina Dysfunction Syndrome. . . . But make no mistake: The infighting over the Paulson Plan among conservatives—always looking for an excuse to bolt the McCain candidacy—neutralized Mr. McCain at the exact moment that the U.S. electorate was focusing like a laser on the crisis. The need for immediate action was manifest and undeniable. . . . Amid all this, on Monday Sept. 29th, House Republicans voted to defeat the rescue plan."

McCain wasn't the only loser. His Republican Party was so divided that it was incapable of contributing to a solution when the nation faced a grave crisis. Obama and the Democrats were the clear beneficiaries of this Republican disintegration. And those GOP actions came when, as Henninger wrote, "the terrified stock market cratered, wiping out individual voter wealth. Four very long days elapsed before Congress approved the plan, but, as with Katrina, voters will only remember the days when the GOP didn't act."

CHAPTER TWENTY-EIGHT

Endgame

"I am crazy addicted to this new dramedy on CBS. I love this show!"

—*Daily Show* host Jon Stewart, speaking of Katie Couric's interviews of Sarah Palin

From the beginning, there was one overriding question about the election of 2008: Could Barack Hussein Obama reassure voters he had the temperament, values, and strength to be president of the United States? During the unnerving days in September, when the markets collapsed, fear spread throughout the country, and doubts arose about John McCain's erratic behavior, the answer to that question had decisively shifted in Obama's favor.

A month before the election, an NBC News/*Wall Street Journal* survey found that voters who thought the economy most important were supporting Obama by fifteen points. By a wide margin, voters said McCain's handling of economic issues made them feel less confident about him. By an equally wide margin, Obama was seen as the candidate who could best handle the issues of housing, the economy, and energy. The voter assessments of McCain grew even worse. They had negative views of the suspension of his campaign to return to Washington and deal with the economic crisis, especially after his waffling about whether to participate in the first debate. Peter Hart wrote in his analysis of those latest numbers, "Up to now, the fundamentals have not translated into a winning position for Barack Obama. In this poll, in large measure due to what voters perceive as an erratic approach by John McCain, those fundamentals have translated into an Obama lead."

Then Sarah Palin again commanded the headlines, but this time not with any positive effect. Now she became a pure negative, and the object not only of new controversy, but also of mockery. Since the GOP convention, when she had become a political meteor, overshadowing McCain and nearly everything else about the campaign, her candidacy had crested. It started to descend at the very time when McCain's campaign became more imperiled.

On the day McCain suspended his campaign, Palin appeared on CBS News in the first of a series of interviews with anchor Katie Couric, following a far more gentle encounter with Sean Hannity of Fox News. The Couric interviews took place during the same week Palin was to meet world leaders at the United Nations to enhance her limited foreign policy credentials and prepare for her upcoming vice presidential debate with Joe Biden.

The Couric interviews also came as the McCain-Palin campaign was being criticized for sheltering her from the media. She had held no press conferences and a miscommunication between her team and McCain's resulted in an embarrassing scene with Afghani President Hamid Karzai: Her handlers had blocked reporters from listening to or filming the opening minutes. Reporters savaged her; it was a terrible start to a difficult week.

The CBS agreement called for Couric to interview Palin over several days to give her greater visibility. In retrospect, that schedule only extended the pain. The Sarah Palin who appeared with Couric was far from the poised and confident politician who had been drawing huge crowds. She was hesitant, halting, and ill at ease. Worst of all, she appeared uninformed.

Early in the interview, Couric pressed Palin to justify her campaign's claim that McCain would restore vigorous government regulation of the financial sector and other parts of the economy. Couric asked her to cite examples of when McCain had sought to regulate the economy, other than his efforts to put restrictions on mortgage giants Fannie Mae and Freddie Mac. After several false starts and pressed by Couric, Palin replied, "I'll try to find you some and I'll bring them to you." Asked what she meant when she cited the proximity of Russia to Alaska as an example of her foreign policy expertise, Palin replied that "Alaska has a very narrow maritime border between a foreign country, Russia, and on our other side, the land boundary that we have with Canada. It's funny that a comment like that was kinda made to—I don't know, you know—reporters."

Couric interrupted: "Mocked?" "Yeah," Palin said, "mocked, I guess that's the word, yeah." Asked to explain how that demonstrated her foreign policy credentials, Palin answered, "Well, it certainly does because our, our next-door neighbors are foreign countries, there in the state that I am the

executive of." Couric kept pressing. "Have you ever been involved in any
negotiations, for example, with the Russians?" Palin mentioned trade mis-
sions, then veered to national security: "As Putin rears his head and comes
into the airspace of the United States of America, where do they go? It's
Alaska. It's just right over the border. It is from Alaska that we send those
out to make sure that an eye is being kept on this very powerful nation,
Russia, because they are right there, they are right next to our state."

A few days later, more of Couric's Palin interviews were broadcast.
They were even more devastating. Asked the name of a Supreme Court
case, other than *Roe v. Wade*, with which she disagreed, Palin drew a blank.
"Hmmm," she began, pausing briefly. "Well, let's see. There's—of course
in the great history of America there have been rulings that there's never
going to be absolute consensus by every American. And there are those
issues, again, like *Roe v. Wade*, where I believe are best held on a state level
and addressed there. So you know, going through the history of America,
there would be others, but." Can you think of any? Couric asked. All Palin
could say was, "Well I would think of any again that could best be dealt
with on a more local level, maybe I would take issue with."

Another seemingly straightforward question brought another baffling
answer. "When it comes to establishing your worldview, I was curious,
what newspapers and magazines did you regularly read before you were
tapped for this to stay informed and to understand the world?" Palin replied, "I've read most of them, again, with a great appreciation for the
press, for the media." "Like what ones, specifically?" Couric asked. "Um,
all of them, any of them that have been in front of me over all these years,"
Palin said. "Can you name a few?" Couric asked. "I have a vast variety of
sources where we get our news, too," Palin said. "Alaska isn't a foreign
country, where it's kind of suggested, it seems like, 'Wow, how could you
keep in touch with what the rest of Washington, D.C., may be thinking
and doing when you live up there in Alaska?' Believe me, Alaska is like a
microcosm of America."

Her poll numbers began to sag. Press reviews were harsh. James Rainey
of the *Los Angeles Times* wrote, "Her third nationally televised interview,
with CBS anchor Katie Couric, found Palin rambling, marginally responsive
and even more adrift than during her network debut with ABC's Charles
Gibson." Some conservative commentators were particularly unforgiving. "I
think she has pretty thoroughly—and probably irretrievably—proven that
she is not up to the job of being president of the United States," David
Frum, a former Bush White House speechwriter, told the *New York Times*.

Conservative columnist Kathleen Parker called for Palin to step aside. "Palin's recent interviews with Charles Gibson, Sean Hannity and now Katie Couric have all revealed an attractive, earnest, confident candidate. Who Is Clearly Out Of Her League," she wrote. Jon Stewart couldn't get enough: "It is October, people, the fall television season is here. I am crazy addicted to this new dramedy on CBS. I love this show!" he said one night. "It is like the first season of *Lost*, only it makes less sense. And when these two get together, I don't want to miss a minute of it. I love cliffhangers! It's the 'Who shot J.R.?' of interviews. Will the Alaskan governor bring me examples, or will we forget all about it because we don't really give a [expletive bleeped over TV] if she has the examples? We just want to see her fumble around some more."

Even inside the McCain campaign, those sympathetic to Palin were alarmed by the Couric interviews. Her answer to the question about the Supreme Court left them bewildered. She had often railed about the *Exxon Valdez* case, but did not have the presence of mind to bring it up. Her answer to what she read was equally distressing. Anyone could have handled that question, her advisers agreed. Instead, they concluded, she had taken offense at what she perceived was an affront to Alaskans, wilderness people cut off from the rest of the world. Schmidt believed the Couric interviews represented one of the worst performances ever by a candidate for national office. Not only were the interviews damaging, but their aftereffects created declining support among crucial swing voters that she was supposed to attract. Palin's appeal now encompassed little more than the Republican base. One senior campaign official said of her performance, "The last couple of weeks of September it degraded. I don't know if it was irretrievable but it was unretrieved."

Palin blamed Nicolle Wallace for the Couric interviews because Wallace had once worked for CBS. Wallace told us later, "I like and respect [Couric] a ton. But I would never give her an interview for any reason other than it was the best decision for the campaign at the time. Obviously, in hindsight, it wasn't the one where our candidate did the best. So if I could take it back, sure I would. . . . It was just ill-timed and unfortunate scheduling."

Another problem with the Couric interviews was that Palin didn't seem to be preparing for them. Instead, she let herself become distracted, understandably perhaps, by her meetings with world leaders at the United

Nations. But she was also oddly determined to finish a questionnaire for tiny Alaska newspaper, the *Matsu Daily Frontiersman*. Her concern about how to answer that paper's questions led to squabbling among her advisers and even to Palin's implied threat that preparing for Couric could wait until the newspaper questionnaire was completed. Apparently Alaska was much on her mind. She worried constantly about her standing at home and, one official said, demanded that the campaign take a poll to see how her popularity was holding up. When told she was still in good favor at home by Schmidt's reading of the poll, she expressed doubt that she was being told the truth, this official said, infuriating Schmidt.

Palin was now days away from her debate with Joe Biden. Those around her could sense that she was upset, even angry, at what was happening to her—upset at her staff, at her own mistakes with Couric, at who knew what. She was not a brooder, but occasionally would let off steam. One adviser was startled by the contrast between the Palin who had galvanized the Republican convention only a month before and the Palin who was preparing for her debate with Biden. "It was like a different person—somebody who was just worn down [and] losing her confidence," the adviser said.

When her campaign began, Palin's staff had prepared cards with facts to help her master the basics of foreign policy. Soon she became dependent on these cards. Now she had scores of them—cards containing facts, names, questions, and answers sharpened and refined through discussion with advisers. Inside the campaign, they became a source of controversy, defended by some as briefing books in a different form, criticized by others as the crutch for a politician who lacked the curiosity to understand issues in depth and wanted everything in easy-to-digest answers.

Palin's knowledge of the world was certainly limited. Later, there were reports that she thought Africa was a country, not a continent. Two advisers told us that report was accurate; several others said it was not literally true. That argument raged within the campaign even after the election. Another report claimed she did not know the countries that were part of the North American Free Trade Agreement. Steve Biegun, who spent considerable time advising her on foreign policy, described both charges as "absurd." He told *National Review*'s Rich Lowry that she knew much about Darfur and about the government's HIV/AIDS initiative in Africa through her church and never was confused about who was in NAFTA. One adviser, who was sympathetic, complained that Palin was stuffed too full of information by a staff that did not trust her. "I finally figured out they were trying to get her to memorize entire passages instead of just letting her very able mind work on its own . . . instead of concentrating on technique—interview technique and debate technique—they were trying to force this on her. . . . I don't think they had a proper appreciation of her own abilities." Others in the campaign became harsher in their judgments of Palin the longer they watched her.

Debate prep began badly. McCain's advisers were worried by reports they had from her traveling team. On Sunday, October 28, Schmidt and Davis went to Philadelphia for a private conversation with Palin. They were moving debate prep to McCain's cabin in Arizona, she was told. Her children would have more freedom to move about and the setting would be more relaxing. They also wanted to keep the number of people involved to a minimum to limit leaks about how she was handling the pressure.

By the day of the debate, the stakes for Palin had risen sharply. That morning, we watched Peter Hart conduct another focus group, among critical swing voters in St. Louis. The voters debated Palin's strengths and weaknesses. To one woman, Palin was a "good strong woman" with "tremendous potential." To another woman, she was frightening: "This isn't on-the-job training," she said. The twelve-member group split five-five between Obama and McCain, with two undecided. When Hart asked how they would vote if the choice were between Biden and Palin, they split eight-four for Biden.

"Nice to meet you," Palin said to Biden as they were introduced onstage at Washington University in St. Louis. "Hey, can I call you Joe?" Her jaunty opening set her tone. As with her convention speech, her actual performance was far better than any of her mock debates. She did not always answer the questions posed by the moderator, PBS's Gwen Ifill, but she knew how to talk into the camera and had her lines down well. "I think we need a little bit of reality from Wasilla Main Street there, brought to Washington, D.C.," she said. Republicans were relieved. "It was the best ninety minutes this campaign has had in two weeks," Republican Tom Rath told us that night. A campaign adviser later said, "She exceeded those terribly low expectations—more than exceeded them. But it was too little too late against the backdrop of the financial crisis and the weight of our difficulties."

For the rest of the campaign, Palin was on the defensive. Colin Powell cited her as one of his reasons for endorsing Obama in mid-October, a personal blow to McCain that called his judgment into question. She struggled against growing resentment among some McCain advisers, who began questioning whether she was the right choice. Sometimes they found her either unresponsive or unreliable as they tried to get answers to rebut ongoing investigative stories about her. Some of these were well documented. She claimed she had said "no thanks" to the infamous Bridge to Nowhere, but did not say she had kept the money for the state. Others were internal struggles that never became public. She initially told Mc-Cain advisers she had no recollection of whether the town of Wasilla charged victims of sexual assault for rape kits and examination. McCain's advisers could not believe that. Campaign officials had trouble getting straight information about whether the Palins were totally without health insurance until Todd Palin got his union card. She said they had no insurance, but campaign aides learned that the family did have catastrophic insurance. One official said he had never had such a difficult time "getting to the bottom of things" in a campaign. The campaign was split into warring camps. While she had strong defenders, doubters became emboldened as McCain's chances diminished. Blind quotes popped up in stories and on blogs. Someone called her a "diva," someone else a "whack job"—characterizations that some of her closest advisers described as vicious and totally unfair. "It was just very hard on her," an aide said. "She took it all, she was such a trouper."

At one point, Davis and Schmidt ordered the campaign's e-mails searched to determine who was leaking damaging information. The search turned up messages that foreign policy adviser Randy Scheunemann sent to William Kristol of the *Weekly Standard* blaming Nicolle Wallace, unfairly, for many of Palin's troubles. In classic McCain campaign fashion, top officials later disagreed over whether Scheunemann had been fired.

In late October, *Politico*'s Jeanne Cummings broke the story of Palin's wardrobe. The Republican National Committee, she reported, had spent $150,000 on clothes for Palin and her family. The story was a huge embarrassment never adequately addressed by Palin and the campaign. "We had a headquarters that said we're not going to comment on strategic spending decisions," one of Palin's advisers said. "Well, you knew we were going to comment on it and comment all at once or drip, drip, drip, slice by slice. The failure was emblematic of the campaign. No one took responsibility. No one owned the issue, followed through on it. It's clear there had been people who were nervous about this, but no one said this is going to come out, we've got to do something about this. It was just shunted aside." Palin bore as much of the blame as anyone. She never seriously questioned how the clothes were being purchased or how much was being spent on her family. The clothes story dogged her to the end of her campaign, providing more fodder for the late-night comedians. Not even Palin's appearance on *Saturday Night Live*, with Tina Fey, could improve her image.

To the end, Palin remained a hero to the Republican base. Few others shared that opinion. McCain strategists were divided over whether the gamble of choosing her had been worth it. Voters were less ambivalent. In those closing campaign days, slightly more than half of likely voters had a negative opinion of her, a sharp drop from her post-convention honeymoon when three-fifths viewed her positively. Three in five judged her not ready to be president. Independent voters, once evenly divided about her, now were overwhelmingly negative. By mid-October, 52 percent of likely voters said her selection made them less confident about the decisions McCain would make as president, according to a *Washington Post*/ABC News poll. On election day, 60 percent of voters said she was not qualified to be president.

The day after the vice presidential debate, David Axelrod was at lunch at Manny's, his favorite Chicago deli. Well-wishers greeted him warmly. "We've polled only in the battleground states and we're at our highest number that we've been in this whole campaign," he said after he was seated. "We've got a lead in Florida, which I think is the big reason that [McCain's] pulling out of Michigan. We're ahead marginally in North Carolina. Wisconsin was close and has now opened up again to a pretty nice lead. We have had good leads in Michigan. We finally marginally pulled ahead in Ohio, first time." Axelrod anticipated a rough few weeks ahead. "I think they're in a fourth-and-long mode and so I think they'll do whatever it takes, whatever they think it'll take," he predicted. "I think there's risk associated with it but I think they know that right now there's a bad dynamic in place for them. So I expect it's going to be very, very rough."

The next morning, the *New York Times* published a front-page story about Obama's relationship with William Ayers, the sixties antiwar radical who had been a founder of the Weather Underground that bombed the U.S. Capitol and the Pentagon. Ayers had never apologized for Weather Underground's violent actions. In a book that happened to be published at the time of the 9/11 terrorist attacks, he said he regretted the group had not done more to stop the war in Vietnam. Now he was a professor at the University of Illinois at Chicago. He and Obama had served on the board of an educational foundation, the Chicago Annenberg Challenge, with other notable Chicagoans. Ayers once hosted a coffee for Obama during his first political campaign. The *Times* article described meetings between Ayers and Obama over the years, concluding, "The two men do not appear to have been close. Nor has Mr. Obama ever expressed sympathy for the radical views and actions of Mr. Ayers, whom he has called 'somebody who engaged in detestable acts forty years ago, when I was eight.'"

McCain's campaign was planning to go after Obama over his relationship with Ayers and had prepared an ad that was to be launched about a week later. The *Times* account accelerated the timetable for the attack. At 11:45 a.m. that morning, Nicolle Wallace sent an e-mail to Palin's traveling party, a copy of which was later given to us. It read, "Goveror [*sic*] and Team: rick [Davis], steve [Schmidt] and I suggest the following attack from the new york times. If you are comfortable, please deliver the attack as written. Please do not make any changes to the below with out approval from steve or myself because precision is crucial in our ability to introduce this." Included was a 164-word script attacking Obama for his relationship with Ayers. The line that attracted the headlines said of Obama, "This is not a man who sees America as you and I do—as the greatest force for good in the world. This is someone who sees America as imperfect enough to pal around with terrorists who targeted their own country."

When she read the message, Palin was enthusiastic. "Yes yes yes," she replied in an e-mail response. "Pls let me say this!!!" Palin delivered those "pal around with terrorists" lines almost exactly as scripted at a Colorado fund-raiser. When she finished, she sent another e-mail back to McCain's high command, "It was awesome," she said in the message.

The attack on Ayers unleashed the nastiest seven days of the campaign. McCain launched attacks on Obama's honesty and seemed to question his character. "Who is the real Barack Obama?" he asked. In New Mexico, he said, "My opponent's touchiness every time he is questioned about his record should make us only more concerned. It's as if somehow the usual rules don't apply, and where other candidates have to explain themselves and their records, Senator Obama seems to think he is above all that." Obama struck back at McCain with a thirteen-minute video, prepared earlier in anticipation of the attacks, reprising McCain's role in the Keating Five scandal involving convicted savings and loan magnate Charles Keating and his relationship with five members of Congress.* Palin told William Kristol during an interview that she thought Obama's links to Reverend Wright should be fair game for criticism, though McCain had ordered his advisers never to raise that issue for fear of being accused of racism. At rallies in Florida, where supporters wore "Sarahcuda" T-shirts, she said, "The heels are on, the gloves are off."

That was the message she was sending McCain to use in his second debate with Obama, Palin said.

The town hall format for that debate at Belmont University in Nashville seemed to favor McCain, but he was not able to take advantage of it. In front of eighty citizen questioners, neither McCain nor Obama dared launch personal attacks. Neither gave an electrifying performance, neither seemed responsive to the potential collapse of the U.S. economy, neither received great praise. To Tom Shales, the *Washington Post*'s TV critic, "The debate had the aura of an almost meaningless ritual being conducted in a soundproof room while outside, panic and calamity were spreading like giant cracks in the earth."

Criticism of McCain was deservedly scathing. He strode about the debate floor gritting his teeth, visibly angry, looking grim. At one point he seemed to go out of his way to demean Obama. While describing legislation that had been backed by Bush, which McCain deemed harmful, he rhetorically asked, "Guess who voted for it?" Then he pointed toward Obama and said, "*That* one!"

On the campaign trail, McCain and Palin's attacks on Obama began to trigger even more hostile reactions toward Obama from some supporters. "No communists" read a sign at a Palin rally in Florida. "Treason!" shouted one person after Palin accused Obama of being critical of U.S. forces in Afghanistan. A speaker at one event asked how Obama could aspire to be commander in chief "when he would not last two hours in one of our military academies." Frank Keating, the former GOP governor of Oklahoma and a McCain campaign co-chairman, raised the issue of Obama's drug use, which Obama had written about in his memoir. "He ought to admit, 'You know, I've got to be honest with you. I was a guy of the street,'" Keating said. "'I was way to the left. I used cocaine. I voted liberally, but I'm back at the center.'"

The anger escalated. In Pennsylvania, McCain's supporters were cap-

---

* The Senate ethics committee cleared McCain of any wrongdoing but criticized him for poor judgment for meeting with federal regulators at Keating's behest.

tured on video calling Obama a terrorist. In Wisconsin, one man stood and said, "I'm mad, and I'm really mad. It's not the economy. It's the socialists taking over our country." The audience rose and applauded. McCain started to respond, and the man shot back sternly. "Let me finish please. When you have an Obama, Pelosi, and the rest of the hooligans up there gonna run this country, we've got to have our head examined. It's time that you two are representing us and we are mad. So go get 'em." As the press bus pulled away, some in the audience flipped a one-finger salute.

Finally, McCain was forced to tamp down the anger. In Minnesota, after a man said he was afraid to raise a child in the United States if Obama were elected, McCain defended Obama. "He is a decent person and not a person you have to be scared of as president of the United States," he said. Minutes later, a woman said she didn't trust Obama and referred to him as an Arab. McCain took back the microphone, shaking his head. "No, ma'am, he's a decent family man . . . that I just happen to have disagreements with on fundamental issues and that's what this campaign's all about." Scattered boos erupted from the audience.

McCain and his advisers were angry with how this was being played in the media. They didn't excuse the extreme comments at their rallies, but believed the press had exaggerated them by playing the words and actions on television of a handful of people at McCain events. In off-the-record calls to reporters, they seethed.

On Saturday, October 11, John Lewis, the Georgia congressman, issued a statement condemning McCain and Palin. "During another period, in the not-too-distant past, there was a governor of the state of Alabama named George Wallace who also became a presidential candidate. George Wallace never threw a bomb. He never fired a gun, but he created the climate and conditions that encouraged vicious attacks against innocent Americans who were simply trying to exercise their constitutional rights. Because of this atmosphere of hate, four little girls were killed one Sunday morning when a church was bombed in Birmingham, Alabama." McCain and Palin, he said, were "playing with fire," and if not careful "the fire will consume us all."

Lewis's statement deeply offended McCain. He admired Lewis, had written generously about him in one of his books. At a forum at the Saddleback Church in August, he had cited Lewis as one of three people he would turn to for advice. He was shocked by the congressman's remarks—whatever had happened during his rallies that week was nothing compared to the racial violence of the 1960s. During the campaign, McCain had tried to reach out to African-Americans. He had gone to Memphis on the anniversary of Martin Luther King Jr.'s assassination and apologized for his opposition to making King's birthday a national holiday. McCain's advisers were enraged at Lewis's statement. Schmidt told us McCain viewed it as "the worst attack on his character in his entire career." Salter called it "the most injurious thing that's ever been said about him." The advisers argued that Obama was running many more negative ads than McCain and was escaping blame for the tone of the campaign. The public didn't agree. Polls showed people believed McCain was running a far more negative campaign than Obama.

Finally, after a week of William Ayers and talk of treason and terrorists and lack of patriotism, everyone stood down. The campaign dialogue returned to more peaceful ground and to arguments more central to the country's real problems. On October 13 McCain delivered a new stump speech, less aimed personally toward Obama and more focused on the economy. Still, he faced the same problem that had plagued him since the spring: lack of a coherent and consistent message. The morning after the Nashville debate, we encountered Salter in the lobby of McCain's hotel. He was still shaking out the cobwebs from a late night of karaoke with Schmidt and some reporters in a nearby bar. Salter, often given to gallows humor, referred to press coverage that was writing off McCain's chances and said, "We've been dead before." Then, with a laugh, "We can't die again."

On October 15, Obama and McCain held their last debate at Hofstra University on Long Island. McCain was at his best, on the offensive throughout the debate. Obama, however, calmly deflected the attacks, unruffled to the end. One headline writer summed it up as "Aggressive Underdog vs. Cool Counterpuncher." McCain tried one last time to distance himself from President Bush. "Senator Obama, I am not President Bush," he said. "If you wanted to run against President Bush, you should have run four years ago. I'm going to give a new direction to this economy in this country." But Obama fired back, "If I occasionally have mistaken your policies for George Bush's policies, it's because on the core economic issues that matter to the American people—on tax policy, on energy policy, on spending priorities—you have been a vigorous supporter of President Bush." Commentators instantly called the debate a draw. Polls instantly gave it to Obama.

The surprise star of the evening was a character named Samuel Joseph Wurzelbacher, who forever would be known as Joe the Plumber. Obama had run into him on a rope line in Ohio several days before the debate. Wurzelbacher complained about Obama's plan to raise taxes on wealthy Americans, saying it would prevent him from buying a small business. Obama said his tax plan was based on fairness. "I think when you spread the wealth around, everybody benefits," he said. The conservative blogosphere picked up the line and claimed that Obama was a socialist. McCain cited Joe repeatedly—he was mentioned two dozen times in the debate—and seized on his criticism of Obama as reinforcement for his own opposition to Obama's economic plan, his health care plan, and their differences about the size of government. Joe, who it turned out did not have a plumbing license and owed taxes himself, became another overnight celebrity, the latest and unlikeliest of the campaign. Republicans turned him into a member of the campaign, having him appear at rallies. He sat for endless interviews. Jay Leno joked, "This plumber has done more interviews in one day than Sarah Palin has done since being chosen by John McCain." Joe the Plumber was one last, weird sideshow in a campaign now rolling steadily toward Obama.

Everything pointed to an Obama victory. National polls gave him a popular-vote lead that bordered on double digits. By late October battleground state polls were moving dramatically in his direction. Across the country, people were already lining up to cast early votes and the Obama ground machine pushed hard to take advantage. Their goal was to bank as many votes as possible before election day—especially voters who were newly registered or had participated only sporadically in the past. Anyone following state-by-state statistics could see the strategy was working. In Colorado, more than half the total votes in 2004 were cast before election day. With a new, more Democratic electorate, that was good for Obama. In Florida, more than a third of the total 2004 ballots were cast early. Governor Charlie Crist was forced to extend voting time by hours each day to reduce long lines at limited numbers of polling places for early voters. In Nevada, more than half the 2004 total was cast early, with big Democratic margins in the two biggest counties. In North Carolina, Democrats had a big margin among early voters as the Republican turnout dropped dramatically.

Obama's organization was now running at full speed. The campaign had taken the best of their work in the primaries and combined it into a new model: massive infrastructure in the states with hundreds of paid staffers in places like Florida, Pennsylvania, Ohio, Colorado, and Virginia coupled with tens upon tens of thousands of empowered and accountable volunteers to knock on the doors and make the phone calls to turn out Obama's vote. All this effort was integrated with the campaign's use of new media to raise money—half a billion online by the end of the campaign—and energize supporters. Their e-mail list numbered thirteen million. Their Internet operation encouraged supporters in any state to download lists of names to call elsewhere in the country to urge them to turn out on election day.

Jen O'Malley Dillon, who had worked for Edwards before joining Obama as battleground states director, told us after the election, "I think [we] had the perfect balance of new technology, old-school organization, faith in the people that they hired, and trust they were going to get the job done. [There was] very little infighting and total empowerment of the team. It was just a very different environment than you see in a lot of presidential races."

The Obama team prized the culture they had created. Jim Messina, hired as chief of staff after the primaries, recalled his discussion with Obama before joining the team. He said Obama told him, "I don't want to hire anyone who's going to come in and kick the shit out of my people. And I demand your absolute loyalty. And we don't leak . . . we have a culture."

As frustrations deepened, McCain's campaign began splintering. Veterans of previous GOP campaigns saw alarming disorganization and lack of crisp decision-making. Palin was accused by critics—some from inside the McCain campaign—of going "rogue," of looking out for herself and a possible 2012 presidential campaign at the expense of McCain. Her defenders insisted she was determined to do whatever she could to help the man who had put her on the ticket, but increasingly she seemed to speak for herself rather than the campaign. When McCain pulled out of Michigan, she sounded incredulous, saying she'd like to campaign there. During a campaign trip in October to New Hampshire, she balked at sharing the stage with former congressman Jeb Bradley because they differed on abortion and drilling in the Arctic wilderness. That same day, she was reluctant to join Bradley and Senator John Sununu for conversation aboard her campaign bus and had to be coaxed out of the back of the bus to talk to them, according to a McCain adviser. She created a distraction at the time of the Hofstra debate by demanding the campaign issue a statement denying that her husband Todd had ever been a member of the Alaska Independence

Party or that that party had ever advocated secession, according to a top official. Schmidt refused.

As election day neared, there was an eruption of accusations and recriminations from inside the campaign, blind quote after blind quote trashing Palin. Some officials denied the worst of the accusations against her; others privately said they were accurate. Opinions about her were so divided that determining the truth was impossible. But the viciousness of the charges and countercharges left a stain on McCain's entire campaign.

CHAPTER TWENTY-NINE

President-elect

"It's the ride of a lifetime."

—David Axelrod, two nights before the election

Obama began his last full day of the campaign on November 3 in Jacksonville, Florida. He had made three stops in Ohio the day before, playing to huge crowds: an estimated sixty thousand in Columbus, eighty thousand in light rain in Cleveland, where Bruce Springsteen warmed up the crowd with a slow-tempo rendition of "This Land Is Your Land" and closed with "The Rising," one of Obama's campaign anthems. Late that night, Obama drew twenty-five thousand at the University of Cincinnati's football stadium. He arrived in Jacksonville around 1:30 a.m. That morning he learned that his grandmother, Madelyn Dunham, who helped raise him, had died after a long illness—a melancholy start to the final forty-eight hours. Obama worked out at the gym and then around 10 a.m. left the hotel for the first of three rallies that day. All were in states won twice by George W. Bush: Florida, North Carolina, and Virginia. All were within his reach.

Plouffe's goal of expanding the electoral map had worked brilliantly. Voter registration efforts over the summer had changed the electorate in some states. Now volunteers were out in force. That final weekend Obama supporters knocked on more than four million doors in Pennsylvania, almost half a million the Saturday before the election in Ohio, while in California volunteers placed a million calls into other states and poured into neighboring Nevada to knock on more doors. Illinois volunteers flooded into Wisconsin, Indiana, Iowa, and Missouri.

McCain held a midnight rally in Miami. His traveling press corps was up at 5:30 for baggage call before a flight to Tampa for the first of seven events that would carry him across the country. He was playing defense, trying to checkmate Obama, but, as Plouffe had hoped, there were too many weak areas to catch them all. A great tidal wave was building behind Obama. Some states that Republicans won in 2004 already appeared lost: Colorado, Iowa, New Mexico, even Nevada. Others were teetering: Ohio and Florida among them. McCain advisers told reporters they detected movement in some places. Pennsylvania was one. So his schedule called for him to stop there during the day. It was the only state on his itinerary that had voted Democratic four years earlier. At Obama headquarters, Jon Carson and the field team scoffed at McCain's talk of winning Pennsylvania. The surge in Democratic registration meant it would take a miracle for McCain to prevail there.

Florida had slipped away from McCain over the summer when his resources were limited and his organization small. Obama had invested heavily there in money, television ads, paid staff, volunteers, and campaign visits. Now he held the upper hand. McCain's team could see the falloff from 2004 in a Tampa rally. Adam Smith of the *St. Petersburg Times* posted a Web site item that last morning recalling that he had been in Tampa two days before the 2004 election. McCain's crowd, he said, was a fraction of what Bush had drawn. From Tampa, McCain plunged on, trying to save Virginia, Indiana, Nevada, and New Mexico before arriving home in the middle of the night for an Arizona rally.

Obama, meanwhile, continued on a final triumphant tour. "We are one day, one moment, from the rebirth of our very nation," DeJuana Thompson told the crowd in Jacksonville as they waited for Obama. "Have you called every person you can think of?" Obama came next. "I have just one word for you, Jacksonville," he said. "Tomorrow!" After Jacksonville, Obama flew to Charlotte, North Carolina. The weather turned foul, as two drenching rains soaked the outdoor rally site before Obama arrived. But the crowd continued to grow and a huge cheer went up as the headlights of his motorcade appeared over the hill in the darkness. An hour earlier, the campaign had released a statement about Obama's grandmother. As he began his speech, the normally reserved and controlled candidate was overcome with emotion. "She died peacefully in her sleep with my sister at her side, so there's great joy instead of tears," he said. But photographers caught a tear rolling down his right cheek.

The storms had backed up traffic at the Charlotte airport and there was a brief reminder that Obama was still a mere candidate for president. His pilot announced that the Obama charter was eighteenth in line for takeoff. Twenty minutes later, after his plane had jumped ahead of a few others, he was airborne for Virginia and the last event of the day. He landed at Washington's Dulles International Airport well behind schedule, but even before he left Charlotte there were reports of a huge crowd building in Manassas.

The symbolism of man and moment spoke powerfully of the changes in America that had taken place in his lifetime: Manassas, the site of the most noted early battle of the Civil War at Bull Run, which sent the Union army fleeing back to Washington; Virginia, which housed the capital of the Old Confederacy in Richmond; Obama, the candidate on the cusp of shattering a racial barrier that many people thought they would never live to see. That was not why Obama's Virginia team had selected Manassas or why his national team had set Virginia as its last stop. Their focus was on practical politics. They were determined to win Virginia, and Manassas was situated near the intersection of two of the most important counties in the state, Loudon and Prince William, both exurban counties critical to the campaign's hopes of converting a state that had not voted for a Democratic presidential nominee since 1964.

Lights flashing, Obama's motorcade sped down the freeway from the airport and then snaked through residential neighborhoods before pulling into the parking lot at the Prince William County fairgrounds. It was then that Obama and his aides could begin to see the mammoth crowd spread out in the park, filling every corner—between eighty and ninety thousand people, which Joel Achenbach of the *Washington Post* called "an artificial lake of humanity." Obama was nearly ninety minutes late but the crowd was eagerly awaiting him however long it took. He delivered his standard stump speech and closed in a powerful voice, "Virginia, your votes can change the world." He worked the rope line and then came back up on the stage again, as if to savor the campaign moment one last time.

The flight home to Chicago went quickly. Before takeoff, Obama thanked reporters for their time on his campaign. Some had been with him for most of the twenty months he had been running, a punishing daily routine that kept them from home for weeks or months at a time. It was now just after midnight. Obama was subdued, grieving over his grandmother's death while knowing that within twenty-four hours he likely would be president-elect, though he gave no public hint of those feelings. "Whatever happens tomorrow, it's extraordinary," he said. As he passed through the cabin, some reporters offered condolences for his grandmother. He shook hands with everyone, then said, "Okay, guys, let's go home." A day earlier, Axelrod had summed up the extraordinary campaign as "the ride of a lifetime." Even those who had traveled Campaign 2008 from start to finish and were physically and mentally exhausted regretted seeing the end come; they sensed there would not soon be another election as dramatic and significant as this one. Before Obama disappeared toward the front of the plane, he offered a final, parting comment: "It will be fun to see how the story ends."

On election day, as polling places began closing in the East, only the size of his victory remained in doubt.

Yet even in the absence of suspense, there was a sense of great anticipation as the states began reporting. A different America began to take shape on the electronic tally boards in the television studios. The eastern seaboard, save for Georgia and South Carolina, was a blue wall. To the Democratic bastion of the Northeast, Obama added Florida, North Carolina, and Virginia. Across the battered industrial heartland, there was a solid bulwark for the Democrats: Pennsylvania and Michigan by double digits, thanks to strong support in the suburbs; Ohio by four points; Illinois, of course, a landslide; and, remarkably, Indiana—Plouffe's dog. The turnaround there was astounding. Four years earlier, Bush won the state by twenty-one points. Obama carried it by a single percentage point, a margin of twenty-eight thousand votes. Only Missouri slipped from his grasp, and by the narrowest of margins. Whatever concerns were voiced during the primaries about Obama's ability to win the big industrial states—supposedly stemming from racial resistance to a black candidate and his difficulty connecting with white voters—were swept aside by the growing alarm over the economy. The Upper Midwest, the scene of fierce battles in 2000 and 2004, was solidly for Obama. Iowa, Wisconsin, and Minnesota all fell to the Democrats by double digits. The West Coast remained firmly Democratic, as it had since 1992. Obama made striking inroads in the Rocky Mountains, where so much time and energy had been invested over the previous months. New Mexico, Republican by less than a percentage point in 2004, went for Obama by fifteen points. Colorado, Bush country by five points in 2004, went for Obama by nine. Fast-growing and rapidly changing Nevada, thought to be competitive until the final weeks, was another rout, with Obama's margin at twelve points.

Four years after Bush's victory sparked talk of a lasting Republican majority, the Republicans looked like a shrinking minority with a southern base and little more. Analyst Rhodes Cook calculated that McCain won the South by seven points. The rest of the nation went for Obama by fourteen. McCain bettered Bush's percentage in just four states, all in the South: Tennessee, Oklahoma, Louisiana, and Arkansas.

Obama's candidacy rejuvenated the Democratic coalition. Ronald Brownstein described Obama's supporters as the "coalition of the ascendant," combining the Democratic base with rising population groups. Obama won the minorities generally loyal to the Democrats—African-Americans and Latinos—but by bigger percentages than Kerry or Gore. Among younger voters, he won overwhelmingly: by two to one among those under thirty and by six points among those thirty to forty-four. His margin among young voters was significantly higher than that of either Gore or Kerry, hinting at a possible generational shift in political affiliation. He enlarged the Democrats' support among upper-middle-class voters, winning those with college degrees as well as those with incomes of more than $200,000 (despite his pledge to raise taxes on many of them). He lost whites without college degrees, but by no more than Kerry or Gore before him. The geographic and demographic shifts left Republicans no immediate answers about how to compete for political power in a country that had moved so quickly away from them.

Obama's 53 percent of the popular vote was the highest for any Democrat since Lyndon Johnson, and he was the first since Jimmy Carter to win by more than 50 percent. His electoral vote totals—365 to McCain's 173—were comparable with those of Bill Clinton in 1992 and 1996, but all the more impressive because he was both an African-American and a northerner. For almost sixty years, the only Democrats who could win the White House were white southerners. In the end, Obama won by nearly 10 million votes, 69,456,897 to McCain's 59,934,814.

Obama's victory was assured when the networks called Ohio shortly before 9:30 p.m., but it wasn't until 11 p.m., when the polls closed on the West Coast, that the networks named him the winner, setting off celebrations across the country and pandemonium in Chicago's Grant Park, where more than 125,000 people waited on a warm November night. In Atlanta, John Lewis, the civil rights leader and Georgia congressman, was speaking in Martin Luther King's Ebenezer Church before a crowd that filled the church and spilled outside. When news came that Obama had carried Pennsylvania and Ohio, Lewis knew Obama had won. "I had an out-of-body experience," he told us later. "I just felt so good. And then later, around eleven o'clock when they declared him the winner, I cried. I just cried."

Valerie Jarrett was backstage at Grant Park when Obama arrived; she had not seen him since the networks had called the race. Her eyes too welled up with tears. "I looked at him and he looked at me and he kind of shrugged and I kind of made a face. And we never said a word," she said. "I gave him a hug and that was it. And I'm so glad we didn't say anything because I couldn't have possibly found the right words to describe how I felt. And the look on his face, he was obviously struggling for what to say to me as well and it was just best to not say a word. I will always remember the look on his face. What I thought—it was, well, it actually worked."

In Arizona, about twenty minutes after the election was called, McCain and Palin came onstage to concede. McCain displayed none of the anger or frustration that had flashed at times during the campaign. His speech was eloquent, gracious, and uplifting, acknowledging the significance of Obama's election. "In a contest as long and difficult as this campaign has been, his success alone commands my respect for his ability and persever-ance," he said. "But that he managed to do so by inspiring the hopes of so many millions of Americans who had once wrongly believed that they had little at stake or little influence in the election of an American president is something I deeply admire and commend him for achieving. This is an historic election, and I recognize the special significance it has for African-Americans and for the special pride that must be theirs tonight. . . . A century ago, President Theodore Roosevelt's invitation of Booker T. Wash-ington to visit—to dine at the White House—was taken as an outrage in many quarters. America today is a world away from the cruel and prideful bigotry of that time. There is no better evidence of this than the election of an African-American to the presidency of the United States. Let there be no reason now for any American to fail to cherish their citizenship in this, the greatest nation on earth."

Palin also had a speech prepared, written by Matthew Scully on his own initiative. Her desire to give it led to one last point of friction between her camp and McCain's. Schmidt was particularly irritated. He believed McCain's concession speech was part of an orderly constitutional process, to acknowledge the opponent's victory and help bind the country. Palin's desire to speak would be highly inappropriate. The misunderstanding—no one in the McCain-Palin operation seemed to have resolved her role for that night in advance—rankled a number of McCain's most senior advisers and created an uproar that night and for days after.

Just before midnight Eastern Time, Obama came onstage in Grant Park, accompanied by Michelle and daughters Sasha and Malia. "If there is anyone out there who still doubts that America is a place where all things are possible, who still wonders if the dream of our founders is alive in our time, who still questions the power of our democracy, tonight is your answer," he said. "I was never the likeliest candidate for this office. We didn't start with much money or many endorsements. Our campaign was not hatched in the halls of Washington; it began in the backyards of Des Moines and the living rooms of Concord and the front porches of Charleston. It was built by working men and women who dug into what little savings they had to give five dollars and ten dollars and twenty dollars to the cause. It drew strength from the young people who rejected the myth of their generation's apathy, who left their homes and their families for jobs that offered little pay and less sleep. It drew strength from the not-so-young people who braved the bitter cold and scorching heat to knock on the doors of perfect strangers, and from the millions of Americans who volunteered and organized, and proved that more than two centuries later a government of the people, by the people, and for the people has not perished from the earth. This is your victory."

He spoke of the challenges ahead. "The road ahead will be long," he said. "Our climb will be steep. We may not get there in one year or even in one term, but, America, I have never been more hopeful than I am tonight that we will get there. I promise you: We as a people will get there. . . . There will be setbacks and false starts. There are many who won't agree with every decision or policy I make as president, and we know the government can't solve every problem. . . . What began twenty-one months ago in the depths of winter cannot end on this autumn night. This victory alone is not the change we seek; it is only the chance for us to make that change."

He closed with the story of Ann Nixon Cooper, age 106, from Atlanta, who had cast her ballot for him that day. "She was born just a generation past slavery; a time when there were no cars on the road or planes in the sky; when someone like her couldn't vote for two reasons, because she was a woman and because of the color of her skin. And tonight, I think about all that she's seen throughout her century in America: the heartache and the hope, the struggle and the progress, the times we were told that we can't, and the people who pressed on with that American creed: Yes, we can."

The words echoed in the urban landscape in Chicago and rippled across the country, the rallying cry that had seen him through difficult days, crushing setbacks, and soaring victories. "Yes, we can!" He spoke of what America had overcome during the century of Ann Nixon Cooper's life, of wars hot and cold, recessions and depression, of moments of inspiration and fear. "And this year," he said, "in this election, she touched her finger to a screen and cast her vote, because after one hundred six years in America, through the best of times and the darkest of hours, she knows how America can change. Yes, we can."

In Grant Park, another huge roar went up from the people: "Yes, we can!"

CHAPTER THIRTY

Interlude

"What was remarkable . . . about our campaign was we never really changed our theory."

—Barack Obama, six weeks after his election

"I think the whole election was a novel," Barack Obama said six weeks after his election. He was seated in his transition office on the thirty-eighth floor of the federal building in downtown Chicago. Next to him on a couch were a football and a basketball, with an "Obama 08" insignia. Other basketballs sat on a bookcase behind his desk. Bulletproof panels had been placed along floor-to-ceiling windows on the side of the office looking out at the city.

The president-elect was welcoming and upbeat, although later that day he would learn during a meeting with his economic advisers that the economic crisis was even worse than they had believed. He appeared refreshed after the long campaign, loose, open, confident. As he escorted us toward his office, he paused to talk to his newly designated chief of staff, Rahm Emanuel, then expressed mock dismay at the mess around the desk of his personal assistant, Reggie Love. Eyeing an open bag of potato chips and papers strewn on the floor, he exclaimed that this was no way for the president-elect's office to look. "Reggie!" he shouted, but Love was nowhere to be seen. Once seated, Obama drank bottled tea and munched on almonds.

So how would the writer and storyteller that he was before becoming a politician tell the story of his election? we asked. "I don't think I was the most interesting character in the election," he said. "If you think about it, you've got the first African-American with a chance at the seat, first woman with a chance at the seat. You've got this aging—scratch aging, because I don't want to offend John [McCain]—but I mean you've got this war hero.

You have a whole cast of characters at the beginning who are fascinating in their own right, in some ways compelling just from a human perspective: John Edwards, Huckabee. And then comes the general election [and] you get Sarah Palin and Joe the Plumber. You've got Reverend Wright, Bill Ayers. It's a pretty fascinating slice of Americana."

He gave a broader perspective. "The way I would tell the story would really have to do with what this campaign said about America and where we've traveled," he said. "The fact that just a little over forty years after the passage of the Voting Rights Act that I can run. That just a few decades after women were admitted to professions like law or medicine in any meaningful numbers, that Hillary could run in a credible way. The generational changes between John McCain's era and our own, and sort of the vestiges of Vietnam, the shift that's taken place in the salience of some of the culture wars that emerged in the sixties that really were the dominant force in our politics, starting with Ronald Reagan, and how that had less power. Which, by the way, includes why the issue of Reverend Wright or Bill Ayers never caught as powerfully as it might have fifteen or twenty years ago. The way the Internet served our campaign in unprecedented ways."

All that indicated a shift to a new country, one "rooted in our deepest values and traditions, but one that points to what this country's going to look like twenty, thirty years from now."

Did he believe his election marked the end of the Reagan era? He took another handful of almonds, rubbing the salt from his hands. "Sorry, I'm starving," he said apologetically before answering.

"What Reagan ushered in was a skepticism toward government solutions to every problem, a suspicion of command-and-control, top-down social engineering," he said. "I don't think that has changed. I think that's a lasting legacy of the Reagan era and the conservative movement, starting with Goldwater. But I do think [what we're seeing] is an end to the knee-jerk reaction toward the New Deal and big government. I think what you saw in this election was people saying, 'Yes, we don't want some big, bureaucratic, ever-expanding state. On the other hand, we don't want a state that's dysfunctional, that doesn't believe in its mission, that can't carry out some of the basic functions of government and provide services to people and be there when they're hurting.' And so, I think what you're seeing is a correction to the correction, right? What we don't know yet is whether my administration and this next generation of leadership is going to be able to hew to a new, more pragmatic approach that is less interested in whether we have big government or small government, [but is] more interested in whether we have a smart, effective government."

And what had he learned about the American people from his campaign? "I have to tell you," he said, "and this is in no way an indication of overconfidence, I was not surprised by the campaign. I felt that, and I said this on the stump, I felt vindicated in my faith in the American people." Drawing on his legal background, he offered "a theory of the case" that he said guided his campaign. "For at least a decade, maybe longer," he said Americans have been "frustrated with a government that was unresponsive; that their economic life was becoming more difficult despite the surface prosperity; that wages and incomes had flatlined and that in this new globalized world people were feeling more and more insecure; that we had never replaced or updated the structures for security that the New Deal had provided with something that made sense for this new economy; that people were weary of culture wars as a substitute for policy; that people were tired of only focusing on what divides instead of what brought us together; that the fifty-plus-one electoral strategies that were generally pursued in national elections were completely inadequate to solve big problems like health care and energy that would require a broader consensus; that people were embarrassed by the decline in America's standing in the eyes of the world and that that would have political relevance to voters who normally might not care that much about foreign policy; and that the American people were decent and good and would be open to a different tone to politics. So that was the theory that we started with. What was remarkable in my mind about our campaign was we never really changed our theory. You could read the speech we gave the day I announced and then read my speech on election night and it was pretty consistent."

He turned to the question of race. His experience in Illinois when running for the Senate in 2004 gave him confidence that America was ready to elect its first black president. "Illinois's a pretty good microcosm of the country and when I started my U.S. Senate race, everybody said a guy with your name, African-American, can't win a U.S. Senate race. And we won," he said. "And my approval ratings I think when I announced for the presidency here in Illinois were like seventy percent. So I thought to myself, If I'm in a big industrial state with twelve percent African-American population and people seem to not be concerned about my race and much more concerned with my performance, why would [that not hold true] across the country?"

He never lost confidence he could overcome racial barriers, though the

Reverend Wright episode had severely tested that belief. In the primaries, his best results were in states with few African-Americans and in those with a high percentage of black voters. His greatest struggles came in states where the racial composition more closely mirrored the national averages. "Our view was never that we had a white working-class problem," he said. "Our view was that we had an age problem. States where there were older white voters, where that was a disproportionate portion of the electorate, were going to give us problems."

As for his campaign itself, he gave a candid assessment of his main competitors. "I was sure that my toughest race was Hillary," he said. "Hillary was just a terrific candidate, and she really found her voice in the last part of the campaign. After Texas and Ohio she just became less cautious and was out there and was working hard and I think connecting with voters really well. She was just a terrific candidate. And [the Clinton campaign] operation was not as good as ours and not as tight as ours, but they were still plenty tough. Their rapid response, how they messaged in the media was really good. So we just always thought they were our most formidable challenge. That isn't to say that we underestimated John McCain, it's just that we didn't think that their campaign operation was as good. And one of the hardest things for me, during the primary, was finding differences with Hillary. I mean a lot of the differences between us, substantively, were pretty modest. . . .

"Going into the general election, I just felt liberated because there was such a stark contrast between John and myself. . . . They made a strategic decision early on to flip on the Bush tax cuts, and in fact double down on them, which locked them into a domestic agenda that was very difficult to separate from George Bush's domestic agenda. So that just gave us a lot of running room on the issues."

It was time to leave, but not before raising one last subject. Obama started his campaign in the shadow of the Old State Capitol in Springfield, we recalled, where Lincoln had delivered his famous "House Divided" speech. Now, as he prepared to return to Washington, his campaign had announced plans for him to follow the last part of Lincoln's train ride to Washington before his inauguration. We wondered how Lincoln, the Illinois lawyer with little national experience, affected Obama's thoughts about his own presidency as another young Illinois lawyer with limited national experience soon to take his presidential oath.

"Lincoln's my favorite president and one of my personal heroes," he answered. "I have to be very careful here that in no way am I drawing equivalence between my candidacy, my life experience, or what I face and what he went through. I just want to put that out there so you don't get a bunch of folks saying I'm comparing myself to Lincoln."

He paused. "What I admire so deeply about Lincoln—number one, I think he's the quintessential American because he's self-made. The way Alexander Hamilton was self-made or so many of our great iconic Americans are, that sense that you don't accept limits, that you can shape your own destiny. That obviously has appeal to me given where I came from. That American spirit is one of the things that is most fundamental to me and I think he embodies that.

"But the second thing that I admire most in Lincoln is that there is just a deep-rooted honesty and empathy to the man that allowed him to always be able to see the other person's point of view and always sought to find that truth that is in the gap between you and me. Right? That the truth is out there somewhere and I don't fully possess it and you don't fully possess it and our job then is to listen and learn and imagine enough to be able to get to that truth.

"If you look at his presidency, he never lost that. Most of our other great presidents, there was that sense of working the angles and bending other people to their will. FDR being the classic example. And Lincoln just found a way to shape public opinion and shape people around him and lead them and guide them without tricking them or bullying them, but just through the force of what I just talked about: that way of helping to illuminate the truth. I just find that to be a very compelling style of leadership. It's not one that I've mastered, but I think that's when leadership is at its best."

The 2008 election was more than an endurance test for the candidates; it was a test of the American people and their institutions. Now that it was part of history, what lessons could be learned from it?

The first, most obviously, involves race.

Since 1619 when a battered Dutch privateer beat around Cape Henry, tacked slowly up the James River, and dropped anchor off Jamestown to deposit the first African-American slaves on the continent, race relations have affected the character of the United States more than any other factor. Black slaves laid the cornerstones for the White House and the Capitol, were sold like chattel in a huge slave market that stood on the site in Washington where the National Archives now houses the Declaration of Independence and the Bill of Rights, and became the source of bloodshed, civil war, discord, and discrimination that plagued the nation throughout its history, dishonoring its professed democratic principles of equality. Whatever happens in Barack Obama's presidency, his election as the first African-American will always form a proud chapter in the American story. For millions watching the election returns, the spontaneous celebrations that erupted in urban neighborhoods that night, the tears in Grant Park, the lines of citizens, most of them African-Americans, trying to buy newspapers the next morning, all testified to a public sense that something shattering—and positive—had occurred.

There are many ways to tell that story. We offer one only. It comes from our last conversation with Fay Citerone, the white, middle-aged professional we had been following throughout the election, who had been wrestling with her initial support for Clinton before switching to Obama. "Listen to this," she told us immediately after the election. "My ninety-two-year-old mom, who is from a very Republican part of Pennsylvania—I think she had a Reagan calendar on her wall—asked me, 'Who are you gonna vote for?' and I said 'Obama.' And she said, 'I think I might, too.' I didn't press it. Then the day before the election, I said, 'Who are you going to vote for?' and she said, 'I'm gonna vote for the black man.' And I said, 'Mom, have you ever voted for a Democrat for president?' And she said, 'No, I don't think I ever have.' She's probably voted in every election in her life. So I asked her about Obama. 'What's the appeal there, what do you like about him?' And she said, 'I think he's very inspiring. That's who we need right now.'

"Three friends told me about black people they worked with who went to the polls at five a.m. Tuesday even though the polls here didn't open until seven. They wanted to be some of the first people to vote. That speaks volumes to me. I think we've come so far in our society that it really didn't matter to white people that he was black. It may have brought about more of a black vote because they had a credible black candidate. But I don't think people cared. Maybe twenty years ago this would have stopped some people from voting for a black candidate. But we've matured so much, American society has, that it just didn't matter anymore."

That may be overly optimistic, but it speaks to the power of what Obama's own story says about America's promise. Here he was, someone who spent much of his youth outside the United States, from a broken family—a black father who abandoned him, a white mother who then married an Indonesian and moved there with him and Barack, only to send the young Obama back to Hawaii to be raised by his white grandparents.

Without major financial resources, or privileged family position, he was still able to attain a splendid education, pursue and realize his dreams.

For many women, the election of 2008 proved unsatisfying. The treatment of Hillary Clinton raised questions about whether sexism is somehow more acceptable than racism. Both Clinton and Sarah Palin endured withering criticism, whether in the media or as the target of late-night comics. There is no way to know how much of Clinton's owed to her being half of a powerful couple who have provoked strong reactions and resentments now for nearly two decades, as opposed to the fact that she is a woman. That she was a polarizing figure is indisputable, though by the end of her campaign she had won over many people with her show of tenacity and resolve. Palin brought much, but not all, criticism upon herself.

The campaign showed that female candidates face their own special obstacles. Clinton joked after the campaign that when Obama awoke each morning, he could go to the gym and exercise. She had to worry about having her hair and makeup done. But there were serious issues that affected her candidacy. Clinton's advisers constantly worried about how to demonstrate that she was capable of being commander in chief in a time of war. Their strategy of running her as the front-runner and inevitable candidate in part grew out of those insecurities—better to show her strong and pre-destined than to allow doubts about whether she was tough enough for the job. Women also come under greater pressure not to show emotions. When Clinton welled up with tears in New Hampshire, she was instantly subjected to questions about whether that moment was real or manufactured to manipulate voters.

Still, her campaign advanced the cause of women's rights—especially their *political* rights. When she talked about her campaign having contributed to the shattering of the glass ceiling, she was expressing much more than what quickly became a political cliché. Over the last two generations, women have assumed more vital roles in American society. They are today by far the greater percentage of those attending college—outnumbering male students by as much as 60 to 40 percent. In the professions, from lawyers to doctors to scientists and researchers, they now comprise more than half of those entering their fields. In athletics too, women now occupy a far greater place than in the past—not the equal of men in pay and celebrity status, but closer in public standing, prestige, and acclaim. Those kinds of statistics would seem to assure women of a more significant place in American life in the future, but the evidence does not support that assumption. Women still fall far behind men in leadership of corporations, in boardrooms, in law firms, in medical establishments. At the end of 2008, for example, Catalyst, a leading nonprofit organization that has been providing statistics about women in business for more than forty years, found that women's overall representation in senior leadership positions has continued to stagnate. Women then represented 46.3 percent of the U.S. labor force, but among Fortune 500 positions they trailed far behind men in the percentage of corporate officers (15.4), board members (14.8), and top earners (6.7). Only 2.4 percent of Fortune 500 CEOs were women. While women in America have made real progress after decades of struggle and protests that slowly brought about changes, sexism still thrives. Far too often women are treated with condescension or as sex objects, suffer discrimination, and fall far behind men in pay and position. And they still lag far behind men in national political leadership. Hillary Clinton's presidential campaign was a signal example both of the power of women to attract wide public support in politics—and of how far they have yet to go. Political leadership still remains a barrier to full equality.

It is crucial to explore the lessons about the process by which Americans elect their president. It remains flawed, as 2008 demonstrated. The battle begins too early, lasts too long, requires ever greater amounts of money, and leaves few people satisfied. Obama's prodigious fund-raising became one of the marvels of the election, evidence of the enthusiasm his candidacy created and seemingly an antidote to the belief that only the wealthiest play an influential role in funding campaigns. But Obama's vast campaign war chest also highlighted the degree to which there was an uneven playing field, particularly in the general election. He could spend freely while McCain, who had accepted public funds and the limits they imposed, could not. He paid little price for rejecting public funding in the fall campaign. Efforts to limit campaign spending have rarely worked, in large part because of constitutional obstacles but also because of ever-present loopholes that have been exploited by candidates or independent groups. But the need to raise huge amounts of money contributes to the early start to each presidential campaign, and despite the growing power of online fund-raising by small donors, candidates still court the biggest givers and fund-raisers. Money still undermines public confidence in the election process.

The role of caucuses and primaries, the timing of the electoral contests, the rush to hold early events, the way delegates are apportioned have all correctly been the subject of long controversy. We offer no easy solution to this problem. In fact, as co-authors we disagree on whether a series of regional primaries, on rotating schedules, would be better (as Johnson believes) than a shortened version of the current caucus/primary process (which Balz favors as a way of testing the candidates by greater exposure to voters in homes and communities). But we agree that the entire election process urgently needs to be reexamined—and reformed.

Another lesson involves the debates. By the end of the primaries, both candidates and voters were experiencing debate fatigue. The debates were too frequent, too long, often too discursive. Democrats debated more than two dozen times, Republicans more than twenty. Only a few significantly shaped the races. Debates during the primaries became more important to news organizations that promote and sponsor them than to voters seeking to form judgments about who should be the next president. In 2008, even more than in past election cycles, they became elaborate staged events with half a dozen or more candidates vying for attention over the course of two hours (or ninety minutes) that rarely examined in depth the critical, complex issues facing the country. Formats that limited candidate responses to sixty or ninety seconds and ranged over many subjects severely limited their usefulness. Too often, they became battles for sound bites and "gotcha" attempts to "get" the front-runner. At the least, we believe McCain's idea of candidates holding a series of joint town hall meetings in which specific subjects of concern were discussed and debated deserved a more positive reception than Obama gave it.

Then there's the media. The media's role in politics always has been, and always should be, controversial. In the American system, the press was granted the extraordinary constitutional right to be wrong in the belief that it would serve as a check on power, a disturber of the peace—even at times reckless and irresponsible—all in the belief that a greater public good emerges from free inquiry. At its best, it is the provider of essential information on which the public can form reasoned opinions. In the new world of media, however, its role becomes more complicated and contentious. The number of media outlets increases extraordinarily. They are abetted by the rise of the blogosphere and the rapid decline of traditional news operations, especially newspapers but also newsmagazines and the traditional three television networks. Opinionated talking heads on cable television dominate much of the political discourse. The round-the-clock, 24/7 news cycle accelerates the pressure to provide instantaneous coverage, so often sensational and lacking in perspective and careful analysis. With all this, the collective arms of the press combine to shape the changing narratives of the long presidential cycle.

In 2008, the performance of the media provided some of its best—and worst—examples of coverage and commentary. We are far from alone in finding that a vicious tone animates many of the blog and cable talk comments from both extreme left and right. As the primary contests began an experiment by one of our colleagues, Gene Weingarten of the *Washington Post*, memorably demonstrated this. Curious to examine the effects of today's information overload on the public, Weingarten locked himself in a room for twenty-four hours with six TVs, two radios, and a laptop set to cycle through the outpouring of eleven blogs and cable news commentary programs. His thoughts emerged in a play-by-play narrative titled "Crime and Unusual Punishment." At first, his reactions were generally positive. As he wrote, "It's complicated, but here it is: There's something real about all this palaver all around me; in its overheated, perfervid way, it's inspiring. You can't get away from that. . . . Unfettered discourse is the sign of a robust democracy. It's a genuine war of ideas out there, being fought by highly committed people who care about the world."

But by the end of his twenty-four-hour immersion in the heated new world of the blogs and attack-and-counterattack cable culture, Weingarten's optimism was shaken: "I cannot tell you how horrible it is," he wrote. "It rattles the very center of your being. If you care about the state of humankind, it fills you with despair. We are as a people bleak and hostile and suspicious, filled with senseless partisanship and willing to believe anything and everything about anyone. We are full of ourselves and we hate. And we do it 24/7."

Weingarten was correct in characterizing the background of public discourse during the election as being bleak, hostile, filled with senseless partisanship and hate. He offered no remedy to a condition that further contributes to growing polarization of American society, making it all the more difficult to achieve public consensus to address complex and growing problems. Nor is there an easy remedy. One of the glories of America's experiment in democracy is the belief that unfettered debate, however vicious and unfair at times, is essential to the functioning of a free society. So one answer to reducing the increasingly destructive political climate lies in continuing to celebrate the First Amendment and its protection of free expression. But at the same time, the public, from political leaders to ordinary citizens, needs to challenge the haters and reassert the values of tolerance, civility, and respect for differences of opinion. That means encouraging uninhibited debate over divisive issues in a diverse society—and to strike a reasoned balance between extremes. And that requires an educational system that stresses teaching citizens these basic elements about a democratic society, and their responsibility to participate, be informed, and appreciate all sides of an argument before rendering a political judgment.

Finally, there's the role of government itself, all the more critical because of the economic collapse and the intervention by Washington to fashion a remedy that so suddenly changed the stakes in the election. Economic warning lights were flashing red for months, if not years. And that raises the far more complex question of what the appointed watchmen were doing during this period, who was watching the watchmen, and what was the proper role of government. Not big, small, liberal, or conservative government, but government that works, government in which people have confidence. The regulatory agencies had become, at best, lax. At worst, they were dismissed as unnecessary. They failed to fulfill their responsibilities. Democrats seize on this as the root of the problem, but in truth neither party can escape blame for what happened.

Whether the economic collapse of 2008 signals a shift in the way Americans feel about the role of government is not clear from the election results alone. At the least, the crisis seems to have shattered the public consensus about following a decades-long Reagan era model of laissez-faire government. That did not answer the question of whether the public wanted a return to big government—or to the principles of government as the neutral umpire, one that strives to allow opportunity to flourish and risk to occur, but also establishes supervision to keep the system from self-destructing. Those principles, and the unanswered questions about the role of government, lay at the heart of the election.

The election of 2008 was not about small issues. It was nothing less than a battle for America. Despite the imperfections of the nominating and electoral process, the excesses of the media, and the failure to plumb below the surface of the greatest issues confronting America, the election of 2008 was as significant as the nation has experienced at least since 1980, if not 1932 and the advent of the New Deal. At the end, the election was defined by the greatest economic crisis since the Great Depression, raising even greater challenges for the American people and their political system. For all its faults, 2008 will be remembered as an election of great consequence and a dramatic turn in direction, one that produced a surge in voter turnout, the engagement of younger voters and African-Americans, and in Barack Obama, John McCain, and Hillary Clinton three politicians notable for their character and resiliency.

The Inauguration

January 20, 2009, the Capitol

O n Barack Obama's inauguration day, the worst of times brought out the best in America.

Obama was taking office facing some of the grimmest conditions a new president could confront. Since his election the Dow Jones Industrial Average had declined by more than a thousand points. Wall Street calculated $7 trillion wiped out during the previous year. The S&P index of the leading five hundred stocks had fallen more than at any time since 1937, with every sector taking double-digit hits and the financial sector losing more than half its value. The government reported the worst job losses since 1945, a decline of two and a half million in the last year, and nearly two million in just the last four months.

Yet despite such terrible news, the enthusiasm of crowds that turned out in record numbers to witness Obama take his oath and the millions of television viewers watching from across the country and around the world showed a joyous anticipation. They had come to Washington from great distances to witness this moment. The city had braced for as many as five million. Final tallies estimated the number at below two million, and this great crowd was ecstatic, exuberantly waving little American flags passed out to mark the moment. Even some with tickets who furiously found themselves stuck in a tunnel due to a security breakdown, making it impossible to reach the Mall in time, anxiously attempted to keep in touch with what was happening, gathering around radios to listen to the proceedings, sharing the inaugural reports with others.

For days, a celebratory mood had swept the capital, reflecting the optimism about the new president across the country. A *USA Today*/Gallup inauguration day survey found people, by nearly six to one, more hopeful about the next four years. The night before, temperatures had dropped well below freezing, amid talk of possible snow. On the morning of the inauguration, the cold remained, but it was clear, the skies were a brilliant blue, the entire scene of masses of people stretching from the Capitol to the Lincoln Memorial sharply illuminated.

The faces that viewers saw on their TV screens were those of Americans eager for success, hopeful that a difficult period was ending, anxious to believe that tomorrow would be better than today.

Every inaugural, especially in the age of television, offers Americans an opportunity to share intimately in the scene playing out before them. So it was with Obama's.

As the cameras panned the inaugural stage, gathered beneath the bunting and flags and secure behind bulletproof glass were the nation's leaders. The Bushes, father and son: one older, more frail; the other, eyes closed, head lowered, the expression at times almost appearing grim. Off to the side, in a wheelchair, after hurting his back lifting boxes, was the outgoing vice president, Dick Cheney, controversial to the end, the result of a series of exit interviews in which he defended the administration's actions. And there were the Clintons, Hillary beaming, Obama's strongest competitor, now about to become the new secretary of state. Beside her a smiling Bill offering words of greetings to distinguished guests. Hovering behind them, barely seen, was the face of Al Gore, yesterday's vice president and almost president.

Then there was the picture of the new, youthful, energetic Obama family: the girls, Sasha and Malia, Malia poised beyond her years in a blue coat, snapping pictures of the crowd; Sasha in pink and orange, standing on a crate so she could see her father sworn in, then giving him a thumbs-up; Michelle, elegant in her beaded lemongrass ensemble. In history's eyes, perhaps most remarkable of all was how so much of America was taking for granted this appealing picture of a black family as they were about to enter the White House to become the nation's first family.

Of the images, the most memorable was of Barack Obama as he stood, tall, slim, alone, in the Capitol doorway before walking down the steps to the podium to take his oath and deliver his address. He paused there, head thrown back, eyes closed, permitting all who watched to guess at what he was thinking at the very moment he was about to enter history. Cool as ever, he surmounted a moment of potential embarrassment as he was being sworn in. In administering the oath, Chief Justice John Roberts inadvertently mangled the words. Obama stood there calmly smiling, his hand on Lincoln's Bible, starting, stopping and starting again in a futile effort to get it right.*

For weeks, anticipation about Obama's inaugural address had been the subject of endless speculation: How would the great orator rise to the occasion, and with what message about the conditions facing the country?

Obama relied on neither soaring eloquence nor poetry, whether ringing FDR words about "the only thing we have to fear is fear itself," or JFK sounding the trumpet again and summoning his fellow citizens to "Ask not what your country can do for you, ask what you can do for your country." Instead of rhetoric, his speech was steeped in realism—sobering words that framed the challenges ahead. He spelled out the errors that had plunged the nation into a time of what he described as "gathering clouds and raging storms" and called for a "new era of responsibility" on the part of every American, in order "to brave once more the icy currents and endure what storms may come."

He unsparingly described the magnitude of problems the nation faced, saying, "That we are in the midst of crisis is now well understood. Our nation is at war against a far-reaching network of violence and hatred. Our economy is badly weakened, a consequence of greed and irresponsibility on the part of some but also our collective failure to make hard choices and prepare the nation for a new age."

After saying these challenges "are serious and they are many" and will not be met "easily or in a short span of time," he drew sustained applause when he said confidently, his voice ringing loudly, that "they will be met."

His message on this inaugural day was of an American renewal, and of the themes that won him such support throughout his long, history-shattering campaign: the necessity for change, for new policies, for appealing to the best, not the worst, in the American character. "On this day," he said, "we gather because we have chosen hope over fear, unity of purpose over conflict and discord. On this day, we come to proclaim an end to the petty grievances and false promises, the recriminations and worn-out dogmas that for far too long have strangled our politics."

Again, a roar of approval from the ecstatic throng stretching out before him.

He reaffirmed America's greatness, then quickly warned that "greatness

---

* At 7:35 the next evening Obama retook his oath of office from Roberts in the White House Map Room. After the chief justice asked Obama whether he was ready, the new president replied, "I am, and we're going to do it very slowly."

is never a given. It must be earned." America's journey, he continued in the same vein, "has never been one of shortcuts or settling for less. It was not the path for the fainthearted, for those that prefer leisure over work, or seek only the pleasures of riches and fame. Rather, it has been the risk-takers, the doers, the makers of things—some celebrated, but more often men and women obscure in their labor—who have carried us up the long rugged road towards prosperity and freedom."

He signaled a notable break in the nation's foreign policy, speaking of a "false choice between our safety and our ideals"—an obvious reference to the Bush policies of torture, detention, and rendition. Of America, he said, "We are ready to lead again."

His speech was widely praised, though naturally there were dissenters. The public was solidly with him. The question that lingered was whether he could translate his words into action and in so doing give hope and confidence to a nation struggling with historic challenges. But that was a story for another day. For now, as the forty-fourth president left the Capitol, Americans paused in celebration. They were proud over this chance for a fresh start under the leadership of a man who had been viewed not so many months earlier as the most unlikely presidential prospect in all of American history.

The events that dominated Barack Obama's first year as president stood in striking contrast to the campaign of 2008. The candidate who brought hope and inspiration to millions struggled as president against the forces of a stubborn recession, a double-digit jobless rate, implacable conservative opposition to his domestic agenda, and a difficult war in Afghanistan. The euphoria that marked election night and Inauguration Day gave way to partisan brawling between Republicans and Democrats and internecine warfare within both political parties. The once soaring Obama watched his popularity steadily recede. By year's end, his approval rating hovered around 50 percent—down from 69 percent at the end of his first hundred days and below the 53 percent of the vote he had won in November 2008.

Politically, it got worse—much worse. On January 19, the eve of the first anniversary of Obama's inauguration, the president and his party suffered a stunning setback: the loss of a Senate seat in Massachusetts that had been held by the late Edward M. Kennedy for nearly half a century. In that special election, Scott Brown, a little known Republican, pulled off an astounding upset that imperiled not only prospects for health care reform but also put Democrats further on the defensive at the beginning of an election year.

The story of Obama's first year thus became a cautionary tale about the differences between campaigning and governing and a reminder that there is nothing linear in the contours of American politics. Obama and his White House team, celebrated for their creativity, competence, and discipline during the campaign, fought with only limited success to translate their winning formulas to the challenges of running the country. The new America heralded by many analysts in the weeks after the 2008 election often looked and acted suspiciously like the old America.

What happened? The answer to that question begins with Obama, who promised so much in both style and substance during the campaign. His candidacy helped create unrealistically high expectations for his presidency. His followers projected onto him attributes and beliefs that may not have been real. His campaign message was built on an inherent contradiction. He promised to usher in a post-partisan era of politics while championing a liberal domestic agenda whose size and shape seemed guaranteed to widen the ideological divide in the country. In office, he had trouble squaring this circle, in part because his Republican opponents in Congress decided early to oppose him on virtually every domestic issue, leading Democrats to label them "the party of No." The loss of Kennedy's Senate seat meant that Obama and the Democrats would face a Republican minority that now held a critical forty-first vote enabling them to enforce a filibuster of any Democratic legislation.

Obama's election changed America's image around the world, but the goodwill did not produce dramatic changes in behavior by U.S. adversaries or significantly more assistance from allies in those conflicts. As president, he often spoke with the same eloquence and intelligence that marked his campaign. He delivered memorable speeches at home and abroad, but his presidency showed the limits as well as the lift of rhetorical leadership.

He had set high ambitions for his presidency, but by moving on many fronts at once threatened to overload the circuits of government. His inspirational candidacy evoked passions among his supporters not seen in many years in American politics. In office, his cool, detached style often left many allies disappointed, especially his most progressive followers. He refused to be bound by the 24/7 political culture that demanded action and interpretation by the minute. He was prepared to let the system work. His patience frustrated followers who may have naively believed the change he promised could come overnight. They wanted a fighter in the White House.

A president's first year in office often becomes a time of disappointment and frustration, stemming both from inherited problems and external crises. Lincoln's first year was consumed by the outbreak of the Civil War, FDR's by the hardships of the Depression, Kennedy's by the disastrous Bay of Pigs invasion, LBJ's by the rising tide of conflict in Vietnam and his unhappy decision to greatly expand America's commitment of troops. Reagan and Clinton, who were two of the most popular recent presidents, suffered setbacks during their first years in office. Reagan survived an assassin's bullet, but an economic downturn sent his polls plummeting to 42 percent by the time of 1982 elections when his party suffered major losses. Clinton's failure to enact health care reform enabled Republicans to regain control of Congress for the first time in forty years. Still, what Obama faced was extraordinary by almost any measure.

When we began this book, we believed that whoever was elected would face some of the most contentious issues the United States had confronted in many years. Still, on three major fronts—the economy, health care, and Afghanistan—Obama took on challenges that proved even more daunting than he and his advisers thought they were on the night he claimed the presidency.

By coincidence, that became clearer to the president-elect on the December day in 2008 when we interviewed him for this book. He was in an upbeat mood when we spoke at midday. Later that afternoon he would be told the full measure of the economic crisis awaiting him. Obama's economic team could see by then that the economy was about to fall off the cliff. But the public did not understand that reality. That presented a problem for the incoming president. Meeting without Obama earlier that day, David Axelrod told the economic team, "America has yet to have its holy shit moment" on the economy. Later, when the advisers met with Obama, Christina Romer, tapped to head the Council of Economic Advisers, went through the reality of the numbers. She repeated for Obama what Axelrod had said earlier. Obama was as startled by her language as by her description of the problem. She outlined the scale of the response that would be needed—a stimulus package approaching one trillion dollars, bigger than the New Deal, just to keep unemployment below 10 percent (which proved to be a miscalculation). When the meeting broke up, Austan Goolsbee, who had served as a principal economic adviser during the campaign, walked up to Obama and said, "That has to be about the worst meeting any president-elect has ever had." Obama replied, "That is not even my worst meeting this week."

The massive economic collapse that he inherited offered Obama two paths. One would be to scale back his ambitious campaign agenda. He could have argued that the economy turned out to be in such a fragile state that all his attention—and all available resources—should be focused on nursing it back to health. That would require pushing for a stimulus package that ended up costing $787 billion. It meant billions more to bail out banks and the auto industry, making the U.S. government part owners of financial institutions and failing car companies. Given the amount of money the government would have to pour into the economy, he might have argued, America could not then afford a costly overhaul of health care or other ambitious initiatives such as combating global warming.

Obama's other path pointed to a big and bold agenda on the model of FDR or LBJ. Rather than using the economy as an excuse for backing off from attending to health care and energy, he could use it as the catalyst for action on all fronts. White House Chief of Staff Rahm Emanuel summed up this view with the admonition, "Never let a serious crisis go to waste." The urgency of the moment and the size of the economic challenges, his advisers believed, might help galvanize the country and unite Democrats and Republicans to work together on issues that in years past had defied the political system's will to act. Obama and his team ultimately found this activist path more appealing. That led him to push immediately for legislation to overhaul the financial regulatory system and to combat global climate change.

Above all, the decision to embrace the second path led Obama to push for an overhaul of the health care system that would tie up the Congress for more than a year. No issue consumed more of his time and energy, sapped more of the president's political capital, or stirred more reaction among conservatives than health care. The health care initiative, on top of all he had done to boost the economy, gave rise to a noisy debate about the size and role of government. Whether it was political opportunism that prompted Republicans to resist, or Obama's failure to craft initiatives that could truly find bipartisan support, the potential for cooperation vanished. The debate over health care energized conservatives and caused Independents who had backed Obama and the Democrats to have second thoughts about the course he was pursuing.

During Obama's troubled first year, we often recalled the style of leadership—Lincolnesque in his telling—that the candidate said he hoped to achieve as president. He described it as seeking "to see the other person's point of view to find the truth that is in the gap between you and me. . . ." Though he conceded that he was no equal of Lincoln, he believed that was "when leadership is at its best." As the year progressed, he could not, however, find a way to guide the country to that gap.

Obama's problems may not have been all that unusual for a new president facing difficult times. What *was* extraordinary about Obama's first year was the swiftness—and viciousness—of the repolarization of the country. The hardening line between Republican and Democrat caught Obama's team by surprise and significantly altered the course of 2009.

Nothing highlighted the conflicts more starkly than what took place in the House chamber on September 9, nine months into his presidency. That Wednesday night Obama was attempting to rally support for his faltering health care initiative. His vehicle was a prime-time address before a joint session of Congress, with millions of Americans watching on television across the country. Obama gave no hint of unease as he began to speak to the joint session, his head cocked back in his by-now familiar stance. The "time for bickering is over," he said. He was halfway through his forty-seven minute speech when he tried to dispel what he called "bogus claims spread by those whose only agenda is to kill reform." It was "a lie, plain and simple" that his plan would create "death panels." It also was untrue that his reform plan would cover illegal immigrants.

Suddenly, from the Republican side of the Congress, a loud shout rang out: "You lie!" Startled, the president turned to his left to see where the shout came from. Vice President Joe Biden and Speaker Nancy Pelosi seated directly behind him looked shocked. Obama paused, then tried to continue. His critics were also wrong in claiming his reform plan would use federal funds to pay for abortions. . . . Again, he was interrupted by another loud shout from the same Republican side: "Not true!"

Now the chamber was in an uproar. Members turned to each other, looking for the source of this stunning outburst. Never before had a president of the United States experienced such direct public disrespect from a member of Congress. The source was an obscure four-term Republican congressman from South Carolina named Joe Wilson. Previously, he had been an aide to the late Strom Thurmond, the staunch segregationist and one-time leader of the Dixiecrats. The public accusation by a member of Congress that a president was a liar became a metaphor for the difficulties Barack Obama was experiencing in carrying out his politics of hope and change. It also was a metaphor for the bitterly divided nation he tried to lead.

By the time Joe Wilson shouted "You lie!" America had fallen back into the strident ideological camps that make it so difficult to achieve consensus—or even compromise—on problems. Obama had never hidden the fact that his domestic agenda tilted to the left. But even before Obama was inaugurated, right wing critics like Rush Limbaugh had declared open warfare. "I hope he fails," Limbaugh said bluntly four days before the inauguration.

In the months that followed, the Right went on a major offensive. Town hall meetings became forums for shouted insults. "Tea Party" demonstrators thronged to rallies across the nation. Obama was accused of being a communist, a socialist, a fascist. Posters depicted him as Hitler, complete with small brush mustache. Glenn Beck, the baby-faced conservative Fox TV talk show host who had called for legions of Tea Party supporters to lead a national movement against Obama and Obamaism, directly accused him of being a racist. The president, Beck told his audience at the end of July, "has exposed himself as a guy, over and over and over again, who has a deep-seated hatred for white people or the white culture." Protestors carrying loaded weapons, including automatic rifles slung over their shoulders, turned up outside events where Obama was speaking. "Birthers" waved banners denouncing him as not even being a natural-born American citizen. They believed he was actually born in Kenya, though copies of his Hawaiian birth certificate had been produced during the campaign.

Part of the responsibility for these protests stemmed from anti-Obama rhetoric leveled almost daily from various Fox News television hosts (which was often challenged from the left in equally polemical terms by some prime-time hosts on MSNBC). But the protests testified to deeper feelings of discontent: rising frustration over the bleak economic news; resentment of the government's bailout of Wall Street tycoons who swiftly began paying themselves bonuses with taxpayer "rescue" money at the expense of a suffering Main Street; concern over a rising tide of national debt and the government's greater role in private and national life; fear over what seemed an increasingly uncertain future.

As the early months of his administration passed, protests against his policies intensified. By August, they were dominating the news. Then Sarah Palin, newly resigned as governor of Alaska, reappeared to introduce the phrase "death panels" to characterize Obama's health care plan. "The America I know and love is not one in which my parents or my baby with Down Syndrome will have to stand in front of Obama's 'Death Panel,'" she said on her Facebook entry of August 7. "Such a system is downright evil." She would become even more prominent—and caustic—weeks later in promoting her book, *Going Rogue.*

By the first anniversary of the election, Obama was also being criticized by former passionate supporters. *Newsweek* marked that anniversary by splashing these words on its cover over a picture of the new president:

YES
HE
CAN
(But He Sure Hasn't Yet)

Under the heading "A Liberal's Survival Guide," Anna Quindlen summed up the view of increasing numbers of Obama supporters. She began by pointing out the difficulties imposed on legislators by the American political system's checks and balances. "What our system has meant during the poisonous partisan civil war that has paralyzed Washington in recent years," she wrote, "is that very little of the big stuff gets done. It simply can't." Then she turned to Obama's record thus far: "The president promised to tackle the big stuff, swiftly, decisively, and in a fashion about which he was unequivocal, and voters took him at his word a year ago. For those who yearned for a progressive agenda that would change the playing field for the disenfranchised, he promised to do good. So far he has mainly done government."

From farther left, the criticism was far harsher. One example: Alexander Cockburn's "A Year of Obama" analysis in *The Nation* began: "A year after Obama's triumphant election, hauling substantial majorities in the House and Senate on his coattails, the progressive sector is trying to warm its hands before the bonfire of all its hopes."

More worrisome, however, was erosion of support among Independent voters. These are the Americans who decide elections. They vote with less regard to party. They are more practical in supporting politicians whose policies and programs they believe will be successful. They are not the shouters and ranters of cable TV or of the Tea Party protestors. For Obama, they are voters who measure his record of success or failure in fulfilling his promises—and the programs to carry them out. Obama built his winning majorities on the support of these Independents, and on women, young voters and, of course, African Americans. The November 2009 elections, in which Republicans captured governorships from the Democrats in Virginia and New Jersey, showed him weaker on virtually every front, except for African-American voters.

The greatest threat to his presidency remained the economy. Unemployment was rising, with more than half a million job losses a month. The nation's output of goods and services was declining at a rate of $50 billion a month. The value of homes was eroding; nearly 14 million Americans now owed more on their mortgages than their homes were worth. By Inauguration Day, unemployment had risen to 7.2 percent. Unhappily, his economic advisers produced an inaccurate forecast then. They said that, with the stimulus package, unemployment would peak at 8 percent. Then the economy would begin to stabilize and recover. They also predicted their economic plan would create—or save—between three and four million jobs. The new jobs did not materialize. In late 2009 unemployment soared to 10.2 percent. The national debt reached historically high levels, hitting an astronomical figure of over $12 trillion and still climbing. Even those grim figures did not reveal the full toll of a sinking economy. In addition to more than 10 percent of Americans without jobs nationally, thirteen states were recording even higher unemployment levels and joblessness was rising in twenty-nine other states.

A year after Obama's election, the lead headline in *The New York Times* posed more long-term problems:

FEDERAL GOVERNMENT FACES
BALLOON IN DEBT PAYMENTS

AT $750 BILLION A YEAR, COST WILL TOP BUDGETS
FOR 2 WARS, EDUCATION AND ENERGY

It was against this dismal background that Obama fought to pass his health reform bill. As the year began, a broad consensus existed about the need for such change. The question was how to accomplish it after the long history of repeated presidential failures beginning with Theodore Roosevelt in 1912 on through every president who had attempted such reform, most significantly Bill and Hillary Clinton's failure fifteen years before. By the end of the year, public support for reform had soured, raising the stakes for Obama and the Democrats pushing to overhaul the system. After intense wrangling, the Senate joined the House in passing a health care reform bill, marking the first time in nearly a century that such a bill had cleared both houses of Congress. Then came the Massachusetts special Senate election, instantly imperiling prospects for enactment of the bill Democrats had spent a year painstakingly trying to pass. In the end, after a bitter and titanic struggle, health care reform was passed by a narrow margin and on March 23, Obama signed it into law.

Internationally, no problem proved more vexing than what to do about Afghanistan. Obama had campaigned as an opponent of the Iraq war but advocated sending more troops to bolster the fight against al-Qaeda in

Afghanistan. In his first months as president, he ordered an additional 21,000 troops into battle. In late summer, his military commanders asked for 40,000 more. Obama deliberated for weeks on the request, triggering charges of dithering from Dick Cheney and other Republicans. Eventually he settled on a plan to send 30,000 more troops to Afghanistan, while trying to reassure a war-weary public they would not be there indefinitely. He set July 2011 as the starting point for their withdrawal, although with hedges and qualifications that left open the possibility of commitment that would last nearly to the end of a possible second term. The policy sparked renewed controversy, fully satisfying neither supporters nor critics of the war and prompting strong resistance from many Democrats. It was now Obama's war, with echoes of Vietnam in the background of the debate.

A week after the decision, Obama traveled to Oslo to receive the Nobel Peace Prize. It was an unexpected honor. Neither the president nor his critics believed he had earned the award. Accepting it a week after ordering an escalation in Afghanistan only heightened the moment. In Oslo, he delivered a speech that underscored the distance he had traveled from his days as a candidate. The young state senator who opposed the 2002 Iraq war resolution when other more experienced Democrats—Hillary Clinton and Joe Biden among them—had supported it, now offered a ringing defense of just wars. He said: "Evil does exist in the world. A nonviolent movement could not have halted Hitler's armies. Negotiations cannot convince al-Qaeda's leaders to lay down their arms. To say that force may sometimes be necessary is not a call to cynicism—it is a recognition of history; the imperfections of man and the limits of reason." Realism coexisted with idealism in Obama's words, testimony to his determination to chart his own course. The Nobel speech brought praise from across the political spectrum. But as so often during his first year, he soon confronted a new barrage of criticism. The issue again was national security and the bureaucratic failure to detect a terrorist intent on blowing up a Christmas Day flight from Amsterdam to Detroit.

The hopes and fears generated by Obama as candidate and president became arrestingly clear one night in the summer of 2009. Pollster Peter Hart convened another focus group, this time of Independents. Seven had supported Obama, four backed John McCain, and one voted for Ralph Nader. The most striking moment came when Hart asked them to recall their feelings the night of Obama's election. It was as if the whole room had been suddenly transported back to the victory celebration in Grant Park. Jeanne Chambers, a nurse who voted for Obama, recalled, "I was very happy because I had voted for him and I think he presented a major sense of optimism, and I think the whole country felt that way."

The McCain voters said they, too, had been caught up in the excitement. "I pledged all my hope for him," said Jennifer Pennington, an account manager for a technical firm. "I didn't vote for him, but I was caught up in that excitement and I cried. I have friends who are African American, and I was caught up in their happiness and I just hoped he did well." Marsha Welder, an account manager at a security firm who voted for McCain, recalled her initial disappointment that her candidate did not win but then said, "Back on that night, I was thinking how proud I was of the country."

Yet, for all the goodwill, these voters expressed genuine reservations about Obama as president. They were not convinced that he was as strong as he needed to be in dealing with the world's problems. Hart asked them to find one word to describe what Obama's backbone is made of. His most enthusiastic backers saw strength. Almost everyone else used less complimentary terms. "Plastic," said one. Others said wood, bamboo, sand, or aluminum foil. Asked what they hoped he had learned in his first months, one said, "I hope he's learned there are a lot of implications to the money he's spending."

Given the magnitude of problems Obama faced, one of the questions that emerged from our chronicle of the 2008 election is whether any of his rivals then, especially John McCain and Hillary Clinton, could have achieved a more successful first year. Admittedly, that's obviously unanswerable but the record suggests it's probably unlikely. As president, both McCain and Clinton would have faced the same intractable problems. Whether either could have demonstrated greater political skills in addressing them, or avoided the polarization that marked Obama's first year, is another irresolvable "what if?" question.

Both of those former rivals resumed active political careers. McCain returned to the Senate. No longer the pure political maverick of previous times, he now became a staunch critic of most of Obama's policies. Clinton forged a new path as Secretary of State. She became one of Obama's most trusted advisers, and won praise for her energetic pursuit of America's interests abroad. But for Obama the record of his first year was, at best, mixed and as he began his second year, Democrats were facing a difficult political landscape and the likelihood of losses in the House and Senate in the midterm elections.

History will write the record of Obama's success or failure. But there were lessons from the first year. Hard times demand hard choices. Hard choices beget controversy, and Barack Obama had more than his share of controversies. "I'm a big believer in persistence," he said in an early press conference. That persistence was tested repeatedly in the months that followed. The choices he made in dealing with the range of competing issues heightened the stakes for his presidency. Where he and his advisers miscalculated was in believing even modest bipartisan cooperation was possible on the big agenda he set out. That miscalculation in the face of enormous problems defined the first year of Obama's presidency.

After one year, this much could be said with assurance. First, the fateful challenges confronting Barack Obama and the United States that made the election of 2008 so significant remain. If anything, they are even more urgent. Second, the record of Obama's presidency and the effort to forge major changes while rekindling a more bipartisan approach to problems is still a story without an end. Ultimately, neither Obama nor the leaders of the Democrats or Republicans will determine that outcome. That resolution lies in the hands of the American people. They will have to decide what kind of country they want, what sacrifices they are willing to make, and what it will take to have a political system that can minimize their differences and achieve desired results. That battle for a better America continues.

DB and HJ
March 23, 2010

Acknowledgments

We owe a debt to many more than we can acknowledge here for assistance during this long book project, but especially want to express our gratitude to Jim Silberman, of James H. Silberman Books, our editor, and Philippa Brophy, our agent, best of counselors and friends. Wendy Wolf of Viking was most encouraging and supportive throughout. We were flattered that she referred to her pair of grizzled co-authors as "the boyz." At Viking, too, we want to thank Barbara Campo, who oversaw the book's production and saved us from an embarrassing error, to Margaret Riggs, who was always helpful, and to Roland Ottewell, our sharp-eyed copy editor. We owe a special debt to Peter Hart, who invited us to attend all of his indispensable focus group sessions during 2007 and 2008 sponsored by the Annenberg Public Policy Center of the University of Pennsylvania. Hart also made available for use in the book the transcripts of those sessions, which, if read now, memorably tell the story of evolving voter attitudes throughout the seemingly endless campaign. We are grateful to President Obama and Senator John McCain for taking time out from their campaigns to give us interviews for this book. For both personal and professional reasons, we want to express again our admiration for the example our friend and colleague David S. Broder has set for all who seek to report on presidential campaigns. He is without peer.

We owe deep thanks to the many people in the Obama, Clinton, and McCain campaigns, as well as to officials in the campaigns of the candidates who did not make it quite so far. They are too numerous to mention by name but they gave generously of their time and their recollections from the beginning of the campaign to long after the votes had been counted. Many show up by name in this book and their contributions have enriched the story we have tried to tell. Others remain anonymous, but their stories were as helpful in providing as complete a record as we could compile. They will not agree with all we have written in these pages, but we cannot thank them enough for helping us understand events through their own eyes.

This book would not have been possible without the support of a marvelous group of editors and reporters at the *Washington Post*. Executive Editor Leonard Downie Jr., Managing Editor Phil Bennett, and National Assistant Managing Editor Susan Glasser were at the helm as we began this project and were exceedingly generous in their encouragement. Executive Editor Marcus Brauchli, Managing Editor Liz Spayd, and National Assistant Managing Editor Kevin Merida were leading the paper as this project turned from reporting to writing in the months after the election and were equally supportive in seeing it through. Other editors to whom we owe thanks are Bill Hamilton, Tim Curran, Rajiv Chandresakaran, Steven Ginsberg, and Marilyn Thompson.

We have drawn from the work of many others at the *Post*—friends and colleagues—who trooped as many or more miles on the campaign trail, sharing reporting and observations and digging up facts and statistics. They include: Anne E. Kornblut, Shailagh Murray, Michael D. Shear, Perry Bacon Jr., Robert Barnes, Peter Slevin, Ruth Marcus, Chris

Cillizza, Juliet Eilperin, Alec MacGillis, Dana Milbank, Lois Romano, Jon Cohen, Jennifer Agiesta, Matthew Mosk, Eli Saslow, Krissah Thompson, Jose Antonio Vargas, Al Kamen, Garance Franke-Ruta, Alice Crites, and Madonna Lebling.

Special thanks to Roger Simon and Marcia Kramer, who provided sustenance on the road and at home, and Ron Brownstein, who offered insights as well as regular phone calls of support. We are indebted as well to colleagues from other news organizations for their reporting and fellowship: Adam Nagourney, Jeff Zeleny, Mark Halperin, John Dickerson, David Chalian, Chuck Todd, Karen Tumulty, and former *Post* colleagues who got away, Michael Abramowitz, Peter Baker, Jonathan Weisman, and Maralee Schwartz.

We are also indebted to Representative John Lewis of Georgia, Representative Joe Sestak of Pennsylvania, Governors Ed Rendell of Pennsylvania and Janet Napolitano of Arizona, for their insights, and to the following: former White House press secretary Mike McCurry, former Republican congressman Robert S. Walker, and veteran political activists and analysts Richard Viguerie, Doug Bailey, Jerry Rafshoon, Ken Jacobs, and Bill Galston. Our interviews with former Immigration and Naturalization Service commissioner Doris Meissner, Dr. Janice Orlowski of the Washington Hospital Center, Major Ray Kimball at West Point, and Harry Meshell in Youngstown were invaluable. In Youngstown, too, we want to thank Mayor Jay Williams, Paul Sracic, Tom Finnerty, Reid Dulberger, David Skolnick, John Hall, and Randy McCartney for their time. Among voters who spoke to us often, we are grateful to Fay Citerone, Karen Kaplowitz, Alan Cohen, and Bob Macauley. Al Garza of the Minuteman Civil Defense Corps that tracks illegal immigrants led us on a memorable trip through the Arizona desert where illegal immigrants continued to enter the United States.

For two years, University of Maryland graduate students attending seminars taught by co-author Johnson compiled helpful studies on all aspects of the campaign. At Maryland, too, Johnson's Ph.D. assistant, Merrilee Cox, was helpful in more ways than he can detail here. And once more, he wants to express his great appreciation for the critical efforts made by his personal assistant, Lisa Larragoite. For more than a decade, she has made possible the completion of three previous books, with this one being the most demanding of all. It couldn't have been done without her.

Balz owes special thanks to Lucy Shackelford for her tireless research; Olwen Price, who carefully transcribed scores and scores of interviews, many conducted in noisy settings; Zachary Goldfarb, who produced a helpful timeline of campaign events; and Karen Skelton, a veteran strategist who helped us understand in a more sophisticated way Obama's pathbreaking field organization. John Balz read the manuscript with a keen eye for style and substance. He saved us from embarrassments and the book is immeasurably better for his contributions. Thanks also to Erica Simmons.

Finally, as co-authors we wish to acknowledge the debt we owe to our best critics and counselors, our wives, Nancy Balz and Kathryn Oberly.

Notes and Sources

As stated in our note to the reader below, quotations in the narrative not otherwise identified are either from our recorded interviews or from our presence while reporting scenes described in the book. In reporting this story, we also had access to countless transcripts of television and other interviews, convention addresses, press conferences, and many speeches described herein. We have cited the timing and place of that material in the text, but for obvious space reasons do not list them all here in the source notes.

ix   **The book's epigraph is drawn from** Theodore H. White, *The Making of the President 1960* (New York: Atheneum, 1961), 3–4.

TAKEOFF

4   **"Privately, they guess":** Barack Obama, *Dreams from My Father: A Story of Race and Inheritance* (New York: Crown, 1995; reissued in 2004), xv.

BOOK ONE: THEY'RE OFF

21   **The first was in October 2002:** Wikisource, http://en.wikisource.org/wiki/Barack_Obama's_Iraq_Speech.

21   **"I began feeling":** Barack Obama, *The Audacity of Hope: Thoughts on Reclaiming the American Dream* (New York: Crown, 2006), 4.

21   **Whatever he said could affect his political future:** David Mendell, *Obama: From Promise to Power* (New York: Amistad, 2007), 174.

22   **Then, as the primary neared, Hull's collapse:** Ibid., 215.

23   **Between sessions in the Illinois Senate:** Eli Saslow, "The 17 Minutes That Launched a Political Star," *Washington Post*, August 25, 2008.

24   **"I'm LeBron, baby":** David Mendell. *Obama*, 2.

24   **"Wait until tomorrow":** Ryan Lizza, "Making It: How Chicago Shaped Obama," *New Yorker*, July 21, 2008.

26   **"Are you going to try to be president?":** Jeff Zeleny, "Testing the Water, Obama Tests His Own Limits," *New York Times*, December 24, 2006.

27   **His seventeen-day itinerary:** Jeff Zeleny, "Kenyans' welcome is heavy with hope; Obama hailed as hero in visit to dad's village," *Chicago Tribune*, August 27, 2006.

34   **"War hero against snot-nosed rookie":** Rick Pearson, "Obama on Obama," *Chicago Tribune*, December 15, 2006.

35   **The epigraph to chapter 2 is drawn from** text of McCain's speech to the Republican convention, Federal News Service transcript, August 30, 2004.

37   **"They let the dogs off the chain":** Robert Draper, *Dead Certain: The Presidency of George W. Bush* (New York: Free Press, 2007), 63.

38   **"agents of intolerance":** David Barstow, "McCain Denounces Political Tactics of Christian Right," *New York Times*, February 29, 2000.

38   **"I endorse Governor Bush":** Dan Balz, "McCain Endorses Bush—Softly; Rivals Meet at Last, Rule Out No. 2 Spot," *Washington Post*, May 10, 2000.

45   **The epigraph to chapter 3 is drawn from** a Mark Penn memo of December 2006. Its first publication was as part of a series of Clinton campaign memos accompanying "The Frontrunner's Fall," by Joshua Green, *Atlantic Monthly*, August 2008. The memo is available at http://www.theatlantic.com/a/green-penn-12-21-06.mhtml.

45   **"When this Hillary gets to the Senate":** David Espo, "Parties assess the new realities in Congress," Associated Press, November 8, 2008.

46   **"I think of her as a pupil of mine":** Joshua Green, "Take Two: Hillary's Choice," *Atlantic Monthly*, November 2006.

46   **"She had an extraordinary grasp of our military culture":** Karen Tumulty, "Hillary: Love Her, Hate Her," *Time*, August 20, 2006.

48   **"triangulation, calculation and equivocation":** Molly Ivins, "It's time for Democrats to put up or shut up," *Fort Worth Star-Telegram*, January 22, 2006.

BOOK TWO: THE PEOPLE

57   **The epigraph to chapter 4 is drawn from** transcripts that were made of all those interviewed during the Peter Hart focus groups throughout 2007 and 2008, sponsored by the Annenberg Public Policy Center at the University of Pennsylvania. Hart made those transcripts available to us for quotation purposes throughout the long election process, which concluded with a final focus group three weeks after the election.

64   **"Looking Inward":** UCLA survey, titled *The American Freshman: National Norms for Fall 2006*, published December 2006 by UCLA's Higher Education Research Institute, and the other vital UCLA survey *The American Freshman: Forty Year Trends*, published April 2007.

BOOK THREE: THE DEMOCRATS

72   **"Well, the question really is":** Anne E. Kornblut and Dan Balz, "In Iowa, Clinton Calls Bush Reckless; Senator Focuses on War in Iraq and Health Care," *Washington Post*, January 29, 2007.

74   **"I've got to vote at noon":** David S. Broder, "Presidential Spring Training," *Washington Post*, April 1, 2007.

77   **"This is a very difficult vote":** Text of Clinton floor speech to the Senate, *Congressional Record*, October 10, 2002, p. S10288.

77   **"I [do not] think it is a smart strategy":** Dan Balz, "Liberal Activists Boo Clinton; Rejection of Iraq Timetable Gets Cool Reception at Conference." *Washington Post*, June 14, 2006.

82   **"so that we can take potentially some action":** Transcript of South Carolina debate, Federal News Service, April 26, 2007.

83   **"Well, I will not promise":** Transcript of South Carolina debate, Federal News Service, July 23, 2007.

84   **"I thought he was irresponsible":** Ed Tibbetts, "Clinton, Obama Trade Barbs in Quad-City Times Interviews," *Quad City Times*, July 24, 2008, http://www.qctimes.com/news/local/article_92348095-c31c-5b38-9f1b-2bc7a0f7abaa.html.

85   **"Change is just a word":** Text of speech released by Hillary Clinton campaign, September 2, 2007.

87   **"The Hillary Clinton who appeared":** Dan Balz, "Can Clinton Be Stopped?" washingtonpost.com, September 24, 2007, http://voices.washingtonpost.com/44/2007/09/24/the_hillary_blitz.html.

89   **"high-value terrorist targets":** Dan Balz, "Obama Says He Would Take Fight to Pakistan," *Washington Post*, August 2, 2007.

95   **"It is absolutely true":** Adam Nagourney and Jeff Zeleny, "Obama Promises Forceful Stand Against Clinton," *New York Times*, October 27, 2007.

97   **"Well, what Governor Spitzer is trying to do":** Transcript of Philadelphia debate, Federal News Service, October 30, 2007.

98   **"This is classic Clinton":** This comment was among the mildest of an outpouring of often vicious blog reactions posted on NewsBusters.org, the official site of the Media Research Center, November 14, 2007.

98 **"In so many ways, this all-women's college"**: Elisabeth Bumiller, "Clinton Returns to her Alma Mater," *New York Times*, November 1, 2007.

98 **"Hillary Clinton seriously blew only one answer"**: James Fallows, "Rhetorical Questions," *Atlantic Monthly*, September 2008.

102 **"When you're attacked"**: Jackie Calmes, "Pool Report 1—Sen. Clinton at Iowa Democratic Party Central Committee Meeting," Pool Reporter: Distributed by Clinton campaign to press. Published in *Politico*, January 27, 2007, http://www.politico.com/news/stories/0107/2491 .html.

103 **"I thought I was funny"**: Anne E. Kornblut and Dan Balz, "In Iowa, Clinton Calls Bush Reckless; Senator Focuses on War in Iraq and Health Care," *Washington Post*, January 29, 2007.

108 **"Worst case scenario"**: Quoted from Mike Henry memo, made available to authors.

109 **"It's not the opinion of the campaign"**: O. Kay Henderson, "Clinton Says She Won't Bypass Iowa, Radioiowa.com Web site, May 23, 2007, http://www.radioiowa.com/gestalt/go .cfm?objectid=BB03571D-AA63-15C7-CBF4AFFAF470E9EE.

114 **"Presidential Cheating Scandal!"**: *National Enquirer*, October 10, 2007.

120 **"Should [Obama] come from behind"**: David Yepsen, "Obama's superb speech could catapult his bid," *Des Moines Register*, November 12, 2007.

121 **"I have said for months"**: Anne E. Kornblut, "Losing Ground in Iowa, Clinton Assails Obama," *Washington Post*, December 3, 2007.

123 **The *Des Moines Register*'s final poll had shocked everyone**: Thomas Beaumont, "Poll: Obama, Huckabee lead into final stretch," *Des Moines Register*, January 1, 2008.

127 **"You know, they said this day would never come"**: Transcript of Obama speech, Federal News Service, January 3, 2008.

134 **"Words are not actions"**: Transcript of New Hampshire debate, Federal News Service, January 5, 2008.

136 **"You campaign in poetry"**: Jeff Zeleny and Patrick Healy, "Not So Fast, Clinton Says About Obama Momentum," *New York Times*, January 7, 2008.

136 **"fairy tale"**: ABC News, video of Bill Clinton, January 8, 2008, http://abcnews.go.com/video/ playerIndex?id=4102345.

137 **"It's not easy"**: Kate Snow, "Clinton Gets Emotional on Campaign Trail," abcnews.com, January 7, 2008, http://blogs.abcnews.com/politicalradar/2008/01/clinton-gets-em.html.

143 **"We know the battle ahead will be long"**: Transcript of Obama speech, Federal News Service, January 8, 2008.

145 **"I listened to you"**: Transcript of Clinton speech, Federal News Service, January 8, 2008.

151 **Solis Doyle was the daughter of Mexican immigrants**: Lynn Sweet, "Chicagoan Runs Hillary's Camp," *Chicago Sun-Times*, June 14, 2007.

158 **"It is wrong"**: ABC News video of Bill Clinton on January 6, 2008, posted on YouTube, http:// www.youtube.com/watch?v=YLDx4NZr2u4.

159 **"watch what and how he says it"**: Domenico Montanaro, "Clyburn on Clinton, Obama," MSNBC's *First Read*, January 26, 2008, http://firstread.msnbc.msn.com/archive/ 2008/01/26/611355.aspx.

159 **"As an African-American"**: Ben Smith, "Bob Johnson on Obama's Past," *Politico*, January 13, 2008, http://www.politico.com/blogs/bensmith/0108/Bob_Johnson_on_Obamas_past.html.

160 **"It'll be, 'When was the last time?'"**: Alec MacGillis, "Clinton N.H. Official Warns Obama Will Be Attacked on Drug Use," washingtonpost.com, December 12, 2007.

160 **"I don't want to present myself"**: Video clips of Obama interview with *Reno Gazette-Journal*, posted on YouTube.com, "Obama: Reagan changed direction, Bill Clinton didn't," http://www.youtube.com/watch?v=HFLuOBsNMZA; "Obama: GOP is the party of ideas for the last 10–15 years," http://www.youtube.com/watch?v=mbaszmcpesc.

160 **"Republicans have had all the good ideas"**: Video shown on NBC's *Meet the Press*, January 20, 2008, transcript available on msnbc.com, http://www.msnbc.msn.com/id/22754999//.

160 **"President Reagan was the engine"**: Jake Tapper, "Obama v. Clinton/Clinton," abcnews .com, January 21, 2008, http://blogs.abcnews.com/politicalpunch/2008/01/obama-v-clinton .html.

162 **"What she said wasn't true"**: Transcript of South Carolina debate, Federal News Service, January 21, 2008.

166   **"Let me say this, South Carolina"**: Transcript of Obama speech, Federal News Service, January 26, 2008.

166   **"Jesse Jackson won South Carolina twice"**: Video clip of Bill Clinton posted on YouTube, January 26, 2008, http://www.youtube.com/watch?v=Qqd2dfjl2pw.

172   **Over the years, Clinton and Kennedy:** Caroline Kennedy, "A President Like My Father," *New York Times*, January 27, 2008.

191   **"You guys need to grow up"**: Peter Baker and Anne E. Kornblut, "Even in Victory, Clinton Team is Battling Itself," *Washington Post*, March 6, 2008.

192   **"We are in for a real fight"**: Joshua Green, "The Frontrunner's Fall," *Atlantic Monthly*, September 2008

192   **"I think everybody here knows"**: Transcript of Austin debate, Federal News Service, February 21, 2008.

195   **"So shame on you, Barack Obama"**: Julie Bosman, "Clinton Criticizes Obama Over Fliers on Trade Sent to Voters in Ohio," *New York Times*, February 24, 2008.

195   **"Could I just point out"**: Transcript of Cleveland debate, Federal News Service, February 26, 2008.

198   **"You know what they say"**: Transcript of Clinton's victory speech, Federal News Service, March 4, 2008.

200   **"God *damn* America!"**: Brian Ross and Rehab El-Buri, "Obama's Pastor: God Damn America, U.S. to Blame for 9/11," ABC News, March 13, 2008, http://abcnews.go.com/blotter/DemocraticDebate/story?id=4443788 & page=1.

200   **"We bombed Hiroshima"**: Ibid.

205   **"my biggest bonehead move"**: Matt Bai, "Working for the Working-Class Vote: Will Gun-Toting, Churchgoing White Guys Pull the Lever for Obama?" *New York Times Magazine*, October 19, 2008.

206   **"You go into some of these small towns"**: Mayhill Fowler, "Obama: No Surprise that Hard-Pressed Pennsylvanians Turn Bitter," *Huffington Post*, April 11, 2008, http://www.huffingtonpost.com/mayhill-fowler/obama-no-surprise-that-ha_b_96188.html.

207   **"Senator Obama's remarks"**: Perry Bacon Jr. and Shailagh Murray, "'Bitter' Is Hard Pill for Obama to Swallow; He Stands by Sentiment as Clinton Pounces," *Washington Post*, April 13, 2008.

207   **"Hillary Clinton's out there"**: Mike Dorning, "Democrats Cling to a Fight; Obama Defends His 'Bitter' Remark, Turns Rebuke on Clinton," *Chicago Tribune*, April 14, 2008.

208   **"I don't believe that my grandfather"**: Transcript of Philadelphia debate, Federal News Service, April 16, 2008.

217   **"Tonight we mark the end of one historic journey"**: Transcript of Obama speech, Federal News Service, June 3, 2008.

218   **"So many people said this race was over"**: Transcript of Clinton speech, Federal News Service, June 3, 2008.

219   **"Although we weren't able"**: Transcript of Clinton speech, Federal News Service, June 7, 2008.

BOOK FOUR: THE REPUBLICANS

228   **"How do we get back"**: Transcript of Reagan Presidential Library debate, Federal News Service, May 3, 2007.

229   **"stands athwart of history"**: George Packer, "The Fall of Conservatism," *New Yorker*, May 26, 2008.

230   **"puzzle palaces on the Potomac"**: Haynes Johnson, *Sleepwalking Through History: America in the Reagan Years* (New York: W. W. Norton, 1991), 68.

231   **"They knew that governments don't control things"**: Ibid.

239   **"baroque circumlocutions"**: Ruth Marcus, "Mitt Romney's Extreme Makeover," *Washington Post*, February 21, 2007.

240   **"President Bush speaks frequently"**: John McCain speech before Council on Foreign Relations, November 5, 2003, http://www.cfr.org/publication/6502/us_situation_in_iraq_and_afghanistan.html.

240   **"My answer is still no"**: McCain interview with Associated Press. Cited by MSNBC, December 15, 2004, http://www.msnbc.msn.com/id/6708495/.

241   **"There's only one thing worse"**: McCain statement reacting to Iraq Study Group. Quoted by Megan Scully in *Congress Daily* on Government Executive Web site, http://www.govexec.com/dailyfed/1206/120706cdpm2.htm.

241   **"To be of value"**: McCain speech at American Enterprise Institute, January 5, 2007, http://www.aei.org/events/filter.,eventID.1446/transcript.asp.

244   **"Everybody says"**: Adam Nagourney, "Far From Inevitable, McCain Retunes '08 Engine," *New York Times*, March 16, 2007.

245   **"I'm not the youngest candidate"**: Transcript of McCain announcement speech, Federal News Service, April 25, 2007.

251   **"It's not like we can just put Rick in a corner"**: Robert Draper, "The Unmaking of a President," *Gentleman's Quarterly*, November 2007, http://men.style.com/gq/features/landing?id=content_6135.

264   **"The surge is apparently working"**: Transcript of New Hampshire debate, Federal News Service, September 5, 2007.

264   **"the willing suspension of disbelief"**: Michael Cooper, "Buoyed McCain Tours Iowa With New Campaign Theme," *New York Times*, September 13, 2007.

265   **"Let me just say"**: Transcript of Florida debate, Federal News Service, October 21, 2007.

265   **"very, very heartened"**: Dan Balz, "Not Waiting for the Nomination, Giuliani Makes All the World His Stage," washingtonpost.com, September 20, 2007, http://voices.washingtonpost.com/44/2007/09/20/post_85.html.

267   **"billed obscure city agencies"**: Ben Smith, "Giuliani Billed Obscure Agencies for Trips," *Politico*, November 28, 2007, http://www.politico.com/news/stories/1107/7073.html.

267   **"When Rudy stopped advertising"**: *Campaign for President: The Managers Look at 2008*, edited by The Institute of Politics, John F. Kennedy School of Government, Harvard University, Rowman & Littlefield Publishers, 2009.

269   **He told one reporter he would like the Rolling Stones to play at his inaugural:** Zev Chafets, "The Huckabee Factor," *New York Times*, December 16, 2007.

270   **"What would Jesus do?"**: Transcript of debate, Federal News Service, November 28, 2007.

270   **"At a previous debate"**: Transcript of debate, Federal News Service, June 5, 2007.

271   **"I knew that if we played"**: Mike Huckabee, *Do the Right Thing: Inside the Movement That's Bringing Common Sense Back to America* (New York: Sentinel, 2009), 99.

275   **"Lazy Like a Fox?"**: *Newsweek*, September 10, 2007.

275   **"Thompson, Lazy as Charged"**: Roger Simon, "Thompson, Lazy as Charged," *Politico*, December 19, 2007, http://www.politico.com/news/stories/1207/7474.html.

276   **"We don't agree with him on every issue"**: "A Leader for All: McCain Can Unite America," *Manchester Union Leader*, December 2, 2007.

276   **calling him a "phony"**: "Romney should not be the next president," *Concord Monitor*, December 22, 2007, http://www.concordmonitor.com/apps/pbcs.dll/article?Date=20071222&Category=OPINION&ArtNo=712230301&SectionCat=&Template=printart.

278   **"I'm past the age"**: Transcript of McCain speech, Federal News Service, January 8, 2008.

278   **"arrogant bunker mentality"**: Michael D. Huckabee, "America's Priorities in the War on Terror," *Foreign Affairs*, January/February 2008, http://www.foreignaffairs.com/articles/63059/michael-d-huckabee/americas-priorities-in-the-war-on-terror.

285   **"If my showing up and endorsing him"**: Transcript of Bush-McCain meeting, Federal News Service, March 5, 2008.

BOOK FIVE: THE ELECTION

299   **The epigraph to chapter 24 is drawn from** Dan Balz, "Obama Going Abroad with World Watching," *Washington Post*, July 19, 2008.

299   **Obama departed Chicago:** Pool Report on Obama departure, by John McCormick, *Chicago Tribune*, Glenn Johnson, Associated Press. Distributed by Obama campaign, July 19, 2008.

301   **"He is an impressive man"**: Transcript of McCain speech, Federal News Service, June 3, 2008.

304   **"At certain times":** Prepared text of Obama speech, released by Obama campaign, June 30, 2008.

307   *Der Spiegel* **published an interview:** "Iraqi Leader Maliki Supports Obama's Withdrawal Plans," *Der Spiegel*, July 19, 2008, http://www.spiegel.de/international/world/0,1518,566841,00 .html.

307   **In the meeting, Petraeus:** Steve Coll, "The General's Dilemma," *New Yorker*, September 8, 2008.

308   **"I could fall asleep standing up":** Pool Report #2, "Obama Meets with Likud leader Benjamin Netanyahu." Reporter, Margaret Talev. Distributed by Obama campaign to traveling press, July 23, 2008.

310   **"almost floated into view":** Jonathan Freedland, "Glastonbury? No, Berlin—Rock Star Welcome for Obama," *Guardian*, July 26, 2008, http://www.guardian.co.uk/world/2008/jul/25/ barackobama.germany.

310   **"Tonight I speak to you":** Transcript of Obama speech, Federal News Service, July 24, 2008.

312   **"completely wrong":** Michael D. Shear, "McCain: Obama 'Completely Wrong' on Iraq," washingtonpost.com, July 21, 2008, http://voices.washingtonpost.com/44/2008/07/21/ mccain_obama_completely_wrong.html

313   **"He's the biggest celebrity in the world":** Alexander Mooney, "McCain Ad Calls Obama 'Biggest Celebrity in the World,'" cnnpolitics.com, July 30, 2008.

314   **"the greatest thing to ever happen to the city":** From the Democratic 2008 Convention blog posting "Denver to host '08 convention," July 30, 2006, quoting the *Denver Post* in 1908 and also the Damon Runyon quotes then, www.demconvwatchblog.com.

315   **"has a vibe so at odds":** Maureen Dowd, "High Anxiety in the Mile High City," *New York Times*, August 26, 2008.

317   **"There was nothing that was going to keep him away":** Susan Milligan, "Kidney Stones Nearly Derailed Speech, Niece Says," *Boston Globe*, August 27, 2008.

322   **"Temple of Obama":** Jeremy Olshan and Geoff Earle, "Temple of Dem on Mt. O-Lympus," *New York Post*, August 28, 2008.

326   **"eye-popping integrity":** Fred Barnes, "The Most Popular Governor," *Weekly Standard*, July 16, 2007.

333   **Salter later told author Robert Draper:** Robert Draper, "The Making (and Remaking and Remaking) of the Candidate," *New York Times Magazine*, October 26, 2008.

334   **"high risk, high reward":** A. B. Culvahouse, speech to Republican National Lawyers Association, April 17, 2009. Carried on C-SPAN. http://www.c-spanarchives.org/library/index .php?main_page=product_video_info&products_id=285343-1.

338   **"It was rightly noted":** Transcript of Palin speech, Federal News Service, August 29, 2008.

338   **"Today, John McCain":** "Sarah Palin: Dems Pounce on McCain Pick," *Huffington Post*, August 29, 2008, http://www.huffingtonpost.com/2008/08/29/sarah-palin-obama- respons_n_122392.html.

343   **"We're familiar with this":** Jeff Zeleny, "Obama Plans Sharper Tone as Party Frets," *New York Times*, September 11, 2008.

343   **"I can see Russia from my house":** *Saturday Night Live*, NBC, October 16, 2008.

345   **The epigraph to chapter 27 is drawn from** "Charlie Gibson Interviews President Bush," ABC News, December 1, 2008.

346   **"just so frozen":** "Bret Baier Interviews President Bush," Fox News, December 17, 2008.

347   **"are at great risk":** Robert Barnes and Michael D. Shear, "McCain: Fundamentals of Economy Are 'Strong' but 'Threatened,'" washingtonpost.com, September 15, 2008, http://voices .washingtonpost.com/44/2008/09/15/mccain_fundamentals_of_economy.html.

347   **"I shall go to Korea":** Eleanor Clift, "Troublemaker: Newt Gingrich, Bedeviling a Bush Again," *Newsweek*, September 25, 2008. Dwight D. Eisenhower speech, Detroit, Michigan, October 25, 1952.

349   **"blow it up":** David M. Herszenhorn, Carl Hulse, and Sheryl Gay Stolberg, "Talks Implode During a Day of Chaos; Fate of Bailout Plan Remains Unresolved," *New York Times*, September 25, 2008.

349 **"I honestly don't believe"**: Dan Balz, "Economic Jabs, Then Punches on World Affairs," *Washington Post*, September 27, 2008.

349 **"This plan sends a strong signal"**: Carl Hulse and David M. Herszenhorn, "Bailout Plan in Hand, House Braces for Tough Vote," *New York Times*, September 28, 2008.

351 **"a tipping point"**: David Cho and Binyamin Applebaum, "'Tipping Point?' Unfolding Worldwide Turmoil Could Reverse Years of Prosperity," *Washington Post*, October 7, 2008.

355 **"Her third nationally televised interview"**: James Rainey, "Palin Talks to Couric—and if She's Lucky, Few Are Listening," *Los Angeles Times*, September 26, 2008.

355 **"I think she has pretty thoroughly"**: Adam Nagourney, "Concerns About Palin's Readiness as Big Test Nears," *New York Times*, September 29, 2008.

356 **"Palin's recent interviews"**: Kathleen Parker, "The Palin Problem," *Washington Post*, September 28, 2008.

356 **"It is October, people"**: *The Daily Show with Jon Stewart*, Comedy Central, October 1, 2008.

358 **"I think we need a little bit of reality"**: Transcript of vice presidential debate, Federal News Service, October 2, 2008.

359 **Jeanne Cummings broke the story of Palin's wardrobe**: "RNC Shells Out $150K for Palin Fashion," Jeanne Cummings, *Politico*, October 22, 2008, http://www.politico.com/news/stories/1008/14805.html.

361 **"The two men do not appear to have been close"**: Scott Shane, "Obama and '60s Bomber: A Look into Crossed Paths," *New York Times*, October 4, 2008.

362 **"No communists"**: Julie Bosman, "Palin Plays to Conservative Base in Florida Rallies," *New York Times*, October 8, 2008.

362 **"'You know, I've got to be honest with you'"**: Michael D. Shear, "McCain Campaign Co-Chair: 'Guy of the Street' Obama Should Come Clean about Past Drug Use," washingtonpost.com, October 9, 2008.

363 **"He is a decent person"**: MSNBC video, posted on YouTube.com, October 10, 2008, http://www.youtube.com/watch?v=Nt3s6bZWQeY.

363 **"During another period"**: Elisabeth Bumiller, "Congressman Rebukes McCain for Recent Rallies," *New York Times*, October 11, 2008.

364 **"Aggressive Underdog vs. Cool Counterpuncher"**: Dan Balz, "Aggressive Underdog vs. Cool Counterpuncher," *Washington Post*, October 16, 2008.

364 **"Senator Obama, I am not President Bush"**: Transcript of debate, Federal News Service, October 15, 2008.

366 **All this effort was integrated**: Jose Antonio Vargas, "Obama Raised Half a Billion Online," washingtonpost.com, November 20, 2008, http://voices.washingtonpost.com/44/2008/11/20/obama_raised_half_a_billion_on.html.

369 **McCain's crowd**: Adam Smith, "Tampa McCain Rally: Where is Everybody?," tampabay.com, November 3, 2008.

371 **Analyst Rhodes Cook calculated**: Rhodes Cook, "One for the Books," *The Rhodes Cook Letter*, December 2008.

372 **"coalition of the ascendant"**: Ronald Brownstein, "Obama Buoyed by Coalition of the Ascendant," *National Journal*, November 8, 2008.

372 **In the end**: Federal Election Commission statistics, January 22, 2009. http://www.fec.gov/pubrec/fe2008/2008presgeresults.pdf.

373 **"In a contest as long and difficult"**: Transcript of McCain speech, Federal News Service, November 4, 2008.

373 **"If there is anyone out there"**: Transcript of Obama speech, Federal News Service, November 4, 2008.

382 **Women still fall far behind**: Recent research from Catalyst, a nonprofit membership organization, with offices in the United States, Canada, and Europe, which studies women's experiences in business.

385 **"It's complicated, but here it is"**: Tim Graham, "WaPo's Magazine Mocks O'Reilly, Limbaugh, Even Olbermann," Media Research Center's NewsBusters.org, March 25, 2008. Weingarten's article was published in the *Washington Post Magazine*, March 23, 2008.

Index